Germans a.

Germans and Indians

FANTASIES, ENCOUNTERS, PROJECTIONS

*

Edited by Colin G. Calloway,
Gerd Gemünden, and
Susanne Zantop

University of Nebraska Press

Lincoln and London

"Compatriots," by Emma Lee Warrior, was previously
published in *All My Relations*, edited by Thomas King
(Toronto: McClelland and Stewart), 1990, and has been
reprinted with kind permission of the author.

"Between Karl May and Karl Marx: The DEFA *Indianerfilme*," by Gerd Gemünden, was previously published
in *Film History* 10, no. 3 (1998): 399–407.

"Blitzkuchen," by Louise Erdrich, was previously published as chapter 13 of *The Antelope Wife: A Novel* (New
York: HarperCollins, 1998).

Library of Congress Cataloging-in-Publication Data
Germans and Indians : fantasies, encounters, projections / edited by Colin G. Calloway, Gerd Gemünden,
and Susanne Zantop.
p. cm. Includes bibliographical references and index.
ISBN 0-8032-1518-5 (cloth: alkaline paper) -
ISBN 0-8032-6420-8 (paperback: alkaline paper)
1. West (U.S.) - Foreign public opinion, German.
2. German Americans - West (U.S.) - History.
3. Frontier and pioneer life - West (U.S.) - Public opinion - History. 4. Indians of North America.
5. Exoticism in literature. 6. German literature - 19th
century - History and criticism. 7. German literature -
20th century - History and criticism.
I. Calloway, Colin G. (Colin Gordon), 1953-
II. Gemünden, Gerd. III. Zantop, Susanne,
1945-2001.
F596 .G47 2002 973.04'97 — dc21 2001052232

Susanne Zantop (1945–2001)

On Saturday 27 January 2001, Susanne Zantop and her husband, Half, were found dead in their home. For their friends and colleagues, it was hard to imagine two people less likely to meet a violent death.

Born in Germany at the end of the Second World War, Susanne was acutely aware of the burden of German history. In her work and her daily life, she insisted on tolerance and respect for others, and she worked to break down barriers to understanding and community. It was this spirit, not a Germanic fascination with American Indian culture, that motivated her to initiate the conference out of which this publication grew. It was this spirit that governed the selection and editing of the papers. Those of us who are left have tried to adhere to that spirit in bringing the project to completion. The book must be Susanne's final say on the subject, but she would never have wanted it to be the last word.

All royalties from this book go to the Zantop Memorial Scholarship Fund at Dartmouth College.

Colin G. Calloway
Gerd Gemünden

Contents

Illustrations

Editors' Acknowledgments

The conference "Deutsche und Indianer/Indianer und Deutsche: Cultural Encounters across Three Centuries" out of which this book developed was made possible by financial support from the German Studies Department and Native American Studies Program at Dartmouth, the Dickey Endowment, the John Sloan Dickey Third Century Professorship, the German Academic Exchange Service, the Hewlett Foundation, the Bildner Endowment, the Ed and Molly Scheu symposium fund, and the Max Kade Foundation, and by the administrative assistance of Margaret Robinson and Linda Welch.

We wish to thank all the participants in the conference and especially those whose contributions are not reflected in the current volume: Maia T. Conrad, Katherine Faull Eze, Gerhard Grytz, Christopher Ronwanièn:te Jocks, Sergei Kan, Wynfried Kriegleder, Diane Krumrey, Rowena McClinton, Elsa Christina Muller, Glenn Penny, Dennis M. Runnels, Barbara Ann Saunders, Ingo Schroeder, Beeke Marie Sell Tower, Darryl K. Stonefish, Dale Turner, and Carola Wessel.

Victoria (Vicki) Hoelzer-Maddox efficiently copyedited the complete first draft of the manuscript and formatted the finished product prior to final submission to the press.

We are grateful to George L. Moses and a second, anonymous reader for their support of the manuscript.

Part 1: Introduction

Close Encounters

Deutsche and Indianer

SUSANNE ZANTOP

In one of the most revealing encounters between Germans and Indians in literature, the Teutonic superhero Old Shatterhand meets, for the very first time, the man who will subsequently become his friend and alter ego, Winnetou, son of the Apache chief Intschu tschuna. This is how Karl May, author of the popular *Winnetou* trilogy, describes Shatterhand's first impressions of his future "blood-brother":

> He was bare-headed . . . and had wound up his hair into a kind of helmet into which he had braided the skin of a rattlesnake, yet without adding any decorative feathers. His hair was so long and heavy that it cascaded down his back. Certainly many a woman would have envied him this magnificent, shiny bluish-black adornment. His face was even nobler than his father's; its color a subtle light-brown with a delicate tinge of bronze. He was, as I now guessed and later confirmed, about my age and had already made a deep impression on me, during this first encounter. I felt that he must be a good person, of extraordinary talents. We scrutinized one another with long, searching glances, and then, I believe, I noticed that his solemn dark gaze with its velvety sheen was briefly illuminated by a friendly light, as if the sun were sending a message to earth through an opening in the clouds.[1]

This passage from an 1890s novel contains, in a nutshell, all the elements that fired German "Indianthusiasm," as Hartmut Lutz calls it in this volume: the exoticized yet sympathetic, even idealizing depiction of the Other; the fixation on hair and skin color as essential markers of difference, typical of European racialized descriptions from Columbus's letters onward; the fantasy of balance, equality, tacit agreement, and respect between the two extraordinary men/cultures as they meet eye-to-eye; the moral-Christian and Enlightenment overtones (sun, light, tolerance); and, last but not least, the erotic attraction to the Other experienced by the European newcomer.[2] Critics and literary scholars have analyzed this encounter in terms of both May's implicit homosexuality and the celebration of homosocial bonding so common in late-nineteenth-century German public discourse.[3] They have fleshed out its nationalist and religious implications and examined its function within a long tradition of "colonial encounters" between Europeans and the "natives" of the New World.[4] Clearly, May's fantasy recasts the familiar stories of John Smith and Pocahontas, Inkle and Yarico, Robinson and Friday, or Cora and Alonzo, by imagining – at least on the surface – a coupling of Europeans and Native Americans that is not marred by racist presuppositions, violence, or exploitation.[5] Unlike Spanish, British, or French colonizers, Germans – May's fiction suggests – were/are able to establish a relationship of mutual recognition and collaboration with American Indians.

It is obvious to us why this vision of a friendship among equals would be enormously attractive to May's male and female German readers, who, throughout the twentieth century, reveled in identifying alternately with the kind, strong Teutonic superman and the equally kind, supple, and beautiful "Indianer": it is profoundly self-congratulatory and self-serving.[6] Hundreds of *Indianer* films, festivals, clubs, or literary May take-offs attest to the continuing fascination of this model, which, I believe, could safely be compared with the black cop–white cop buddy fantasies that have recently populated U.S. films and in which the moral stature of the white hero is enhanced by the presence of a dark-skinned sidekick. With eighty to one hundred million copies in twenty-eight languages in circulation, May's works, since their inception, have generated a whole culture industry that almost obsessively reiterates and thereby reproduces the idea of a special affinity between Germans and Native Americans based on shared experiences.[7]

Indianthusiasm, of course, existed in other European countries as well – Marmontel's novel *Les Incas* (1777) in the eighteenth century and Chateaubriand's tragic story *Atala ou les amours de deux sauvages dans le désert* (1801) in the nineteenth century led to sentimental identifications all over Europe with the plight of Indians. The Indian hobbyist movement, as Christian Feest reminds us in this volume, is alive and active in England, the Czech Republic, and Russia, to name just a few.[8] Nor is the desire to impersonate characters from different times or different ethnic groups a peculiarly German endeavor: Renaissance games and Civil War impersonations, for example, are a favorite pastime in the United States, and American school children of all ethnic backgrounds regularly dress up as Pilgrim Fathers or Mothers when Thanksgiving approaches. It seems, however, that the identificatory enthusiasm for things *Indian* – which predated and outlasted Karl May's fictions by over a hundred years – has particularly flourished in German lands. Peter Bolz, in his introduction to a recent exhibit on North American Indians in the Anthropological Museum in Berlin, attributes this enthusiasm to Germans' "deep-rooted longing for political freedom and freedom of movement" during political and economic oppression, that is, throughout the nineteenth and first half of the twentieth centuries.[9] Gerd Gemünden and I have established similar connections between a collective sense of inferiority, resulting from military and political defeat, and a collective identification with "the Indian" as the underdog – in the late eighteenth century, when the occupied German states were trying to redefine themselves against imperial(ist) France, as well as in the late twentieth century, when East and West Germany were attempting to situate themselves vis-à-vis the powerful capitalist-"imperialist" West, particularly the U.S. and particularly during the Vietnam era.[10] Hartmut Lutz, in turn, sees a link between Germans' quest for a national territory and national identity in the nineteenth century and their sentimental self-projections as the *Indianer* of Europe, colonized and oppressed by others yet longing to be free.[11] Not surprisingly, the clichéd image of the Indian freely roaming the prairie has more to do with national needs at specific historical moments in Europe than with Indian people and their experiences on the North American continent.

More important than the "cliché-ridden relationship" (Bolz) between Germans and Indians, however, is the fact that the discussions of the relationships themselves have been replete with clichés – not just clichéd conceptions and stereotypical depictions of Indians, but also stereotypical accounts of Germans and their supposed national character or alleged (sinister) motivations. Recent traumatic events – the Holocaust, World War II, and the Cold War – have revived conceptions formed over centuries and hardened them into caricatured notions of the Other on all sides, be they noble or ignoble savages, neo-imperialist capitalists or the harbingers of democracy, evil Krauts or Nazi *Übermenschen*. More often than not, these binary confrontations obfuscate specific historical constellations and internal multiplicities and replace their careful, nuanced study.

The mutual projections and conventional preconceptions formed the point of departure for our conference "Deutsche und Indianer/Indianer und Deutsche: Cultural Encounters across Three Centuries," held in May 1999 at Dartmouth College, and the volume that emerged from it. When Colin Calloway, chair of Native American Studies at Dartmouth, my colleague Gerd Gemünden in the Department of German Studies, and I sat down together to organize a conference on Germans and Native Americans, our purpose was precisely that: to question the self-serving myths and rehistoricize a debate that had

Susanne Zantop

all too often remained caught in the limited perspective of a field or an approach or been invested with national or ideological interest. We hoped to achieve a productive confrontation by bringing together Germanists, Americanists, and scholars of Native American studies; European and North American historians, anthropologists, art historians, and literary critics; Germans, Native Americans, and others. We all had, from very different perspectives and independently of one another, reflected on European perceptions of and interaction with Native Americans: Colin Calloway, for example, in his recent study titled New Worlds for All: Indians, Europeans, and the Remaking of Early America (1997); Gerd Gemünden in his reflections on German Indianerfilme mentioned above; and I in my book Colonial Fantasies: Conquest, Family, and Nation in Precolonial Germany, 1770–1870 (1997), which analyzes German representations of South America and South American Indians. Now, we hoped, we could broaden our own knowledge and limited perspective by joining forces with others working in the field and by establishing a dialogue between those interested in representation and the imaginary, on the one hand, and those who are after historical "facts" and "experience," on the other.

From the start, we were perfectly aware that the terms "Germans" and "Indians" are problematic: Who were these "Germans" anyway? The inhabitants of the first German nation formed in 1871, the German Empire? The multiethnic inhabitants of the three-hundred-plus "German" mini-states and principalities, the remainders of the Holy Roman Empire of German Nation in the eighteenth century? Or all German-speaking peoples, whether they live(d) in Switzerland, Austria, Russia, or Germany? And who were "the Indians"? The hundreds of tribes and nations that populated America before, during, and after the European conquest and colonization? Native Americans living on reservations in the United States or Canada? Or all those who can claim descent from European and indigenous ancestry? Purposefully, we therefore left the German names in the title to indicate that Deutsche as well as Indianer were ironically used terms that had more to do with fantasy than with any lived actuality, terms that needed to be interrogated.

In fact, the questions we asked ourselves were aiming to differentiate the somewhat monolithic picture left to us by nineteenth-century literature. We wanted to find out how Native Americans and German settlers on the North American continent had negotiated their interactions in their everyday encounters across the centuries; whether these interactions were exclusively characterized by violence, oppression, and cultural and physical displacement, or whether there was also peaceful cohabitation and cultural exchange; whether all European settlers were behaving the same way, at the same time,

6

or whether one could distinguish between them according to nationality, creed, or the region they came from or lived in. We furthermore wanted to explore how Native Americans perceived Germans, both inside the United States and in Europe: whether they considered them a separate, "different" category or lumped them together with all "whites" or all "Europeans"; how they responded to German realities during their visits to Europe as members of circuses or ethnic exhibits in the nineteenth century, or as tourists, students, activists, or members of the U.S. army in the twentieth. In other words, we were interested in the ways in which these multiethnic encounters in various "contact zones," to use Mary Louise Pratt's term, affected the pictorial and written documents that were produced throughout the centuries and how these in turn shaped perceptions.[12]

The response to our call for papers was overwhelming: we received over eighty proposals and many more inquiries from all over western Europe and North and South America. Clearly, we had tapped into a subject that was of more than academic importance to many people – to academics as well as to businessmen involved in trading in Native American artifacts, to teachers of North American studies as well as to Germans living on Indian reservations, to descendants of mixed German-Indian marriages as well as to novelists, film makers, or members of Karl May fan clubs. Several Native Americans proposed to offer "workshops" and run sweat lodges for German visitors; some Germans wanted to speak about "adventure vacations" on reservations or about organizing trips to sites mentioned in May's novels ("Winnetours"). Significantly, there were almost no proposals by Native American scholars to counter this outpouring of Indianthusiasm.

Perhaps this lack of Native American *scholarly* interest in German-Indian relations should not surprise us: from a Native American perspective, "Germans" are part of the larger picture of European militiamen, explorers, or settlers who invaded and appropriated Native territory. Why, after all, *should* Native Americans be interested in Germans? Obviously, there are more pressing topics to investigate. By the same token, we were surprised to discover how many Native American novelists in both the United States and Canada are actually writing about German-Indian relations in their fictions. German protagonists are a separate, clearly distinguishable category figure, for example, in novels and short stories by Louise Erdrich, Lee Maracle, Richard Wagamese, Emma Lee Warrior, Tomson Highway, to name just a few. All these writers explicitly or implicitly address the question of how fantasies of a special affinity or mutual prejudices affect the interaction of both "ethnicities." Over and beyond simple confrontations – as Renate Eigenbrod and

Ute Lischke-McNab suggest – they concentrate on what is "between the 'two' cultures," the space in which new meaning can emerge.[13]

To counter the problematic gap in scholarly contributions and the ensuing imbalance in our program, we therefore decided on a two-tier approach: to ask Native American colleagues to provide commentary and critical responses to the panelists during the conference and to reprint fictional texts by Native American authors in our anthology. Christopher Ronwanièn:te Jocks (Mohawk, assistant professor of religion and Native American studies), Dale Turner (Anishinabe, assistant professor of government and Native American studies), and Darryl Stonefish (Delaware, tribal historian of the Moravian Band Delaware Nation in Thamesville, Ontario) graciously agreed to chair sessions. Dan Runnels (Salish) set the tone by opening the conference with a prayer in Salish; Christopher Jocks and Daryl Stonefish added personal memories and oral history to the, at times, somewhat "academic" analyses; and Dale Turner offered his reflections on European representations. Indian conference participants made their own critical comments from the floor and spoke up whenever they perceived a tone of cultural condescension or insensitivity in any of the presentations. A central message of the conference was that there are various ways of remembering and approaching a conflicted history and that personal memories and oral history can enlighten and subvert the official story. Another important lesson – particularly for the European participants – was the realization that even well-intentioned academic discourse can appear extremely arrogant and closed-minded if it does not contain a reflection of its own epistemological interest, that is, reflections on the terminology, perspective, and goals of the presenter. Ultimately, all interventions served to remind us that "reality" – historical and contemporary – can be approached in many different ways, and that neither academic research nor personal memory *necessarily* grants better access or provides deeper insights.

Much of what we learned in this – for us – first academic encounter between two "ethnically" oriented departments entered into this volume. Of the many fascinating and detailed studies presented at the conference, we chose those that were most encompassing and offered more general information. For example, rather than including four different accounts of relations between Moravians and Indian tribes in four different regions, we selected one representative essay to encourage readers to engage in further research and study. In some instances, we solicited papers to cover an area that had not received enough attention during the conference. The fictional narratives, in turn, were designed to provide the humorous, occasionally ironic, sometimes bitter commentary that had accompanied and enriched the oral presentations.

Emma Lee Warrior's poignant short story "Compatriots" (1987) opens the anthology. We felt that her ironic account of eager Hilda in search of "real" experiences among the Blackfoot Indians and of Helmut Walking Eagle, the off-putting German Indian impersonator (and profiteer), would set the tone for the whole enterprise: for our questioning of the motives, desires, and investments of Germans in search of Indian "authenticity," on the one hand, and, on the other, of Native American responses to this new form of cultural intrusion and appropriation. Rather than celebrating "difference" or an essential Germanness or Indianness, Warrior's thoroughly modern tale explores the mutual (mis)perceptions and (mis)understandings as "stranger" meets "stranger."[14]

The anthology closes with Louise Erdrich's chapter "Blitzkuchen" from her recent novel *The Antelope Wife* (1998). Not only does her mixed German-Indian descent and her former presence at Dartmouth make Erdrich an obvious candidate for a book on German-Indian connections produced by Dartmouth professors, but her tale of captivity and assimilation provides us with much food for further thought. In fact, it raises all the issues that the academic contributions seek to address in their own way: the mutual fears based on traumatic experiences in a variety of war settings; the power relations between colonizer and colonized, captor and captive; the tensions between tradition and innovation and the possibilities of cultural transfer and "transculturation." In her dense and beautifully suggestive prose, Erdrich envisages a transcendence of stereotypes and traditional hatreds: when the twice-captive German prisoner of war Klaus emerges from under the gunnysack to reveal his hedgehog hair and inoffensive looks, when he bakes his famous Blitzkuchen, and when the Indians and this one German share in the quasi-religious ritual of a common meal, all animosity and revenge fantasies melt away. As Klaus is adopted into the tribe, his sweet "German" cake, composed of "Indian" ingredients, becomes part of the tribe's food ritual and memory and a metaphor for all forms of mixing that take place when two cultures meet. As Erdrich's utopian vision, however, makes clear, this is not a meeting on European terms, since the German – prisoner of war of the Americans and captive of the Indians in one – does not act from a position of power. He literally bakes for his life. Peaceful adoption of cultural practices, Erdrich suggests, can only take place when the ones in power consciously refrain from resorting to violence; in other words, when power is used toward positive change.

This "frame" for the anthology is enhanced by Christian Feest's overview of German perceptions of Indians in which he warns against an overreliance on national categories and on the self-delusive concept of a "special affinity" between the two. The bulk of the contributions are subdivided into three sections, each of which is introduced by a general overview. The first of these sections focuses on actual historical encounters between German settlers and Indian inhabitants of the newly formed colonies. In his survey of German-Indian history, Colin Calloway proposes that generalizations based on nationality are problematic – a point that is reiterated by the other contributors in this section as well: each historical moment needs to be examined in its specificity if it is to reveal information about attitudes, responses, or actions of "Germans" or of the "Indians" with whom they cohabitated. More often than not, German settlers seem to have behaved like other immigrants (Barsh), except for when their religion or social status placed them in the position of outsider (Dally-Starna and Starna; Riordan) – a position, as we know from Erdrich's chapter, that can create a greater sensitivity toward the surrounding culture and a greater willingness to collaborate or even assimilate. And more often than not, the Native Americans' behavior varied, depending on how they were treated and what their stakes or alliances were in a particular confrontation. The first section is rounded off by a reversed motion: the travel of an Indian delegate, the Ojibwa George Copway, or Kah-ga-ga-gah-bow, eastward, to the World Peace Congress in Frankfurt, Germany, in 1850 (Peyer). Above and beyond its entertainment value, the anecdote of Copway's romantic travel to German lands yields insights into certain ramifications of cultural contacts between Indians and Germans that we still contend with today: the enthusiasm and expectations of a German audience reared on sentimental identification with American Indians from novels, upon encountering, at last, a "real Indian" – and the tragic conflict in which this places the Native traveler, who finds himself forced to perform a role, to become an "Indian impersonator" alienated from his own life experiences.

In the second section, Projections and Performances, the question of German projections, representations, and imitations is pursued in greater detail. In his sweeping survey of German intellectual history, Hartmut Lutz argues that paper-Indians had a kind of redemptive function for Germans, who throughout the nineteenth century were searching for foundational fictions that would bestow on them a national "mission," a manifest destiny and identity. He proposes that texts like Tacitus's Germania and characters like the Cheruscan chief Arminius or the heroic Siegfried of the Nibelungen saga emphasized the "tribal," "savage" origins of Germans, who, in the figure of May's Winnetou, imagined for themselves a "red brother," one who did not despise but loved them. Ironically, this search for an adoring "brother" only extended to distant peoples, not to minorities within Germany, such as the Jews or the Gypsies living on German soil. As Lutz tries to show, within this complex social pathology, anti-Semitism and Indianthusiasm were only different sides of the same coin.

In his contribution Jeffrey Sammons focuses less on imaginary configurations than on literature based on actual encounters: the writings of Charles Sealsfield (Karl Postl), Balduin Möllhausen, and Friedrich Gerstäcker, who traveled through North America in the nineteenth century and transformed their experiences into novels or tales that—while ethnographically more accurate than Karl May's—are still shaped by their political-ideological agendas, their commercial interests, and the expectations of their reading public. Karl Markus Kreis, in turn, analyzes the narratives of two other, quite different, real encounters, as he contrasts the description of Indians in newspaper accounts of Wild West shows with those in reports from Catholic missions on Indian reservations. These narratives, too, tell us more about European readers and missionaries and their fantasies than about the Native Americans they interacted with.

In a part devoted to performance, documentary filmmaker and Yurok anthropologist Marta Carlson and drama/performance specialist Katrin Sieg take a look at the Indian hobbyist movement in Germany. While Sieg reports about field work she has undertaken among several *Indianer* clubs in order to gain a better understanding of the quite varied motivations and concerns behind this drive toward Indian impersonation, Carlson, speaking from a Native American perspective, precisely calls for the kind of soul-searching and self-analysis that *Indianerclubs* in Germany have, so far, failed to engage in. The two essays, Sieg's longer investigation and Carlson's shorter commentary, are therefore to be read in tandem, as two of many possible ways to approach a subject that Philip Deloria, for example, has explored for the U.S. context in his *Playing Indian* (1998).

Like Katrin Sieg's essay, Gerd Gemünden's contribution on the DEFA *Indianerfilme* situates cultural production, in this case, East German cinema, in its historical-political context. Gemünden looks at the many movies with Indian topics that were produced in the former GDR and analyzes them in juxtaposition to similar productions in West Germany. Read against the backdrop of the Cold War, these "Easterns" reveal their "political unconscious" and hidden agenda: the anti-Americanism and anticapitalism that allies East German communists with "Indian warriors" fighting the U.S. system. Again, it is useful to read this contribution in connection with others, since the patterns Gemünden discovers are also discernible in the different motivations of Indian impersonators uncovered by Sieg and Carlson.

Renate Eigenbrod and Ute Lischke-McNab introduce the fourth section, titled "Two-Souled Warriors: The Conjunction of Germans and Indians Revisited," based on a quote from Erdrich's Blitzkuchen chapter. The two essays – Eigenbrod's analysis of narratives by Canadian First Nations writers and Lischke's introduction to Louise Erdrich's *Antelope Wife* – highlight the attempt of these Native American writers to rethink and revise the stereotypes that have colored the depiction of both Indians and Germans, without glossing over differences. In the "two-souled warrior always fighting with themself" Erdrich alludes to both Goethe's Faust ("Two souls, alas, cohabit in my breast") and to her own predicament, the "triple whammy" of her mixed Chippewa-German-Jewish background.[15] As Erdrich, Eigenbrod, and Lischke-McNab point out, ethnic categories alone do not do justice to the diversity and multiplicity within Indian and German populations or even within individuals. The Native American writers remind us that there is no such thing as "authenticity" or a fixed "identity": cultures, be they German or Indian, are in constant flux; individuals have multiple, shifting, at times warring identities. Yet as the writers insist, divisions along gender, class, regional, sexual, or religious lines not only create further fragmentation – they also allow for affiliations and solidarity above and beyond ethnicity.

The collection of articles in this anthology constitutes only a beginning. Many more authors and topics deserve closer scrutiny. One could imagine an essay on the impact of German anthropologists such as Franz Boas on the study of Native Americans; one can envisage studies of the ethnographic and ethnomusicological collections in the nineteenth century, the role and function of Native Americans in European art and of Europeans in Native American art, and, above all, an investigation of the experiences and impressions of Native Americans among Germans in Europe. Some of this work is currently being done in this country in the form of Ph.D. theses and in Germany, where North American studies programs and departments of ethnohistory are flourishing. In order to encourage further study, we have included an extended, albeit selected bibliography of primary sources and secondary work on German-Indian relations. This bibliography is designed not just to reflect the texts on which this anthology is based, but to reveal needs and opportunities for future investigation – and for future dialogue.

Notes

1. May, *Winnetou: Reiseerzählung*: 59. My translation.

2. For a historical overview and analysis of the tradition of emphasizing hair and skin color, see my *Colonial Fantasies* or my 2000 essay "Der Indianer."

3. Honour, *New Golden Land*, 244. See also Lutz *'Indianer' und Native Americans*, 27; or Schmidt, *Sitara*, 32.

4. See Hohendahl; Zantop, " 'Indianer.' "

5. For the encounter literature, see Hulme, *Colonial Encounters*; Zantop, *Colonial Fantasies*; or Hölz, *Fremde*.

6. The equality of the two protagonists is, of course, only superficial, on the levels of both plot and narrative perspective: Winnetou is literally subsumed into white Christian society when he eventually recognizes that Christianity is the "better" religion; he also dies in volume 3 of the trilogy, whereas his "brother Charly" is allowed to continue his heroic quest in many more novels. And, as the quote indicates, the perspective on the Indian is that of the European, who gets to describe, categorize, define, and delimit the Other on his terms.

7. Augstein, "Weiter Weg," 130.

8. See Feest's essay in this volume. One could argue, however, that the fact that there is more research on German Indianthusiasm in Germany than in other countries – which, according to Feest, accounts for a greater awareness of Germans' supposed proclivity – indicates a greater preoccupation with the relationship to begin with.

9. See Bolz, "Indianer und Deutsche," 14.

10. See Gerd Gemünden's contribution in this volume as well as his work on Herbert Achternbusch in *Framed Visions*. Zantop, "Colonial Legends."

11. Significantly, the term *Indianer* is associated in the German imagination above all with North American Indians and, in particular, with Plains Indians. For our conference and for this volume we therefore decided to exclude contributions on Central and South America, although there are, of course, many accounts of encounters between Germans and indigenous peoples in those regions, sometimes even framed by German *Indianer* fantasies. See, for example, chapter 3 of Leo Spitzer's account of Austrian-Jewish exiles in Bolivia (*Hotel Bolivia*).

12. See Pratt, *Imperial Eyes*.

13. I am indebted here to Hartwig Isernhagen's essay "(Un)translatable?," especially p. 14.

14. For a detailed presentation of the short story for German students of English, see Enter and Lutz's article " 'Compatriots,' " 86–94.

15. The image of the two warring souls is firmly established within the European cultural context. As Büchmann's collection of proverbs, *Geflügelte Worte*, points out, Goethe's Faust passage was anticipated by Wieland's drama *Die Wahl*

Susanne Zantop

des Herkules (1773) and by Racine's *Cantiques spirituels* (seventeenth century), in both of which the protagonist is torn apart by the two souls at war inside him (156-57). I do not know whether Erdrich is the first to introduce this image into Native American literature, or whether – as I suspect – it already has a long tradition there too.

Compatriots

EMMA LEE WARRIOR

Lucy heard the car's motor wind down before it turned off the gravel road a quarter of a mile west of the house. Maybe it was Bunky. She hurried and left the outhouse. She couldn't run if she wanted to. It would be such a relief to have this pregnancy over with. She couldn't see the color of the vehicle, for the slab fence was between the house and the road. That was just as well. She'd been caught in the outhouse a few times, and it still embarrassed her to have a car approach while she was in there.

She got inside the house just as the car came into view. It was her aunt Flora. Lucy looked at the clock. It was seven-thirty. She wondered what was going on so early in the morning. Flora and a young white woman approached the house. Bob barked furiously at them. Lucy opened the door and yelled at him. "I don't know what's wrong with Bob; he never barks at me," said Flora.

"He's probably barking at her," explained Lucy. "Not many whites come here."

"Oh, this is Hilda Afflerbach. She's from Germany," began Flora. "Remember? I told you I met her at the Calgary Stampede? Well, she got off the seven o'clock bus, and I don't have time to drive her all the way down to my house. I took her over to my mother's, but she's getting ready to go to Lethbridge. Can she stay with you till I get off work?"

Lucy smiled. She knew she was boxed in. "Yeah, but I've got no running water in the house. You have to go outside to use the toilet," she said, looking at Hilda.

"Oh, that's okay," her aunt answered. "She's studying about Indians, anyway. Might as well get the true picture, right? Oh, Hilda, this is my niece, Lucy." Flora lowered her voice and asked, "Where's Bunky?"

"He never came home last night. I was hoping it was him coming home. He's not supposed to miss any more work. I've got his lunch fixed in case he shows up." Lucy poured some water from a blue plastic water jug into a white enamel basin and washed her hands and face. "I haven't even had time to make coffee. I couldn't sleep waiting for him to come home." She poured water into a coffeemaker and measured out the coffee into the paper filter.

"I'd have some coffee if it was ready, but I think I'd better get to work. We have to punch in now; it's a new rule. Can't travel on Indian time anymore," said Flora. She opened the door and stepped out, then turned to say, "I think the lost has returned," and continued down the steps.

The squeak of the dusty truck's brakes signaled Bunky's arrival. He strode toward the door, barely acknowledging Flora's presence. He came in and took the lunch pail Lucy had. "I stayed at Herbie's" was all he said before he turned and went out. He started the truck and beeped the horn.

"I'll go see what he wants." She motioned to Flora to wait.

When Bunky left, she went to Flora. "Maybe it's a good thing you came here. Bunky didn't want to go to work 'cause he had a hangover. When he found out Hilda was going to be here all day, he decided he'd rather go to work."

"If I don't have to leave the office this afternoon, I'll bring the car over and you can drive Hilda around to look at the reserve, okay?"

"Sure, that'll be good. I can go and do my laundry in Spitzee." She surveyed the distant horizon. The Rockies were spectacular blue and distinct. It would be a nice day for a drive. She hoped it would be a repeat of yesterday, not too hot, but, as she stood there, she noticed tiny heat waves over the wheat fields. Well, maybe it won't be a repeat, she thought. Her baby kicked inside of her, and she said, "Okay, I'd better go tend to the guest." She didn't relish having a white visitor, but Flora had done her a lot of favors and Hilda seemed nice.

And she was. Hilda made friends with the kids, Jason and Melissa, answering their many questions about Germany as Lucy cooked. She ate heartily, complimenting Lucy on her cooking even though it was only the usual scrambled eggs and fried potatoes with toast and coffee. After payday, there'd be sausages or ham, but payday was Friday and today was only Tuesday.

"Have you heard of Helmut Walking Eagle?" Hilda wanted to know.

"Yeah, well, I really don't know him to talk to him, but I know what he looks like. He's from Germany, too. I always see him at Indian dances. He dresses up like an Indian." She had an urge to tell her that most of the Indians wished Helmut would disappear.

"I want to see him," Hilda said. "I heard about him and I read a book he wrote. He seems to know a lot about the Indians, and he's been accepted into their religious society. I hope he can tell me things I can take home. People in Germany are really interested in Indians. They even have clubs."

Lucy's baby kicked, and she held her hand over the spot. "My baby kicks if I sit too long. I guess he wants to do the dishes."

Hilda got up quickly and said, "Let me do the dishes. You can take care of the laundry."

16

"No, you're the visitor. I can do them," Lucy countered. But Hilda was persistent, and Lucy gave in.

Flora showed up just after twelve with the information that there was a sun dance going on on the north side of the reserve. "They're already camping. Let's go there after work. Pick me up around four."

"I can't wait to go to the sun dance! Do you go to them often?" Hilda asked Lucy.

"No, I never have. I don't know much about them," Lucy said.

"But why? Don't you believe in it? It's your culture!" Hilda's face showed concern.

"Well, they never had sun dances here – in my whole life there's never been a sun dance here."

"Really, is that true? But I thought you have them every year here."

"Not here. Over on the Blood Reserve they do and some places in the States, but not here."

"But don't you want to go to a sun dance? I think it's so exciting!" Hilda moved forward in her seat and looked hopefully at Lucy.

Lucy smiled at her eagerness. "No, I don't care to go. It's mostly those mixed-up people who are in it. You see, Indian religion just came back here on the reserve a little while ago, and there are different groups who all quarrel over which way to practice it. Some use Sioux ways, and others use Cree. It's just a big mess," she said, shaking her head.

Hilda looked at Lucy, and Lucy got the feeling she was telling her things she didn't want to hear. Lucy had chosen this time of day to do her wash. The Happy Suds Laundromat would be empty. As a rule, the Indians didn't show up till after lunch with their endless garbage bags of laundry. After they had deposited their laundry in the machines, Lucy, Hilda, and the kids sauntered down the main street to a cafe for lunch. An unkempt Indian man dogged them, talking in Blackfoot.

"Do you know what he's saying?" asked Hilda.

"He wants money. He's related to my husband. Don't pay any attention to him. He always does this," said Lucy. "I used to give him money, but he just drinks it up."

The café was a cool respite from the heat outside, and the cushioned seats in the booth felt good. They sat by the window and ordered hamburgers, fries, and lemonade. The waitress brought tall, frosted glasses, and beads of water dripped from them.

"Hello, Lucy," a man's shaky voice said, just when they were really enjoying their lunch. They turned to look at the Indian standing behind Hilda. He was definitely ill. His eyes held pain, and he looked as though he might collapse from whatever ailed him. His hands shook, perspiration covered his face, and his eyes roamed the room constantly. Lucy moved over to make room for him, but he kept standing and asked her, "Could you give me a ride down to Badger? The cops said I have to leave town. I don't want to stay 'cause they might beat me up."

"Yeah, we're doing laundry. I've got Flora's car. This is her friend, Hilda. She's from Germany."

The sick man barely nodded at her, then, turning back to Lucy, he asked her, "Do you have enough to get me some soup. I'm really hungry." Lucy nodded and the man said, "I'll just sit in the next booth."

"He's my uncle," Lucy explained to Hilda as she motioned to the waitress. "His name is Sonny."

"Order some clear soup or you'll get sick," Lucy suggested to her uncle. He nodded, as he pulled some paper napkins out of a chrome container on the table and wiped his face.

The women and children left Sonny with his broth and returned to the Laundromat. As they were folding the clothes, he came in. "Here, I'll take these," he said, taking the bags from Lucy. His hands shook, and the effort of lifting the bags was clearly too much for him. "That's okay," protested Lucy, attempting to take them from him, "they're not that heavy. Clothes are always lighter after they've been washed."

"Hey, Lucy, I can manage. You're not supposed to be carrying big things around in your condition." Lucy let him take the plastic bags, which he dropped several times before he got to the car. The cops had probably tired of putting him in jail and sending him out each morning. She believed the cops did beat up Indians, although none was ever brought to court over it. She'd take Sonny home, and he'd straighten out for a few weeks till he got thirsty again, and he'd disappear as soon as he got money. It was no use to hope he'd stop drinking. Sonny wouldn't quit drinking till he quit living.

As they were pulling out of town, Lucy remembered she had to get some Kool-Aid and turned the car into the Stop-n-Go Mart. Hilda got out with her and noticed the man who had followed them through the street sitting in the shade of a stack of old tires. "Hey, tamohpomaat sikaohki," he told Lucy on her way into the store.

"What did he say? Sikaohki?" queried Hilda.

The Kool-Aid was next to the cash register, and she picked up a few packages and laid them on the counter with the money. When the cashier turned to the register, Lucy poked Hilda with her elbow and nodded her head toward the sign behind the counter. Scrawled unevenly in big, black letters, it said, "Ask for Lysol, vanilla, and shaving lotion at the counter."

They ignored the man on the way to the car. "That's what he wants; he's not allowed to go into the stores 'cause he steals it. He wanted vanilla. The Indians call it 'sikaohki'; it means 'black water.'"

Although the car didn't have air-conditioning, Lucy hurried toward it to escape the blistering heat. When she got on the highway, she asked her uncle, "Did you hear anything about a sun dance?"

At first he grunted a negative "Huh-uh," then, "Oh, yeah, it's across the river, but I don't know where. George Many Robes is camping there. Saw him this morning. Are you going there?"

"Flora and Hilda are. Hilda wants to meet that German guy, Helmut Walking Eagle. You know, that guy who turned Indian?"

"Oh yeah, is he here?" he said indifferently, closing his eyes.

"Probably. He's always in the middle of Indian doings," said Lucy.

"Shit, that guy's just a phony. How could anybody turn into something else? Huh? I don't think I could turn into a white man if I tried all my life. They wouldn't let me, so how does that German think he can be an Indian. White people think they can do anything – turn into Chinese or Indian – they're crazy!"

Sonny laid his head back on the seat and didn't say another word. Lucy felt embarrassed, but she had to agree with him; it seemed that Indians had come into focus lately. She'd read in the papers how some white woman in Hollywood became a medicine woman. She was selling her book on her life as a medicine woman. Maybe some white person or other person who wasn't Indian would get fooled by that book, but not an Indian. She herself didn't practice Indian religion, but she knew enough about it to know that one didn't just join an Indian religious group if one were not raised with it. That was a lot of the conflict going on among those people who were involved in it. They used sacred practices from other tribes, Navajo and Sioux, or whatever pleased them.

The heat of the day had reached its peak, and trails of dust hung suspended in the air wherever cars or trucks traveled the gravel roads on the reserve. Sonny fashioned a shade behind the house underneath the clothesline in the deep grass, spread a blanket, and filled a gallon jar from the pump. He covered the water with some old coats, lay down, and began to sweat the booze out. The heat waves from this morning's forecast were accurate. It was just too hot. "Lordy, it's hot," exclaimed Lucy to Hilda as they brought the laundry in. "It must be close to ninety-five or one hundred. Let's go up to Badger to my other aunt's house. She's got a tap by her house and the kids can cool off in her sprinkler. Come on, you kids. Do you want to go run in the sprinkler?"

The women covered the windows on the west side where the sun would shine. "I'm going to leave all the windows open to let the air in," said Lucy, as she walked around the house pushing them up.

Lucy's aunt's house sat amongst a clutter of junk. "Excuse the mess," she smiled at Hilda, waving her arm over her yard. "Don't wanna throw it away, it might come in handy." There were thick grass and weeds crisscrossed with paths to and from the clothesline, the outhouse, the wood stove. Lucy's aunt led them to an arbor shaded with huge spruce branches.

"This is nice," cooed Hilda, admiring the branches. Lucy's aunt beamed, "Yes, I told my old man, 'Henry, you get me some branches that's not gonna dry up and blow away,' and he did. He knows what's good for him. You sit down right here, and I'll get us some drinks." She disappeared and soon returned with a large thermos and some plastic tumblers. They spent the afternoon hearing about Henry, as they watched the kids run through the sprinkler that sprayed the water back and forth. Once in a while, a suggestion of a breeze would touch the women, but it was more as if they imagined it.

Before four, they left to pick Flora up and headed back to Lucy's. "It's so hot after being in that cool cement building all day!" exclaimed Flora, as she settled herself into the car's stifling interior. "One thing for sure, I'm not going home to cook anything. Lucy, do you think Bunky would mind if you came with us? I'll get us some Kentucky Fried Chicken and stuff in town so you don't have to cook. It's too hot to cook, anyway." She rolled up a newspaper and fanned her face, which was already beginning to flush.

"No, he won't care. He'll probably want to sleep. We picked Sonny up in town. Both of them can lie around and get better. The kids would bother them if we were there."

It was a long ride across the Napi River toward the Porcupine Hills. A few miles from the Hills, they veered off until they were almost by the river. "Let's get off," said Flora.

Hilda gasped at what she saw before her. There was a circle of tepees and tents with a large open area in the middle. Exactly in the center of the opening was a circular structure covered with branches around the sides. Next to this was a solitary unpainted tepee. Some of the tepees were painted with lines around the bottom; others had orbs bordering them, and yet others had animal figures painted on them. Smoke rose from stoves outside the tepees as people prepared their evening meals. Groups of horses stood languidly in the waning heat of the day, their heads resting on one another's backs and their tails occasionally flicking insects away. The sound of bantering children and yapping dogs carried to where they stood.

"Let's eat here," the kids said, poking their heads in to look in the bags of food. Flora and Lucy spread a blanket on the ground, while Hilda continued to stand where she was, surveying the encampment. Flora pointed out the central leafy structure as the sacred area of prayer and dance.

"The tepee next to it is the sacred tepee. That's where the holy woman who is putting up the sun dance stays the entire time. That's where they have the ceremonies."

"How many sun dances have you been to?" asked Hilda.

"This is my first time, but I know all about this from books," said Flora. "Helmut Walking Eagle wrote a book about it, too. I could try to get you one. He sells them cheaper to Indians."

Hilda didn't eat much and kept looking down at the camp. "It's really beautiful," she said, as if to herself.

"Well, you better eat something before you get left out," advised Lucy. "These kids don't know when to stop eating chicken."

"Yeah," agreed Flora. "Then we can go down and see who's all there." Hilda had something to eat, and then they got back into the car and headed down toward the encampment. They drove around the edge of the camp and stopped by Flora's cousin's tent. "Hi, Delphine," said Flora, "I didn't know you were camping here." Lucy knew Flora and Delphine were not especially close. Their fathers were half-brothers, which made them half-cousins. Delphine had grown up Mormon and had recently turned to Indian religion, just as Flora had grown up Catholic and was now exploring traditional beliefs. The same could be said about many of the people here. To top things off, there was some bad feeling between the cousins about a man, some guy they both had been involved with in the past.

"Can anybody camp here? I've got a tepee. How about if I camp next to you."

Delphine bridled. "You're supposed to camp with your own clan." Flora looked around the camp. "I wonder who's my clan. Say, there's George Many Robes, he's my relation on my dad's side. Maybe I'll ask him if I can camp next to him."

Delphine didn't say anything but busied herself with splitting kindling from a box of sawn wood she kept hidden underneath a piece of tarp. Jason spied a thermos under the tarp and asked for a drink of water.

"I have to haul water, and nobody pays for my gas," grumbled Delphine, as she filled a cup halfway with water.

"Oh, say," inquired Flora, "do you know if Helmut Walking Eagle is coming here? This girl is from Germany, and she wants to see him."

21

"Over there, that big tepee with a Winnebago beside it. That's his camp," Delphine answered, without looking at them.

"Is she mad at you?" Jason asked Flora.

"Yeah, it must be the heat," Flora told him with a little laugh.

Elsie Walking Eagle was cooking the evening meal on a camp stove outside the tepee. She had some folding chairs that Lucy would've liked to sit down in, but Elsie didn't ask any of them to sit down though she was friendly enough.

"Is your husband here?" asked Flora.

"No, he's over in the sacred tepee," answered Elsie.

"How long is he going to take?"

"Oh, he should be home pretty soon," Elsie said, tending her cooking.

"D'you mind if we just wait? I brought this girl to see him. She's from Germany, too," Flora said.

Lucy had never seen Helmut in anything other than Indian regalia. He was a smallish man with blond hair, a broad face, and a large thin nose. He wore his hair in braids and always wore round, pink shell earrings. Whenever Lucy saw him, she was reminded of the Plains Indian museum across the line.

Helmut didn't even glance at the company but went directly inside the tepee. Flora asked Elsie, "Would you tell him we'd like to see him?"

"Just wait here. I'll go talk to him," Elsie said, and followed her husband inside. Finally, she came out and invited them in. "He doesn't have much time to talk with you, so . . ." Her voice trailed off. The inside of the tepee was stunning. It was roomy, and the floor was covered with buffalo hides. Backrests, wall hangings, parfleche bags, and numerous artifacts were magnificently displayed. Helmut Walking Eagle sat resplendent amidst his wealth. The women were dazzled. Lucy felt herself gaping and had to shush her children from asking any questions. Helmut looked at them intently and rested his gaze on Hilda. Hilda walked toward him, her hand extended in greeting, but Helmut ignored it. Helmut turned to his wife and asked in Blackfoot, "Who is this?"

"She says she's from Germany," was all Elsie said, before making a quick move toward the door.

"Wait!" he barked in Blackfoot, and Elsie stopped where she was.

"I only wanted to know if you're familiar with my home town Wiesbaden?" said Hilda.

"Do you know what she's talking about?" Helmut asked Elsie in Blackfoot. Elsie shook her head in a shamed manner.

"Why don't you ask her questions about Germany?" He hurled the words at Hilda, then, looking meanly at his wife, he added, "She's been there." Elsie flinched and, forcing a smile, waved weakly at the intruders and asked them in a kind voice to come outside. As Lucy waited to leave, she looked at Helmut, whose jaw twitched with resentment. His anger seemed to be tangibly reaching out to them.

"Wow!" whispered Hilda in Lucy's ear.

Outside, Flora touched a book on the fold-out table. Its title read *Indian Medicine* and in smaller letters, *A Revival of Ancient Cures and Ceremonies.* There was a picture of Helmut and Elsie on the cover. Flora asked, "Is this for sale?"

"No, that one's for someone here at camp, but you can get them in the bookstores."

"How much are they?" Flora asked, turning the book over.

"They're twenty-seven dollars. A lot of work went into it," Elsie replied.

Helmut, in Blackfoot, called out his wife's name, and Elsie said to her unwelcome callers, "I don't have time to visit. We have a lot of things to do." She left them and went in to her husband.

"Do you think she wrote that book?" Lucy asked Flora.

"He's the brains; she's the source," Flora said. "Let's go. My kids are probably wondering what happened to me."

"I'm sorry I upset her husband. I didn't mean to," said Hilda. "I thought he would be willing to teach me something, because we're both German."

"Maybe you could buy his book," suggested Lucy.

"Look," said Flora, "if you're going to be around for a while, I'm going to a sun dance this next weekend. I'm taking a few days off work. I have a friend up north who can teach you about Indian religion. She's a medicine woman. She's been to Germany. Maybe she even went to your home town."

"Oh, really!" gushed Hilda. "Of course, I'll be around. I'd love to go with you and meet your friends."

"You can come into the sweat with us. First, you'll need to buy four square yards of cotton . . ." began Flora.

But Hilda wasn't really listening to her. She looked as if she were already miles and miles away in the north country. Now, a sweat, she thought, would be real Indian.

Germany's Indians in a European Perspective

CHRISTIAN F. FEEST

"Of all Europeans, the German has the greatest love for the Indian," the German travel writer Hans Rudolf Rieder wrote in the epilogue to his book *Lagerfeuer im Indianerland*. "It is almost as if a piece of the Indian was in each one of us."[1] Already in 1924, Lisa Barthel-Winkler had written: "In *Winnetou* Karl May delineates the Indian drama. It is also the German drama. . . . Who has grasped the meaning of the Indian drama, has also grasped the meaning of the German drama."[2] Under the pseudonym Barwin the same author published a novel in 1943, in which Pontiac is depicted as a fascist leader who, in his attempt to save his race against British duplicity, is assisted by a young German appropriately named Kraft.[3]

In 1939, the year in which Rieder stressed the special relationship between Germans and Indians, Commissioner of Indian Affairs John Collier spread the rumor that the German government had declared the Sioux to be "Aryans" and that the nationalist "German-American Bund" was now attempting to incite the Indians to resist the draft.[4]

A German colleague told me how as a boy during the Second World War during his visits to the Karl-May-Museum in Radebeul, he pondered the question whether the Indians were now the allies of the Germans, because both nations were at war with the United States. A similar reasoning may have stood behind Karl May's decision to make the Apaches the heroes of his Indian novels and the special friends of his German Westerner Old Shatterhand: after all, May had been inspired to write about adventures in the American-Mexican border region of the Southwest in the course of his translation of Gabriel Ferry's *Le coureur de bois*, in which the Comanches were depicted as the allies of the French in their battle against the Apaches. If one's enemies' enemies were one's friends, it followed that shortly after the Franco-German War of 1870-1871, the Apaches must be on the side of the Germans.[5]

Although Karl May first personally encountered Native Americans long after writing his Indian novels, Lisa Barthel-Winkler used him as a key witness on German-Indian affinities; moreover, as late as the 1960s, the U.S. State

Department recommended that its staff read May's novels for a better understanding of the German psyche. This recommendation was prompted perhaps in part because, according to Albert Speer, Adolf Hitler had extolled May's Apache hero Winnetou as "the very model of a company commander," or because in 1944 the German Army High Command had ordered three thousand volumes of May's novels as handbooks for partisan warfare.[6]

Rather than piling up more evidence of this kind, I would like to place the presumed affinity between "Germans" and "Indians" in a wider European perspective and offer some comments on the assumption of what might be called "German exceptionalism." I would also like – again in a wider perspective – to outline some of the needs and opportunities for further research and reflection.

At the outset it may be useful to clarify the terms "German" and "Indian." The Columbus year of 1992 reminded us that there were no Indians living on the continent later to be known as America when the errant Italian sailor arrived on its shores. "Indians," as a conveniently simplified cover term for the multitude of different peoples inhabiting what only for Europeans was a "New World," is a European invention, and it has been "Indians" who have inhabited the European (and Euro-American) mind ever since. Much of the history of European-Indian relations is thus part of a history of European ideas, their development, and their diffusion. The "Indian" is nothing more nor less than a concept created by the white man for his own use and enjoyment.[7]

The spread of the concept is in fact a convenient measure for the Europeanization of other parts of the world. When in 1971 I began my research for a brief survey on "Indians in Non-English Literature," I wrote letters to Turkey to ask whether anybody knew of Turkish literature on Indians.[8] My correspondents at that time were puzzled and possibly mildly amused at the idea that Turks should take any interest in such exotic subject matter. Apparently, not even Karl May's *Winnetou* novels had been translated into Turkish (which is strange since the trilogy was translated even into artificial languages such as Esperanto and Volapük); otherwise, my Turkish correspondents would have learned from May's preface to the first volume that the Indians were the Turks of America, a vanishing race. My contacts occurred some years before the appearance of the now famous Indian bumper sticker asserting "I'm glad Columbus wasn't looking for Turkey." The confusion between Indians and turkeys, however, has a long tradition. In fact, the name "turkey" for the fowl is based on the same mistake as is the term "Turkish wheat" for "maize," and, indeed, some regional variants of German still use the designation "Indian" for the feathered animal. In the meantime, however, the Turks have caught up with western Europe and have begun looking for both Columbus and the Indians, and so the *Turkish Journal of American Studies* publishes a surprisingly large number of essays especially on contemporary Native American literature, but also on other Indian subject matter. (There is, by the way, also a growing interest in India in the study of "the other Indians.")

The major problem in dealing with the notion of "the Indian" on a conceptual basis lies, of course, in its apparent function as an expression of "otherness," both threatening and inviting, that serves to define the "self" through oppositional contrasts. As a result, the images of "the Indian" produced by Europeans over the past five hundred years have varied tremendously, not only because of the inherent dichotomy, but also because of the ever-changing needs of those who have come to employ it.

As to "the Germans," I must confess that especially during those eleven years in an earlier part of my life when I was a German citizen without ever having lived in Germany, I had been led to believe that, indeed, there were "Germans." Now that I have lived and worked in Germany as an Austrian citizen, I have found to my amazement that I had been grossly mistaken. What one finds referred to as "the Germans" in the literature and media is, in fact, an assortment of rather different peoples who speak a variety of languages and who seem to find a semblance of unity when it comes to soccer. In a recent survey, a representative sample of persons living in Germany was asked to rank their identities as inhabitants of their region, as Germans, and as Europeans. The result appears to corroborate my more anecdotal observations: the vast majority of those surveyed thought of themselves first and foremost as inhabitants of their region, a rather substantial number thought of themselves as Europeans, and only a small minority identified themselves primarily as Germans. Thus, the first affinity between Indians and Germans may be that both categories are largely fictional.

Social identities are, of course, always socially constructed, so it is not overly surprising to find them change over time. This is particularly true for German identity formation, whose complex history I cannot fully review here (for more on German identity, see Hartmut Lutz's paper in this anthology). But it is clear that Germanness occupied many people in the German-speaking world, especially during the late eighteenth and nineteenth centuries in connection with the invention of the idea of "Volkstum" and/or "nationhood" and the rise of the nation-state, as national identity occupied other European peoples during the same period, for the same reasons. It is indeed likely that early forms of Pan-Indianism, like the attempts of Pontiac or Tecumseh to forge supratribal alliances, are related to these developments in Europe either through the diffusion of ideas or through the manner in which these indigenous political movements were perceived by Euro-American observers.

The question of national unity is a prominent theme in German Indian fiction as well, in both the nineteenth century and the first half of the twentieth century. That this should be so is, of course, not a reflection of any real affinity, but a function of the ideological need, more prevalent in those past periods than it is today, to affirm the claim of German unity. The failure to attain such unity is seen in novels, such as the Tecumseh series by Nazi hack writer Fritz Steuben, as the primary cause of the Indians' doom.[9]

Yet it is perceived affinities such as the shared need for national unity in a world dominated by Anglophones and Francophones conspiring against Germans and Indians that has led several of the authors to assert the existential affinity of the two more or less fictional peoples. This conclusion is based on a now unfashionable essentialist view, which considers the shared historical experience or commonality of fate, best expressed by the German term "Schicksalsgemeinschaft," one of the central features defining ethnicity or "Volkstum." There were other such perceived affinities in the past. Florike Egmond and Peter Mason have recently shown how in early-seventeenth-century Germany the perception of the ancient Teutonic peoples was already related to images of American Indians.[10] After all, the case can be made that the Germans, as depicted in the writings of Tacitus, were the Indians of the Romans. But so were the Gauls and the Picts.

For the promoters of the Virginia Company of London, such perceived similarities were translated into appeals for public support of the colonization of Virginia and the Christianization of its Native inhabitants. A broadside published in 1615 to announce a lottery for the benefit of the Virginia Company of London shows the images of two Native Virginians together with a poem that begins with the following lines:

Once, in one State, as of one Stem
Meere Strangers from Ierusalem,
As Wee, were Yee; till Others Pittie
Sought, and brought You to That Cittie.[11]

Similarity turned into identity when, in 1669, Morgan Jones, a Welshman, was captured by the Doegs in North Carolina and, according to his own account, was saved from certain execution by the fact that his presumably last words ("Have I escaped so many dangers, and must I now be knocked on the head like a dog?") uttered in Welsh were understood by his captors, who thus recognized him as a relative and set him free.[12] While hardly significant in the official colonial propaganda, this and related tales supporting the legendary pre-Columbian discovery of America by Prince Madoc supply evidence for the perceived affinity and even consanguinity of the colonizers and the colonized.

Although the Germans never had much need to legitimize any colonial ventures of their own in North America, the theme of a Nordic ancestry of the Indians, especially those of the Northeast, occasionally turns up in popular fiction of the Nazi period, where a Viking ancestry, courtesy of Eric the Red, is claimed at least for the chiefly lineages.[13] It also appears in Swedish fiction, where a Native descendant of Swedish colonists becomes a Pan-Indian hero.[14] On a much deeper level, a Hungarian linguist has suggested a relationship between the Finno-Ugrian language family and the Pomoan languages of California.[15] Although this suggested evidence for a common ancestry of the Hungarians and the Indians has so far not met with the approval of either the Finno-Ugrianists or even the most daring Pan-Penutianists, it shows that the desire to identify with the Indians is a widespread European phenomenon, rather than just a German aberration.

Even if the idea of a shared German-Indian ancestry remained a pipe dream, the proposition of an ultimate merging of Germans and Indians was actually suggested in negotiations leading to the "private treaty" of 1847 between the German colonists of New Braunfels in Texas and the Comanches.[16] In proposing the treaty, the colony's leader, Baron Otfried Hans von Meusebach, not only promised that the Germans and the Comanches should "live together like one people of brothers." He told the assembled Comanches: "If our people will have lived together with yours for some time and we have come to know one another, it may well be that some will want to intermarry. Soon the warriors of our tribe will learn your language. If they are then so inclined and agree upon marriage, I know of no obstacle, and our peoples will become the better friends."[17] The treaty is proudly referred to by Texas-Germans (and some Germans as well) as "the only Indian treaty never broken," but these and other fair promises it contained were never redeemed, as the Comanches were soon to learn when the Germans did not come to their succor when they were expelled from the region by the Americans.

The idea of legitimating the conquest through an amalgamation of colonizers and colonized had, of course, already been put into practice to some extent by the French. Among the English, the marriage between Pocahontas and John Rolfe was for a long time regarded as a sufficiently symbolic act to serve the same purpose, but not as an example deserving widespread emulation. In the early eighteenth century, however, William Byrd, the Virginian trader, pointed to the French practice as a possible model for the English as well.[18] A similar suggestion of about the same period is found in an anonymous proposal for a better way to civilize the Indians submitted to the Bishop of London: it suggests that presents of trade goods should be placed at strategic points along the borders of the Indian country in order to attract some of the Indians, who would then be taken into English homes where they would learn the language and ultimately intermarry with their hosts. The resulting offspring, brought up in Christian civility but still speaking their Native language, could then be sent back to the Indian country as missionaries to convert their relatives.[19]

On an individual, rather than a collective level, Indian ancestry has been claimed by an assortment of French, English, Polish, and German writers and artists, who were thus attempting to transform themselves in the eyes of the world into real Indians. The most famous of all was, of course, the Englishman Archie Belaney, who successfully mutated into Grey Owl.[20] But the Iroquois identity of French writer William Camus is as dubious as the Blackfoot (or Cheyenne) descent of the German Nazi painter Elk Eber or the Shawnee affiliation of the Polish writer Sat-Ohk.

Another rather popular Pan-European method to become an Indian is, of course, what has traditionally been called "hobbyism" and more recently, especially by those practitioners who think of their activity as an avocation rather than as a pastime, as "Indianism." The phenomenon of non-Indians emulating what they believe to be "Indian" lifestyles actually encompasses a number of distinct, although probably related, practices. These range from children playacting Indians in a rather stereotypical manner, inspired by fictional representations of Indian life in novels and films, to rather serious attempts to imitate more or less specific indigenous cultures, although the imitation of Plains Indian cultures, which most closely approach the popular Western understanding of "the Indian," is the most common. Other related practices of cultural transvestism (with varying emphases on the emulation of dress styles and values) include the Indian ballets so popular in the seventeenth century, temporary or permanent changes of the social identity of persons actually accepted as members of Native groups, or the activities of boy scouts.[21] The origins and interrelationships of these practices are still imperfectly understood, and their evaluation by Native and non-Native observers has ranged from acceptance to puzzlement to rejection as outright blasphemy or as an inappropriate form of "cultural appropriation."[22]

Few observers have doubted the possibility and validity of voluntary or even forced changes in the social identity of Euro-American captives or cultural renegades living among Native American groups and forsaking the affiliation with their culture of origin in favor of an alternative lifestyle, or of assimilation of persons of Native American descent into white society. But many of the very same commentators who have expressed a heartfelt understanding of the desire of disenchanted members of white societies to "go Native" have harshly criticized Indian hobbyists, whose activities they brand as insensitive, exploitative, and demeaning. Ward Churchill, to cite only one recent example, has accused them of insincerity because they pursue an economic survival strategy in the very capitalist world they attempt to escape in their spare time.[23] At the same time, however, one is reminded of John Barth's speculation in *The Sot-Weed Factor* about "some unreckoned law of compensation," according to which for every Indian who assimilates into white society there must be a white person who turns into an Indian.[24] As an anthropologist reared in the tradition of accepting cultural otherness, while at the same time trying to understand and explain it, I accept the practice of hobbyism as a subcultural reality, which cannot be criticized just because it deviates from my own cultural norms. I am as puzzled by these subcultural practices as I am puzzled and intrigued by other cultures, and I can only regret that so little serious attention has been devoted to understanding and explaining them beyond the assertion that they are a form of cultural escapism. The phenomenon could be more fruitfully compared to the "cultural conversion" (or is it only a "travesty of lifestyles"?) of cultural renegades.[25]

Like other observers, Churchill described hobbyism as a peculiarly German phenomenon. But this is clearly a misrepresentation of the facts; nor is the phenomenon related – as some others have suggested – to the writings of Karl May. Not only does hobbyism have a substantial tradition in the United States, but it occurs nearly everywhere in western, northern, central, and eastern Europe.[26] In some regions it appears to be a fairly recent phenomenon, but it has deep historical roots in countries such as Great Britain, the Netherlands, France, and the former Czechoslovakia. Although there are recent video documentaries on Indian hobbyism in the Czech Republic and in Russia, the prominence of German hobbyism may be attributable to the fact that it has been covered earlier and more frequently in the media and that it has even been the subject of some serious research.[27]

Another fact that is frequently overlooked is the relatively minor scope of this kind of cultural transvestism. Even if the number of organized Indian hobbyists in Germany ranges between ten thousand and twenty thousand and may seem large when compared to the residential population of most Indian reservations, hobbyists are scattered across the country and amount at best to as little as .0025 percent of the total population.

Christian F. Feest

Undoubtedly, the functions of German hobbyism, which has a recorded history of about one hundred years, have changed greatly over time.[28] This is particularly apparent in the former GDR or what are now called the "new states" of the Federal Republic of Germany. In the old GDR, hobbyism provided, among other things, a safe way to dream about America and about alternatives to the prevailing drab and conformist lifestyle, because the government found it hard to crack down on groups of its citizens who identified strongly with a minority oppressed by American imperialism.[29] Even other groups of cultural imitators, such as those wishing to be cowboys or Confederate soldiers, sought refuge under the umbrella of the Indian clubs. Contrary to the situation in Western Europe, where hobbyists were often frowned upon by members of political Indian support groups, hobbyism and solidarity peacefully coexisted in the East German clubs. Since the unification of Germany, at least some of the East German groups have developed a certain nostalgia for the old socialist system, in part because the ideological reservations the old government had created for them have now been opened up to competition and free-market forces.[30]

Since dependable studies of hobbyist groups outside Germany are even rarer than studies of those in Germany, it is not possible to determine whether the motivations for the practice are the same and to what extent local factors are responsible for specific expressions of the same phenomenon.[31] There has been a recent surge of interest in European Indian hobbyism among Native Americans, and one hopes that they will be able to avoid the mistakes they have accused anthropologists of making in their studies of Native American cultures.

There is sufficient evidence that in the past quite a few Germans managed to be accepted by Native American groups as members in good standing and that some even moved up to positions of political leadership. These include not only Solomon Bibo, a German Jew from Westphalia who was elected Governor of Acoma Pueblo in the 1880s, but also a compatriot from the principality of Waldeck, encountered in 1778 as an Indian chief by the British mercenaries during their sojourn in Florida.[32] That such transformations were not the product of a specific German-Indian affinity is indicated by the similar fate of Englishmen and Frenchmen during the colonial period. The likelihood of a white man becoming an Indian chief was so generally accepted in the nineteenth century that after the Battle of the Little Bighorn rumors circulated that even Sitting Bull himself was, in fact, a disenchanted American who had joined the Lakotas to guide them to victory over his former country's army. As in the case of the fictional chiefs of Norse descent, these equally imagined white roots of Sitting Bull also provided a neat explanation for the unusual military genius of a leader of so-called savages, an idea also exemplified by Karl May's Apache hero Winnetou, whose outstanding abilities are in part explained by the instructions Winnetou received from his German teacher, who had emigrated after the revolution of 1848 and ended up with the Mescaleros.

It is well known that Europeans of various descriptions came to live with and transform into Native peoples in North America.[33] This phenomenon is neatly illustrated by an anecdote related by Father Alfons Stelzig, a German priest from Prague, who for some time served the spiritual needs of German communities in Texas in the 1840s. Once, or so his story goes, the German settlers were attacked by a group of apparently hostile Indians. Just when Stelzig thought he was about to be tomahawked by a horrible-looking "savage," the Indian paused, fell on his knees, and asked the father in Czech: "Ježis Maria Josefe! Pane Stelzig kde pak se tu berou?" [Jesus, Mary, and Joseph! Mr. Stelzig, what are you doing here?] The Indian turned out to be Wenzel Přihoda, Stelzig's former bootblack in Prague, who had married into the tribe.[34] Given the somewhat precarious relationship between Germans and Czechs in Prague, it is indeed fitting that the two men should have ended up on opposite sides on the other side of the Atlantic as well. Taken in isolation or in conjunction with the living tradition of Czech Indian hobbyism, a strong case could be made for the special nature of Czech-Indian relationships.

Robert Dunlap Clarke, claimed, tongue in cheek, that Sitting Bull was a polyglot and that this ability extended to writing German poems. An officer on General Terry's staff, Clarke included in his second edition of *The Works of Sitting Bull in the Original Latin and French* (1878) a long poem presumably written by the famous exile in Canada, the various parts of which were in six different languages, including ancient Greek and German. That the German was rather poor by any standard should certainly not be blamed on its presumed author. At the time the little volume was published, however, Sitting Bull had already had his first recorded encounter with a Native speaker of German, Bishop Martin Marty of Switzerland, who had tried unsuccessfully to convince Sitting Bull to return to the United States.

More significant for our investigation of German-Indian relationships, however, was an encounter that occurred three years later, shortly after Sitting Bull had surrendered at Fort Buford and had been confined with what remained of his loyal followers at Fort Randall in South Dakota. In October 1881 he was visited by a young German journalist and artist, Rudolf Cronau, who had been sent to the United States as a special correspondent by the largest German family journal of the day, *Die Gartenlaube*. It says something about his priorities that Cronau instantly proceeded to Washington to get permission from both the Secretary of the Interior, Carl Schurz (himself a German), and the Army command to visit Indian reservations. It is not clear why Cronau first went to Standing Rock, where he stayed for three weeks, camping with the Hunkpapa away from the agency, although it is possible that the notoriety of Sitting Bull had led him there. After sketching as many Lakotas as were willing to sit for him, Cronau moved on to Fort Randall, where he was well received, partly because so many of the soldiers were of German origin. These included the quartermaster, named Retzius, and his clerk, Fritz Schenk of Switzerland, whose teacher in his native Bern had been Rudolf Friedrich Kurz, the artist, who had spent some years among various tribes on the upper Missouri and was now telling his students how much fun it had been to live with the Indians.[35]

Cronau quickly established contacts with Sitting Bull, who seemed happy to find someone who would write letters for him to Washington, and who in return was ready to pose for the artist. While sketching him, Cronau (according to his own account) tried to teach Sitting Bull some German, at the same time attempting to pick up some Lakota words himself. If we can trust Cronau (and there may be reason not to), the old Hunkpapa and the young German quickly became friends. When he departed just a week later, the assembled Lakotas gave "Iron Eye," as they called the bespectacled journalist, a tearful good-bye. They asked him to come back soon, which he never did, although he claimed to have left good friends behind. On parting, Cronau presented Sitting Bull with his photograph, inscribed on its back: "To my friend Tatanka-Iyotanka from Rudolf Cronau, special artist of *Die Gartenlaube.*"

Cronau's report on Sitting Bull was published by the *Gartenlaube* under the title "A Red Napoleon," a dubious epithet ten years after the Germans' latest war with France. It was republished twice in two different books that Cronau threw on the market in order to exploit the presence of Indian shows in Germany. The first show consisted of a group of Oglalas from Pine Ridge whom Cronau accompanied across Germany and Austria and who were somewhat inappropriately billed as "Sitting Bull Sioux Indians." The second one was Buffalo Bill's first appearance on the Continent. Shortly afterward Cronau returned to the United States, where he took up residence and became an American citizen. Sitting Bull had been killed in 1890, and in 1895 Cronau learned from a friend that a dealer in Los Angeles was offering for sale some personal belongings of Sitting Bull, including the photograph he had given to him in 1881. The photograph, he was told by the dealer, had been worn by Sitting Bull suspended from his neck by a rawhide string on the day he was shot and was, in fact, showing stains of his blood. Cronau declined to buy the whole lot at the asking price of one thousand dollars but investigated the case of the photograph to the extent that it became clear that Sitting Bull had certainly not carried it over his heart at the time of his death. Almost forty years later, Cronau finally acquired the picture from George Heye, the founder of the Museum of the American Indian, who had bought the collection. Cronau's account of the story of the photograph, first published around the time of his death presumably in one of the German-American journals to which he regularly contributed, culminates in the description of how Sitting Bull had worn Cronau's picture at the time of his death![36]

This account has sometimes been taken as an illustration of the deep affinity between Germans and Indians. What stronger image can one evoke than the most famous of all Indians wearing on his chest the picture of his German friend on the day he lost his life? Clearly, Cronau's visit to the Lakotas and to Sitting Bull created a lasting impression in his mind, and Sitting Bull even may have remembered the artist whose photograph he kept and whose influence on the style of his pictographic autobiographies produced at Fort Randall is clearly apparent. The evidence for a special relationship, however, is largely imaginary and apparently only the final stage of Cronau's clever marketing of his own work.

Sitting Bull's own repeated contacts with Germans are nothing but a reflection of the strong presence of Germans in late nineteenth-century America. At Fort Randall he was visited again by Bishop Marty (who was accompanied by a young Swiss missionary), and after he returned to Standing Rock, he received repeated visits from Father Bernard Strassmaier and perhaps other German Benedictines who were running the Catholic mission on the reservation. Sitting Bull never converted, and his German may not have improved notably in the course of his prolonged exposure to native speakers of the language, whom the Lakotas came to call "Bad Speakers," because the Germans' English may have been even worse than their own.

When Sitting Bull died, however, considerable attention was given to the event in Germany. Within months, several docu-fictional accounts appeared by authors such as Pistorius, Frey, Foehse, and Herold.[37] Five years later, Sitting Bull featured prominently in a German book on the occultism of the Indians.[38] Can we interpret this as an indication of a specific German interest in Indians in general and in Sitting Bull in particular? Probably not. Once again, the second visit of Buffalo Bill's Wild West shows provided a ready market for literature of this kind. And although I have not researched the other European literatures as diligently as I have the German publishing field, it appears that Sitting Bull received comparable attention elsewhere. In fact, the earliest European book on Sitting Bull appeared in France, years before anything was published about him in German: Joseph Bournichon's *Sitting Bull, le héros du désert. Scènes de la guerre indienne aux États-Unis.*[39] 1891 also saw the publication of a book on Sitting Bull in Danish, and a few years later a book in Swedish was published.[40] Given the much smaller number of speakers of Danish and Swedish, the interest was at least proportional to that shown by the Germans. Moreover, most of the early German literature on Sitting Bull was apparently based on American sources (with little additions taken from Cronau) and thus can hardly be regarded as a significantly *German* contribution to the field.

As the numerous titles published in the twentieth century reflect, things then changed. Books such as Georg Goll's *Dakota: Der Freiheitskampf der Sioux* of 1929 or Rudolf Daumann's two-volume novel published in the GDR in 1956-1957, for example, have strong anti-American accents, although one was written from a conservative-nationalist and the other from a socialist point of view.[41] In terms of sheer numbers, German books on Sitting Bull seem to outnumber publications in other languages, but this may in part reflect my inadequate coverage of the non-German literature. But whether written in French, Italian, or Swedish, they all have a marked pro-Indian bias, with earlier works depicting Sitting Bull primarily as a warrior and more recent books exploiting the newly fashionable stereotype of Indian spirituality.[42]

To summarize, it can be said that little of what Germans dreamed about with respect to their Indian affinities had not similarly been dreamed about by other Europeans. Most importantly, however, the German claim of a special bond or affinity between themselves and "the Indians" is far from unique. "We are the Indians of Europe" is something that has been asserted, not only by Germans, but also by members of various other European nations, from the French to the Finns (who – no matter how blonde and palefaced they are – often regard their non-Indo-European language as a distinct mark of this affinity). The claim is usually accompanied by the additional assertion that the fascination is mutual. Witness, for example, the expressed (and ultimately fulfilled) wish of Two-Two, who had come to Germany in 1914 as part of a Lakota troupe performing for Circus Sarrasani, to be buried on the Catholic cemetery in Dresden.[43] One foundation myth related by a French hobbyist group recalls the mythical encounter of a French farm worker in the American West with a group of Indians, who after getting to know the foreigner exclaimed in surprise: "You [the French] are the Indians of Europe!"[44]

The claim of exceptionalism thus appears to be something that is typical for certain segments of European societies but not universal either in Germany or elsewhere in Europe. Casual observers of the situation have sometimes accepted these claims at face value and have interpreted them as representing a feeling shared by Germans (or other Europeans) at large, but the vast majority of Germans (or British or Hungarians) would consider the suggestion of a spiritual kinship between themselves and Indians absurd.

The question then is: Why has the claim of a specific German-Indian relationship received such wide attention, while similar claims about other nations have been disregarded? My answer would be because German scholarship has devoted so much critical reflection to this phenomenon and to other aspects of the German interest in "Indians," which, of course, is also more prominent than, for example, the Hungarian or Danish interest because of the proportionally larger size of the German-speaking population and immigration into North America. Emigration may indeed be seen as a major factor in determining the interest in America in general and in the Indians in particular in the respective countries of origin.[45]

Even if we accept the Karl May phenomenon as one of unusual proportions, in part a result of the extraordinarily clever marketing of his works by his publisher, the fact remains that scholars have devoted much more attention to the second rank of German writers of Indian fiction such as Charles Sealsfield, Balduin Möllhausen, Friedrich Gerstäcker, and Fritz Steuben, than to comparable French authors such as Gabriel Ferry and Gustave Aimard, without whose writings Karl May would have been nearly unthinkable.[46] While Gabriel Chinard's studies of 1911 and 1934 remain the major surveys of French Indian fiction, several such surveys of German Indian fiction were made in the past, and there seems to be a ready market for more of the same.[47] The writings of Emilio Salgari, comparable to Karl May's in scope and success, have hardly been recognized and discussed by the world at large or even by Italian scholars.[48] Sat-Ohk, the Polish writer who claimed to be of Shawnee descent, is almost unknown outside Poland and the former GDR, where his works appeared in translation.

While I would like to see more studies of non-German fiction on Indians, which would help us place German writings in their proper European perspective, the German literature itself remains to be explored more fully. In a bibliographical survey I did many years ago, I was able to identify about one thousand titles of Indian fiction published in Germany between 1875 and 1900.[49] Many of these booklets are from 32 to 128 pages long and were published in several competing popular series. Taken together, they may have had a greater impact on German views of Indians than did the works of Karl

May, who actually emerged from this much larger group. Almost no attention has been devoted to these minor writings, partly because only a few have found their way into libraries. It has therefore been much easier to write yet another book on Karl May than to deal with his minor contemporaries. No comparative survey has been done on the size of this kind of literature in other languages, which would ultimately provide us with a sound basis for comparative purposes and for a sound measure of the relative interest in "Indians" by Germans and other Europeans.

In the case of visual representation, the German contribution has received much less recognition. Art historians have, of course, been aware of the importance of the art schools of Düsseldorf and Munich for nineteenth-century American painting, and the Indian-related work of German-American painters such as Charles Wimar, Albert Bierstadt, or Winold Reiss has been noted, because their works are available in American collections.[50] The work of Karl Bodmer, on the other hand, was not fully appreciated until the majority of his drawings came into American ownership in the 1950s.[51] Serious American interest in Balduin Möllhausen, who also produced paintings, has also been fairly recent.[52] Many other German, Swiss, or Austrian artists, such as Adolf Hoeffler, Lukas Vischer, Johann Baptist Wengler, and even Rudolf Friedrich Kurz, who depicted Indians, still remain relatively unknown, because their work is held mostly in European repositories.[53] This is even more true for artists whose work does not focus on the stereotypical Plains Indians – and for other European painters of Native American subject matter, such as the Frenchman Henry Farny, the Dutchman Cornelius Krieghoff, and the Swede Carl Oscar Borg.

In the case of photography, much work has been produced by German-Americans, from John Hillers through Eugene Buechel and Frederick Weygold to Ulli Steltzer, Helga Teiwes, and Christine Turnauer, but European photographers of Indians also include Italians, Swedes, Frenchmen, and Hungarians.[54] Archival resources of German photographs of Native Americans have only recently received some of the attention they deserve, for example, the late nineteenth-century Pueblo photographs of Aby Warburg or Karl von den Steinen.[55] Virtually unknown treasures exist in other European archives, such as the 1904 Hopi photographs of Ole Martin Solberg in Oslo.[56] Unlike some of the paintings, these photographs have not yet been studied. Until recently, the same was true of "Indian" movies. As Gerd Gemünden's contribution to this volume suggests, Indianerfilme can tell us much about the social and cultural needs of East and West Germans in the 1960s and 1970s.

With paintings and photographs, we have already moved from pure imagination of "the Indian" to interaction with real people. Scholars and missionaries left more tangible evidence of their encounters with Native Americans. In the case of missionaries, we find another illustration of the fact that the ready availability of the sources has affected scholarly discourse and consequently the general view of the relative importance of certain kinds of European-Indian relationships. Because of Thwaites's monumental collection *Jesuit Relations and Allied Documents*, the work of European missionaries in North America came to be equated with the work of French Jesuits in New France.[57] While the French Jesuits certainly played an important role on the continent, the ready availability of French texts in English obfuscated the work not only of mostly German Jesuits in the Greater Southwest, but also the great variety of European missionaries working in the United States throughout the nineteenth century. I have mentioned the German Benedictines on Standing Rock Reservation and could equally have referred to the German Jesuits on Pine Ridge and Rosebud — were it not for the ubiquity of German and other European missionaries among Native Americans. The question that should concern us here is whether we have any reasons other than accessibility to look at German missionaries in isolation from the rest of the field, in other words, to look at them as a specific expression of German-Indian relationships. While undoubtedly missionaries as well as other Europeans carried their specific cultural baggage into their encounters with Native Americans, some of the material suggests that ethnic difference was secondary to denominational differences or to cultural differences between the various Catholic missionary orders.

Another aspect of missionary encounters with Native Americans has only recently started to attract the attention of scholars, namely, their activity as collectors of Native material culture. I mention this factor specifically, because in the Western tradition of scholarship, which relies almost exclusively on words, the important information contained in artifacts is all too often overlooked. Not only do artifacts provide access to otherwise unrecorded information about cultures, but the aspect of selectivity inherent in any collecting is also an equally important insight into how the collectors perceived other cultures. One of the reasons for the relative neglect of these collections is that few of them have been properly identified and access to them is difficult.[58]

Separate ethnographic collections were, of course, the first institutions of the new scholarly discipline concerned with nature and classification of cultural differences, which emerged in the 1770s and whose earliest designations, "Ethnographie," "Völkerkunde," and "Ethnologie" were all coined within a

Christian F. Feest

few years in the German-speaking part of Europe together with the concept
of "culture," which became so basic to anthropology.[59] Taken in conjunction
with the importance of the work of Alexander von Humboldt in the early
nineteenth century, it is not surprising to find that German scholarly involvement with Native Americans got off to an early start. Among the early
achievements were Adelung and Vater's linguistic classification of American
Indian languages, followed by the more influential one of the Swiss-American
Albert Gallatin, the first (and notably bilingual) anthology of American Indian
poetry by Johann Christoph Adelung, a first book-length treatment of American Indian religions by the Swiss Johann Georg Müller, and one of the earlier
summaries of North American prehistory by Emil Schmidt. Another result
was the ethnographic work on the Upper Missouri by Maximilian Prince of
Wied; in terms of its importance in the history of ethnography, this work has
hardly been adequately recognized, in part because the only English translation available is inadequate and abbreviated.[60] But once again, scholarly
approaches to Native American subject matter was (and is) not a German pre-
rogative – the history of such scholars in other countries has been much less
well documented. If we disregard immigrants who became famous North
Americanists (Alexander Goldenweiser, Edward Sapir, and Paul Radin), Claude
Lévi-Strauss and Åke Hultkrantz are the best known European scholars outside Germany with research interests in Native Americans. But there are the
Dutch anthropologist Herman ten Kate, the Dutch linguist C. C. Uhlenbeck,
the Belgian Frans Olbrechts, the Romanian George Deveraux, the Dane Kaj
Birket-Smith, and many more from other countries.[61]

The work of Franz Boas with American Indians was the result of his unexpected encounter with a group of visiting Bella Coolas in Berlin in 1886. This
episode, finally, gives me the opportunity to refer at least briefly to the largely
unrecovered treasures hidden in the material relating to the encounter between Native Americans and Europeans in Europe, which for the study of
European-Indian relations in general and German-Indian relations in particular is of the utmost importance. This material is important because in
these encounters, which occurred between the sixteenth and the twentieth
century and whose number and frequency is generally underestimated, the
situation of the encounter in America is reversed: Whereas travelers, missionaries, artists, or scholars working in the field appear as isolated individuals,
and thus their cultural background retreats behind the task of grasping the
collective cultural difference of another group, the opposite is generally true
for the perception of Native American visitors to Europe. Here it is the visitors who are isolated from the cultural context, a situation that provides a

much clearer view of the cultural background of their observers. Bernd Peyer's paper on George Copway in this volume examines this particular kind of encounter and elucidates the interest inherent in studying the reception of Native American visitors in Europe and particularly in Germany.

As in most of the other subjects I have referred to, the larger number of existing studies of Native American visits to Germany is not a true indication of their relative frequency, but a skewed result of scholarly interest. Even the most preliminary surveys of the situation in other European countries reveal comparable enthusiasm when it come to Indians.[62] I firmly believe that in order to make sense of the specific nature of German-Indian affinities and relationships, it will be necessary to look at similar relationships across Europe.

Notes

1. Rieder, *Lagerfeuer*, 446.
2. Barthel-Winkler, "Drama," 343.
3. Haible, *Indianer*, 198–99; after World War II, Barwin turned to writing soapy dime novels for women, but her Pontiac book was republished in 1956 and even translated into Dutch.
4. Bernstein, *American Indians*, 25–26, 183 n. 15.
5. See Feest, "Indians and Europe?" 611.
6. Wood, "Role of the Romantic West," 316–17.
7. Berkhofer, *White Man's Indian*; see Lutz, "Indianer" und "Native Americans."
8. Feest, "Indian in Non-English."
9. Friedrichs, "Tecumseh's Fabulous Career"; Haible, *Indianer,* 148–281.
10. Egmond and Mason, *Mammoth*, 181–84.
11. Feest, "Virginia Indian," 8–10.
12. Owen, *British Remains*, 103–6.
13. See Gymir, *Sontschem.*
14. Linderholm, *Roda kampar.*
15. Sadovszky, *Discovery of California.*
16. Reproduced in Klotzbach, *Solms-Papiere,* 120.
17. Anonymous, "Texas."
18. Feest, "Pride and Prejudice."
19. Anonymous, "Proposals."
20. Smith, *From the Land.*
21. Taylor, "Indian Hobbyism Movement."
22. For example, Baskauskas and Medicine, "*Speaking the Spirit*"; Rickard, "Alterity."

23. Churchill, "Indians 'R' Us?"

24. Barth, *Sot-Weed Factor*, 696.

25. Kohl, " 'Travestie' "; see also Katrin Sieg's contribution on Indian hobbyism in this volume.

26. Powers, *Yuwipi*; also Deloria, *Playing Indian*.

27. For example, Baskauskas and Medicine, "Speaking the Spirit."

28. Conrad, "Mutual Fascination"; Bolz, "Life among the 'Hunkpapas.' "

29. Turski, "Indianist Groups"; see van der Heyden, "Native American Studies"; for a similar situation in Poland, see Nowicka, "Polish Movement."

30. While a substantial portion of German cultural impersonation is devoted to American role models, such as Indians, cowboys, and Confederates, the practice also extends to other historic cultures, such as the Middle Ages. It remains open to speculation whether those of our contemporaries who emulate the lifestyle depicted in the *Star Trek* series do so because of its basically American philosophy; at least, this example further illustrates the generally fictional nature of role models for playacting.

31. Bolz, "Life among the 'Hunkpapas' " is an exception with regard to comparisons of German and non-German hobbyists' motivation and local factors, see Dubois, "Indianism"; Maligne, "Cheval Debout"; N. N. "Indianism"; R. Hämäläinen, "We are the Mystic Warriors."

32. Regarding Bilbo, see M. L. Marks, *Jews among the Indians*, 122. For a discussion of the Waldeck-born chief, see Woringer, "Waldeckischer Indianerhäuptling."

33. See, for example, Hallowell, "American Indians"; Jacquin, "Indiens Blancs"; Kohl, "Travestie."

34. Feest, "Österreicher," 44.

35. Cronau, *Im Lande der Sioux*; Feest, *Sitting Bull*, 18–21, 81.

36. Cronau, "My Visit"; Feest, *Sitting Bull*, 18–21.

37. Pistorius, *Aufstand*; Frey, *Büffelauge*; Foehse, *Letzte Sitting Bull* (Last Sitting Bull); and Herold, *Sitting Bull*.

38. Kuhlenbeck, *Occultismus*, 35–48.

39. Bournichon, *Sitting Bull*.

40. For the Danish, see Stenholt, *Sitting Bull*; for the Swedish, see *Sitting Bull, Sioux-Indianers Siste Höfding*, 1908.

41. Goll, *Untergang der Dakota* (republished in 1940); Daumann, *Sitting Bull*.

42. See Feest, *Sitting Bull*, 112–15.

43. Conrad, "Mutual Fascination"; see also Markus Kreis's contribution in this volume.

44. Renaud, "Far West."

45. See, for example, Rusinowa, "Indians"; Borsányi, "Emerging Dual Image."

46. See, for example, Lowsky, *Karl May*; Wollschläger, *Karl May*.

47. Regarding French surveys, see Chinard, *L'Éxotisme américaine* (1911) and

L'Amérique (1934). For German surveys, see Feest, "Indian in Non-English"; Lutz, "*Indianer*" *und* "*Native Americans*" and the literature cited there; see also Jeffrey Sammons's contribution in this volume.

48. See Busatta and Salgari, "Writer."

49. Feest, "Indian in Non-English."

50. See R. Stewart et al., *Carl Wimar*; Hendricks, *Albert Bierstadt*; and J. C. Stewart, *Winold Reiss*.

51. Goetzmann et al., *Karl Bodmer's America*; see Kittlitz, "Karl Bodmer."

52. Husemann, *Wild River*; see Jeffrey Sammons's contribution in this volume.

53. See Andreas, *Adolf Hoeffler*; Anders et al., *Lukas Vischer*; Feest, "Johann Baptist Wengler"; and Kläy and Läng, *Romantische Leben*.

54. Regarding German photographs, see Fowler, *Western Photographs*; Buechel, *Rosebud*; Haberland, "Nine Bella Coolas"; Arndt, *Rote Wolke*; Steltzer, *Indian Artists*; Teiwes and Lindig, *Navajo*; and Turnauer, *Portraits*. For other European photographs, see Marino, "Carlo Gentile"; H. W. Hamilton et al, *Sioux*; Coutancier, *Peaux-Rouges*; and Korniss, *In the Land*.

55. Guidi and Mann, *Photographs at the Frontier*; Sanner, "Karl von den Steinen."

56. See Laniel-Le François, "Hopi."

57. Thwaites, *Jesuit Relations*; see Codignola, "Battle."

58. See Kasprycki, "Matters of Faith."

59. Vermeulen, "Emergence."

60. See Feest, *Indians of Northeastern North America*.

61. See Hovens, *Herman F. C. ten Kate* and Swiggers, "C. C. Uhlenbeck."

62. See Giordano, *Indiani* and the various essays in my *Indians and Europe*.

Part 2: Historical Encounters

Germany in the eighteenth century

Historical Encounters
across Five Centuries

COLIN G. CALLOWAY

Like the Scots and the Irish, German people have had a long history of diaspora in America. The Thirty Years War (1618–1648) and subsequent European conflicts sent people fleeing from devastated homelands to Hungary and Russia in the east. In the eighteenth century the main tide of emigration of German-speaking peoples shifted west. Despite efforts to stem this *Amerikaauswanderung*, perhaps about one hundred thousand German-speaking people migrated to North America before 1800, with the numbers peaking between 1749 and 1755. Most of the emigrants were Protestants, lured to America by promises of free land, low taxes, and religious toleration; a variety of private and official schemes brought settlers to lands as far north as Nova Scotia and as far south as Georgia. Most landed at Philadelphia, and by the time of the American Revolution, the population of Pennsylvania was about one-third German; that of the entire mainland British colonies almost 10 percent. As Liam Riordan shows in his essay, many English Pennsylvanians shared Benjamin Franklin's fears that German people would "swarm into our settlements, and by herding together, establish their language and manners, to the exclusion of ours." German-speaking immigrants came from different regions and spoke many different dialects of German, but English colonists tended to lump them all together, often with immigrants from Holland, as Dutch.[1]

This stream of German immigration paled in comparison with the flood of mass migrations that followed the failed revolutions of 1848 and the social and economic dislocations of rapid industrialization. Four million people fled the German Empire for the United States before 1914; between 1830 and 1930 at least one out of every six immigrants to the United States was German-speaking. By 1900 they and their children constituted 10 percent of the nation's total population, and in some areas of the Midwest the percentage was much higher: in Nebraska, for example, nearly half the inhabitants trace their ancestry to German-speaking immigrants. As evidenced by German town names scattered across the country, German people played an important role in the repeopling of North America and they left their mark on the land and the culture that was becoming the United States.[2]

They also experienced varied and extensive contacts with the Native American inhabitants of the continent – after all, the "free land" that lured them was once Indian land – but one would never know it from a perusal of the historical literature. Library shelves contain volumes on Spanish-Indian relations, French-Indian relations, and British-Indian relations, but encounters between Indian peoples and German-speaking peoples remain virtually ignored. Despite enduring stereotypes, informed generalizations about Germans in America's history are almost impossible. Germany as a nation was not founded until the later nineteenth century, and German-speaking immigrants came to America from Austria, Hungary, Russia, Rumania, Yugoslavia, Switzerland, and Alsace, as well as from Germany itself. Those who came differed widely in religious denomination, politics, class, and culture.[3] They entered Indian country as individuals, families, and groups, not as representatives of a colonizing nation. Consequently, many of their encounters with the Native inhabitants became subsumed under the general rubric "Indian-white relations." Nevertheless, a brief survey of historical sources reveals that encounters between German people and Indian people ranged the spectrum between war and peace, occurred on two continents, and have stretched across five centuries to the present.

Germans in Indian Country

German individuals and groups were involved from the very beginning in the European invasion of Indian America. In fact, the very first German contact with Native people in North America may have predated Columbus: Leif the Lucky, son of Erik the Red, who founded an Icelandic colony on the west coast of Greenland late in the tenth century, made his first voyage to "Vinland" around 1000; the sagas tell that one of Leif's crew was "a Southerner named Tyrkir," who appears to have been a German.[4] For the most part, Germans approached Indian country for much the same reasons as other Europeans did and behaved in much the same way as they did, and Indians responded to them accordingly. But Germans also often occupied a somewhat marginal situation in colonial America and the United States, and on occasion they developed their own particular relations with Indian people. Those relations prompted Indians to identify them sometimes as friends, sometimes as intermediaries with other, more aggressive Europeans, sometimes as the prime aggressors in frontier conflicts.

A few German speakers were among the colonists who settled at Jamestown in 1607. Two German artisans, whom Captain John Smith sent to build a house for chief Powhatan in 1608, took up residence with the Indians and advised Powhatan to attack the English. They tried to enlist allies from Jamestown to secure weapons for the Indians and plotted to murder Smith. Powhatan had the two men put to death, lest they betray him as they had Smith.[5]

The first distinctive German settlement in America was established in 1683 when thirteen Dutch and German families from Krefeld founded Germantown in Pennsylvania.[6] In 1710 Swiss and German Protestant refugees founded a colony at New Bern on the Neuse River in North Carolina, but it was almost immediately destroyed a year later when the local Tuscaroras' accumulated grievances against white traders exploded in war. Baron Christoph von Graffenried, "Governor of the German Colony in North Carolina," was captured by the Indians. Although his English companion, trader and traveler John Lawson was tortured and killed, von Graffenried was released. He blamed the English for the war and made a treaty with the Tuscaroras that "in times when the English and the Indians are in strife," he would be "entirely neutral." The New Bern settlers were to mark their houses with "the sign of Neuse, N" on the understanding that no injury or damage would be done to them. But the Tuscaroras were in no mood for distinctions and, said von Graffenried, "my poor people's houses although the doors were marked with a sign, had to be burned."[7]

Beginning in the 1730s, exiled Protestants from Salzburg, in what is now Austria, immigrated to Georgia. Ordered from their homeland in 1731, the Salzburgers took up residence in James Edward Oglethorpe's new colony, where they were joined by Calvinists from Switzerland and Lutherans from Württemberg. At one point, Georgia had a higher percentage of German inhabitants than did Pennsylvania. Baron Philip George Friedrich von Reck, a young Hanoverian nobleman in charge of transporting the Salzburg immigrants, did sketches and paintings of Uchees, Creeks, and Cherokees and penned a brief report on the Indians living in Georgia. Baron von Reck described the Creeks as "honest, open-minded, truthful, not interested in personal gain," but he did not hold other Indians in such high regard. Most Salzburgers seem to have had a poor opinion of, and poor relations with, their Indian neighbors.[8]

German-speaking people entered Indian country in ever-increasing numbers in the eighteenth century, as both traders and settlers. Like their Scotch-Irish contemporaries, German immigrants who entered the Delaware Valley in the eighteenth century inherited a frontier culture that had been shaped by seventeenth-century pioneer Finns and Swedes through contact with the Indian inhabitants.[9] German latecomers often looked with disdain on their backwoods predecessors, but they adopted many of their ways, followed their paths, and on occasion enjoyed the same kind of shoulder-rubbing intimacy with Indian people that the Finns had achieved with neighboring Delawares.

In New York's Mohawk Valley, German people settled in such numbers that eighteenth-century travelers through the area characterized it as culturally German. In fact, the German settlers lived in close proximity to the Indian inhabitants of the region, and German and Iroquois ways of living and speaking mingled quite freely. One traveler at the time of the American Revolution reported hearing spoken on a regular basis: English, High Dutch, Low Dutch, French, Mohawk, Oneida, Onondaga, Cayuga, Seneca, and Tuscarora.[10] Catherine Weissenberg, a runaway indentured servant, became a housekeeper and common-law wife to Sir William Johnson, the Irish trader who lived in the valley and became British superintendent of Indian Affairs. She bore him three children and came to know many Iroquois people during the course of her husband's commercial and diplomatic dealing with them. After she died in 1759, a Mohawk woman, Molly Brant, took her place in Johnson's household. During the Seven Years War, Johnson expressed doubts about the loyalty of the Germans in the Mohawk Valley. He said they taught the Indians to distinguish between Germans and English, claiming that the English oppressed and sought to "root out" the Germans. But Friedrich Rohde, a geologist from Cologne who traveled through the valley in 1802, when most of the Mohawks and Oneidas had been forced into exile during and after the Revolution, saw that it was not the Germans who were rooted out. The first settlers were Palatine Germans, he wrote, and they "settled down right among the Indians." "However, they multiplied so rapidly and vigorously that the Indians grew mistrustful and finally fell into open warfare in order to drive them out. Now and then you can still see the ruins of forts and old blockhouses that served these Mohawk Germans as refuges in emergencies. The outcome was that the Indians moved on, the Germans kept their property, and to this day maintain it as conquered land and their possession."[11]

Germans settled in French as well as English colonies. Some thirteen hundred people recruited from various parts of Germany were among the colonists brought to Louisiana by the French Company of the Indies between 1717 and 1721. They settled at various points along the Mississippi and the Gulf Coast, giving their name to the German Coast. Like most colonial inhabitants in the Lower Mississippi Valley, German settlers lived by farming, herding, hunting, gathering, fishing, and trading. They often occupied lands that

Indians had previously cultivated, and they interacted with the local Houma, Tunica, Chitimacha, and Acolapissa Indians, as well as with French colonists and African slaves. Like other colonists, they suffered terribly in the famine and fever that struck in 1719-1721 – "Most of those found dead by the heaps of shells were Germans," wrote one French lieutenant – and they fled from Indian attacks to take refuge in New Orleans when the Choctaws revolted in 1748.[12]

Though most Germans in eighteenth-century America lived east of the Mississippi, a handful ventured west long before the United States laid claim to the region: Spanish sources reported a German hunter among the Comanches in the mid-eighteenth century and in 1749 some German traders participated in a huge Comanche trade fair of more than four hundred tepees on the Arkansas River, along with French and Wichita traders.[13]

Living in Indian country meant that German people, like other colonists, sometimes were vulnerable to Indian captivity and sometimes became "white Indians." In January 1757, for example, Sir William Johnson received a message from the Shawnees. This was not unusual in Johnson's line of work, but in this case the messenger, called Ooligasha or Owilgascho in Shawnee, was a German named Peter Spelman, "who has lived these seven years past amongst the Indians." In April, Johnson was trying to start negotiations for the return of a German girl named Elizabeth Hilts, who had been captured from German Flatts and was living at Onondaga. Hans Fife, a German who was captured by the Senecas and then redeemed at the end of the Seven Years' War, "being a profligate Person," immediately escaped back to the Senecas and fought with them against the British in Pontiac's War.[14] Fears that captives might "turn Indian" were widespread in the colonies, and quite well founded, although there is no evidence to suggest that German people were any more likely to do so than were French, English, Scots, or Irish.

Mediators and Moravians

The eighteenth-century frontier was a messy place of cultural mixing and recurrent conflicts. In Pennsylvania, German-speakers endured hostility from English authorities and neighbors but made a place for themselves in a complex multicultural landscape of intertribal rivalries and competing colonial interests (see Riordan, this volume). German settlers, traders, Indian agents, and missionaries mingled with Indian peoples along the Pennsylvania and Ohio frontiers. In 1745, for example, German colonists arrived at the Indian town of Shamokin on the Susquehanna River and opened a Moravian mission.

Located at the forks of the Susquehanna, Shamokin was a trading center, a crossroads of peoples and cultures, a busy place, a volatile community, and a bit scary for the missionaries. After a garrison was established there in 1758, soldiers, their wives and camp followers, traders, missionaries and their families rubbed shoulders with Delawares, Tutelos, Mahicans, Shawnees, Oneidas, Cayugas, and various other passersby. At any time, it seems, one might hear drunken brawling, creative cursing, and hymns sung in English, German, and any number of Indian languages. The Oneida chief Shickellamy welcomed the Moravians with gifts of food, helped build the mission, and taught them how to plant their fields. He also gave them Iroquois names because, he said, the Germans' names were "too difficult to pronounce." When Shickellamy's granddaughter died, the little girl was buried with her face painted, dressed in a shirt German women sewed for her, and placed in a coffin German men built for her.[15] Ten years after the mission was built, the so-called French and Indian War broke out, and Delaware Indians along the Susquehanna Valley attacked German and Scotch-Irish communities they had formerly lived alongside. Conrad Weiser reported that one war party attacked a German family named Kobel. The father, though wounded, was able to hold them off with his gun, but the Indians captured his wife and their eight children. Separating the children from the mother, the Indians "spoke to them in High Dutch: *be still, we won't hurt you.*" Then they killed the mother. The children immediately fled, and most escaped. Another German child, Catherine Smith, was taken captive by Delawares and liberated when Colonel John Armstrong and three hundred Pennsylvania troops attacked and destroyed the Delaware town at Upper Kittaning on the Allegheny River in 1756.[16]

In such complex contexts and turbulent times, German peoples sometimes exercised important roles as interpreters and culture brokers. The French earned a reputation for their willingness to meet Indians on their own terms and their ability to sustain middle grounds of coexistence in Indian country, but some German individuals and groups appear to have been equally effective in negotiating across cultures.[17]

One such individual was Conrad Weiser (1696-1760), a German farmer who, in the middle years of the century, "practically made a career of Indian business." Born in Germany, Weiser settled with his family in southeastern New York. He lived among the Mohawks, was adopted by them, developed a facility in Iroquoian languages, and became an interpreter. Weiser recognized that effective translation required more than learning Indian words; he maintained it was necessary "to converse with the Indians and study their Genius," and he left his son with the Mohawks so they could teach him the language of the council fire. After moving to western Pennsylvania, he played a pivotal role as a negotiator and intermediary in tribal relations with the colonial governments of Pennsylvania, Maryland, and Virginia and was appointed Indian agent for Pennsylvania in 1741. Weiser routinely enlisted the assistance of Iroquois friends in dealing with the rituals and nuances of Indian diplomacy. He understood that important business often took place outside of formal negotiations: during the council of the Onondaga chiefs in 1743, he met men like Shickellamy and the Onondaga orator Canasatego "in the Bushes to have a private Discourse."[18]

Weiser also pointed others down the path of Indian diplomacy. Daniel Claus, who had come to America in 1749 at the peak of eighteenth-century German immigration, was on the verge of heading for home when he met Weiser. Weiser persuaded Claus to accompany him to Onondaga so he could "introduce him to the Natives of America & shew him the Curiosities &ca of their Country."[19] Claus went on to a long career and a prominent position in the British Indian Department, as did his son, William.

German-speaking missionaries of the Moravian Church worked in Indian country from Georgia to Newfoundland.[20] The Unitas Fratrum was born in 1457 as a Protestant reform church pioneering worship in the vernacular, Scripture as the guide for life, congregational hymn singing, and education for both sexes. Counter-Reformation activity in Bohemia and Moravia kept it an underground religion until, in 1727, the members found a hospitable refuge on the estate of Nikolaus Ludwig Reichsgraf von Zinzendorf in Saxony, where they renewed their church. From there, the Moravians or "Mährische Brüder," as Zinzendorf called them, began missionary work that carried them to four continents. In 1735 they established a North American missionary base in Savannah, Georgia, where they carried out work among Cherokees and Creeks. David Zeisberger, who was born in Moravia and moved with his family to Saxony, emigrated to join the Savannah community. After the community failed, he moved inland with the Moravians when they established a new center at Bethlehem, Pennsylvania, in 1741, and began missionary work among the Delawares. Zeisberger helped negotiate Indian-white relations, learned to speak Mohawk and Onondaga, and was adopted into the Onondaga tribe in 1749. Then he began concentrating his mission among the Delawares, who also adopted him. He learned their language and moved with them to the Ohio Valley (Delawares had been moving west since the 1720s, and in the 1770s the Ohio Delawares invited the missionaries and their Christian Indians to settle in the Muskingum Valley).[21] The Moravians established mission towns at Schönbrunn, Gnadenhütten, Lichtenau, and Salem, and some four hundred Christian Indians lived in these towns. After American militia massacred the residents of Gnadenhütten in 1782, Zeisberger migrated west with his followers to new settlements in Michigan and Ontario. He worked for sixty-three years as a missionary to the Indians.[22]

Johann Gottlieb Ernestus Heckewelder (who was actually born in England) came to North America with his parents to join a Moravian colony in Quebec and helped establish a Christian Delaware community. Appointed Zeisberger's assistant, Heckewelder served for fifty years as pastor and advocate for Indians who converted to the Moravian faith. The federal government recruited him to assist in treaty negotiations with Indians. Heckewelder wrote an account of the Indians of Pennsylvania whose lives he shared, which not only provided detailed descriptions of Indian culture but also presented some scathing indictments of white policies and practices toward Indian people.[23]

Moravians compiled an extensive record – and kept extensive records in the form of diaries – of encounters with Indian peoples, in an era and area of dramatic change and disruption. Moravians tried to distance themselves from the colonists responsible for so much of the disruption, and they assured Indians that they were "a separate people and from other white people quite different." Some Indians, as the essay by William Starna and Corinna Dally-Starna suggests, seem to have agreed. Unlike English missionaries, the Moravians' method of missionizing Indians was to live among them and learn from them. In James Merrell's words, "they fed the hungry, lodged the weary, and pitched in to harvest corn or chop wood," and they counted upon a Christian example to win Indian souls.[24] Moravians adopted Indian methods of farming and hunting, often wore Indian clothing, and in some cases, married Indian converts.

As did Christian missionaries elsewhere, Moravians and their new religion produced divisions in Indian communities already disrupted by war, disease, and alcohol. Nevertheless, the Moravians' reputation for pacifism, communalism, and fair dealings won them friends and converts in Indian country. Even the prominent Delaware warrior and diplomat Teedyuscung, "the chief of sinners," received baptism in 1750. He took the name Gideon and lived at Gnadenhütten for a time, before he broke with the Moravians and moved to Wyoming on the Susquehanna in 1754.[25]

The Moravians' reputation allowed them to function as mediators in the disputes that recurrently flared up in the regions where they lived and worked. Moravian missionary Christian Frederick Post, serving as an ambassador from Pennsylvania, made two trips to the Ohio country in 1758 in an effort to achieve peace with the Indians. Known to the Delawares as Wal-

Fig. 1. *The Power of the Gospel*, painted by Christian Schussele in Philadelphia in 1862, presents an imaginative reconstruction of David Zeisberger preaching to the Delawares. The painting is six feet high by nine feet long and hangs in the Moravian Church Archives Building in Bethlehem, Pennsylvania. Courtesy, Moravian Archives, Bethlehem PA.

Fig. 2. Moravian missionaries baptizing Indian converts. Native women on the right and men on the left await baptism while two Indian assistants look on. Photo courtesy, New York Public Library.

langundowngen, Post had two Indian wives, marrying a Wampanoag and then a Delaware woman in turn. Known for his calm disposition and his love of Indians, Post was accompanied on his peace mission by Pisquetomen, a fiery Delaware known for his hatred of Pennsylvania colonists; they were, notes James Merrell, "an odd couple."[26]

In 1753 some Moravians left Pennsylvania and founded Wachovia in North Carolina. They explored the possibilities of establishing a mission among the Cherokees, but not until 1801 was the Moravian mission at Springplace established. Most Cherokees were reluctant to accept missionaries, but the Moravians seemed like a safe bet because they were known not to display the anti-Indian attitudes of most frontier whites—"we love all people, no matter what their color," they told the Cherokees. Nevertheless the Springplace mission got off to a shaky start and made slow progress among the Cherokees, who seemed more interested in getting schools for their children than in attending church.[27]

War and Peace on the Frontier

English settlers often disparaged the fighting abilities of their German neighbors, depicting them as hard-working farmers who "understood nothing of Indian warfare."[28] German settlers in turn distanced themselves from the British in their dealings with Indians: when British officials warned Germans in rural New York of impending attacks by Indians, the Germans laughed, "slapping their hands upon their buttocks," and asked "why should the Indians wish to harm us?"[29]

But Germans did their share of fighting against and alongside Indians. At least one German accompanied Francisco de Coronado's multiethnic expedition into the Southwest in 1540-1542: Juan Fioz, a native of Worms, was a bugler in the army.[30] German recruits fought with the French and their Indian allies during the Seven Years War in North America, and some switched sides after the British captured Fort Niagara in 1759.[31] A German regiment was raised to fight in South Carolina's Cherokee War in 1759.[32] During the American Revolution, Hessian mercenaries who fought for the British came into contact with Britain's Indian allies and into conflict with Indians who had enlisted in support of the American cause. During the skirmishes around New York in the summer of 1778, Hessians fought against Indians from the village of Stockbridge in New England.[33] Some Hessian mercenaries who had been taken prisoner and stayed on after the war married Indian women from the town of Mashpee on Cape Cod, which lost many of its men during the Revolution.[34]

German people also participated in the wars for the West waged between Indians and the United States in the nineteenth century, both as settlers moving on to Indian homelands and as soldiers charged with dispossessing the Indians. As always, Germans were present on the moving frontier. For example, a census for the district of Cape Girardeau in Missouri in 1803 (the year the formerly Spanish region was transferred from France to the United States) recorded Germans living alongside Scots, Irish, and other settlers who had moved west from Kentucky and Tennessee, in an area inhabited by Shawnees, Delawares, and other Indian peoples who had crossed the Mississippi to escape American expansion and by indigenous peoples like the Osages who resented and resisted the arrival of the immigrant tribes.[35]

On most frontiers Germans were usually "secondary settlers," but in west Texas in the mid-nineteenth century they pushed the frontier into Comanche country.[36] In 1842 a group of German noblemen formed the Verein zum Schutze deutscher Einwanderer in Texas (the Society for the Protection of German Immigrants in Texas). In 1845 the society founded the town of New Braunfels. The following year they moved northwest to found a second colony at Fredericksburg, north of the Pedernales River, and purchased a land grant between the Llano and Colorado rivers, in the midst of Comanche hunting territory. The governor of Texas feared the German intrusion would spark a Comanche war (at a time when the United States was at war with Mexico). He dispatched Major Robert S. Neighbors as a special agent to try to prevent it. The immigrants formed armed militia units for their defense, but, unlike most Anglo-Americans who went west in the nineteenth century, they had no prior experiences or legacy of hatred to prime them for conflict with Indians. In March, guided by emigrant Shawnees and using Delaware interpreters, Hans Baron von Meusebach (known in English as John O. Meusebach), commissioner general of the German immigration company, went into Comanchería to negotiate. He met in their villages with head chiefs of the Paneteka band of Comanches—Buffalo Hump, Santa Anna or Santana, and Mopechucope, also known as Old Owl. In May the chiefs came to Fredericksburg to sign a treaty. The Germans and the Comanches agreed that each should be free to go where they pleased and to visit each other's settlements; that each should support the other against their enemies; that Meusebach and company should be free to conduct surveys; and that both parties would "use every exertion to keep up and even enforce peace and friendship between both the German and the Comanche people and all other colonists and to walk in the white path always and forever." The Germans promised three thousand dollars in presents and provisions and the treaty opened 3.8 million acres of Comanche land to German settlement.[37]

For a while, Comanches and Germans did walk the white path. Santana had previously visited Washington DC, and he and Mopechucope worked for peace. German settlement patterns, which clustered lots around a village, required less land than the dispersed settlement patterns of Anglo-Americans. The German settlers were initially inept hunters and depended on the Comanches to supply them with food. Comanches brought in deer, bear, and buffalo meat and honey. Germans traded their farm produce with the Comanches, sometimes, it seems, bought stolen horses from them, and gave gifts to reinforce good relations. Comanches came and went freely in Fredericksburg. This period of peaceful coexistence gave rise to a myth, perpetuated by later immigrants, that German-Indian relations in Texas were characterized by peace and friendship. But peace was short-lived. Santana and Mopechucope died in the smallpox epidemic that swept Comanchería in 1848 or in the cholera epidemic the following year; German confidence and pressure on Comanche land increased. Immigrants crossing Comanchería en route to the California gold mines and the growing presence of state and federal government in Indian relations added to tensions. The conflicts that erupted may have been with northern Comanche bands rather than with the southern Panetekas who signed the 1847 treaty, but by the early 1850s, Comanches were raiding German settlements, stealing German horses, and killing German people. The pattern continued through the '60s and '70s.[38]

Some Germans were captured by Kiowas and Comanches.[39] Former provisional president of Texas David Burnet, who had once lived for a couple of years with the Comanches while they nursed him back to health from tuberculosis, explained how young captives sometimes were remade into Comanche persons: "When boys and girls are captured, they are not subject to any systematic punishment, but are immediately domiciliated into the family of the captor. If docile and tractable, they are seldom treated with excessive cruelty. They are employed in menial services, and, occasionally, in process of time, are emancipated and marry into the tribes, when they become, de facto, Comanche."[40]

German boys who had been captured and adopted by Kiowas and Comanches sometimes grew up and fought with them against Americans. Herman Lehmann, the son of German immigrant parents who lived near Fredericksburg, was captured in 1870 at eleven years of age by Mescalero Apaches and lived for nine years among the Indians. He fought as an Apache against his adoptive people's enemies – Indian and white. After killing an Apache in a drunken brawl, he fled to the Comanches and joined them in raids against frontier settlements. Reluctantly, he was persuaded to return to his mother in Texas, where he took up a life he described as comprising "Work, Wedlock and Things Worse." In one skirmish, Texas Rangers mistook Lehmann for Rudolph Fischer, another German boy who had been captured as a youth and raised by Indians. According to Lehmann, Fischer was adopted by the Comanches and, after about ten years with them, was brought back to his people near Fredericksburg, "but he had become so thoroughly Indianized that he was not content to remain and resume the white man's ways." After spending about a year with his parents, he returned to the Comanches, where he had a wife and child.[41] Another German captive came to be named "Kiowa Dutch."[42] Other captives displayed no reluctance to escape from southern Plains Indians. A Southern Cheyenne war party attacked the immigrant family of "John German" during the Red River or Buffalo War in 1874, killed the parents and older sister, and carried off four young daughters. The girls were subsequently recovered but reported they had been raped.[43]

Encounters between Germans and Indians continued long after hostilities abated, and survived in the memories and folklore of German-Texan families. Louise Ernst Stöhr, "who came from a very cultured family," recalled her feelings of isolation living on a frontier farm. The Indians who lived just to the west "would bring back horses and cows that strayed away, in exchange for milk and butter." She imagined that they were lonely too.[44]

In Arizona, Germans made up as much as 10 percent of the army in Arizona and participated in campaigns against the Apaches in the 1870s and 1880s. Like their Anglo-American neighbors, German miners, merchants, farmers, and missionaries disrupted the world of the Yavapais. They took over Indian lands, lobbied for the removal of Indian people, participated in the exploitation of Indian reservations, and, in some cases, participated in Indian hunting expeditions.[45]

In the 1850s, German settlers who moved on to the lands of the Dakota, or eastern, Sioux in southern Minnesota fueled growing Dakota anger toward their non-Indian neighbors and the United States government. The Dakotas (the Mdewakanton, Sisseton, Wahpeton, and Wahpekute bands of the Sioux) ceded lands in treaties in 1837 and 1851; by the terms of the 1851 treaties, they agreed to settle on reservations. While the Dakotas resented their confinement, watched their children go hungry, and saw the money promised to them by the treaties diverted into traders' pockets, German settlers arrived in the upper Minnesota Valley under the sponsorship of a Chicago immigrant society. In 1854 they established the town site of New Ulm at the junction of the Big Cottonwood River. During the winter months some of them took shelter in the Indians' abandoned summer lodges. When the Dakotas returned in the spring, there was an ugly confrontation. Dakota women "became enraged and struck the ground with their fists to indicate that that land belonged to them;" young warriors threw down survey flags and killed cattle. But the army arrived before open violence broke out, and the Dakotas withdrew.

The Indians were told that New Ulm was on land they had ceded to the government. But the reservation borders were not surveyed until 1858, leaving room for further conflicts as more Germans, and some Scandinavians, settled on the edge of the reservation in the late 1850s. The Germans were farmers; Dakota men were undergoing a difficult transition as the United States government and its agents pressured them rather than the women, who traditionally raised corn, to take to a life behind the plow. The government failed to honor its treaties, and the Dakotas saw their new German neighbors as the aggressive embodiments of an alien way of life and a policy of dispossession that was being imposed upon them. During negotiations for another treaty in 1858, the Mdewakanton Dakota chief, Little Crow or Taoyateduta, complained that the Germans scared away the Indians' game and encroached on the reservation: "[Y]ou gave me that line," he told the treaty commissioners, but "your Dutchmen [Germans] have settled inside of it." He wondered why the government had not removed them. New Ulm became a center for liquor-trading and German farmers frequently supplied Indians with alcohol, but there was little reciprocal exchange. Thrifty German pioneers saw no reason to share what they had with Indians, offending Dakota people for whom sharing and generosity was a way of life; hungry Dakotas had little to barter, and Germans often regarded them as beggars. Dakotas called the Germans *iasica*, "bad speakers," a derogatory term that placed them outside of the Dakota world where humans were bound by ties of kinship and reciprocity.[46]

When the so-called Great Sioux Uprising broke out in Minnesota in 1862, Germans were among the first targets, and many were mutilated as the Dakotas vented their pent-up anger. A captive heard the Mdewakanton warrior Shakopee, or Little Six, sing a war song that translated as "The Dutch [Germans] have made me so angry. I will cut off their heads while they are still breathing."[47] Dakota warriors attacked German farms and assaulted New Ulm. Though New Ulm held, furious Dakotas killed some four hundred settlers — Shakopee told another captive "my arm is lame from killing white people."[48] Dakotas also hid and protected some settlers, but Germans generally received no quarter. One exception, Helen Tarble, who lived in a German community near the reservation for four years before the war, had had good relations with the Dakotas, practicing the virtues of generosity and reciprocity that marked her as a human being in Dakota eyes. When the Dakota warriors captured the Tarbles and their neighbors during the outbreak, Mrs. Tarble begged for mercy in Dakota. The Indians brutally killed those from whom they had received abuses and insults but spared Mrs. Tarble and her children, assuring them they need not fear for their lives. Mrs. Tarble was taken captive but allowed to do much as she pleased.[49]

After the army defeated the Dakotas, a military commission condemned three hundred Dakota men to death for their part in the war and its atrocities. As the chained prisoners and their dependents were being moved in carts to a stockade near Mankato, a mob attacked them in New Ulm, killing two of them. George Crooks, or Wakanajaja (Holy Lightning), was six years old at the time and never forgot when the settlers attacked the caravan and killed his sixteen-year-old brother: "We were pounded to a jelly, my arms, feet, and head resembled raw beef steak. How I escaped alive was always a mystery to me. My brother was killed and when I realized he was dead I felt the only person in the world to look after me was gone and I wished at the time they had killed me." President Lincoln commuted the sentences of most of the Dakotas, but thirty-eight were hanged, the largest single mass execution in American history. The bitter legacy of the conflict, and of Dakota-German relations in Minnesota, endured for generations.[50]

As the United States' conflicts with the Sioux shifted farther west, Germans fought and died on the northern plains – with General George Crook at the Battle of the Rosebud and with Marcus Reno and George Armstrong Custer at the Little Big Horn. John Finerty, a war correspondent for the *Chicago Times* who accompanied Crook's army, reported that the majority of the rank and file were "of either Irish or German birth or parentage."[51] German immigrants constituted 15 percent of the Seventh Cavalry in June 1876, a total of 126 men. As members of that regiment, they served alongside men from the United States (57 percent of the regiment) and immigrants from Ireland, England, Scotland, Canada, Switzerland, France, Italy, and Denmark; they also served alongside Arikara, Crow, Shoshoni, and other Indian scouts and allies.[52] Many, including the regiment's chief trumpeter, Henry Voss, born in Hanover, Germany, died with Custer.[53] Others were more fortunate. Charles Windolph had emigrated from Prussia in 1870 to avoid being drafted into the Franco-Prussian War. But America did not live up to its promise as a land of opportunity. Unable to find work in New York, Windolph joined the army –

the very life he had left home to avoid. Six years later, on the night of 26 June 1876, he found himself pinned down, with other survivors of Major Marcus Reno's battalion of the Seventh Cavalry on a hill overlooking the Little Big Horn River, after having been routed by Lakota and Cheyenne warriors who swept out of their village to repulse Reno's charge. That night, as Charles Windolph looked down into the valley, his mind plagued with terrible scenes from the day's disaster and agonizing questions about what had happened to Custer's men, he expected to be killed: "We felt terribly alone on that dangerous hilltop," Windolph recalled in later life. "We were a million miles from nowhere. And death was all around us." But late the next day, the Indians struck their lodges and moved off toward the Big Horn Mountains. On the morning of the twenty-seventh, an army relief column arrived. Charles Windolph did not die on Reno Hill. He died in 1950, at the age of ninety-eight, the last American soldier to survive the Battle of the Little Big Horn.[54]

German soldiers played their part in the brutal mopping up campaigns that followed the Little Big Horn. For example, Captain Adolphus von Leuttwitz, a native of Prussia who had enlisted as a private in the Union Army in 1862 and rose through the ranks, lost a leg as a result of the wound he sustained when the army attacked and destroyed American Horse's village of Oglalas and Miniconjous at the Battle of Slim Buttes in September 1876. According to John Finerty, who knew him, "This gentleman had served in the Austrian and Prussian armies, had fought at Montebello, Magenta, Solferino, all through the Italian campaign of '59, had distinguished himself at Gettysburg and other great battles of our war, and had escaped relatively unscathed. Yet his hour had come, and he fell wounded in a miserable Indian skirmish, the very first man."[55] German soldiers also participated in the Seventh Cavalry's slaughter of Miniconjou people at Wounded Knee in 1890.

German peoples continued to settle Sioux lands at the end of the nineteenth century, but there was not always conflict. German Jesuits founded St. Francis mission on the Rosebud Reservation in 1886 and Holy Rosary Mission on Pine Ridge two years later (see Markus Kreis's paper in this volume) and were assisted by Franciscan nuns from German-speaking communities. In the 1880s and 1890s, many Germans whose ancestors had settled in Ukraine migrated to Dakota Territory. These German-Russian immigrants were Catholics, but they had no church or clergy of their own and longed for them. The Sioux at the Standing Rock Reservation had a Catholic church and clergy, whether they wanted them or not. In the early years of the twentieth century, each Sunday in winter when the Missouri River was frozen, German-Russians would cross the ice to the Catholic church on the Standing Rock

Sioux Reservation, sit in the back pews behind the Sioux, listening to sermons delivered in Sioux, and join the Sioux in singing Latin hymns.[56]

Mary Brave Bird, who grew up on the Rosebud Reservation, said the St. Francis mission school "was a curse for our family for generations." She attended the school in the 1960s and found the conditions unbearable. "Many of the nuns were German immigrants, some from Bavaria, so that we sometimes speculated whether Bavaria was some sort of Dracula country inhabited by monsters." Mary rebelled and ran away. Her mother, who had also attended the school, did not speak of it much but acknowledged that she had received a quality education, "even if they had to beat the knowledge into you." Mary's mother was baptized into the Catholic faith by Father Eugene Buechel, who had come to Rosebud as a young man in 1902 and spent the rest of his life on the reservation. Lakotas remembered him as "quite a remarkable man." He founded a museum, collected and cataloged native healing herbs, and compiled a huge dictionary and grammar of the Sioux language. "My mother told me that through his books she not only learned English, but got a better understanding of her own Lakota language." Like other missionaries, Buechel used to travel by horse and buggy with a portable altar to say mass in small hamlets and isolated homesteads around the reservation. "People liked him because he could speak Sioux flawlessly, ate whatever Indian food was put before him, and always had his pockets full of little gifts for the children." Other German missionaries were not so well liked.[57]

Travelers, Scientists, and Artists

Germans also visited Indian country as travelers, scientists, and artists. Their recorded impressions regularly display the biases, prejudices, and cultural myopia of their times as they projected their own interpretations and values onto Indian America. In the new age of democratic politics that followed the French Revolution, titled and educated German visitors, like their French counterparts, identified strongly with the warrior elites in Indian societies as fellow aristocrats confronting a world of wrenching changes.[58]

One of the earliest German travel accounts was written by John Lederer, an immigrant from Hamburg who made three expeditions into the Virginia and Carolina backcountry in 1669-1670 in hopes of finding a route through the Appalachians. Lederer was the first European to explore the Piedmont and Blue Ridge Mountains and leave a written record. He visited Indian villages, traveled with Indian guides and interpreters, and left extensive observations on Native life and culture, as well as advice on how to trade with Indians.[59] On

the other side of the continent, Georg Wilhelm Steller, a young German naturalist, accompanied Danish sea captain Vitus Bering on his Russian-sponsored
expedition to the coast of Alaska as early as 1741–1742.[60] George von Langsdorff,
a Baltic German, made ethnographic reports of the area during his voyages
in the first decade of the nineteenth century.[61] So did Otto von Kotzebue,
another Baltic German working for the Russians, who led an expedition to
coastal Alaska in 1815–1818 during the course of a voyage around the world and
again in 1823–1826, and whose name was given to an Inupiaq village and to the
sound that surrounds it, twenty-six miles above the Arctic Circle. He was accompanied by a German poet of French descent, Adelbert von Chamisso, who
produced his own account of the voyage.[62] In 1823, a young German duke, Paul
Wilhelm of Württemberg, traveled up the Missouri, recording information
on the Potawatomis, Kansas, Iowas, Omahas, Otos, Osages, Poncas, Pawnees,
Arikaras, Sioux, and other Indian peoples he encountered.[63] Paul Wilhelm of
Württemberg made several trips to the United States, and in 1851 Heinrich
Balduin Möllhausen, who had immigrated to the United States from Germany at age twenty-four, two years before, joined his grand tour to the Rocky
Mountains as expedition artist. Möllhausen returned west in 1853 as drafts-
man and topographer on Lieutenant Amiel W. Whipple's three-year boundary
survey along the thirty-fifth parallel, from Arkansas to California. In 1857–
1858 he made a third trip as artist for Joseph C. Ives's mapping survey of the
Colorado River. He provided illustrations to accompany the published reports of the expeditions, his own western diaries were published in 1858, and
he later became a prolific writer on the Indians of North America, publishing nearly two hundred books.[64] (On Möllhausen, see also Jeffrey Sammons's
essay in this volume). Around the same time, the well-traveled German geog-
rapher and ethnographer Johann Georg Kohl wrote *Kitchi-Gami*, an account
of life among the Lake Superior Ojibwas based on his observations and conversations with Ojibwa people in northern Wisconsin during the summer of
1855. Unlike Americans Lewis Cass and Henry Schoolcraft, who had written on
the Ojibwas, Kohl displayed empathy for people undergoing difficult changes
(the year before his visit, the Wisconsin Ojibwas were placed on four reservations, at Lac Courte Oreilles, Lac du Flambeau, Red Cliff, and Bad River),
listened to their stories, and changed his attitudes toward Indians in the light
of personal contact: "When I was in Europe," he wrote, "and knew them only
from books, I must own I considered them rude, cold-blooded, rather un-
interesting people, but when I had once shaken hands with them, I felt they
were 'men and brothers.'" Kohl became one of the most important German
ethnographers before the professionalization of anthropology.[65]

Naturalist and ethnologist Alexander Philipp Maximilian von Wied-Neuwied hired Swiss artist Karl Bodmer to accompany him on a two-year scientific tour of the United States. Leaving St. Louis in April 1833 aboard the American Fur Company steamboat Yellowstone, Maximilian and Bodmer traveled up the Missouri River, spent the winter at Fort Clark in North Dakota, and returned to St. Louis the following spring. Like the American artist George Catlin before him, Bodmer made sketches and watercolors of the Indian peoples of the Missouri River. His work provided the illustrations of Native American life that accompanied Maximilian's published account of the expedition, *Travels in the Interior of North America,* published in German in 1839, and are widely regarded as some of the finest ethnographic records of nineteenth-century northern Plains cultures.[66]

Rudolph Kurz, a young Swiss artist, went West in 1846 to study the Indians Catlin and Bodmer had painted. He spent six years on the Mississippi and Missouri and produced sketches of Indian peoples he met.[67] Seven years later Carl Wimar, a German-born artist who settled in St. Louis and specialized in painting scenes from the American frontier, also traveled up the Missouri to see Indians firsthand. He made numerous detailed sketches, but his paintings reflected the attitudes of mid-nineteenth-century America: Indians were either "savage foes" or "noble red men" doomed to extinction. In many of Wimar's pictures, Indian subjects are portrayed against the background of a symbolically setting sun.[68] Friedrich Richard Petri saw Indians rather differently. Petri, who attended the Royal Academy of Fine Arts in his native Dresden, emigrated in the aftermath of failed revolution in Saxony and arrived in Texas in 1851. Living on the western frontier of Texas, he farmed for a living, but he also did pencil and watercolor sketches of Comanches and Lipan Apaches, as well as of Delawares and Shawnees who served as guides at the nearby army post, Fort Martin Scott, which German farmers supplied with food. Although Petri lived only six years in Texas before his death by drowning at age thirty-three, he was there at a time when Indians frequented the German settlements – even his own cabin – and he seems to have gotten to know some of them. Nineteenth-century stereotypes depicted Indians as lacking in humanity, but Petri did not: his sketches capture "Indians and settlers in casual and friendly conversations, here an Indian child eating a melon, there Indian youths spraddled languidly on their ponies."[69] Later in the century, Aby Warburg followed the tradition of Bodmer, Kurz, and Wimar in a new medium. Visiting America for his brother's wedding in 1895, the young Hamburg art historian traveled west to Arizona and recorded aspects of Pueblo life and culture by camera.[70]

Colin G. Calloway

Fig. 3. After Karl Bodmer, "The Travelers Meeting with the Minatarre Indians near Fort Clark;" engraving with aquatint, hand-colored. An interpreter introduces Prince Maximilian to a group of Hidatsa Indians on the Upper Missouri, winter 1833–1834. Maximilian is the shorter man; Bodmer, the artist, is the taller man next to him at far right. Courtesy, Joslyn Art Museum, Omaha NE; Gift of Enron Art Foundation.

Ethnographers, Linguists, Anthropologists, and Collectors

The first German field researcher who was specifically and exclusively an ethnographer, rather than an all-purpose naturalist, was Adolf Bastian (1826–1905). Bastian did not visit North America (he did travel to South America and the West Indies), but his career marked a turning point in German anthropology. He was one of the key organizers of the Gesellschaft für Anthropologie, Ethnologie und Urgeschichte (Society for the Study of Physical Anthropology, Ethnology, and Prehistory) in 1869 in Berlin, editor of its journal *Zeitschrift für Ethnologie*, and also founded the ethnology section of the Berlin Museum and the Royal Museum of Anthropology in Berlin.[71]

While most of the famous German ethnographic expeditions in the late nineteenth and early twentieth centuries were undertaken in Africa, Asia, and South America, some scholars conducted significant field research and gathered items for museums in North America, especially along the Pacific Coast and in Alaska. Prominent among them were Johan Adrian Jacobsen (1853–1947) and Aurel Krause (1848–1908). Jacobsen was a Norwegian-born explorer who in 1881–1883 undertook a major expedition to the coast of British Columbia and Alaska as well as to the interior of Alaska, collecting over seven

Fig. 4. Lipan Indian with breastplate by F. Richard Petri, circa 1850s.
Courtesy, the Texas Memorial Museum, accession #2257-1.

thousand Indian, Yup'ik, and Inupiaq ethnographic specimens on behalf of
the Royal Berlin Ethnological Museum. Unlike Jacobsen, whose primary goal
was artifact collecting, Aurel Krause, accompanied by his brother Arthur, concentrated on ethnographic research. He focused on the Tlingit Indians of
southeastern Alaska, with whom he spent the entire winter of 1881–1882. His
description of Tlingit economy, social life, and religion, published in German in 1885, was the first detailed study of this people and became a standard
reference work for generations of American scholars of that culture.[72]

The most famous German-born scholar of North American Indian ethnology and linguistics was Franz Boas (1858–1942), who began his scholarly
career as a student of physics, mathematics, and geography at several German
universities, but who became more interested in human culture.

Fig. 5. "Preliminary sketch for Bartering with an Indian by F. Richard Petri, circa 1850s." Courtesy, the Texas Memorial Museum, accession #2269-3 C.

Boas's first ethnographic expedition to the Inuit of Baffinland in 1883-1884 was largely financed by a newspaper, the *Berliner Tageblatt*, an indication of the wide interest in Indians among the German reading public. Boas's intention was to study the influence of the environment on the seasonal migration and subsistence habits of the Inuit, a project that reflected the environmental determinism popular among German geographers of his time, but his experience among the Inuit convinced him that the effect of the environment on human life was mediated through culture – the subject of his subsequent work.

In 1886 Boas went to the field again, this time to study the culture of the Bella Coola Indians of British Columbia. His interest in these people had been aroused when he encountered a group of Bella Coolas "on exhibition" in Berlin. Boas's lifelong interest in the indigenous peoples of the Northwest Coast, and especially the neighbors of the Bella Coola, the Kwakiutl, resulted in a dozen books and numerous articles.

Boas immigrated to the United States in 1889 and, after a series of university and museum appointments, became professor of anthropology at Columbia University in 1899. In the course of several decades at Columbia he trained a large number of American anthropologists (beginning with Alfred Kroeber [1876-1960], the first doctorate in anthropology in the United States), many of whom specialized in Native American ethnography, linguistics, physical anthropology, and archaeology. Because of their apprenticeship under Boas, several generations of North Americanists were influenced to a significant degree by the German intellectual tradition. Moreover, several of the most prominent early Boasians who went on to do pioneering research in North American ethnology and linguistics, most notably Kroeber and Robert Lowie (1883-1957), came from German-speaking families and had been raised in an environment strongly influenced by German intellectual culture. Boas established a new direction for research into languages. In the eighteenth and nineteenth centuries scholars had concentrated on collecting vocabulary – and German linguists J. C. Adelung, J. Vater, and Johann Carl Buschmann did pioneering work among North American Indians – but Boas emphasized grammatical categories and the place of language in its cultural context. He documented an extraordinary array of North American Indian languages and established models that were followed by scholars of North American Indian languages throughout the twentieth century.[73]

Germans and German-Americans in the late nineteenth and early twentieth century also compiled collections of artifacts from their tours of Indian country. Thousands of objects were shipped across the Atlantic to be placed in museum collections in Germany and Austria. Sons of German immigrants continued the practice in America. George Gustav Heye amassed materials that eventually became the basis for the National Museum of the American Indian. Rudolph Haffenreffer created the King Philip Museum as a tribute to the history of the Indians of New England. In the 1920s, when the prevailing opinion maintained that there were no "real Indians" left in New England, Haffenreffer took pains to have local Indian people involved in his museum. In the 1950s his museum was donated to Brown University and renamed the Haffenreffer Museum.[74]

In the late twentieth century, Germans joined the flocks of scholars, tourists, cultural voyeurs, New Agers, and wannabees who regularly turn up in Indian communities. Like all visitors they have not always been welcome and have sometimes outstayed their welcome. They have sometimes been culturally insensitive and often displayed normal human clumsiness, and they have sometimes exploited their hosts and abused their hospitality. But Indian scholars from Canasatego to Charles Eastman to Vine Deloria have pointed out that Indian America has a lot to teach Europe if Europeans are willing to look and listen. Germans, perhaps more than any other nation, have demonstrated the willingness to do so.

Indians Discover Germany

From the very first contacts between Europe and North America, Indians crossed the Atlantic on their own voyages of discovery and encountered a new world "over there." Anthropologist Harald Prins estimates as many as two thousand American Indians had made the trip to Europe by the time English Pilgrims sailed to America on the Mayflower. Most turned up in the port cities of England, France, and Spain, but Prins reports an intriguing historical snippet: "In the yeere 1153 . . . It is written, that there came to Lubec, a citie of Germanie, one Canoa with certaine Indians."[75] German broadsides dated 1566 depict an Eskimo woman and child who had been captured by French sailors and taken to the Netherlands, but the illustrations were derived from Dutch woodcuts and it is doubtful that the captive Eskimos themselves reached Germany.[76]

The earliest known visit to Germany by North American Indians occurred in 1720, when Captain John Plight, "an Indian trader, militia officer, and all-purpose rascal" from Charleston, South Carolina, took over two Creek "princes" and displayed them and their tattoos for money.[77] The earliest Indian sailors from New England who went to sea in the eighteenth and nineteenth century sometimes traveled the world on whaling and trading ships. Since as many as one-third of the New England whaling crews were of Indian, African, and Indian-African descent, it is unlikely that Paul Cuffe, of African and Pequot descent, was the only New England Native to dock in German ports like Bremen.[78]

Before long, Indian travelers were turning up in Germany where, in the nineteenth century, there was great demand for *Völkerschauen*, educational displays, that presented families of people living in replicas of their native habitations and demonstrating their native ways and traditions. In the 1820s American captain Samuel Hadlock exhibited a traveling show of "Eskimos from Baffin's Bay" in Europe. The family of Inuit toured Germany in 1824–1825, visiting Hamburg, Leipzig, Berlin, Potsdam, Dresden, Munich, Strasbourg, and other cities. The German sculptor Johann Gottfried Schadow sketched their portraits.[79]

George Copway, "the most widely acclaimed Indian writer of the antebellum era," attended the Third World Peace Congress in Frankfurt am Main, Germany, in August 1850. A Canadian Anishinabe or Ojibwa Methodist, Copway represented the "Christian Indian of America" and gave a speech before the congress. He was disappointed by his performance but was warmly received in Germany (see Bernd Peyer, this volume).

In 1885 Johan Adrian Jacobsen, the Norwegian collector of artifacts, also brought Inuit to Germany, although one group of eight people he had hired in Labrador in 1880 caught smallpox and died. In 1885 Jacobson contracted with a group of nine Bella Coola Indians from the Northwest Pacific Coast to tour

Germany as a troupe, performing traditional dances and staging other cultural events. The Bella Coolas received twenty dollars a month plus room and board, and they also made and sold carvings during their tour. They stopped in more than two dozen German cities, attracted considerable attention, and inspired Franz Boas to make the Northwest Coast his life's work, although the press frequently pointed out that they did not look like Indians were supposed to look. Tedium, travel, and a grueling schedule that often required two performances a day took their toll. By the time the tour ended in the summer of 1886, the Bella Coolas were tired of performing and tired of Germany.[80]

"Show Indians" in Germany

In the late nineteenth and early twentieth century, many Indian people – primarily Oglala Lakotas from the Pine Ridge Reservation in South Dakota – visited Germany as members of the traveling Wild West shows and the Sarrasani Circus. They signed up for these stints for money, for adventure, or simply to escape the deadening hand of United States policy on the reservations. Everywhere they went in Europe, they were tourists as well as entertainers.[81]

The first Oglalas traveled to Germany in 1886 with Frank Harvey. Other Oglalas toured Europe with "Mexican Joe" in 1887 and with Dr. William "Doc" Carver's "Wild America" in 1889. After tours of the eastern United States and England, William F. "Buffalo Bill" Cody took seventy-two Indians to Germany in 1890 as part of his show's European tour that also included France, Spain, and Italy. Cody's Indians toured Munich, Vienna, Berlin, Dresden, Leipzig, Bonn, Koblenz, Frankfurt, and Stuttgart, and "caused a sensation," writes George Moses. "The enthusiasm in Germany seems to have been greater than anywhere else in Europe." Critics in the United States expressed concern about the Show's exploitation of their Indian participants, and some alleged that Cody mistreated his Indians. Despite the generally favorable reception in the German press, Hamburg newspapers reported that the Indians were ill-treated and underfed.[82] Buffalo Bill's show returned to Germany in 1891. Ninety-eight Sioux joined the show, including Kicking Bear, Short Bull, and twenty-one other Lakotas who had been arrested for their part in the so-called Ghost Dance Outbreak the previous year. Cody added new acts to the show, including equestrian squads from around the world, and the Indians performed alongside German guards from the German emperor's Ulan regiment.[83] "Show Indians" returned to Germany with Buffalo Bill in 1906, again to enthusiastic newspaper coverage.[84]

Other shows followed. During the Trans-Mississippi Exposition of 1898 in

Fig. 6. Sarrasani circus troupe of Lakotas on board the steamship *Westphalia*, bound for Germany, circa 1928. Photo courtesy, National Archives and Records Administration-Central Plains Region, 75.PR.2801.

Omaha, Nebraska, five hundred Indians from thirty-six tribes participated in the first "Great Indian Congress," whose purpose was to help non-Indian visitors better understand the ways of life of the various tribes. Between 1907 and 1912, under the direction of Colonel Frederic T. Cummins, this ethnological show toured Europe, including Germany, as "Colonel Cummins's Wild West and Indian Congress."[85] In 1912, Hans Stosch-Sarrasani recruited twenty-two Oglalas for his circus. The Sarrasani Circus traveled throughout Europe but was based in Dresden, where it provided shows to audiences in a six-thousand-seat arena. The outbreak of World War I in August 1914 disrupted the tours. Sarrasani moved his Indians to Denmark. Indians from Cummins's troupe became stranded. Lacking passports and papers, they were arrested in Hamburg as Serbian spies, before the American consul secured their release, and they escaped to London via Denmark and Norway.[86] After the war, Sarrasani resumed business, and groups of Oglalas performed with the Dresden circus in the 1920s.[87]

Many scholars trace the appeal of Karl May's western novels and the continuing German fascination with the American West to the visits of these "Show Indians." Like some modern Germans, they were, in a sense, "playing Indian." Their participation in the shows may have been a function of their exploitation and economic marginalization, but, as George Moses suggests, "playing Indian could also be interpreted as defiance." At a time when their cultures were under siege back home and they themselves targeted for assimilation and disappearance, some Indians found in the Wild West shows an opportunity to celebrate their cultures in arenas far from the prying eyes of Indian agents.[88]

Indian Soldiers in Two World Wars

While Germans participated in larger conflicts in Indian country in the eighteenth and nineteenth centuries, Indians participated in larger conflicts in and against Germany in the twentieth century. After the United States entered World War I in 1917, more than seventeen thousand Native Americans registered for military service. While the German press exploited United States treatment of Native peoples to score propaganda points, the American press reveled in the image of the first Americans joining their white brothers in a war for democracy: "Indians see Germany trying to do to all the world what the white man did to the Indian," explained one newspaper. Many Indians, too, saw themselves fighting for freedom. "The Indian fights because his country, his liberties, his ideals and his manhood are assailed by the brutal hypocrisy of Prussianism," said Seneca Arthur C. Parker, president of the Society of American Indians. Chauncey Yellow Robe said Indians fought against "German savagery . . . [t]o save the world for civilization, freedom and democracy."[89]

About ten thousand Indians served in the American Expeditionary Force, and Native American soldiers fought in every major engagement on the Western Front in 1918. Indians killed and were killed by Germans. As in subsequent wars, Indian soldiers were assigned dangerous assignments as scouts, snipers, and messengers on the assumption that they possessed natural talents for such roles. Their casualty rates were high: Russel Barsh estimates that at least 5 percent of Indian servicemen died in action, compared with 1 percent for the AEF as a whole. Many performed courageous deeds and some won military honors; some were taken prisoner and served out the war in German camps. In the last months of the war, the U.S. Army used Native-speaking Indian soldiers to transmit military messages and perplex German code-breakers. Choctaw, Osage, Sioux, Cheyenne, and Comanche telephone operators prefigured the achievements of the famous Navajo "code-talkers" in World War II.[90]

Service in the war gave many Indians their first opportunity to observe German culture and ways of life and gave some Germans reared on Karl May their

Fig. 7. Wilson and the last of the Mohicans: "You cowards! If you would not have allowed us to wipe you out, you could now fight for America's freedom!" Cartoon by Eduard Thöny published in *Simplicissimus*, 1 May 1917.

first opportunity to see real Indians. Looking at each other through blood-red lenses and influenced by wartime propaganda, however, many Indians and Germans saw only "savage Huns" and "savage redskins." Lakotas began to include the term *iya sica*, "bad speakers," in song texts as a designation for Germans but also as a generic term for enemy in both world wars.[91]

When the United States entered the Second World War against the Axis Powers in 1941, Indians again rallied to the cause (while in some cases making it clear that they did so as allies, not as subjects, of the United States). Navajos and other Southwestern tribes signed a multitribal resolution to outlaw the use of the swastika. Southwestern Indians had formerly employed the motif in blanket weaving, basket making, and sand painting, but Nazi Germany's adoption of the symbol gave it new and sinister connotations: "a symbol of friendship among our forefathers for many centuries has been desecrated," stated the resolution.

Some twenty-five thousand Indians served in the military, more than one-

Fig. 8. Banning the swastika, February 1940. Florence Smiley and Evelyn Yathe, Navajos of Tucson, Arizona, signing the imposing parchment document that formally outlawed the swastika symbol from designs such as basket and blanket weaving. Four tribes, Navajos, Papagos, Apaches and Hopis, banned the symbol in use by the Indians long before it came to have a sinister significance. © Bettmann/CORBIS.

third of the able-bodied male population between ages eighteen and fifty. Several hundred Indian women served as nurses, Wacs, and Waves. Indian soldiers fought Germans on the Normandy beaches and with General Patton in Germany; Indian airmen flew bombing missions from England with the Eighth Air Force, raining destruction on cities like Dresden and Cologne.[92]

Although they fought in a modern, machine-age war, Indian people sometimes approached the conflict in traditional ways. As a young man, Crow tribal historian Joe Medicine Crow interrupted his studies toward a masters degree in anthropology at the University of Southern California to serve in World War II. Though descended from a long line of Crow war chiefs, Medicine Crow enlisted as a private. Nevertheless, he distinguished himself in battle in traditional Crow fashion: he counted coup on an enemy and captured a German horse.[93] Ho-Chunk (Winnebago) families passed from one family to another a German scalp that had been brought back from the war, and each family held a victory dance. After the fourth ceremony the scalp was returned as the family war bundle or put in a grave.[94]

Colin G. Calloway

Continuing Connections

Indians continued to serve in the armed forces in Germany after World War II. A small group of Indian soldiers stationed in Germany during the Cold War organized the Native American Association of Germany (which has recently started a campaign to reeducate Germans raised on the fantasies of Karl May about the realities of Native American history).[95] Other Indian people visited Germany as tourists. In the 1960s and 1970s, German student movements expressed solidarity with the American Indian Movement, and AIM members marched in East Berlin's May Day parade.[96] Some young Germans made pilgrimages to the encampment of Lakota medicine man and AIM spiritual leader Leonard Crow Dog – "And, of course, there were the Germans," commented Mary Brave Bird, who was married to Crow Dog at the time.[97] For many young West Germans AIM became a symbol of resistance against an oppressive capitalist system. AIM support groups sprang up throughout Germany to raise money and to try and inform the general public about current events in Indian country. At the same time, AIM paid attention to international diplomacy, and AIM leaders visited Germany. Clyde Bellecourt toured Europe in 1974, and the next year Dennis Banks and Vernon Bellecourt authorized the first representative office in West Berlin.[98] AIM leaders and other Indian activists have continued to visit and find support in Germany.

In recent years, responding to German fascination with all things Indian, more and more Native scholars, artists, and performers have traveled to Germany, individually or under the auspices of companies, selling cultural events to receptive audiences. In the spring of 1999, "Indian Village Europe," an American Indian exposition and park, opened at Schloss Schönau, south of Vienna. Chief Jim Billie of the Florida Seminoles spoke at the opening ceremony, along with the Canadian ambassador to the United States, the Austrian Minister of Environment and Family, and other dignitaries. Donlin Many Bad Horses blessed the opening with a Cheyenne prayer, members of the Hoop Dance Academy from Pine Ridge performed, and the Arrow Space Rock band from Pine Ridge played during the evening. The opening was broadcast live on Austrian television and recorded for transmission throughout the German-speaking countries a few days later. Many Indian people have appeared at the village, performing songs and dances, telling stories, and giving demonstrations of Native arts and crafts.[99] Germany offers a large market for Native American goods, with sales of jewelry alone reaching nine million dollars in 1998 and with significant potential for expansion.[100] Many Germans belong to Indianer clubs, where they don feather headdresses and play Indian (see Katrin

Sieg's essay in this volume). Though these hobbyists often feel they are showing respect for Indians, many Native Americans criticize them for exploiting Indian people by appropriating their culture (see Marta Carlson's comment in this volume).

Some Germans feel and claim a special affinity with Indians. Indians and Germans have often intermarried and still do: Luther Standing Bear was married in Germany, to an Austrian or German nurse; Oscar Howe and N. Scott Momaday both took German wives. But as Russel Barsh suggests in his case study from the Pacific Northwest (this volume), the data do not demonstrate that marriages occurred with sufficient frequency to justify notions of a special relationship between the two peoples.

Unlike the Spanish, French, British, or Americans, Germans did not enter Indian country as members of a colonizing nation, but they participated in the colonizing process. Their relations with the Indian people whom they encountered defy easy characterization. History furnishes instances of coexistence, cooperation, and mutual respect, but, on balance, relations between Indian people and German people seem to have been not much different from those between Indians and other groups of Europeans. People made war, people made love, and, as in any cultural encounters, things were usually pretty complicated.

Notes

I am grateful to Christian Feest, Hartmut Lutz, and Bernd Peyer for reading and offering suggestions on a draft of this essay.

1. Fertig, "Transatlantic Migrations," 192-235; Wokeck, "Harnessing the Lure," 204-43; Roeber, "'Origin,'" 220-83; Grubb, "German Immigration," 417-36; Franklin, *Papers* 4:234, 484-85; Fogleman, *Hopeful Journeys*.

2. Tanner, *Settling of North America*, 116-17; Luebke, *Germans in the New World*, 175.

3. Luebke, *Germans in the New World*, xiii.

4. Magnusson and Pálsson, *Vinland Sagas*, 55; G. Jones, *Norse Atlantic Saga*, 192-94. I am grateful to Christian Feest for bringing Tyrkir to my attention.

5. Sheehan, *Savagism*, 114; J. Smith, *Travels and Works* 2:456, 463, 466-67, 476-77, 487.

6. Luebke, *Germans in the New World*, 159.

7. Graffenried, *Account*, 83, 238, 262, 281-82.

8. G. F. Jones, *Georgia Dutch*, esp. 258-65 for Indian relations; Reck, "Short Report," 1:135-48.

9. Jordan and Kaups, *American Backwoods Frontier*.

10. Snow, Gehring, and Starna, *In Mohawk Country*, 245, 247-48, 258, 262, 289, 340, 364, 375, 380, 392; McGregor, "Cultural Adaptation," 6-34.

11. Johnson, *Papers* 9:676; Snow, Gehring, and Starna, *In Mohawk Country*, 374.

12. Meinig, *Atlantic America*, 195; Usner, *Indians*, 32-33, 36, 46-54, 93, 200; Rowland, Sanders, and Galloway, *Mississippi Provincial Archives*, 14, 29, 40, 136, 216.

13. Hackett, *Pichardo's Treatise*, 324; P. Hämäläinen, "Western Comanche Trade Center," 499.

14. Johnson, *Papers*, 9:591-92, 674; Lucier, *Pontiac's Conspiracy*, 146.

15. Merrell, "Shamokin," 16-59; Merrell, "Shickellamy," 244.

16. *Pennsylvania Archives*, 2, 512, 755.

17. White, *Middle Ground*, provides close analysis of the processes involved.

18. Merrell, *Into the American Woods*, quotes at 33, 59, 66. See also P. A. W. Wallace, *Conrad Weiser*. For the 1743 council see *Journey to Onondaga*, esp. 116-17.

19. Merrell, *Into the American Woods*, 72; Claus, *Journals*, pt. 2.

20. Different aspects of the Moravian-Indian encounter were explored during the 1999 conference at Dartmouth during a "Moravian round-table," chaired by Darryl K. Stonefish, Tribal Historian for the Moravian Band of the Delaware Nation at Thamesville, Ontario. These and other scholars of Moravian history have since developed their own computer network. Five papers were presented; the most complete paper is printed in this volume as representative.

21. McConnell, *Country Between*, 225-32.

22. Wessel, "Missionary Diaries," 31-37; Olmstead, *Blackcoats*; Olmstead, *David Zeisberger*; De Schweinitz, *Life and Times of David Zeisberger*.

23. Heckewelder, *History, Manners, and Customs*.

24. Merrell, *Into the American Woods*, 84.

25. A. F. C. Wallace, *Teedyuscung*, 39-53.

26. Post, "Journal," 175-291; Merrell, *Into the American Woods*, 85, 242; Champion, "Christian Frederick Post," 308-25, assesses the Moravian's role in the Treaty of Easton and securing Indian alliance.

27. McLoughlin, *Cherokee Renascence*, 72-75. See also Fries, *Records of the Moravians*.

28. Perkins, *Border Life*, 98; id., "Distinctions and Partitions amongst Us," 223.

29. Quoted in Roeber, "Origin," 278.

30. "Muster Roll of the Expedition," in Hammond and Rey, *Narratives*, 100.

31. Pouchot, *Memoirs*, 223.

32. Roeber, "Origin," 277.

33. Baurmeister, *Revolution in America*, 205; Ewald, *Diary of the American War*, 145.

34. Hawley, "Account."

35. "Statistical Census," 2:403-13.

36. Jordan, *German Seed in Texas Soil*, 40-54, 118.

37. Hoerig, "Relationship," 423-31; Biesele, "Relations," 116-29; Newcomb,

"German Immigrants," 47–63; Kavanagh, *Comanches*, 303–5; Deloria and DeMallie, *Documents of American Indian Diplomacy* 2:1493–94. On Meusebach see his granddaughter's biography, King, *John O. Meusebach*, esp. 11–23 for the Comanche negotiations.

38. Hoerig, "Relationship," 433–51; Winfrey, Day, et al., *Texas Indian Papers*, 2: 279; 3:38–40, 134, 244; 4:134–37, 327–29.

39. Winfrey, Day, et al., *Texas Indian Papers*, 4:88, 330, 426–28.

40. Regarding Burnet's experiences, see Lamar, *New Encyclopedia*, 145; for Burnet's account, see Winfrey, Day, et al., *Texas Indian Papers*, 3: 92.

41. Lehmann, *Herman Lehmann*, quote on 105; cf. Gillett, *Six Years*, 43–44; Winfrey, Day, et al., *Texas Indian Papers* 4:88; cf. 426.

42. Wharton, *Satanta*, 58–59.

43. Berthrong, *Southern Cheyennes*, 392, 395, 400–1.

44. McCoy, "Tales of the Grandmothers," 218.

45. Grytz, "Old Shatterhand."

46. G. C. Anderson, *Kinsmen of Another Kind*, esp. 240–43, 259; id., *Little Crow*, 130–31; quote on 101. On German hatred of the Dakotas in 1862, see Tolzmann, *Sioux Uprising*. Thanks to Christian Feest for this reference.

47. Anderson and Woolworth, *Through Dakota Eyes*, 77; G. C. Anderson, *Little Crow*, 138.

48. Anderson and Woolworth, *Through Dakota Eyes*, 247.

49. G. C. Anderson, *Kinsmen of Another Kind*, 263–65; Tarble, "Story of My Capture."

50. G. C. Anderson, *Kinsmen of Another Kind*, 276–78; Anderson and Woolworth, *Through Dakota Eyes*, 227, 233, 261–62.

51. Finerty, *War-Path and Bivouac*, 115.

52. Scott, Willey, and Connor, *They Died With Custer*, 90–94.

53. Scott, Willey, and Connor, *They Died With Custer*, 25.

54. The information on Charles Windolph is taken from Welch and Stekler, *Killing Custer*, 287–89, 295.

55. Finerty, *War-Path and Bivouac*, 10–12, 282–83.

56. Jahner, *Spaces of Mind*.

57. Crow Dog, *Lakota Woman*, 31–35; Brave Bird, *Ohitika Woman*, 19–20. (During the time she was married to Leonard Crow Dog, Mary Brave Bird took her husband's name.) Manhart, *Eugene Buechel*.

58. See Liebersohn, *Aristocratic Encounters*.

59. Lederer, *Discoveries*.

60. Steller, *Journal of a Voyage*.

61. Langsdorff, *Voyages and Travels*.

62. Kotzebue, *Voyage of discovery*; Chamisso, *Voyage around the world*. A third ac-

count of the voyage was written in French by the accompanying painter, Louis Choris.

63. Württemberg, *Paul Wilhelm.*

64. Lamar, *New Encyclopedia of the American West,* 727-28; Möllhausen, *Diary of a Journey.*

65. J. G. Kohl, *Kitchi-Gami.* Information on Kohl is taken from the introduction to this edition by Robert E. Bieder; quote on xxxi.

66. Prince Maximilian of Wied's *Reise in das innere Nord-America in den Jahren 1832 bis 1834* was published in Koblenz in 1839-1841. The English version, "Travels in the Interior of North America, 1832-1834," is less complete.

67. Kurz, "Journal."

68. Stewart, Ketner, and Miller, *Carl Wimar.*

69. Newcomb, "German Immigrants," quote on xvi; McGuire, "Observations on German Artists," 190-93.

70. Guidi and Mann, *Photographs at the Frontier.*

71. I am grateful to my colleague Sergei Kan for providing information on the early years and prominent figures of German anthropology.

72. Krause, *To the Chukchi Peninsula;* id., *Tlingit Indians.*

73. Goddard, *Languages,* 26, 43-44, 290.

74. Krech, *Passionate Hobby,* esp. McMullen, " 'The Heart Interest,' " 167-85; Krech, "Rudolf F. Haffenreffer," 49-89; and Kidwell, "Every Last Dishcloth," 105-38; 232-58.

75. Prins, "To the Land of the Mistigoches," 175-95; see esp. 177-78 and 191, n. 9 for the reported voyage in 1153.

76. Sturtevant and Quinn, "This New Prey," 61-65.

77. Feest, *Indians and Europe,* 615.

78. Barsh, " 'Colored' Seamen"; Foreman, *Indians Abroad,* 109-13.

79. Wright, "The Traveling Exhibition"; Israel, "Johann Gottfried Schadow," 215-33; 235-41; Foreman, *Indians Abroad,* 126-28; Bankmann, " 'Esquimaux-Indians,' " 21-26.

80. Haberland, "Nine Bella Coolas," 337-74.

81. Moses, *Wild West Shows;* Napier, "Across the Big Water," 383-401.

82. Moses, *Wild West Shows,* 91; Fiorentino, " 'Those Red-Brick Faces,' " 408.

83. Moses, *Wild West Shows,* 109-12, 118-19.

84. Moses, *Wild West Shows,* 189.

85. Bolz, "Life Among the 'Hunkpapas,' " 482.

86. Moses, *Wild West Shows,* 187.

87. Moses, *Wild West Shows,* 262-63; Conrad, "Mutual Fascination, 463-70.

88. Moses, *Wild West Shows,* 277.

89. Barsh, "American Indians," 276-303, quotes on 288-89.

90. Britten, *American Indians;* Barsh, "American Indians," 278.

91. Theisz, "Bad Speakers," 427–34.

92. Bernstein, *American Indians*, 40, 54–55.

93. Medicine Crow, *From the Heart of Crow Country*, ix.

94. Lurie, *Mountain Wolf Woman.*

95. "Ich bin ein Cowboy," 124.

96. Christian Feest, personal communication.

97. Brave Bird, *Ohitika Woman*, 48.

98. Peyer, "Who Is Afraid of AIM?," 551–61

99. Bronitsky and Associates, press release, 12 May 1992. The Web site for Indian Village Europe is *http://www.silverbird.at.*

100. Stamps, "Germany," 21–22.

American Indians and Moravians in Southern New England

CORINNA DALLY-STARNA AND
WILLIAM A. STARNA

Emerging from a religious revival led by Count Nicholas Ludwig von Zinzendorf in the early decades of the eighteenth century, the Moravian Church, or Herrnhuter Brüdergemeinde, sought to advance its distinctive brand of Protestantism through a network of foreign missions. The church's first venture in North America, begun in 1735 on the Ogeechee River in coastal Georgia, was short-lived. Falling victim to deadly epidemics of dysentery and other maladies, and also to their pacifistic inclinations, which rendered them a liability to a colony under threat of invasion by the Spanish in adjacent Florida, the Moravians moved to Pennsylvania.[1] There, in 1741, they established Bethlehem, the North American headquarters of the Moravian Church and its mission activities.

In July 1740 a ship carrying the Moravian brother Christian Henry Rauch from Europe arrived in New York. There Rauch learned that a number of Indians were in the city conducting business with colonial officials.[2] Determined to bring the word of God to the Indians, Rauch managed to locate their delegation and met with two of its members, Tschoop and Shabasch. Both of these men were Mahicans from the village of Shekomeko, located in the highlands east of the Hudson Valley.[3] The Indians reportedly told Rauch that they wished to improve themselves and be instructed in the way of salvation.[4] Finding his way to Shekomeko, Rauch would begin the Moravians' nearly thirty-year mission to the Indians in this part of colonial America.

Shekomeko was only one of several small Indian villages situated in the rugged and remote expanse of territory between the Hudson and Connecticut Valleys, which, in turn, was bifurcated by the north-to-south-flowing Housatonic River. It sat just a few miles west of the New York-Connecticut border in the northeast corner of what is today Dutchess County. Neighboring Indian villages included Pachgatgoch and Wechquadnach in the northwestern quadrant of the colony of Connecticut, a hard day's walk from Shekomeko; Potatuck, some twenty miles down the Housatonic from Pachgatgoch; and the

Corinna Dally-Starna and William A. Starna

large mission village of Stockbridge, which the Reverend John Sergeant had established in southwestern Massachusetts about 1736.[5] In contrast to the well-populated Massachusetts Bay towns lying to the east and the flourishing Anglo-Dutch communities to the west, much of the Housatonic drainage retained the characteristics of a frontier, with a scattering of colonial villages, crossroads, and farmsteads.[6]

The Indian villages in the Housatonic Valley were multiethnic communities composed of local groups, immigrants from the Hudson Valley, and refugees from decades of colonial wars in eastern and southern New England. Mahicans were the dominant population in Shekomeko and also in Stockbridge, where they were known as the Housatonic or Stockbridge Indians.[7] At Pachgatgoch and Wechquadnach, the Moravians identified virtually all of the Indians living there as "Wompanoos."[8] "Wapanoo" or Wampanoag, "easterner," appears to have been the Munsee term for any non-Delaware people living to the east of their homeland in the central and lower Hudson River Valley.[9] Nevertheless, the records suggest that these "Wompanoos" were ethnic Mahicans, Wappingers or "Highland Indians," Potatucks, Pequots, Mohegans, and possibly Paugussetts, in addition to other Indian residents of unknown affiliation in the region.[10]

Relatively little has been published on the Indians of the Housatonic Valley and its environs for any time period. English-language records from western Connecticut are concerned primarily with ordinary governmental matters and generally lack information of ethnological value. A comprehensive history of the Moravian missionary effort there and nearby in New York has yet to be written. A major obstacle to accomplishing such a task, whether for the missions of western Connecticut or for those outside the Northeast, is that nearly all the extensive historical record left by the Moravians is in German script and remains in archives as a fundamentally untapped resource. Only recently have American, Canadian, and German scholars undertaken the daunting task of translating these materials and begun writing regional and topical studies.

Most historical treatments of the area, for example, De Forest's (1851) history of Connecticut's Indians and Orcutt's (1882) monograph on the Indians of the Housatonic and Naugatuck Valleys, were completed in the nineteenth century. Ethnological works, and there are only a few, are limited to regional surveys and the Stockbridge community.[11]

This essay, then, represents a modest first step in filling a historical void, especially as it concerns the middle decades of the eighteenth century. Our analysis is confined primarily to the Indian people of the Housatonic Valley and the Moravian missionaries who lived and labored among them. To be sure, the Moravians would go on to establish other Indian missions in places such as Shamokin and Gnadenhütten in Pennsylvania, Fairfield in Ontario, White River in Indiana, and Springplace in Georgia. But the missions discussed here offered the Moravians some of their first intimate views of Indian life in the maelstrom of change, which had begun with the arrival of Europeans more than a century earlier and was fast approaching the crisis years of the American Revolution.

Undeniably a good deal can be said about the Moravians themselves and their religious efforts to introduce Christianity to the Indians in Connecticut, New York, and elsewhere in the Americas.[12] But our purpose here is not to follow that well-traveled path. Our interests lie instead in drawing out from the nearly one thousand manuscript pages of mission records translated thus far, specifically those from Pachgatgoch and Wechquadnach, the details surrounding the social interaction that endured between Moravians and Indians and the ethnological context within which this interaction took place.

The encounter between the Moravians and the Indians residing in the villages of Pachgatgoch and Wechquadnach was unmarked by anything resembling the hackneyed "clash of cultures" portrayal. For well over a century there had been no lack of secular contact between Indians and Euro-Americans in New England, and Protestant ministers and missions had long been fixtures there. However, this is not to say that the arrival of the Moravians did not engender some tension and even opposition from the Indians. Indeed, Rauch's initial efforts at Shekomeko to proclaim the word of God were met with scorn and derision from many of the Indians. And near the end of his first year there, opposition from a portion of the community, which reportedly had been incited by local whites, forced him to take refuge for a time with a local farmer.[13] But the occasional negative reaction that the Moravians may have sparked among the Indians was nothing unusual and very much a part of the missionary enterprise.[14]

Most of the Moravians who served in the missions were familiar with Indian people. They had mingled with Native people who passed through or lived in and around Bethlehem, experience that was most likely to their benefit. Yet cultural factors also proved advantageous in facilitating their interaction. The forms of social organization found among Moravians and Indians exhibited similarities that may have, on the one hand, rendered the conduct and attitude of the Moravians not only familiar to the Indians, but also understandable and, ultimately, acceptable. On the other hand, it is conceivable that the Moravians, consciously or unconsciously, took some comfort in observing these similarities among the Indians.

Moravians organized their religious communities into collectives or sodalities known as "choirs." Here individuals were assembled into groups and assumed their roles and responsibilities in the community on the basis of age, gender, and marital status: children, boys and unmarried men, girls and unmarried women, married people, widows and widowers.[15] The full range of Moravian behaviors, experiences, and obligations took place within these segregated social units.

A less doctrinaire variant of this kind of social organization was found among American Indians, including those residing in southern New England. As is the case in most other small-scale polities, Indian communities customarily exhibited a relatively well-defined, gender-driven division of labor and forms of age-grading within the general population that were roughly analogous to the social segregation found in Moravian choirs. Among adult Indians, women's and men's roles were distinct. The responsibilities of seventeenth-century Native women included childcare, food gathering and preparation, weaving, and making clothing. Men hunted, fished, and took part in raids and warfare.[16]

This sexual division of labor, as the Pachgatgoch and Wechquadnach records demonstrate, persisted well into the eighteenth century. By then, however, the variety of tasks had changed somewhat. The records reveal that men alone hunted, made dugout canoes, felled trees from which they separated the annual rings used to produce splints for basket making, constructed wigwams, hauled logs to be split into firewood, and built fences.[17] Women continued to do what women traditionally had done, such as care for children and prepare food.[18] But they also wove reed mats, carried in clay used for chinking chimneys and plastering dwellings, and gathered wild fruits.[19] Moreover, groups of "single women" were observed going into the woods to make brooms.[20]

In other instances and as required, men and women joined together to form work groups. Both sexes tended village fields, planting and harvesting corn, beans, and other crops.[21] Fishing, too, appears to have been a communal activity, although there are indications that some fishing parties were made up exclusively of men.[22] Teams of men and women were mobilized to go into the forest and nearby swamps to cut and gather materials to make brooms and baskets and an assortment of wooden utensils, which were then sold to whites in order to obtain food and clothing.[23]

Men and women also hired themselves out to white farmers, especially during planting and harvest times, where they were paid in meals and drink, often to their detriment with hard cider and rum, or with much-needed clothing.[24]

Moravians and Indians lived, worked, and worshipped together in the same communities through good times and bad. The obvious cultural and historical differences that distinguished these two peoples were partially mitigated by the social intimacy that arose from their living virtually in each other's laps. Throughout this experience, and in keeping with the practices of their church, the Moravians encouraged the Indians to reflect on their own spiritual lives. This could only be accomplished through fervent, ceaseless, and often lengthy dialogues with the Indians over the "state of their hearts," a central theme of Moravian theology. When not at work in their homes and gardens, teaching school, or holding services, the Moravians were talking to the Indians, individually or in small groups, wherever and whenever they could.[25] The brethren, often assisted by their wives, probed into the lives and thoughts of the Indians, scrutinizing and questioning family relationships, marital responsibilities, the rearing of children, or any other issue that they could tie to their moral and spiritual well-being. Frequently at the center of these discussions was the misuse of alcohol and its pernicious effects on Indians and their communities, a topic to which we will return.

A key to appreciating this social intimacy is language. No one doubts its centrality in negotiating the misconceptions and intricacies that attend the meeting of dissimilar cultures. As the Jesuits in Canada learned, there were but two courses open to them in this regard: "[T]hey could teach their numerous hosts to speak French or church Latin, or they could themselves learn a native tongue."[26] They chose the latter, albeit with varying degrees of success. Among the Indians in the Housatonic Valley, however, a somewhat more complicating set of factors was at work.

With few exceptions, the Moravians' first language was German, although they also spoke English. The Indians, of course, conversed in their own languages and dialects, and in the multiethnic villages of Shekomeko, Wechquadnach, and Pachgatgoch, these were numerous.[27] In addition, an unknown number of Mahicans and other River Indians spoke Dutch, having had decades of practice that followed from their trading relationships with the residents of what once was New Netherland and later the colony of New York.[28] At the same time, contact with colonists and missionaries in southern New England obliged many to learn English, and they did. The outcome was that the Moravians preached to the Indians mostly in English, often with the help of Native interpreters who conveyed their words to the Indians in a language identified as "Wompona."[29]

The importance placed on the use of English in the Housatonic Valley villages is illustrated by the experiences of Brother Büninger. Shortly after his arrival in Pachgatgoch, the Indians approached Büninger, complaining that he had not held a meeting with them in two days.[30] When he confessed that he was without his interpreters, both of whom had gone to the seaside, and therefore could not preach, the Indians asked him why he needed interpreters. After all, he spoke English! In 1752, Sensemann, who had spent more time at Pachgatgoch than any other of the Moravians, wrote that because he did not have an Indian to interpret for him, he held a service in English.[31]

There is little evidence that the Moravians made a serious effort to either preach in or teach German to the Indians, nor would this have made much sense.[32] Although there were earnest attempts to learn the Indian languages, it is doubtful that the majority of the Moravians reached high levels of fluency; none of the brethren spent sufficient time among the Indians to do so. And as the scholarly Jesuits had discovered, they, like the Moravians, were in age beyond the best years for learning a language. Thus, the linguistic skills the Moravians did manage to acquire, while acceptable for everyday conversation, were insufficient to convey theological abstractions or ecclesiastical missives. Revealing what may have been his own understandable linguistic frustrations and, perhaps, inadequacies, Brother Büninger observed that "the dear Brethren are lacking in their language suitable words to express themselves when interpreting. For example, they do not have any suitable words for *Grace, Blessing,* and *Redemption.* We advised them to incorporate these particular words into their language, as one language often borrows one word from another language."[33]

The intimacy of religious discourse between Indians and Moravians did little to cloud their cultural differences, which, although conceded, would not be reconciled. But neither did these differences generate significant intolerance, provoke a disruptive incivility, or deter the occasional cooperative effort or thoughtful gesture. What is noteworthy, however, is the degree of separateness that, at the same time, characterized most aspects of their secular lives.

Outside of religious activities, the Moravians, along with their Indian hosts, expended a substantial measure of their energy on economic pursuits. Farming, of course, was critical for their own and the Indians' survival. Still, in carrying out this task, the brethren and the Indians cultivated and kept separate fields. At Pachgatgoch, the Indians provided the Moravians with two plots of land on which they planted corn, beans, and oats. They cut meadow hay and cornstalks to use as winter feed for their livestock.[34] Turnips, potatoes, and cabbage were grown in small house gardens.[35] The Indians, on the other hand, appear to have restricted themselves to growing corn and beans.

The physical separation of their fields (and their homes) was often bridged by the Indians with offers of assistance, which included working the Moravians' crops.[36] There is no indication that the brethren reciprocated in kind, but instead they furnished the Indians with cooked meals in exchange for their labor.[37]

Indian hunters at times supplied the Moravians, who did not hunt or fish themselves, with deer and bear meat as well as with fish, thereby supplementing the foodstuffs that the brethren purchased from white merchants in nearby towns.[38] Other courtesies the Indians extended included gifts of turkey meat, apples, flat corn bread, white bread, and beans.[39]

Firewood was a critical and scarce resource in the Housatonic Valley and elsewhere in southern New England.[40] Some of the Indians, particularly single women and the elderly, tried to ease this situation by moving each fall to their "winter huts," or wigwams, on the mountain west of Pachgatgoch, where supplies were more readily available.[41] For others, the gathering of firewood dominated community life, and it was no different for the Moravians, whom the Indians often helped in this task.[42] In January 1751, Brother Sensemann wrote that, during the course of a fierce and cold wind, he tried to dissuade the Indians from cutting firewood for him. The men nonetheless insisted and hauled in three sleds full. In return Sensemann gave the headman's wife some dried beans, corn, and meat with which to prepare a feast, which was held at the brother's house.[43] The next winter Sensemann reported: "Because our firewood was almost used up, the other day an Indian Sister had secretly carried a load of wood to the front of our house."[44]

It is difficult to determine to what extent the Indians' actions to supply the Moravians with labor, food, and firewood were demonstrations of altruism, expressions of a traditional pattern of reciprocity, an unadorned strategy to meet real and immediate needs, or, more likely than not, a combination of these factors. We would only point out that the mid-eighteenth century was a difficult period for Indian people in southern New England and elsewhere in the East. For decades they had suffered from the effects of epidemic disease, warfare, land loss, alcohol abuse, social upheaval, and mistreatment by colonial governments.[45] The spread of colonial settlements, rapid Euro-American population growth, and the clearing of forests for lumber and the requirements of agriculture and stock raising diminished the available habitat for game animals such as the white-tailed deer, greatly reducing their numbers.[46]

There is no question that a part of the assistance the Indians provided the Moravians, occasionally in the face of their strong opposition, was calculated

Corinna Dally-Starna and William A. Starna

to serve a singular purpose: to be fed as payment for their labor. In virtually every instance where groups of villagers either delivered firewood or planted, hoed, and harvested for the Moravians, they were provided a meal.[47] The Indians' unyielding resolve to bring Sensemann firewood in the dead of winter, just mentioned, may have been contrived to get badly needed food. Winter and spring were generally the hungry times for Indian people. Stored surpluses would be in short supply or exhausted, wild plant foods unavailable, and the harvest would not begin until late summer.[48] It was for want of food that adult Indians hired themselves out to white farmers to plant and harvest crops and cut timber.[49] In 1755 Brother Rundt reported that he had admonished the Indians at Pachgatgoch for "running out to the worldly people and begging them in importunate ways for some food and drink," and by doing so, "had sought out themselves the opportunity for their heart to suffer harm most easily."[50] Going to the Moravians with offers of assistance in return for badly needed provisions made perfect sense to the Indians.

Offers of assistance and sharing by the Indians, either as individuals or in groups, may have been sincere gestures of goodwill and expressions of concern about the welfare of the Moravians. At the same time, such behavior may have served to maintain or enhance the status of headmen and other influential people or factions in the villages. The formation of religious alliances between Native and preacher, which then could be used for political gain, is nothing new in the history of missions.[51] Furthermore, the Moravians understood, as had the Jesuits before them, that to gain admission to and remain in a Native community and ultimately to be permitted to promote their religious teachings there, they would have "to create a rock-ribbed Christian faction among the tribesmen, preferably from leading families and lineages who could withstand the disdain of their more conservative neighbors."[52] Economic exchange helped create and solidify these vital relationships.

The one or two Moravians stationed at any one time in the Housatonic Valley villages were not in a position to exercise a great deal of Christian largess to the Indian populations there. They grew what food they could, raised a few livestock— mostly pigs and cows—purchased staples and meat from white merchants, and, if there was a choice and the means, ate foods that were familiar to them, such as bread soup and turnips.[53] Although Indian corn, whether sweet, roasted, or cracked, was a large part of the Moravians' diet, it was not always appreciated. A case in point is Brother Sensemann's complaint that Indian bread upset his stomach.[54] He also did not relish the hard work of pounding dried corn into flour using the Indians' heavy log mortar and pestle. "The pounding is very toilsome," he wrote, on the same day that he intended to borrow an Indian woman's horse to haul two bushels of corn to a nearby mill to have it ground.[55]

The reasons behind some of the Moravians' neglect to participate any more than they did in task or subsistence-sharing relationships with the Indians are uncertain. The brethren's behavior may simply have been a reflection of the paternalistic attitudes clerics commonly held about their flocks or those of whites convinced of their own presumed "racial" superiority. Perhaps it was because the brethren at Pachgatgoch, who frequently were accompanied by their wives, rarely numbered more than one or two at any one time. Given the requirements of their religious duties, they may have had little time to spare for anything else, including helping the Indians. Nevertheless, where religious tasks were concerned, the brethren and the Indians worked side-by-side, for example, building and repairing the school and the meeting house.[56]

A few of the Moravians took a much greater part in the everyday affairs of the Indians than did some of their brethren. In the winter of 1751, Brother Sensemann labored hard with the Indians to dig out the village spring and line it with stones. That evening, however, he prepared his own supper and ate alone.[57] In the end, Sensemann's secular life and that of the other Moravians remained very much removed from that of the Indians.

Whatever inferences can be drawn about the sharing and redistribution of resources and labor in the Native villages of the Housatonic drainage, by Indians or by Moravians, there nonetheless remains the plain and poignant language of Brother Büninger: "Here I must praise the Indian Brethren and Sisters' readiness to serve others, for they are, on all occasions when I am in need of their help, willing with all their heart. A good many [times] they have done [things] for me without [being] asked ... because they saw that it was necessary."[58]

The parallel but mostly separate lives led by the Moravians and Indians extended also to features of their religious conduct. In contrast to the Jesuits, other Protestant sects, and also to their brethren in the Ohio country, who strove mightily to undermine Native religious systems, the Moravians at Pachgatgoch appeared unusually indifferent.[59] Much of this attitude may have stemmed from the philosophical underpinnings of the church. In his account of how the United Brethren preached the gospel and managed their missions to the Indians, Bishop Spangenberg, a leading theologian of the Moravian Church, related two directives: first, in their dealings with the Indians, to avoid any debate over which is the true church, and instead, "simply to preach Christ," and second, to "leave every one to his own religion."[60]

This evident toleration for religious views other than their own was of considerable spiritual but also practical benefit to the Moravians; it presented less of a threat to the surrounding and competing Protestant mission communities and their political supporters. Moreover, their noninterventionist approach may have rendered them more acceptable to the Native people at Pachgatgoch and Wechquadnach.

Whatever the Moravians' aspirations, the Indians remained, for the most part, unintimidated by the daily routine of their religion. At Pachgatgoch, Indians, both men and women, continued the practice of using the sweat lodge, which frequently forced the cancellation or rescheduling of the regularly held evening service.[61] Yet in an example of religious syncretism, the Moravians were told that, during a men's sweat, the Indians had agreed to stay close to the Savior so as not to return to their "former way[s]."[62] Although the Moravians were somewhat less accepting of other Native practices, for instance, Indian medicine, there is not a single recorded case of a brother disparaging or attempting to intrude on the Indians' custom of attending the sweat lodge.

The most divisive and troublesome factor affecting relations between Moravians and Indians in the Housatonic Valley villages was alcohol. It was both an impediment to Moravian accomplishments and a threat to the survival of the Indian communities. The ravages wrought by alcohol in Indian communities in the Americas is a well-known and extensively chronicled historical reality.[63] And the Indians of New England fared no better than the rest.[64] Drinking and its destructive effects were a constant source of controversy, strife, and struggle.

For the Moravians, drinking by the Indians was, on the one hand, a wedge issue that frustrated their efforts to draw the Indians to Christ and, on the other, the force that unraveled many of their hard fought victories. The Moravians' efforts to keep the Indians from drink and "close to the Lamb" was an unending battle. "Before they knew the Savior," the Indians bluntly told Brother Sensemann, they came together "to drink, to dance, to fight, and for all kinds of indecent ways of life."[65]

Complicating matters for everyone were the frequent trips the Indians made outside of their villages to work for white people and to sell their handcrafted goods. Forays south to Long Island Sound and to nearby towns, the Moravians worried, were "very dangerous" to the Indians.[66] Even the late fall move of the Indians to their "winter huts," away from their villages and the Moravians, was considered "a dangerous time for the poor hearts because they disperse so."[67] The risk posed was the easy access to alcohol, unchecked by the supportive presence of the Moravian brethren and their religious message.

It was, moreover, a risk that the Indians understood and feared and against which they tried to protect themselves.[68]

The Indians, of course, were well aware of the hazards of drinking. Brawls, assaults, and disputes were disruptive occurrences, alcohol-induced illnesses and death a reality, and the threat to the solidarity and thus the survival of the community irrefutable.[69] It is here that the interests of the Moravians and Indians converged.

The Indian villages in the Housatonic Valley, while they served as bases for mission activities in the middle decades of the eighteenth century, had been in place for many years prior to the arrival of the Moravians. Toward that end, it is our contention that the Moravians' presence and their religious teachings were used by the Indians, with considerable positive effect, to shield themselves from the lethal impact of alcohol and the possibility that their communities might fail to survive. This is not to say that Indian people in western Connecticut were little more than religious cynics or only nominally receptive to the Christianity that the Moravians introduced to them.[70] There were many bona fide Indian converts, an unknown number of whom would follow the Moravians to Bethlehem when they were forced to abandon the mission in the 1760s. But we agree with historian James Axtell, who, with ethnological insight, argues that Indian societies in colonial America were "pragmatically incorporative" when it came to other faiths, not to mention the cultural practices of non-Indians.[71]

The writings the Moravians left suggest that the Indians in the Housatonic Valley took what they believed to be useful from the European religious culture that was presented to them and fashioned for themselves a means to maintain the integrity of their communities. They listened and often took to heart the cautions and counsel that the Moravians regularly offered about the menace of alcohol. However, leaving their villages to live in their winter wigwams or to hunt, fish, work, or sell their goods was for some a test of their sobriety, one that they are reported to have failed many times. Still, the Indians seem to have understood that, in coming home again, they would be met by the forgiving brethren and, importantly, by their own people. As the history of the missions in North America shows, Indians accepted, "in just the amounts necessary," what they thought would be advantageous to maintain their cultural identity.[72] For the people of Pachgatgoch and Wechquadnach, there is every indication that the Moravians' teachings and their concern for the spiritual welfare of their "brown flock" were not simply passively or uncritically received, but were turned to good use: to appeal for temperance in the form of a religious message and thereby help ensure cultural survival.

Corinna Dally-Starna and William A. Starna

The evangelical achievements of the Moravians among the Indians, at least initially, were equal to and may have exceeded those of other Protestant missions in New England.[73] In large part, this success can be attributed to their conscious forbearance in the exercise of the "civility must precede Christianity" mandate of their competitors and to their adherence to a cultural relativism that echoed the approach taken by the Jesuits in their Canadian missions.[74] But what the Moravians did accomplish pales in comparison to the feat of the Housatonic Valley Indians. Pachgatgoch, known today as the Schaghticoke Indian Reservation, remains in the hands of Indian people, members of the Schaghticoke Tribe. They have survived.

Notes

The multi-year project to translate the original German language records of the Moravian mission in Connecticut is sponsored and funded by the Mashantucket Pequot Tribal Nation through the auspices of the Mashantucket Pequot Museum and Research Center, Theresa H. Bell, Executive Director. We would like to thank the nation for its support of this scholarly effort.

1. De Schweinitz, *Moravian Manual*, 38-40; Fries, *Moravians in Georgia*.

2. Loskiel, *History of the Mission*, 2:8-9; Reichel, *Memorial*, 31.

3. Loskiel, *History of the Mission*, 2:8.

4. Reichel, *Memorial*, 31-32; Frazier, *Mohicans*, 61.

5. Colee, "Housatonic"; Axtell, *Invasion*; Frazier, *Mohicans*.

6. Colee, "Housatonic," 69-70.

7. Colee, "Housatonic."

8. *Records of the Moravian Mission among the Indians of North America* [hereinafter, MR], n.d., 34/3191/1; 27 Dec. 1751, 4/115/14/1.

9. Goddard, *Eastern Algonquian*; Salwen, *Indians*, 175.

10. MR, boxes 111-15, *passim*; Salwen, *Indians*; Goddard, *Eastern Algonquian*.

11. Salwen, *Indians*; Conkey, Boissevain, and Goddard, *Indians*; Colee, "Housatonic"; Wojciechowski, *Paugusset*; Frazier, *Mohicans*.

12. See, for example, Fries, *Moravians in Georgia*; Gipson, *Moravian Indian Mission*; Wallace, *Thirty Thousand Miles*; Hamilton and Hamilton, *History*; Wessel, *Missionsvorstellung*; Smaby, *Transformation*; Price, *Alabi's World*; Faull, *Moravian Women's Memoirs*.

13. Loskiel, *History of the Mission*, 2:11; Reichel, *Memorial*, 33-35.

14. Axtell, *Invasion*.

15. Spangenberg, *Account*, 91.

16. Bragdon, *Native People*, 177.

17. MR, 9 Apr. 1750, 3/114/2; 6 July 1750, 3/114/2; 20 Oct. 1750, 3/114/2; 29 Mar. 1751, 3/114/3; 14 Jan. 1752, 3/114/5/1; 12 Sept. 1752, 3/114/7.

18. MR, 31 Aug. 1762, 4/15/12.

19. MR, 27 Apr. 1750, 3/114/2; 9 Sept. 1754, 4/115/2; 14 and 29 July 1755, 4/115/3.

20. MR, 1 Mar. 1751, 3/114/3.

21. MR, 24 May 1751, 3/114/3; 18–19 Sept. 1760, 4/115/10/1.

22. MR, 4 June 1750, 3/114/2; 28 May 1755, 4/115/3.

23. MR, 29 Mar. 1752, 3/114/5/1; 3 Nov. 1760, 4/115/10/1.

24. MR, 24 July 1751, 3/114/4; 16 Oct. 1758, 4/115/8; 29 Sept. 1759, 4/115/9/1; 15 Sept. 1760, 4/115/10/1.

25. MR, 20 May 1755, 4/115/14/7; Spangenberg, *Account*, 87; Langton, *History*, 74.

26. Axtell, *Invasion*, 81.

27. Goddard, *Eastern Algonquian*.

28. Frazier, *Mohicans*; Loskiel, *History of the Mission*, 2:8, 15.

29. MR, 25 Dec. 1751, 3/114/5/1.

30. MR, 18 May 1750, 3/114/2.

31. MR, 29 Mar. 1752, 3/114/5/1.

32. MR, 10 Oct. 1752, 3/114/7.

33. MR, 16 Jan. 1755, 4/115/3; italicized words are in English in the original.

34. MR, 14 Oct. 1762, 4/115/12.

35. MR, 30 Apr. 1750, 3/114/2; 24 and 29 May 1751, 3/114/3; 3 June 1760, 4/115/9/1; 3 May and 10 Sept. 1762, 4/115/12.

36. MR, 1 May 1750, 3/114/2; 24 May 1751, 3/114/3; 3 July 1762, 4/115/12.

37. MR, 10 May 1759, 4/115/9/1.

38. MR, 5 and 19 May 1751, 3/114/3; 30 Jan. 1752, 3/114/5/1; 27 Sept. 1752, 3/114/7; 22 Mar. 1762, 4/115/12.

39. MR, 15 and 20 Feb. 1751, 3/114/3; 3 Mar. 1751, 3/114/3; 1 Apr. 1754, 3/114/9.

40. Cronon, *Changes*, 120–21.

41. MR, 5 and 12 Nov. 1750, 3/114/2.

42. MR, 4–5 Nov. 1751, 3/114/4.

43. MR, 24 Jan. 1752, 3/114/5/1.

44. MR, 5 Dec. 1752, 3/114/7.

45. Jennings, *Invasion*; Salisbury, *Manitou*; Campisi, *Mashpee Indians*; Mandell, *Behind the Frontier*; Richter, *Ordeal*.

46. Cronon, *Changes*; Jordan and Kaups, *American Backwoods*.

47. MR, 14–15 Mar. 1754, 3/114/9; 1 June and 7 Dec. 1762, 4/115/12.

48. MR, 24 Feb. and 30 June 1755, 4/115/3; 8 Feb. 1760, 4/115/9/1.

49. MR, 18 Oct. 1751, 3/114/4.

50. MR, 16 Nov. 1755, 4/115/3.

51. Campisi, "Fur Trade" and "Oneida," 482; Axtell, *Invasion*.

52. Axtell, *Invasion*, 78.

53. MR, 8 Aug. 1752, 3/114/7; 29 July 1750, 3/114/2.

54. MR, 22 Jan. 1751, 3/114/5/1.

Corinna Dally-Starna and William A. Starna

55. MR, 3 Nov. 1752, 3/114/7.

56. MR, 9–11 and 27 April 1750, 3/114/2; 18 July 1755, 4/115/3.

57. MR, 6 Dec. 1751, 3/114/5/1.

58. MR, 21 Aug. 1750, 3/114/2.

59. Gray and Gray, *Wilderness Christians*; Gipson, *Moravian Indian Mission*; Axtell, *Invasion*.

60. Spangenberg, *Account*, 40, 64.

61. MR, 1 Nov. 1750, 3/114/2, 15 Aug. and 29 Sept. 1751, 3/114/4, 22 Jan. 1752, 3/114/5/1.

62. MR, 3 Feb. 1755, 4/115/3.

63. Mancall, *Deadly Medicine*.

64. Axtell, *Invasion*; Frazier, *Mohicans*; Mandell, *Behind the Frontier*.

65. MR, 20 Feb. 1752, 3/114/5/1.

66. MR, 14 May 1750, 3/114/2; 30 July 1751, 3/114/4.

67. MR, 28 Oct. 1750, 3/114/2.

68. MR, 12 June 1751, 3/114/3; 31 July and 11 Sept. 1754, 4/115/2.

69. MR, 28 Oct. 1751, 3/114/4; 19 May 1759, 4/115/9/1.

70. Axtell, *Invasion*, 282–86.

71. Axtell, *Invasion*, 286.

72. Axtell, *Invasion*, 286.

73. Loskiel, *History of the Mission*, 2:155; Axtell, *Invasion*.

74. Axtell, *Invasion*; see also Spangenberg, *Account*, 92, 97, 99–100.

"The Complexion of My Country"

The German as "Other" in Colonial Pennsylvania

LIAM RIORDAN

A major theme of colonial American history concerns the development of racial consciousness from the massive transatlantic migrations of the early modern era and the consequent social configurations and confrontations arising in New World societies. As the title of a popular general text by a leading early American scholar suggests, "Red, White, and Black" represent subjects of central importance.[1] However, this essay argues that the tripartite racial formation among European settlers, Indians, and enslaved Africans was also a far more variegated meeting of cultural groups with multiple distinct interests and self-understandings. While a stark racialist rendering of colonization appeared at the very start of European expansion, it was less consistent and less persuasive in the colonial era than generally assumed.[2]

The convenient abstraction of racial identity quickly falls apart when its reliability is examined in specific social contexts. Understanding how group identities coalesce and change requires examining how such cultural formations were experienced in particular places. The diversity of mid-eighteenth-century Pennsylvania provides an especially telling site for exploring how ethnic and religious differences among settlers as well as among Native American groups contested the utility of race as an explanatory principle for early American society.[3] Pennsylvania's proprietary officials (who were almost invariably British or of British descent), German colonists, and Quaker political leaders often bitterly disagreed with one another, while Delaware Indians struggled to defend their interests, not only versus varied colonists, but also against the powerful Iroquois Confederacy, which sought to exploit Delaware weakness. Delaware group identity itself was a creation of colonial experience, although by the mid-eighteenth century the term had been adopted by Native peoples and achieved a stunning tenacity that persisted in spite of multiple forced migrations.[4]

German settlers and Delaware Indians in Pennsylvania were often deeply antagonistic toward one another but at the same time occupied structurally similar positions in relation to dominant British and Iroquois authorities, whose power largely depended upon restraining the validity of independent action by their respective subordinate ethnic groups. Indeed, proprietary officials and Iroquois leaders in mid-eighteenth-century Pennsylvania enhanced their positions by cooperating across the racial divide at the highest level of diplomatic negotiation, while hoping to enforce conformity within their own ranks and expecting their elite counterparts to deliver the same.

The point in recovering the varied ethnic dimensions of colonial America is not to replace a rigidly racialized sense of the colonial past with a fixed ethnic one, but instead to see how these sensibilities helped to shape one another and changed over time. Ethnic and religious identities informed cross-cultural contact and could challenge as well as reinforce racial categorization depending on particular local conditions. "Ethnic" perspectives, meant generally here as subracial cultural groups, can counter the dominance of racialized narratives about the past by recovering alternative senses of self whose significance has been muted by the ability of ductile racial categories to appear as permanent features of the social landscape.

This essay begins by examining Anglo-American hostility toward Germans in mid-eighteenth-century Pennsylvania and then considers the varied alliances and antagonisms among proprietary and Quaker leaders, German settlers, Delawares, Iroquois, and Christian Indians who were brought together in a series of Indian conferences conducted in the town of Easton from 1755 to 1762. Throughout, we will see that ethnic and religious perceptions constantly modified the racial categories that are more readily identifiable today. Whether viewed from the Iroquois council fire at Onondaga, the Delaware village at Wyoming, the proprietary country estate of Pennsbury, the Quaker Meeting House in Philadelphia, or the German union church in Easton, group identity significantly shaped everyday life and politics in multicultural Pennsylvania.

People of German descent in colonial British America provide the best example of the contested nature of white racial identity in early America. By the middle of the eighteenth century, between one-third and three-fifths of Pennsylvania's colonial population consisted of non-English-speaking immigrants from central Europe and their children. Although the founding of a modern German state did not occur until the late nineteenth century, this large body of German-speaking people from a variety of territories, but particularly from the southwestern Rhineland, took on a new corporate identity in Pennsylvania, often termed "Dutch" or "Palatine," the latter after a particularly important location of emigration.[5] This sizable group of non-Britons frightened Pennsylvania leaders, who took strong steps to limit and divert German immigration. As early as 1727, the Pennsylvania assembly passed a law requiring the "late inhabitants of the Palatinate upon the Rhine and Places adjacent" to swear a special oath of loyalty to the king and the proprietors of Pennsylvania.[6]

German immigration to Pennsylvania had begun with the origins of the colony in the 1680s, but the crucial surge started in the 1720s and continued to build until the Seven Years War (1756-1763) disrupted Continental emigration. Thus, the German presence in Pennsylvania peaked in the 1750s during a time of major political change in the colony. While the colony experienced a significant transition with the death of its first generation of Pennsylvania-born leaders, a fundamental challenge arose with its first sustained Indian wars from 1755 to 1765. The obvious threat of war that had emerged by 1753 was especially trying for Quaker pacifists who controlled the assembly. In the midst of this turmoil, the loyalty of Germans within the colony became a burning concern for Pennsylvania's Anglo-American political leaders.

Benjamin Franklin provides sterling access to their fears. In a frequently reprinted 1755 essay, he asked his readers, "Why should Pennsylvania, founded by the English, become a Colony of *Aliens*, who will shortly be so numerous as to Germanize us instead of our Anglifying them, and will never adopt our Language or Customs, any more than they can acquire our Complexion."[7] Franklin targeted a perennial concern raised by immigration. How would foreign newcomers join society without causing social turmoil? Even more striking, however, is his extreme separation of the swarming "Palatine Boors," as he described Germans elsewhere in this account, and the English. Indeed, his sense of their fundamental difference went beyond cultural distinctions of language and custom to include "complexion." More than simply learned behavior, in Franklin's view, the embodied difference of Germans prevented them from fully joining Anglo-American society.

Given today's widespread belief that all Europeans are white, Franklin's distinctions may seem puzzling, but he definitely presented Germans as physically different from Englishmen. His final paragraph begins, "[this] leads me to add one remark: That the Number of purely white People in the World is proportionately very small." Even among Europeans, "the Spaniards, Italians, French, Russians and Swedes, are generally of what we call a swarthy Complexion; as are the Germans also, the Saxons only excepted, who with the English, make the principal Body of White People on the Face of the Earth."[8] Interestingly, Franklin readily divided Germans into at least two distinct groups. Saxons from the northeast, whose fifth-century invasion of England he implicitly acknowledged elsewhere as shaping the English people, he accepted as white.[9] Meanwhile, the Palatines of the southwest and the numerous Rhenish groups that made up the overwhelming majority of Pennsylvania Germans were cast among the larger number of swarthy and inferior people. Clearly, whiteness encompassed and excluded groups in mid-eighteenth-century Pennsylvania different from those it embraces today.

Franklin and other Anglo-American leaders of Pennsylvania in the 1750s consistently located the German threat to the colony as stemming from their failure to understand the proper meaning of English liberty. As such, they were associated with Africans, who were supposedly at a similar low level of political development. Thus, Franklin described Germans in racialized terms in another instance: "Not being used to Liberty, they [i.e., Germans] know not how to make a modest use of it; and as Kolben says of the young Hottentots, that they are not esteemed men until they have shewn their manhood by beating their mothers, so these seem to think themselves not free, till they can feel their liberty in abusing and insulting their Teachers."[10] Franklin suggested not only that Germans were too different to join Anglo-American society but also that their ignorance and unruliness might subvert all English rights in the colony. As he concluded, "In short unless the stream of their importation could be turned from this to other Colonies . . . they will soon so out number us, that all the advantages we have will not be able to preserve our language, and even our Government will become precarious."[11] Franklin and his colleagues believed that the German presence threatened English liberties. As John Murrin has argued regarding New York, the other major British colony with a sizable non-English-speaking European population, the defense of English rights often found expression through "ethnic aggression." To celebrate the rights of "free-born Englishmen" cannot properly be understood as ethnically neutral.[12]

The widespread hostility toward Germans circulating in mid-century Pennsylvania was more than the armchair philosophy of casual observers. William Smith, along with allies like Franklin, built upon such ideas to create the Charity School movement, which aimed to reshape German-speakers in Pennsylvania by offering them free education in schools that would teach English ways.[13] Shifting our attention from Franklin's imagining of a radically different German "other" to the campaign that perspective inspired exposes the limitations of sweeping racial categorization. Moreover, the Charity School movement demonstrates the strengths and the limits of Pennsylvania-German solidarity. In spite of the movement's anti-German inspiration, its policies presumed that German difference could be overcome through education. As the head of the London-based Society for the Relief and Instruction of Poor Germans explained to its Pennsylvania trustees, the society aimed to provide religious and English instruction to German Protestants so that they "may become better subjects to the British government and more useful to the colonies."[14] In a similar vein, William Smith, the group's ardent champion, explained in a letter to two other trustees that "the Scheme is chiefly to *anglify and incorporate*."[15] The elite leaders of the Charity School movement did not intend incorporation to imply equality in any sense. Rather, the anglicization of Pennsylvania-German children was supposed to instill the hierarchical values of the eighteenth-century Anglo-American world and especially the loyalty owed to colonial proprietary authority and imperial royal authority.

Initially, at least, such expectations for converting Germans into anglicized subjects seemed likely to succeed, especially since the two most prominent German church leaders in Pennsylvania supported the society and shared its leaders' wariness about the unruliness of German settlers. To the Lutheran Henry Melchior Muhlenberg, the colony abounded in "vagabonds" who exploited the idea of a "free Country" by "turning Liberty into Licentiousness." Therefore, the Charity School movement could play a crucial role by transforming Pennsylvania Germans into "loyal Subjects to the sacred Protestant throne of Great Britain."[16] The Dutch Reformed minister Michael Schlatter, who later became the society's first superintendent, showed less restraint in observing to the proprietor Thomas Penn "that the Large body of Germans that inhabite your territorie are in danger of growing savage, if there are not some wide measures taken to reclaim them." To Schlatter, "the Annals of the German History prove" that their "uncultivated Tempers has often made Sovereigns tremble on their Thrones." He favored the Charity School movement as especially necessary since Pennsylvania Germans could still be redeemed as "good subjects," although "at present [they] can scarcely be called men."[17] Leaders of varied backgrounds shared the sense that political stability rested upon the ethnic character of a government's subjects and that ordinary Germans were a threat to good order.

These German church leaders' disdain toward common Pennsylvania Germans paralleled that of Anglo-American political leaders and demonstrates that the colony's German community was far from monolithic in the 1750s. Status differences separated Pennsylvania Germans who had achieved varying degrees of assimilation, and this difference found expression, not only in class and urban-rural terms, but also in fundamental religious distinctions. For example, Christopher Saur, the influential printer in Germantown and spokesperson for a German sectarian perspective, condemned the Charity

School movement. As he explained in a letter to Conrad Weiser, Saur felt that the leaders of the society "care very little either for religion or for the cultivation of the Germans, they rather want the Germans to stick out their necks by serving in the militia in order to protect the property of these gentlemen." Saur considered free schooling a pernicious bribe to secure German votes and ultimately turn Pennsylvania-born children against their German parents. In the end, he charged that "the scheme is only for the rich and the English."[18] The Charity School movement met relatively swift defeat from a Pennsylvania-German public who feared the nefarious goals of its Anglo-American organizers. Ethnic hostility toward Germans inspired the reform movement, just as surely as ethnic hostility against its anglicizing goals caused its downfall. Nevertheless, the movement's appeal to certain German leaders, especially from Lutheran and German Reformed Church groups, indicates that Pennsylvania-German solidarity was far from absolute. That the German sects tended to be pacifists and allied with Quakers in the assembly, while the German church groups were beginning to develop stronger ties to the Penn family's proprietary political network became even clearer with the outbreak of sustained conflict with Indians in 1755.

As much as Franklin and the Charity School movement provide a brow-raising point of entry to the "German problem" in colonial Pennsylvania, we need to know more about the specific experiences of Pennsylvania Germans. Up to this point our consideration of German ethnic identity has mostly adopted the perspective of English colonial leaders who cast their gaze outward from London and Philadelphia, but the remainder of this essay moves our vantage point to the town of Easton, the seat of Northampton County, a two-day journey north of Philadelphia on the Delaware River. Like any other Pennsylvania-German town that we might select, it immediately draws us into overlapping contests about ethnic identity. Most of all, examining events in Easton in the decade after its 1752 founding requires that we add American Indians to our assessment of how ethnic and racial identities informed perception and action in multicultural Pennsylvania. The terms white, English, German, Christian, Delaware, Iroquois, and Indian each gave distinctive meanings to events and had clear social consequences for individuals.[19] Furthermore, each identity took shape in relationship with one another, and none were absolutely fixed except in the most oppressive circumstances.

The political implications of group identity in Easton, Pennsylvania, can only be properly understood by briefly tracing the origins of the colony and its subsequent expansion beyond Philadelphia. A permanent European presence in the Delaware Valley preceded English colonization by nearly a century, but when the English did arrive in the 1680s, they did so in peculiar fashion as architects of a predominantly Quaker colony. Early English settlers primarily occupied the rich farm areas around Philadelphia, later known as the "old counties" of Philadelphia, Chester, and Bucks.[20] Quakers, however, did not long remain a majority of the population, and even William Penn's sons spurned the Society of Friends to return to the Church of England. This development helped produce the fundamental political division of mid-eighteenth-century Pennsylvania, where Quakers controlled the assembly, while the Anglican proprietors controlled the governor's office and its broad patronage powers.[21]

German mass migration to Pennsylvania started in the 1720s before the division between the two leading English groups crystallized into stark political opposition. The Germans mostly settled beyond the English core of the original three counties, where they soon created a "German crescent" arcing around Philadelphia to enter northern New Jersey as well as Maryland and extending down the Shenandoah Valley into the Virginia backcountry. The dramatic population growth and territorial expansion fueled primarily by German immigration required the creation of new counties outside the English center. Starting with the founding of Lancaster County to the west in 1729 and culminating with Berks County and Northampton County to the north in 1752, colonial Pennsylvania grew to include eight counties and the separate jurisdiction of Philadelphia City. All five of the new counties, with the exception of Cumberland, were predominantly German.[22]

Not surprisingly given the previously discussed hostility toward Germans, this growth caused considerable concern on the part of colonial leaders. As the proprietary councilor Thomas Graeme explained in a 1750 letter to Thomas Penn, "the present clamor of a great many people here of all Ranks . . . is that the Dutch by their numbers and Industry will soon become masters of the Province and also a majority in the legislature." Governor Hamilton and the Quaker assembly supported Graeme's simple solution, which became law: the boundaries of the new counties were drawn to "comprehend to a trifle the whole body of Dutch and consequently forever exclude them from becoming a [political] majority."[23] This scheme sent twenty-six representatives to the assembly from the three English-dominated old counties and Philadelphia, while the five newer counties elected just ten assemblymen. Such a strategy was far from unusual in the English political tradition, all the more so since the new counties were initially sparsely populated by colonists. Nevertheless, the population in the new counties roughly matched that of the older ones by the 1770s, and the underrepresentation of the non-English counties became a significant issue in the Revolutionary politics of Pennsylvania.[24]

Easton's very name and location bespoke the entwined politics of race and ethnicity that repeatedly emerged in the exercise of power in colonial Pennsylvania. The proprietors planned that the town would operate as a stronghold supported by their patronage. Indeed, the town and county were named after the family estate of Thomas Penn's new wife in Northamptonshire, England, and the town's main streets likewise reflected proprietary familial significance.[25] But the identity politics called into play by Easton's creation went well beyond the assertion of proprietary power. The "Forks of the Delaware" at the confluence of the Lehigh and Delaware Rivers, where Easton would later be planted, was the center of contested terrain in the infamous Walking Purchase of 1737, whereby proprietary officials manipulated the terms of William Penn's 1686 deed, which was itself almost certainly falsified.[26]

At the first major Indian conference at Easton in November 1756, the newly installed Governor William Denny unwisely pushed the Delaware leader Teedyuscung to explain what grievances had led the warring Delawares to align themselves with the French. When Teedyuscung offered a general response about past abuses, Denny demanded that he explain the complaints in greater detail. To this Teedyuscung responded, "I have not far to go for an Instance; this very Ground that is under me (striking it with his Foot) was my Land and Inheritance, and is taken from me by fraud."[27] The Delawares had been pushed from the Forks of the Delaware to a new settlement on the Susquehanna River at Wyoming by the Walking Purchase, and Teedyuscung clearly hoped to gain redress for that abuse in return for ending Delaware support for the French.

Although the proprietors' legal frauds surrounding the Walking Purchase were despicable, their land grab was also facilitated by Iroquois support in displacing the more vulnerable Delawares. A 1742 conference produced a famous expression of this proprietary-Iroquois alliance and demonstrates the sharp disagreements separating Indian groups in the colonial era. The Iroquois helped enforce the Walking Purchase when the Onondaga speaker Canasatego levied one of the best-remembered public shamings of the colonial period. Turning to Delawares at the meeting, he charged, "Cousins, Let this Belt of Wampum serve to Chastize you; You ought to be taken by the Hair of the Head and shaked severely till you recover your Senses and become Sober. . . . How came you to take upon you to sell Land at all? We conquered You, we made Women of you. You know you are women, and can no more sell land than women."[28] Canasatego's pronouncement is a fitting counterpoint to Franklin's invocation of physical difference to explain German inferiority. There, Germans' fundamental otherness was described through embodied racial difference; here, an Iroquois spokesman relied on embodied gender difference to express its dominance over another group. Before the founding of Easton but crucial to its transformation into colonial territory, an alliance between proprietors and Iroquois compelled Delaware submission to a brazen seizure of their land. Although it would never be enough to reverse this abuse, Delawares established a parallel alliance with Quakers, who organized the Friendly Association for Preserving Peace with the Indians by Pacific Measures in 1756 as a specific countermove to the proprietary-Iroquois union. Struggles over land determined the basis of power in British colonial America and shaped Delaware-Quaker and proprietary-Iroquois alliances that transcended simplistic racial logic.

While ethnoreligious identity provided one means for reaching across the racial chasm, so too did understandings of gender. Nancy Shoemaker has recently argued that scholars have for too long focused on what divided European and Indian gender values without recognizing that they also shared the fundamental view that manliness was a metaphor for courage and activity, while effeminacy invoked fear and weakness. These shared gender assumptions were especially clear when it came to waging war, since everyone agreed that men were proper warriors and that women were not. Thus, Shoemaker concludes that "women" and "men" were "ready-made metaphorical tools for clarifying what one nation expected from another."[29]

Shoemaker's observations about the place of gender values in colonial-Indian diplomacy are especially interesting in the case of Pennsylvania, where Quakers' public commitment to pacifism imperiled their masculinity.[30] That such atypical colonists controlled the Pennsylvania assembly despite being a small minority in the colony by the mid-eighteenth century is extraordinary. Not surprisingly, the Pennsylvania-Indian wars beginning in 1755 forced many Quakers to resign from public office the following year. This mid-century decline in Quaker political power was a turning point in colonial Pennsylvania, but Quaker withdrawal from the assembly was not as complete as often assumed. Although Quakers held fewer seats after 1756, they never withdrew completely from political office in the colonial period.[31]

On the colonial frontier and in Indian conferences, however, the femininity implied by pacifism and the group liability of being identified as women were unequivocally negative. The Delaware leader Teedyuscung repeatedly insisted that the people of his nation had become men again by throwing off their petticoats.[32] Conrad Weiser, Pennsylvania's most influential Indian interpreter, recalled a particularly explosive moment from an Easton treaty negotiation when Teedyuscung metaphorically offered the English a petticoat, "the same as his ancestors received from the, then, Five Nations." To this an English officer angrily responded that if Teedyuscung "insisted upon an Answer to that Belt: The Point of the Sword should decide it."[33] Relying on a classic image of entwined masculine and martial virility, the officer distanced himself, and the proprietors he represented, from the taint of Quakerly pacifism. Finally, accusations of female status were not only cast upon groups without power. When Pennsylvania's Governor Denny, a disagreeable person by most accounts, left an Easton treaty meeting before the final ceremonies were performed, the Iroquois "ridiculd him" and suggested that Weiser "search him to see if he was a man or woman."[34]

The key individual overseeing local developments in Easton for the proprietors was William Parsons. Initially sent to conduct land surveys, he stayed on as the proprietors' land agent and held several legal appointments, including justice of the peace and county recorder. Parsons despised Easton's rough conditions and especially its raw settlers, of whom he wrote, "I can truly say that I never saw or heard of so much Scheming, low Contrivance, and Insincerity."[35] His criticisms seem linked to the strong local German presence; as he explained to provincial authorities in Philadelphia, "this new world has taken a great turn of late and now we must acknowledge that the earth with the fullness thereof belongs to the Dutch, at least they think so."[36]

While the urbane leaders of the Charity School movement sought to assimilate Pennsylvania Germans to English ways, local men like Parsons, who had more sustained contact with ordinary settlers, maintained a harsher racialized vision. Money raised for a local German school led Parsons to wonder "whether it be man or beast that the generous benefactors are about to civilize." Indeed, educating Germans "seems to me like attempting to wash a blackamoor white."[37] The Charity School movement was never as benign as its publicly stated commitment to bilingualism and integration claimed, and the racialized views expressed by local English leaders like Parsons contributed to the movement's failure. As the overseeing body of the Reformed Church in Pennsylvania declared when withdrawing its support from the society, "the Directors try to erect nothing but English schools, and care nothing for the German language."[38]

William Parsons's extreme opposition to Easton's German settlers must have been refigured somewhat when the town became embroiled in violence with Indians in the fall of 1755. In December, Parsons described a desperate scene and warned that unless major support arrived immediately, the Indians "will very soon be within sight of Philadelphia."[39] As the French and Indian War pushed back the frontier of colonial settlement in Pennsylvania,

Easton residents increasingly worried about their vulnerability. In a June 1757 petition requesting munitions from the governor's council, the townsmen viewed "their Situation [as] much more Dangerous than any other part of the Province on this side of the Susquehanna . . . [because] every Indian, almost, that comes here says this Town stands upon their Land."[40] Clearly, all settlers in Easton shared a basic understanding about the threat posed to them by Indians. As Parsons explained that same season, Easton "stands upon the very Land which the Indians claim, and is upon that Account alone much more in danger of an Attack from the Savages than any other place."[41]

The war without question encouraged German "blackamoors" and Englishmen to rally together against "savages." In fact, the Quaker assembly's reluctance to establish a colonial militia and the prohibition on Quaker enlistment in the subsequently organized voluntary militia provided a crucial institutional avenue for Pennsylvania German social ascendance in colonial society. For those church Germans on the colonial frontier who lacked pacifistic religious tenets, the Indian wars and militia duty brought them into close cooperation with Anglo-American proprietary interests.

The enormous violence brought on by the French and Indian War soon made Easton a crucial place for attempts to end the bloodshed. Although still a small town that had been founded by just eleven settler families in 1752, six years later Easton hosted a treaty meeting that brought over five hundred Indian representatives to town and scores more women and children not accounted for in the official minutes.[42] Six major conferences had been held there by 1762, and a closer look at the treaty process can help us see how the meetings themselves fundamentally revolved around the presentation of reliable group identities. In fact, treaty conferences can usefully be approached as elaborate efforts to articulate and maintain dependable group boundaries. Colonists and Indians were obviously contending sides, but this dualistic opposition needed to be deflected since successful treaties required reconciliation. In order for the work of peace to go forward, treaty conferences needed shared interests to come to the fore through a ritualistically crafted "middle ground."[43]

The detailed minutes of the 1761 treaty meeting in Easton reveal the highly staged context within which Indians and colonists negotiated at these formal events. The elaborate use of belts and strings as communication vehicles structured the meeting. Governor James Hamilton, for example, opened the conference "with the usual Ceremonies of giving them a String, to bid them heartily welcome, and another to wipe the Sweat from their Bodies." This "At the Wood's Edge Ceremony" had begun among Iroquois villages before colonization and was adopted by colonists because it helped bind groups together in conference settings.[44] Beyond this particular ceremony, belts were required presentation devices for all weighty matters, and agreements were confirmed by joining belts together or by having Indian women sew new belts from wampum exchanged at the conference.[45]

The central use of belts demonstrates that the communication forms relied upon in these meetings were not entirely the product of colonists' control. As one scholar astutely noted, treaty descriptions lead one into an apparent "world of strange values, betokened by belts of wampum," but such objects brought into play the fundamentally human "tangle of forces . . . that continue to drive our modern world: ambition, idealism, fear; the defense of systems of government; the making and breaking of empires."[46] But these shared rituals should not lead us into believing that treaty meetings were purely cooperative events. Close contact at conferences also produced shock, disgust, and even further violence. For instance, Peter Snyder recalled a story handed down in his family about his great-grandmother who, as a twelve-year-old at the 1758 Easton treaty, had a terrifying encounter with a drunken Indian woman who chased her at knife point from the Indian camp in the center of town.[47] Moreover, all the Easton treaty conferences were held in the midst of a war that regularly intruded upon negotiations. At the particularly charged 1757 meeting, the interpreter Conrad Weiser arrived to find a group of New Jersey men who had come committed to "Cutt off the Indians that are now here." Later, when a false alarm about a nearby Indian attack circulated, Weiser noted that "The cry of the common people, of which the town was full, was very great against the Indians."[48] Even as treaties depended upon cooperation, they also reinforced the dislike and awareness of major differences separating colonists and Indians.

But the dualistic opposition of colonist and Indian, now so easily comprehended as racial distinction, itself required careful maintenance to prevent myriad divisions among the English and the Indians from undermining the stable group boundaries that the treaty process required. Large conferences brought together a vast range of Indian groups. At Easton's 1758 conference, an impressive array of Native nations gathered, including representatives from each of the Iroquois Confederacy as well as Nanticokes and Conoys, Tutelos, Chugnuts, Chehohockles alias Delawares, Unamies, Munsees or Minisinks, Mohicans, and Wappingers or Pumptons, each carefully delineated in the official minutes by their number and key leaders. This represented not just displaced Delaware Valley groups, but the array of backcountry Indian nations that had resettled by 1730 into the upper Susquehanna Valley from as far south as Maryland and Virginia. Originally from three distinct language groups, they had relocated under Iroquois protection in what one scholar has termed a "veritable united nations," but that also might be likened to refugee camps.[49] In these circumstances, intra-Indian disagreements could be more pointed than those across the supposed racial chasm. At Easton in 1756, a Seneca named Newcastle insisted that his suspicion of having been bewitched by Delawares be documented so that should he die the cause would be communicated to the Six Nations. While Newcastle explained this to the governor, the Delaware leader Teedyuscung "bolted into the Room" and "fell into a violent passion with Newcastle."[50] When Newcastle fell incapacitated by a life-threatening illness the next morning, poisoning seemed a likely accusation.

This conflict represented more than just personal animosity, for it built upon the ongoing contention about the Delawares' status as women that the Iroquois spokesman Canasatego had pronounced in 1742. Teedyuscung hoped to use his ties with warring western Delawares and the French to make strong claims upon both the proprietors and the Iroquois who desperately sought Delaware neutrality and peace in the west. At the 1756 conference Teedyuscung announced, while presenting a belt from the Six Nations, "formerly we were Accounted women, and Employed only in women's business, but now they have made men of us, and as such are now come to this Treaty having this Authority as a man to make Peace." But Newcastle provided quite another interpretation of the same belt. He told Conrad Weiser that the belt actually reinforced the Delawares' status as "our women" and further chastised the subordinate Native group for having "suffer'd the String that ty'd your Pettycoat to be cut loose by the French and you did lay with them and so became a common Bawd, in which you did very wrong."[51]

Teedyuscung's assertion of authority scandalized the Iroquois so deeply that he was beaten by a Tuscarora for "affecting the Great man" at the 1758 Easton conference.[52] Signs of dissent among the Indians were widespread at the meeting, and even before Teedyuscung arrived, the British Indian agent George Croghan had "a bad opinion of this Treaty," because "the Indians are Much Divided and Jelious of Each Other."[53] The disputatious Delawares and especially their self-aggrandizing leader Teedyuscung led the Cayuga Tokahaia to raise systematic doubts about the treaty process in 1761, because its messages were sent "by straggling Indians, Delawares and others, upon whom there is no dependence." They lose belts, forget messages, drink them away, and "if they happen to reach us, they are nothing but Nonsense."[54]

Proprietary commentators clearly aimed to diminish Teedyuscung's legitimacy by emphasizing his conflicts with other Native groups, but his argument with Newcastle over the meaning of the Six Nations belt was just one of many fundamental disagreements that divided autonomous Native nations during the French and Indian War. In addition to the Delaware-Iroquois split, the Forks of the Delaware remained home to a large number of Christian Indians. Moravian missionaries, headquartered since 1741 at nearby Bethlehem, carried out the most successful Indian conversion effort in British colonial America.[55] Job Chilloway, for instance, was among the Jersey Indians displaced to the Forks, who, given his name, was probably a baptized Moravian like his brother Wilhelm. Job Chilloway not only was employed by the Pennsylvania government and successfully sued in its courts, but was also among the handful of Indians to possess a patented title to land in colonial Pennsylvania.[56]

In addition to the Moravian influence among Christian Indians around Easton, the Presbyterian missionaries John and David Brainerd also had worked in the region. These missionary efforts meant that acculturated Christian Indians were a frequent enough presence in Northampton County that their status as Indian often went unrecorded. Nevertheless, Christian Indians lived dangerously in colonial society. For example, Moses Tatamy, a principal convert of David Brainerd, was unusual in his degree of acculturation, which included acquiring a deed to three hundred acres of land upriver from Easton. But this adaptation to English property holding and his regular work as an interpreter failed to spare his family from tragedy and later economic reversal. His son William was killed while carrying messages to set up Easton's 1757 conference; the wife of another son, Nicholas, continued living in Easton as late as 1796, when she was among the poorest taxed inhabitants of the town. As James Merrell has demonstrated, far from enjoying a liberated middle ground, Christian Indians occupied a fraught cultural category whose hybridity generally caused rejection by colonists and Indians alike.[57]

For the treaty system to work, all sides needed to accept the reliability of unified overarching identities, especially those that were projected upon others. When pan-Indian and pan-English identities collapsed, sharp crises ensued that exploded into violence. While records produced by colonists often pointedly emphasized disagreements among diverse Indian groups, disarray on the English side was no less profound. The bilingual Christian Delaware Joseph Peepy condemned the inconsistency of English leaders so starkly at Easton in 1761 that he offered "no belt or string upon this occasion." Furthermore, he charged that Virginia's governor and the British Indian Superintendent William Johnson, unlike the Pennsylvanians, did "not speak or do right to us," and asked pointedly, "how comes it . . . that you do not all speak alike," for "when we look towards [the three leaders] . . . we esteem you all as one."[58] Both sides sought reliability from others who, they hoped, might possess greater solidarity than they knew to exist among themselves. When Superintendent Johnson finally attended a conference at Easton in 1762, he was stunned by Quaker accusations that he aimed to help the proprietors confirm their illegal seizure of Delaware land. From Johnson's perspective atop the colonial hierarchy of Indian negotiations, such dissent among Englishmen was intolerable. He left the conference complaining that he "would do nothing more in such a Mob and such treatment he never had met before."[59] Johnson was unprepared to cope with the diversity of interests among colonists in multicultural Pennsylvania.

Just as control of land deeply divided Iroquois and Delaware, the greatest threat to colonial solidarity in Pennsylvania came, not from antagonism toward German settlers nor from the hostile political disagreements separating Quaker and proprietary political factions, but from Connecticut-based settlers who claimed land along the northern and western borders of established Pennsylvania territory. These colonists had begun to move down the Delaware River and across the Blue Mountains to the Susquehanna in the mid-1750s and threatened the new Delaware settlement at Wyoming as well as the essential proprietary claim to manage all Indian land purchases in the region.[60]

Matters came to a head at the 1761 Easton treaty meeting, where Teedyuscung expressed resentment at the role forced on him by the proprietors to repel the violent Connecticut settlers. Intercolonial conflict seemed imminent as the migrants from New England claimed an enormous swath of land from the Delaware above Easton to the Susquehanna. Governor Hamilton demanded to know how the Connecticut settlers could possibly claim this huge tract when the oldest belt of agreement between Indians and Pennsylvania authorities had established that all land sales would be handled through William Penn and his descendants. What Indians had made a treaty with Connecticut men? The answer, not surprisingly, was that it had been performed by "straggling Indians," specifically, in this case, the Oneida leader Thomas King. Hamilton hoped to restore the system that enriched the proprietors by ordering that King be punished and declared such private sales "of no force."[61] This brewing internal colonial struggle over western land exploded in the almost forgotten Pennamite Wars, whose outcome was ultimately sidetracked by the intrusion of the American Revolution. What remains clear, however, is that local groups pursued their distinct interests in ways that fundamentally undercut reliable white or Indian solidarity in colonial America. Such broad common understandings were forged because those fictions were necessary, especially for treaties to occur, but their meaningfulness is easily overstated.

Brokers that moved among diverse cultural groups performed the crucial work of binding this multicultural landscape together. More often than not they were individuals deemed liminal in the societies they inhabited, as in the case of the German-born Weiser and the Moravian missionaries or that of the Christian Indians who frequently served as Indian interpreters.[62] The significance of their work was tellingly commemorated at the 1761 Easton conference less than a month after Weiser's death. At the opening speech of the conference, Seneca George presented eight strings, two black belts, and three white belts to stress the need for reconciliation and the difficulty of communicating without Weiser, whom he described as "a great Man, and One Half a Seven Nation Indian, and one Half an Englishmen."[63] Recognition of Weiser's vital role extended beyond mere posthumous praise, for as early as 1742 he had been championed by an Iroquois spokesman as "equally allied to us both, He is of our Nation and a Member of our Council as well as Yours."[64]

When Governor Hamilton spoke after listening to three days of Indian presentations at the 1761 conference, he immediately returned to Seneca George's powerful image. Hamilton agreed that Weiser's death marked a major loss and, in yet another demonstration of the degree to which colonists and Indians shared symbolic forms, stated that I "heartily join [you] in covering his body with bark." But Hamilton insisted that Weiser had only been "by adoption one of the Six Nations, though by birth one of us."[65] The governor insisted that colonists who worked closely with Indians could not actually become Native people in a fundamental way, directly countering Seneca George's view of Weiser as "One Half a Seven Nation Indian." But the governor's attempt to control the interpreter's identity distorted Weiser's actual life history: he had been born in Württemberg and arrived in New York as a thirteen-year-old in 1710. Although others probably saw him as a Palatine, the governor of Pennsylvania in 1761 insistently embraced Weiser as "one of us."

Analysis of group identity needs to include individual examples and assess their place in broader processes of categorization. Weiser surely stands at a complex intersection of multicultural Pennsylvania: German born, he was a trustee of the Charity Schools to anglicize German-speaking children; successful and much sought after by both colonial and Indian leaders to serve as an intermediary, he forbade such a career path for his own children; a spiritual wanderer who never fully embraced any particular Christian faith, he also never seriously considered adopting Native spirituality. Governor Hamilton's final claim upon Weiser was apt, for he certainly never considered himself an Indian; indeed, he more closely represented the model Pennsylvania German that English authorities sought to produce: honorable, dependable, and readily counted as one of us.

What, then, does Weiser's example mean for the racial othering of Germans that opened this essay? Was that othering a passing hostility caused by booming German immigration and already in eclipse by increasing solidarity among "English" or "British" colonists during the French and Indian War? Such a trajectory can be traced with some social-scientific certainty, but the German ethnic attachment persisted with both positive and negative attributes. Barely a decade later, another major war descended upon Easton and again produced Indian conferences and convinced young men to fight. The American Revolution was particularly decisive in racializing Native Americans as a savage "other," since, unlike the French and Indian War, natives had decided with overwhelming, though never universal, solidarity to side with the British. That aspect of the Revolutionary struggle is well known to those who care to examine its significance for Native Americans.[66]

Far less obtrusive, however, was the persistence of strong ethnic othering by Anglo-Americans during the American Revolution. James McMichael was among the troops who camped in Easton before setting out on General John Sullivan's brutal Revolutionary campaign into Iroquois country. But what McMichael saw in the Pennsylvania-German town disturbed him as much as anything he saw among the Indians. As he marched away from Easton, he observed: "I was looked upon as a barbarian by the inhabitants, and they appeared to me like so many human beings scarcely endowed with the qualifications equal to that of the brute species." Others offered a similar view, like Samuel Shute, who found Easton a miserable place with only "three elegant buildings in it, and about as many inhabitants that are [in] any ways agreeable. Take them in general they are a very inhospitable set – all High Dutch & Jew." In contrast, McMichael found Morristown, New Jersey, "very hospitable" because its residents were "all professors of the Presbyterian religion, which renders them to me very agreeable."[67]

McMichael's sensibility seems crude, but it is substantively no different from Benjamin Franklin's more refined argument for limiting German immigration in favor of "white" Englishmen twenty-five years earlier. As Franklin then noted, "perhaps I am partial to the Complexion of my Country, for such Kind of Partiality is natural to Mankind."[68] Examining group identity still elicits sensitivity (even among characteristically latitudinarian scholars) because it touches upon a deep impulse to make sense of the world by knowing and often disliking what you are not. Group consciousness often functions through negation, more through criticism of others than through a positive assertion of self. For instance, the trustees of the Society for the Relief and Instruction of Poor Germans believed that their work countered ethnic awareness or, as they termed it, "the narrow Distinctions that blind the Vulgar."[69] Similarly, many today shy away from multiculturalism because they fear group identity as an easily exploited facade. These opponents of ethnic distinction are correct insofar as cultural identities can be manipulated and used coercively. However, to shun ethnic assertions and to fail to grapple with how they have helped to inform individuals' understandings of their world reinforces the permanence of embodied difference as the only legitimate grounds for demarcating group identity. The complexion of one's country has many facets that are enriched by transcending strictly material markers. This recovery of difference from the multicultural landscape of colonial Pennsylvania points to the changing significance of group identities and the variations within groups that often are inaccurately portrayed as persisting without change over time.

Notes

1. Nash, *Red, White, and Black*.

2. The term "other" is employed with intended irony in this essay's title. By considering Germans as a racialized group in mid-eighteenth-century Pennsylvania, as argued in the essay, I depart from a central thrust of postcolonial theoretical literature, which has emphasized colonization and racial formation as a fundamentally dualistic contrast between the West and subjugated others. Important work in this tradition includes Said, *Orientalism*; Fanon, *Black Skin*; and Todorov, *Conquest of America*. Two excellent starting points from the recent literature on the complexity of white racial formations are Roediger, *Wages*, and Jacobson, *Whiteness*.

3. For an excellent study of ethnicity among colonists in British America, see Landsman, *Scotland*. On African ethnicities being converted into racial identity through enslavement, see Gomez, *Exchanging*. For a study that places the key development of pan-Indian (i.e., racial) consciousness in the late-eighteenth century, see Dowd, *Spirited Resistance*.

4. On the diverse origins of the Delawares, see Hunter, "Documented Subdivisions"; Weslager, *Delaware Indians*; and Goddard, "Delaware."

5. Although identification of Germans as Dutch may be a corruption of "Deutsch," it was a well-known term in early modern England for Rhenish people. The "Low Dutch" basically referred to the modern Netherlands, and the "High Dutch" indicated people from the middle and upper Rhine; see Fogle-

man, *Hopeful Journeys*, 197n. The best study of the general contours of eighteenth-century migration to Pennsylvania is Wokeck, *Trade in Strangers*.

6. Quoted in Weber, *Charity School Movement*, 9. On the specifically German nature of the registers created by this law, see Wokeck, *Trade in Strangers*, 38.

7. Franklin, *Observations Concerning the Increase of Mankind* (1751), reprinted in Franklin, *Papers*, 4:234. Although this work was first published anonymously in 1755, Franklin's authorship was widely known. He probably wrote the piece in 1751 and circulated similar opinions in private letters that were themselves copied and recirculated in the colonies, Britain, and continental Europe. Editorial comments in the *Franklin Papers* pay scrupulous attention to the broad network of Franklin's "private" correspondence. For other examples of Franklin's fear of German corruption, see *Papers*, 4:120–21; 5:21, 159.

8. Franklin, *Papers*, 4:234.

9. Franklin to Peter Collinson, 9 May 1753, in Franklin, *Papers*, 4:479–80.

10. Franklin, *Papers*, 4:484. Franklin refers to Peter Kolben, *Present State*, 1:123–24. The most important study of Germans in colonial British America has carefully examined their gradual assimilation of an English concept of political liberty; see Roeber, *Palatines*. The best introduction to the Dutch and German presence in colonial British America is Roeber, " 'Origins.' "

11. Franklin, *Papers*, 4:484–85.

12. For an insightful analysis of English and Dutch conflict in late seventeenth-century New York, see Murrin, "English Rights." The dynamic relationship between English and British group identities in eighteenth-century Pennsylvania is beyond the scope of this essay. Recall, however, that Daniel Defoe described Englishmen as composed of "a Mixture of all kinds . . . [a] Het'rogeneous Thing" derived from "a Mongrel half-bred Race." Linda Colley offers a compelling analysis of the development of British identity in *Britons*; for her discussion of the Defoe quote, see 15–16.

13. The citation of anti-German views by Pennsylvania political leaders at midcentury could continue at length. One of the most comprehensive and influential was Smith's anonymously published *Brief State*, which denounced Germans as Francophiles and Quaker-supporting pacifists and, thus, wholly unreliable subjects. Such opinions led Smith to organize the Charity School movement. For a detailed discussion of Pennsylvania politics with attention to Smith's role, see Tully, *Forming American Politics*.

14. Samuel Chandler to (Governor) James Hamilton, (Chief Justice) William Allen, (Provincial Secretary) Richard Peters, (Postmaster General) Benjamin Franklin, (multilingual Indian interpreter) Conrad Weiser, and [Anglican Reverend] William Smith, 15 March 1754, reprinted in Franklin, *Papers*, 5:238. The trustees' titles have been added in parentheses to underscore their prominence. Conrad

Weiser, who is discussed further in this essay, was the only German speaker among the Pennsylvania trustees.

15. Smith to Richard Peters and Benjamin Franklin, February 1754, Franklin, *Papers*, 4:212.

16. Muhlenberg, 3 August 1754, read at the first meeting of the society, reprinted in Franklin, *Papers*, 4:421,418. The small network of Pennsylvania-German elites who worked closely with English political authorities is suggested by the fact that Muhlenberg married Conrad Weiser's daughter Maria.

17. Schlatter to Thomas Penn, 12 June 1750, quoted in Rothermund, "German Problem," 13.

18. Saur to Conrad Weiser, 16 September 1755, translated and reprinted as appendix 20 in Rothermund, *Layman's Progress*, 171, 172.

19. The Iroquois were themselves a composite group generally referred to by the English in the eighteenth century as the Six Nations. The confederacy began as an alliance among Seneca, Cayuga, Onondaga, Oneida, and Mohawk, perhaps in the late fifteenth century, with the Tuscarora joining as the sixth nation in the early 1720s. On the significance of adoption and assimilation for forming Iroquois identity, see Richter, *Ordeal*, 66-74. Whenever possible I identify individual Native people by their tribal affiliation, from which position certain leaders were empowered as spokesmen for the broader Iroquois Confederacy.

20. The best study of Quaker colonization is Levy, *Quakers*. For a concise assessment of the distinctiveness of Quaker spirituality, see Dunn, "Saints."

21. On the Quaker Party's control of the assembly from 1739 to 1755 and their successful reformulation in 1756, see Tully, *Forming American Politics*, 145-59.

22. For a regional description of Pennsylvania German settlement, see Fogleman, *Hopeful Journeys*, 80-86.

23. Graeme to Thomas Penn, 6 November 1750, reprinted as appendix 13 in Rothermund, *Layman's Progress*, 163.

24. On the political underrepresentation of the new counties, see Gipson, *British Empire*, 3:173-77. For a close study of the ethnic dimension of politics in Pennsylvania culminating with ratification of the federal Constitution, see Ireland, *Religion*. For a recent study of ethnoreligious representation in Pennsylvania politics that draws conclusions quite different from my own, see Splitter, "Germans."

25. Weaver, *Forks of the Delaware*, ix.

26. Francis Jennings has scrutinized the Walking Purchase in several publications; for his stinging denunciation of the proprietors and their alliance with the Iroquois, see *Ambiguous Iroquois Empire*, 325-46 and 388-97. For a view that agrees that the Walking Purchase was a crude fraud but questions its significance for later events, see A. F. C. Wallace, *Teedyuscung*, 251.

27. Treaty Minutes, 13 November 1756, quoted in Auth, *Ten Years' War*, 67.

28. Canasatego quoted in Jennings, *Ambiguous Iroquois Empire*, 344. This speech and its implications for Native gender values have produced a large historical and anthropological literature. For two examples in addition to Jennings, see P. A. W. Wallace, *Conrad Weiser*, 35–39, 195–96, and Shoemaker, "Alliance."

29. Shoemaker, "Alliance," 254.

30. On the feminine quality of Quaker political culture, see Tully, *Forming American Politics*, 350–51.

31. On Quaker persistence in office, see Ryerson, "Portrait," and Tully, "Quaker Party."

32. Teedyuscung repeated this point at Easton conferences in 1756, 1757, and 1758 and, as discussed later, was seen as an upstart for it by the Iroquois Confederacy and the proprietors. See P. A. W. Wallace, *Conrad Weiser*, 449, 484, 540.

33. Weiser quoted in P. A. W. Wallace, *Conrad Weiser*, 525.

34. Quoted in Merrell, *Into the American Woods*, 264. Though gendered political struggles informed some Indian diplomacy and were especially common in Quaker Pennsylvania, they appeared throughout the Atlantic world as with the famous transvestitism charge levied against Lord Cornbury, governor of New York and New Jersey from 1702 to 1708; see Bonomi, *Lord Cornbury Scandal*.

35. Parsons to Benjamin Franklin, 15 January 1753, reprinted in Franklin, *Papers*, 4:410.

36. Parsons to Samuel Rhoades, 17 August 1751, quoted in Chidsey, *Frontier Village*, 83.

37. Parsons to Richard Peters, 1754, quoted in Chidsey, *Frontier Village*, 86–87.

38. Reformed Coetus minutes, 24 August 1757, quoted in Weber, *Charity School Movement*, 59.

39. Parsons to James Hamilton and Benjamin Franklin, 15 December 1755, reprinted in Franklin, *Papers*, 4:294.

40. Easton petition to Richard Peters, 26 June 1757, quoted in Auth, *Ten Years' War*, 81.

41. Parsons quoted in P. A. W. Wallace, *Conrad Weiser*, 472.

42. *Minutes of Conferences*, 1758. Any history of Pennsylvania-Indian relations in the war period includes assessments of the Easton treaties. My references are usually to Paul Wallace's biography of Weiser because it contains the most detailed day-by-day narrative and often includes long primary source quotations.

43. White's influential study established this key concept for examining Indian-white relations; see *Middle Ground*.

44. *Minutes of Conferences*, 1761, 3; Merrell, *Into the American Woods*, 19–27. As will become clearer in the following discussion, Merrell's important Pennsylvania study offers an important corrective to misreadings of White's work as pointing toward the "middle ground" as a fundamentally harmonious zone of coopera-

tion. Instead Merrell traces a "sickening plummet" where familiarity bred deep contempt (*Into the American Woods*, 37-38).

45. The typography of Franklin's printed treaties attempted to capture the rhythm of negotiations that were shaped by the exchange of material objects. For careful facsimile reproductions, see Boyd, *Indian Treaties*. Nevertheless, official treaty minutes were carefully edited for publication and must be interpreted with care. An essential reference guide is Jennings, *History*.

46. P. A. W. Wallace, *Conrad Weiser*, 522.

47. Henry Manuscripts, Easton volume, 21-22, Historical Society of Pennsylvania.

48. Both quoted in Merrell, *Into the American Woods*, 269.

49. *Minutes of Conferences*, 1758, 3; Jennings, *History*, 41. On the interethnic nature of late eighteenth century Indian villages, see Calloway, *American Revolution*.

50. Account by Parsons and Peters, quoted in P. A. W. Wallace, *Conrad Weiser*, 447.

51. Both quoted in P. A. W. Wallace, *Conrad Weiser*, 449, 450.

52. Richard Peters Journal, 20 September 1758, quoted in P. A. W. Wallace, *Conrad Weiser*, 196. For a less negative view of Teedyuscung's leadership, see Auth, *Ten Years' War*.

53. George Croghan to Sir William Johnson, 21 September 1758, reprinted in Johnson, *Papers*, 3:4.

54. *Minutes of Conferences*, 1761, 4-5, 11.

55. The best assessment of Moravian-Indian relations in Pennsylvania is Merritt, "Kinship." A more accessible introduction to her work is "Dreaming." For the internal development of Moravian Bethlehem, see Smaby, *Transformation*.

56. Job Chilloway's participation in colonial society can be traced in *Minutes of the Provincial Council*, 9:754, and "Minutes of the Committee," 6:55. Also see, Hunter, "Documented Subdivisions," 37.

57. For accounts of Tatamy, see Hunter, "Moses," 71-88; Chidsey, *Frontier Village*, 62; and Merrell, *Into the American Woods*, 88-92, 145. Only 2 of 184 people in Easton were taxed less than the "widow Tattemy" in 1796, Easton Tax List, Northampton County Archives.

58. *Minutes of Conferences*, 1761, 10.

59. Johnson quoted in Merrell, *Into the American Woods*, 266-67. Also see Johnson to the Commissioners for Trade, 1 August 1762, Johnson, *Papers*, 3:847-48.

60. For a Native view of the Connecticut intruders, see A. Wallace, *Teedyuscung*, 50-66, 223-28, 254-64. On European settlement on the Susquehanna, see Mancall, *Valley of Opportunity*.

61. *Minutes of Conferences*, 1761, 12-13.

62. In addition to Merrell on go-betweens, see Richter, "Cultural Brokers," and Tiro, "James Dean."

63. *Minutes of Conferences*, 1761, 3.

64. Quoted in Pardoe, "Many Worlds," 28.

65. *Minutes of Conferences, 1761,* 8.

66. On the Indians' American Revolution, see Calloway, *American Revolution,* and Graymont, *Iroquois.*

67. McMichael, "Diary," 15:207, 204; Shute, "Journal," 268. I have been able to identify only two Jewish households in Easton in the 1770s, one of them related to the prominent Hart mercantile family of New York City; Easton's first synagogue would not be organized until 1839.

68. Franklin, *Papers,* 4:234.

69. Pennsylvania Trustees of the Society to the London Trustees, 24 September 1756, reprinted in Franklin, *Papers,* 6:533.

Since this book went to press several essays have appeared relating to German-Indian relations. See, in particular, John B. Frantz and A. G. Roeber, guest eds., "Special Issue: Pennsylvania Germans," *Pennsylvania History* 68, nos. 1–2 (winter/spring 2001).

German Immigrants and Intermarriage with American Indians in the Pacific Northwest

RUSSEL LAWRENCE BARSH

In December 1914 I was sixteen years old and came to America. The quality of my mind and its information at that time was such that, on sailing for America from the port of Rotterdam, I bought two pistols and much ammunition. With these I intended to protect myself against and fight the Indians. I had read of them in the books of Karl May and Fenimore Cooper, and intently hoped for their presence without number on the outskirts of New York City. – Ludwig Bemelmans, *My War with the United States*

In this era of postmodernist cultural studies, it is wise to recall that ideals pervading literature and popular culture may tell us very little about everyday human behavior. Reifying the literary and artistic works of a society renders scholarship easy by focusing on readily accessible data such as novels and poetry but assumes that these elite products are important factors in everyday decision making by a significant part of the population. While literary and artistic expressions are undoubtedly tethered to everyday life in many ways, we should seek rather than neglect the contradictions.

The historical German fascination with idealizations of American Indians is a case in point. There is no disputing the pervasive image of the Indian in German literature, popular culture, or scholarship, or the extent to which the Indian has represented a secret wish, a return to the free, idiosyncratic individualism of tribal lifestyles. But to what extent have Germans acted affirmatively on their fascination, and not merely by speaking and organizing among themselves (appropriation) but through everyday social relationships?

German immigration to British America began modestly in 1683 with the arrival of the *Concord* at Philadelphia and the founding of Germantown. Mainly farmers, early German immigrants were initially concentrated in Pennsylvania and western New York, where they were instrumental in the settlement of the Ohio valley and the construction of the Erie Canal.[1] With

Table 1: Number of U.S. immigrants by decade and nationality, 1850–1890 (in thousands)

	1850s	1860s	1870s	1880s
Ireland	914	436	437	655
Scotland	38	39	88	150
England*	386	568	460	657
Canada	59	154	384	393
German Empire	952	787	718	1,453
Austrian Empire	–	8	73	354
Scandinavia	25	126	243	656
Russia	–	3	39	213
All others	224	194	370	716

*Includes unspecified British Isles

the great increase of German immigration beginning in the 1850s, however, the center of gravity of German settlement shifted westward. By the 1880s, Germans had surpassed the Irish as the largest foreign-born element in the American population, and the new center of gravity of the German-American population had become the agrarian Midwest, chiefly Ohio, Illinois, Michigan, and Wisconsin.[2] Table 1 shows the nationalities of immigrants to the United States by decades from the 1850s to 1880s.[3]

An analysis of German immigration and frontier intermarriage with Indians in the Pacific Northwest suggests little relationship between loving the image of the Indian and loving the real Indian as a fellow human being in the flesh. To be sure, the Germans who came in contact with Indian tribes along the Northwest frontier were not intellectuals, but subsistence farmers and day laborers. They may have read Karl May and James Fenimore Cooper but were less influenced by Romantic ideals than by deeper European prejudices and the pragmatism of the stomach. Immigrants who did bring Romantic idealism with them to the New World may have been embarrassed and even repelled by the reality of American Indians as less-than-ideal beings who were impoverished, Americanized, and frequently resentful of European immigrants.

Nationality and Marriage Patterns

European immigrants differed considerably in their propensity for selecting men and women of their own nationality as marriage partners, to judge from the reported parentage of the American-born population in 1880. Data from Wisconsin, Minnesota, and Washington Territory can be used to illustrate this phenomenon. Wisconsin and Minnesota were major destinations for the post-1850 wave of German immigration. Washington had barely begun to attract settlers in the 1850s, by contrast, and it still lagged far behind Wisconsin and Minnesota in terms of population growth in 1880 when persons of German birth or parentage comprised 16 percent of its adult citizens. At the same time, Indians were still a respectable 11 percent of the population in western Washington's Puget Sound country in 1880, while Indians represented less than 0.5 percent of the population in Wisconsin and Minnesota.

Table 2 presents the parentage of the American-born population of Wisconsin, Minnesota, and Washington Territory in 1880. Nearly half of the American-born population of Wisconsin had at least *one* German-born parent, for example, and of those with at least one German-born parent an impressive 84 percent had *two* German-born parents. Ethnic endogamy (marriage within an ethnic group) among persons of German ancestry in Wisconsin, in fact, may have been as high as 93 percent, if those with an American-born parent (9 percent) had German-born grandparents. Table 2 therefore offers a conservative estimate of endogamy, since American-born partners may have been of the same original European ancestry as their foreign-born spouses.[4]

Table 2 suggests that, on the whole, Germans were more endogamous than Irish or British immigrants and less endogamous than Scandinavian immigrants.[5] German, Scandinavian, and Irish immigrants were all more likely to marry outside their nationality in Washington Territory than in either Minnesota or Wisconsin, however. The greater rate of mixing in Washington Territory may have been the result of a relatively small number of settlers and the relatively industrialized character of the early Northwest settlements, with their salmon canneries and logging camps. The foreign-born element of the Washington population was also somewhat higher, at 55 percent compared to 48 percent in Minnesota and 42 percent in Wisconsin.

In compiling data on parentage for publication, the Census Bureau did not distinguish American Indians from other American-born persons. It is necessary to examine the original manuscript forms ("schedules") utilized by census enumerators to calculate the frequency of marriages between Ameri-

Table 2: Parentage of the American-born population in Wisconsin, Minnesota, and Washington, 1880

	Wisconsin	Minnesota	Washington
Total number one or both parents German	49	33	19
Of these ... German : German (%)	84	81	68
German : American (%)	9	11	28
German : Other (%)	6	8	3
Total number one or both parents Irish	17	19	25
Of these ... Irish : Irish (%)	73	73	53
Irish : American (%)	16	16	30
Irish : Other (%)	11	11	16
Total number one or both parents Scandinavian	9	26	6
Of these ... Scandinavian : Scandinavian (%)	87	92	50
Scandinavian : American (%)	7	4	22
Scandinavian : Other (%)	6	4	27
Total number one or both parents British	13	8	25
Of these ... British : British (%)	52	40	39
British : American (%)	34	39	44
British : Other (%)	14	21	17

Totals may be affected by rounding.

can Indians and particular nationalities of non-Indians. Table 3 summarizes all of the mixed marriages I could identify in 1900 census schedules for the ten Washington counties bordering Puget Sound, broken down by the nativity of the non-Indian spouse. The respondents had been asked for their race and birthplace as well as for the birthplace of each of their parents. This information enabled me to include mixed marriages among the respondents and among the respondents' parents. Since I had data on two generations of marriages ending in 1900, I decided that it was best to make comparisons with the composition of the region's non-Indian population in 1880, that is, with the

Table 3: Nativity and marital choice, Puget Sound, 1880–1900

	Percent of mixed marriages[a]	Percent of total population[b]
American-born	49	72
Foreign-born	51	28
Canadian	8.9	6.3
English and Welsh	10.3	4.4
Scottish	5.6	1.4
Irish	3.9	3.6
Scandinavian	5.6	3.4
German	7.8	3.4

a. Marriages existing or identifiable from living persons' parentage in 1900.
Total number: 359.
b. Total population enumerated in 1800: 24,146.

pool of eligible partners at approximately the midpoint of those two generations.

Two conclusions are suggested by table 3. Foreign-born settlers were significantly more likely to choose Indian marriage partners than were their American-born neighbors. Among foreign-born settlers, this pattern was strongest for Scottish settlers, who were four times more likely to marry Indians than would be predicted merely from their proportion of the region's total population. English-born and German-born settlers were each 2.3 times more likely to marry Indians than their proportion of the total population would have predicted. The least propensity to marry Indians was found among Irish immigrants.

Several issues emerge from these data. Germans were indeed more likely to choose Indian partners than were American-born settlers, but this tendency appears to reflect a larger pattern of behavior among foreign-born immigrants rather than a distinctively German characteristic. In fact, the group most likely to choose Indian partners was the Scots, who had figured so prominently in the process of métissage with Indian nations of the Canadian prairies nearly a century earlier.[6] Table 3 is only broadly consistent with table 2, moreover, suggesting that recent immigrants' reasons for marrying outside their own group were somewhat different from their reasons for choosing Indians as partners. German settlers tended to be more endogamous than Scandina-

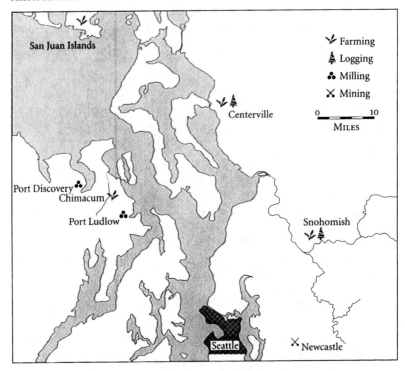

Seven ethnically diverse settlements near Puget Sound, 1880

vians in Washington Territory, on the whole, but Germans also tended to be more interested in Indians as marriage partners than were Scandinavians.

Some Puget Sound Case Studies

To explore these patterns further, I chose seven representative, ethnically diverse Puget Sound settlements with varied economic bases and at least some intermarriage with Indians in the late nineteenth century. They include a relatively old but isolated farming community on Orcas Island in the San Juan archipelago and more recently settled farming and logging settlements at Centerville on the Skagit River, the middle Snohomish River, and the Chimacum valley on the west side of the sound (map 2 and table 4). Two recently established mill towns on the west side of the sound, Port Ludlow and Port Discovery, were also included, as was Newcastle, a coal-mining town near present-day Seattle, where a relatively large number of Germans, Welsh, and Poles had been employed in the area's short-lived coal industry.

Puget Sound Indians were already engaged in profitable trade with the

Table 4: Economy and employment in seven Puget Sound settlements, 1880

Settlement and Economy	Orcas Islands FARMING	Chimacum FARM/LOGGING	Centerville FARM/LOGGING	Snohomish FARM/LOGGING	Discovery SAWMILL	Pt. Ludlow SHIPYARD	Newcastle COAL MINING
Total number Employed	68	64	183	292	157	90	245
farmers (%)	65	47	44	30	14	2	4
laborers (%)	16	48	33	56	64	57	82
tradesmen (%)	12	–	6	6	20	42	10
business/profession (%)	3	3	8	11	4	1	4

Laborers includes loggers and miners.

Hudson's Bay Company and the American Fur Company by the 1820s, but the area did not attract permanent settlers until the 1850s, when small bands of Anglo-Canadian and American farmers established themselves on Whidbey Island, the San Juan Islands, and Point Elliott (Seattle). In the wake of an American show of force – the shelling of villages by the gunboat *Massachusetts* – Salish leaders reluctantly recognized American sovereignty over most of Puget Sound under treaties signed in 1854 and 1855. Despite a brief outburst of armed resistance to American settlements the following year, ending in the burning of several fortified villages by militiamen and the hanging of Salish leader Leschi, relations between settlers and Indians were peaceful and businesslike, sustained by settlers' reliance on Indians to supply them with fish and labor.[7] Impeded by the sound's dense rain forests, however, settlement was slow compared with Portland (terminus of the Oregon Trail), the Willamette Valley of western Oregon, and the prairies of central Washington along the Columbia River.

Puget Sound was therefore a relatively new and remote frontier in the 1850s, when Germans already comprised 37 percent of all immigrants to the United States, second in importance only to the Irish. By 1880 there were 2,263 German-born persons living in Washington Territory, of whom roughly one-third (37 percent) had settled on the shores of Puget Sound. A few of them became captains of industry, such as logging and lumber magnate Frederick Weyerhaeuser. Most arrived with little money and lived modestly as farmers and laborers. What follows are profiles of seven economically and ethnically diverse communities in which many of the sound's earliest German settlers lived (see tables 4, 5, and 6).

Table 5: Population and nativity in seven Puget Sound settlements, 1880

	Orcas Islands	Chimacum	Centerville	Snohomish	Discovery	Pt. Ludlow	Newcastle
Total Adults	123	87	223	447	214	128	333
American Indian (%)	41	46	10	25	22	12	2
American (%)	32	18	39	45	36	34	28
Canadian (%)	9	2	5	5	6	13	7
English (%)	6	23	4	6	14	15	11
Scotch-Irish-Welsh (%)	2	3	4	4	6	6	39
Scandinavian (%)	2	17	32	5	6	11	1
German (%)	3	5	6	4	3	2	4

Some of the oldest farms in Puget Sound are found on Orcas Island in the San Juan archipelago, which remained largely agricultural until the 1970s. The islands also remained a refuge for many Indian groups, such as the Samish, the Saanich, and the Cowichan peoples, that chose to continue coasting the sound freely as fishermen. Many early settlers chose Indian women as partners, and in 1880 three-fifths of all of the married couples on Orcas Island were mixed (table 6).[8] There were only three German men on the island in 1880; one came with his German wife, while another married Jenny (or Ginny), a Tsimshian woman from British Columbia whom he met while employed by the Hudson's Bay Company. Although American-born settlers outnumbered English and Canadian settlers by a factor of two to one, more English and Canadians married Indians. It should be noted that most settlers' Indian wives came from British Columbia, so the mixed population of the islands truly represented a "new people."

High rates of intermarriage also characterized the less isolated, more economically and ethnically diverse agricultural settlements that developed elsewhere in Puget Sound, such as Centerville and Chimacum.

Centerville (now Florence) was a growing farming and logging town at the mouth of the Skagit River, with two general stores, a telegraph office, a saloon, a butcher, a glove maker, a dressmaker, a cigar maker, an organ builder, a physician, a land surveyor, two teachers, and a Lutheran church with a Norwegian pastor. The community included seven Indian couples, two

Table 6: Marriage and Intermarriage rates in seven Puget Sound
settlements, 1880

	Orcas Islands	Chimacum	Centerville	Snohomish	Discovery	Pt. Ludlow	Newcastle
Total Adults	123	87	223	447	214	128	333
Married (%)	71	79	53	65	47	57	50
white : white (%)	22	26	22	66	58	56	95
white : indian (%)	61	62	61	19	13	44	4
indian : indian (%)	17	12	17	15	29	–	1

of them on farms, the rest subsisting from wage labor. There were also eight
mixed households with white husbands – none of them German – and Indian
wives. The Germans of Centerville were mainly northerners, from Hamburg
and Schleswig-Holstein. All but one of them were farmers, and, unlike most
American-born and Norwegian farmers in the area, they were nearly all unmarried.[9] This cannot be attributed to differences in age; most unmarried
German farmers were under forty years of age. The Germans had all immigrated to the sound directly from Europe, however, while a large proportion of
American-born and Norwegian-born settlers had first lived in another region
of the United States, where they had married.[10]

The Chimacum valley on the opposite side of Puget Sound was first farmed
by two English seamen, William Bishop and William Eldridge, who settled
there in the 1850s with local Indian wives. Although both men later remarried
to English women, they were joined by many other mixed couples. Chimacum remained a small hamlet in 1880, with a post office (William Bishop
served as postmaster), a saloon, and a land surveyor's office. Nearly all permanent settlers were farmers; transient Chinese contract laborers worked in the
surrounding forest as loggers and bolt cutters. Interestingly, nearly half of
the men living with Indian women were Norwegians and Finns. These data
suggest that highly localized conditions rather than broad social forces were
affecting relationships between foreign-born men and Indian women.

On the whole, settlers remained near tidewater in 1880, but farms and logging camps stretched along the Snohomish River for twenty miles into the interior. The "city" of Snohomish was already established as the county seat with
its courthouse, sheriff, auditor, court clerk, a single lawyer, and a small news-

paper. The town commercial center also boasted seven lumber merchants, a hotel, two saloons, two grocers, two druggists, three dry-goods stores, a shoemaker, two blacksmiths, and a physician, as well as a land office and a surveyor. The river was still home to many Snohomish and Snoqualmie Indians who chose to remain near their ancestral village sites rather than move to the Tulalip Indian Reservation. The 1880 census found six Indian cabins on the west edge of Snohomish city, presided over by an "Indian Doctor." The other men were working as loggers, and their wives worked in town at the hotel. Farther upstream near present-day Monroe, a large number of Indian and mixed households were found near what Snohomish Indians today remember as "the Krieschel place," for John Krieschel, one of two Prussians who settled there with Indian wives. Nine more German men were farming or logging nearby along the river, two of them with German wives and two with American-born wives. They were equally divided between Prussians and Saxons, and southerners from Baden and Bavaria. Unlike Germans at Centerville, a majority of Snohomish valley Germans worked as laborers and tradesmen rather than as farmers.[11]

On the more recently settled west side of the sound, Port Ludlow was a young company town with a vertically integrated (logs to launch) shipyard, a hotel, and a general store. There were single-family houses as well several company bunkhouses for single men. Two widowed women worked as laundresses. Many nationalities were represented among the workers and, in contrast with longer-settled Centerville or Snohomish, a majority of them were not American-born but recent immigrants. Most of the men were unskilled laborers, but there were also many craftsmen such as millwrights, ship carpenters, joiners, and coopers. Americans and Canadians comprised a majority of the skilled trades (67 percent), while other nationalities dominated the unskilled sector (61 percent). The director of the shipyard was Canadian. Among the large number of mixed marriages at Port Ludlow were two (14 percent) involving German men and Indian women.

Like nearby Port Ludlow, Port Discovery was a relatively recently settled logging and mill center in 1880. There was the mill, wharves, and company steamboats and repair yard, as well as a hotel, a general store, a saloon, a school, and a stagecoach line running to Port Townsend. Ships were not built at Port Discovery; the dimensional lumber was exported to Seattle and San Francisco. The owner of the sawmill was a child of Scots who had settled in Ohio, and the teachers and company engineers were Anglo-Americans, but the captain of the steam ferry, Otto Brown, was a Prussian. American-born skilled mill workers and tradesmen were at the top of the social hierarchy, while a majority of the unskilled laborers were recent immigrants and local Indians. Interestingly, the company nurse, Jennie Alia, was an unmarried Indian woman from British Columbia. Nearly a fifth of the men working at the mill were Indians, and most of them lived in town with Indian wives. This contrasts with Port Ludlow, where there were no all-Indian households. While Germans (all of them from the north) worked at the Port Discovery mill, none were married to Indians.[12]

The mining town of Newcastle near Seattle provides an extreme for purposes of comparison. King County coal was an important industry until the 1920s, and the ethnicity of the coal fields was quite distinct from Puget Sound's milling and farming centers. Germans, Poles, Welsh, and Irish were far more visible in the coal fields, where they outnumbered American-born and Canadian workers. Indeed, more than half (57 percent) of Newcastle's North American-born workers and their wives had Irish, English, Scottish, or Welsh parents. Mining at Newcastle was dominated by immigrants from the British Isles, while the Americans and Canadians were mainly unskilled laborers. Newcastle's Germans, mostly Prussians (79 percent), also worked as unskilled laborers. There were very few marriages with Indians at Newcastle, which perhaps is explained more by economic than cultural factors. Dozens of Indian families could still be found living in nonreservation hamlets along the Duwamish, Cedar, and Green Rivers of southern King County, within a day's wagon ride from Newcastle. There was no demographic integration of Indian and non-Indian farms around Newcastle, however, and only two Indians were employed by the mines. Puget Sound farmers, loggers, and mill hands elsewhere probably had relatively more frequent contact with Indians as neighbors and fellow workers than did the miners or laborers of Newcastle.

Interpreting the Case Studies

Excluding Newcastle, where intermarriage was negligible, selected Puget Sound communities suggest that men immigrating from Canada, the British Isles, and Germany were all more likely to choose Indian women as wives than were their American-born neighbors (table 7). Only men from the Scandinavian countries seemed reluctant to establish partnerships with Indian women. Even this pattern was subject to local variation, however, for in the Chimacum valley Scandinavians were disproportionately more likely to marry local Indian women. Overall, then, the main factor affecting marriage choice was probably immigration itself, rather than the nationalities of the immigrants. Immigrants presumably arrived with little money or property

Table 7: Nativity of Indians' non-Indian spouse in seven Puget Sound settlements, 1880

	Orcas Islands	Chimacum	Centerville	Snohomish	Discovery	Pt. Ludlow	R : P
American	10	2	5	13	2	5	38 : 38
Canadian	8	1	–	–	1	–	10 : 6
English	3	4	1	1	3	3	16 : 9
Scotch-Irish	2	–	–	7	–	1	10 : 4
Scandinavian	–	7	–	2	–	1	9 : 11
German	1	1	–	4	–	2	8 : 4
Other	1	2	2	–	–	2	

R = Proportion of all mixed marriages (N = 96) in these settlements.
P = Proportion of total adult population (N = 1,222) in these settlements.

and may have sought out Indian women as domestic helpers and piecework laborers. Judging from local oral history, a large number of Indian women knitted socks, sewed dresses, dug clams, and wove baskets to supplement their households' income.

A secondary factor may have been immigrants' occupational niches. Two-thirds (66 percent) of the non-Indian men who married Indian women in the case-study communities made their living as farmers, more than twice the proportion of farmers among the employed adult population of these communities as a whole (31 percent). A large proportion of non-Indian husbands were laborers only in Port Ludlow, a shipbuilding town where there were only neighboring farmers of any description. Only at Centerville were non-Indian spouses of Indian women either businessmen or professionals. This pattern suggests that Indian wives were valued as resources for immigrants "starting from scratch" as self-sufficient farmers within an unfamiliar landscape. Traditional ecological knowledge, such as knowledge of the local topography, soils, medicinal plants, and wild foods, may have been crucial to the survival of an immigrant who knew nothing about local conditions and, indeed, may never have farmed in his country of origin. Census schedules tell us nothing about what immigrant men did before they arrived at Puget Sound, but most of the family oral histories I have recorded at Chimacum identify non-Indian forebears as having originally come as sailors or laborers.[13]

A third factor may have been the ratio of single men to single women in recently established Puget Sound settlements.[14] On Orcas Island there were two single men for every single woman over the age of sixteen. At more recently settled and economically more diversified Chimacum, Snohomish, and Centerville, the ratio of single men to single women ranged from 7:1 to 14:1, while in the industrialized settlements of Port Ludlow, Port Discovery, and Newcastle, the ratio of single men to single women rose from 18:1 to 24:1. There was a critical shortage of potential wives throughout the area, especially in industrializing areas where there was abundant seasonal employment for unattached and therefore relatively mobile men in logging, fishing, and long-shoring. If foreign-born men were less likely than American-born men to bring wives with them to Puget Sound and therefore more likely to seek wives only after their arrival in Puget Sound settlements, they had a strong incentive to overcome the prejudices they may have borne against women of color.

Indian women may have been making important choices as well. The ratio of Indian women to Indian men in Puget Sound was generally high; it was nearly 2:1 at Chimacum, Centerville, and Orcas Island, where the rate of intermarriage with white men was also very high. In addition, nearly all of the non-Indian men with Indian wives were farmers, while all of the Indian men with Indian wives were laborers or fishermen. Indian women who married settlers were therefore upwardly mobile. As the region's Indian communities faced the stresses of disease, loss of traditional livelihoods, poverty, and dispersal to pursue employment, the extreme shortage of single European women in Puget Sound gave Indian women options that Indian men lacked.

Despite the manifest popularity of American Indian imagery in the literature and popular culture of nineteenth-century Germany, socioeconomic realities appear to best explain the extent to which German immigrants chose Indian women as wives on the Puget Sound frontier. Single white women were extremely scarce in Puget Sound's growing settlements, and, like other foreign-born settlers arriving unmarried and without capital, German immigrants tended to look upon single Indian women with less prejudice than did their American-born neighbors. Like other foreign-born men, Germans found Indian wives particularly desirable as partners in claiming farmland out of the rain forest.

Interesting cultural questions remain unanswered by quantitative methods, however. Once established with their Indian wives within extensively mixed communities such as Orcas Island, Chimacum, or the Snohomish River, did German men exert a distinctive cultural influence on their offspring?

Some students of *métissage* in Canada have argued that the Scottish and French streams of intermarriage during the fur-trade era resulted, for some time at least, in two distinctive cultural streams among the "new people" who called themselves half-blood or *métis*.[15] Ordinarily, the children of mixed ancestry in Puget Sound (and elsewhere in the United States) did not identify themselves as a distinct national population, but either as Indians of the mother's tribe or as whites. Within the mother's tribes, on the whole, I have found little evidence of lasting ethnic markers or consciousness in Puget Sound – except perhaps in the case of descendants of Chinese, Japanese, or Filipino men, most of whom came to the area as low-status contract cannery workers.

In the oral histories of Snohomish Indian families, for instance, there are occasional references to the origins of European forebears: English, Irish, Scottish, Dutch, Finnish, Norwegian, and Prussian. But nationality was not associated with social distinctions between family lines. Indian descendants of Prussian immigrant John Krieschel shared influence over the Snohomish of the Sultan-Monroe area with the Indian descendants of John Elwell, who had come from Maine. Although most of the Krieschels were loggers and mill workers and the most influential of the Elwells a ferry captain, these occupational differences were unrelated to ethnic origins.

In the Chimacum area, mixed-ancestry families were a majority for a long time and continue to form a distinct social group there. As noted earlier, the main lineages were of English, Finnish, and Dutch ancestry, but the only social distinctions among Indians were based on class rather than on ancestry. The Hickses, who lived a more traditional way of life fishing and clamming near Irondale spit, were often described as more "Indian" but of somewhat lower status, although they could trace their roots to England the same as the Bishops, who were prosperous dairy farmers and exercised leadership in the community until the 1920s (when superseded by the Woodley-Strand family of Irish-Finnish ancestry). If Snohomish Indians' European ties had any influence on their self-perceptions or social distinctions among themselves, no trace of this remains in oral histories or contemporary behavior.

Germany has branches buried in the Indian tribes of Puget Sound, but they are largely unacknowledged by contemporary Indians. To them, the Germany left behind by some of their ancestors has long since been replaced by the Germany of the American mass media. At the individual level, however, I wonder whether the Germany of popular culture today has any greater bearing on personal relationships between Indians and Germans than the Indian of German popular culture a century ago had on such relationships then.

Appendix

Nativity and Occupation of Non-Indian Spouses in Puget Sound Mixed Marriages, 1880. British Columbia nativity denoted by asterisk.

CENTERVILLE

Caldon, James (Louise)	England	broker
Goodridge, Sam (Jennie)	Maine	farmer
Harvey, Pedro (Sara)	Chile	log dealer
Irvine, John (Emma)	Maine	storekeeper
Morrison, William (Sara)	Maine	fisherman
Perkins, James (Nellie)	Maine	farmer
Preston, C[harles](Peggy)	Maine	log dealer
Silvey, John (Betty)	Portugal	farmer

CHIMACUM

Anderson, Charles (Margaret)	Norway	farmer
Clawson, Peter (Mary)	Norway	farmer
Fortman, Nicholas (Susan*)	Holland	farmer
Glanville, John (Jennie*)	England	farmer
Lindley, John (Annie)	England	farmer
Malmquist, Edward (Lizzie)	Sweden	farmer
Reif, George (Annie*)	Saxony	farmer
Roberts, Joseph (Mary)	Virginia	farmer
Smith, John (Emma)	Nova Scotia	farmer
Strand, Edward (Boeda)	Finland	farmer
Thomas, Daniel (Matilda)	England	farmer
Thompson, Henry (Ellen)	Norway	farmer
Van Trojen, John (Elizabeth)	Holland	farmer
Weber, David (Mary)	England	farmer
Williams, Charles (Sallie)	Finland	farmer
Williams, John (Jennie)	Finland	farmer
Woodley, Frank (Clara)	California	farmer

NEWCASTLE

Bankson, Charles	Sweden	coal miner
Pierce, Daniel (Mary)	New Hampshire	carpenter
Tucker, William (Ellen)	Illinois	farmer

ORCAS ISLAND

Bridge, J. H. (Betsy)	New York	cooper

Burke, Alfred (Annie*)	Massachusetts	farmer
Cowen, George (Narwacha)	Ireland	laborer
DeShaw, John (Betty*)	Canada	fisherman
Dingman, George (Jenny*)	Holland	farmer
Dixon, Thomas (Elizabeth)	Illinois	farmer
Fauchet, Peter (Catherine)	Canada	farmer
Gasperell, Charles (Ellen)	Iowa	farmer
Gray, John (Lucy*)	Kentucky	farmer
Guthrie, James (Ziermath)	Scotland	farmer
Hichens, E. (Nina)	England	farmer
Lawrence, Louis (Matilda*)	Canada	farmer
Lotte, Freeman (Louise)	Canada	farmer
May, Emil (Elizabeth)	Massachusetts	farmer
McGee, James (Emma*)	Canada	farmer
Moore, William (Sarah*)	South Carolina	farmer
Nichols, M. W. (Adele)	Maine	farmer
Perkins, Henry (Mary*)	Maine	fisherman
Seward, David (Mary*)	Canada	laborer
Shattuck, Charles (Mary*)	Massachusetts	farmer
Smith, Robert (Lucy*)	England	farmer
Smith, William (Kitty*)	England	farmer
Stevens, John (Emma*)	Canada	farmer
Trudell, Louis (Mary*)	Canada	farmer
Verick, John (Jennie*)	Prussia	farmer

PORT DISCOVERY

Borger, Thomas (Fannie)	Pennsylvania	farmer
Eves, James (Jennie*)	England	farmer
Keymes, James (Elizabeth)	New Brunswick	farmer
Meyers, George (Susan)	New York	sawmill laborer
Smith, Charles (Mary*)	England	farmer
Woodman, James (Mary)	England	farmer, mill clerk

PORT LUDLOW

Alexander, Samuel (Sophia*)	Scotland	teamster
Bain, Alexander (Marie)	New York	logger
Bain, Andrew (Julia)	France	laborer
Coleman, Charles (Kate)	Norway	laborer
Cooper, John (Mary)	Baden	laborer
Corn, Jefferson (Annie)	Ohio	laborer
Delaney, Brown (Annie)	New York	logger

Hawkins, Horace (Annie*)	New York	laborer
Johnson, Christian (Kate*)	Prussia	laborer
Lumaskie, Cosimo (Lucy*)	Italy	fisherman
Murphy, William (Lucy*)	England	laborer
Palmer, William (Jane*)	Vermont	laborer
Pemmant, William (Jane)	England	laborer
Stubbs, William (Mary*)	England	laborer

SNOHOMISH RIVER
Snohomish City Area:

Clark, Benjamin (Susan)	New York	farmer
Gilbreath, John (Betty)	Ireland	farmer
Hatch, Ezra (Josie)	Massachusetts	farmer
Nailor, John (Louisa)	Wisconsin	laborer
Short, Charles (Eliza)	Ireland	farmer
Walker, George (Betsy)	Maine	farmer

Monroe area ("Krieschel Place"):

Anderson, Peter (Nellie)	Prussia	logger
Doyle, Patrick (Mary)	Ireland	farmer
Greenwood, George (Michie)	Scotland	farmer
Hawkins, William (Mary)	Illinois	farmer
Krieschel, John (Mary)	Prussia	farmer
MacDonald, William (Kate)	Scotland	camp cook
Saunders, George (Mary)	England	carpenter
Williams, Thomas (Louisa)	Norway	farmer

Sultan vicinity:

Allen, George (Mary)	Scotland	farmer
Clark, James (Mary)	Tennessee	farmer
Elwell, George (Eliza)	Maine	farmer
Elwell, John (Susan)	Maine	farmer
Haggerty, Ned (Jennie)	Ireland	laborer
Harriman, Charles (Elizabeth)	Maine	[farmer]
Henry, —— (Kate)	Prussia	[log camp]
Johnson, Andrew (Helen)	Sweden	farmer
Kelsey, Gus (Susan)	New York	farmer
McClung, Henry (Martha)	Pennsylvania	farmer
Taylor, Charles (Mary)	Wisconsin	farmer
Williams, David (Sally)	Prussia	laborer
Woods, Salem (Adelaide)	New York	farmer

Notes

1. M. A. Jones, *American Immigration*, 111. German immigrants' relationships with other ethnic groups have attracted little academic attention. An exception is Horton and Keil, "African Americans and Germans," 17–183.

2. Census Office, *Statistics*, 1:649.

3. Brown and Roucek, *Our National*, 10–11.

4. The number of children per marriage is a confounding and unreported factor. If German-German couples tended to have fewer children than did German-American couples, for example, German-German couples would be underrepresented in the tabulation. The timing of different waves of national immigration is also a possible confounding factor.

5. "British" for these purposes included English, Scottish, and Welsh, and Irish who identified themselves as having been born in the British Isles; Canadians were tabulated separately as immigrants from "British America."

6. Peterson and Brown, *New Peoples*.

7. Barsh, "Puget Sound Indian Demography."

8. Detailed family histories can be found in Jones-Lamb, *Native American Wives*.

9. Only one-sixth (17 percent) of the Germans were married or widowed, compared to 64 percent of the Americans and 70 percent of the Norwegians. Americans and Canadians dominated business and the trades at Centerville, Scandinavians worked either as farmers (53 percent) or laborers, and Germans were nearly all farmers (93 percent).

10. Norwegian farmers came via Dakota Territory (6), Minnesota (2), Kansas, Iowa, and Wyoming; the Americans came via Missouri, Kansas, Nebraska, Colorado, and Oregon.

11. More than half of the Germans in the seven case-study communities were Prussians, and most of the remainder came from Saxony, Baden, and Schleswig-Holstein. There were too few to make any useful comparisons by origins within the German Empire.

12. On the other hand, two of the American-born men with Indian wives, Borger and Myers, were probably of German ancestry, although both they and their parents reported American nativity.

13. One-fourth (27 percent) of the Indian wives of non-Indian settlers in the case-study communities had been born in British Columbia. Just as many of these northern women married *farmers* (65 percent) as did Indian women born in Washington Territory (66 percent). While this suggests that women's knowledge was *not* an asset in marriages to farmers, it should be borne in mind that the international boundary ran through the middle of Salish territory, and Salish women were likely to have close kinfolk on both sides (Suttles and Lane, "Southern Coast Salish").

14. Pierson (*Black Yankees*, 119–20) claims that sex ratios explain the high frequency of marriages between Indian women and African-American men in colonial New England. He offers no direct evidence in support of this claim, however.

15. For example, Slobodin, *Métis*.

A Nineteenth-Century Ojibwa Conquers Germany

BERND PEYER

A solitary Ojibwa represented the "Christian Indians of America" at the Third World Peace Congress held in Frankfurt on the Main on 22–24 August 1850. During the third sitting, he delivered a passionate speech highlighted by the dramatic presentation of a peace pipe to the president of the congress. Whereas the reporters for the London and Paris papers, whose readers had since grown weary of romantic accounts about Indians, tended to ridicule his "Cooperish" performance at this international event, the German reception of "Higaga-Bu, Häuptling der Chipawakis," as George Copway came to be known here, was jubilant. Disillusioned with the political repressions following the abortive revolution of 1848–1849, the German public was still highly receptive to idealistic interpretations of Indian ways of life. Copway subsequently met with numerous German dignitaries in Frankfurt, Heidelberg, Wiesbaden, Düsseldorf, and Cologne. He spent a "merry evening" with the renowned poet and forty-eighter Hermann Ferdinand Freiligrath, who requested Copway to stand as godfather to his youngest son. Copway's exotic features were captured in bronze by a noted Frankfurt sculptor, and an epic poem that he falsely claimed to be the author of was translated into German. His appearance at the Peace Congress has been brought up repeatedly in the Frankfurt media and since become a permanent feature of this city's long and eventful history.

George Copway, or Kah-ge-ga-gah-bow ("Standing Firm"), already had a remarkable and somewhat controversial career behind him when he embarked upon his journey to Europe in the summer of 1850. Born in the fall of 1819, as a member of a band of Southeastern Ojibwas living in the vicinity of Rice Lake, Ontario, he was brought up in a traditional woodland mode of existence until his conversion to Christianity at the age of eleven. He attended a Methodist mission school at Rice Lake from about 1830 to 1834 and was then recruited as a missionary by the American Methodist Episcopal Church. Copway served at various missions in the Great Lakes region of the United States from 1834 to 1837, after which he was sent to the Ebenezer Method-

Fig. 9. Portrait of George Copway, frontispiece for *The Life, History, and Travels of Kah-ge-ga-gah-bowh*, 2d ed. (Philadelphia: James Homestead, 1847).

Fig. 10. Plaster bust of George Copway fashioned by Eduard Schmidt von der Launitz in 1850. Courtesy, Institut für Stadtgeschichte, Frankfurt am Main.

ist Church Manual Labor School in Jacksonville, Illinois, to prepare for his ordination. Following his graduation and ordination late in 1839, Copway continued to do missionary work in the United States and Canada up until 1846, when the Canadian Conference of the Wesleyan Methodist Church expelled him on the charge of having embezzled tribal funds. He then moved back to the United States, where he soon emerged as a fairly successful public speaker and author. Copway published two popular books, *The Life, History, and Travels of Kah-ge-ga-gah-bowh* (1847) and *The Traditional History and Characteristic Sketches of the Ojibway Nation* (1850), both of which went through several editions and were circulated in England as well. In 1850 he also produced a lengthy epic poem under his name titled *The Ojibway Conquest*, which appears to have been written by another author. Around 1849 Copway outlined an ambitious plan for the creation of a Northwestern Indian Territory to be designated as "Kah-ge-ga" in a pamphlet addressed to the Thirty-first Congress of the United States under the title *Organization of A New Indian Territory* (1850). This unrealistic scheme was not very original – an almost identical plan had been formulated by Secretary of War John Bell in 1841 – but it did receive the temporary support of numerous of his newly acquired friends in the literary and political circles of the East.[1]

"Rev. George Copway, Chief of the Ojibway Nation," as he now presented himself before the public, was thus at the height of his second career in the early summer of 1850, when he received an impromptu invitation by Elihu Burritt, a leading figure in the American peace movement and founder of the League of Universal Brotherhood, to represent the "Christian Indians of America" at the Third World Peace Congress in Germany.[2] Armed with letters of recommendation from notable American authors like Henry Wadsworth Longfellow and Francis Parkman, Copway embarked from Boston on 10 July 1850, on a long journey that would take him through parts of England, Scotland, France, Belgium, and Germany. Shortly after his return to New York at the close of that same year, Copway published a 346-page account of his experiences titled *Running Sketches of Men and Places* (1851).

Copway was obviously not the first American Indian to visit the Old World. It has been estimated that by the time the Pilgrims landed in Massachusetts in 1620, perhaps as many as two thousand Indians had already made the transatlantic crossing – most of them involuntarily – and many others followed suit in the coming centuries.[3] Unfortunately, these early travelers left no written testimonials of their experiences abroad. Even though some of the popular eighteenth-century French and English narratives of Indian visitors were ascribed to real individuals (e.g., Addison's "King Sa Ga Tean Qua Rash Tow"), these can hardly be regarded as authentic documentation.[4]

Thus, while the basic conception of an Indian travelogue may not have been entirely new at the time, a firsthand report like *Running Sketches* is still somewhat of a literary sensation. It needs to be pointed out, however, that Copway was actually preceded by a fellow Canadian Ojibwa traveler, George Henry, or Maungwudaus (1811–1888), who published a brief account of his extensive European tour with George Catlin's traveling exhibition in 1845. Unlike Copway, however, Maungwudaus and his Ojibwa-Ottawa dance troupe only reached the Belgian border to Germany.[5]

Copway arrived in Liverpool about two weeks after his departure from Boston and, finding that he had some time to spare before his scheduled crossover to the mainland, immediately plunged into a bustle of social calls and public speaking engagements. Determined to perform the role of a model Christian Indian, Copway established a number of self-imposed rules of behavior for the duration of his European sojourn: "I will uphold my race – I will endeavor never to say nor do anything which will prejudice the mind of the British public against my people – In this land of refinement I will be an Indian – I will treat everybody in a manner that becomes a gentleman – I will patiently answer all questions that may be asked of me – I will study to please the people, and lay my own feelings to one side." In keeping with the usual protocol for Indian visitors since the days of Pocahontas (alias Lady Rebecca), the "tall, well-proportioned, and handsome man, with the manners and graceful dignity of a perfect gentleman" was in turn lionized by the crème de la crème of British society. His weekly schedule of appointments with various lords and ladies reads like a foppish excerpt from a veteran socialite's itinerary: "Sabbath morning – go to Mr. Gambardilli. Evening – at Under Secretary's house, Dr. Wiseman to be there. Monday evening – Tea at Mr. S——, New Broad street. Tuesday – Dine at E. Saunders', George Street – a celebrated Dentist. Wednesday – Hampton Court, with Mrs. Gibson's Pic-nic party. Thursday, August 8th – To Breakfast with R. Cobden, at 9 1-2 o'clock. Evening – Dine at Lord Brougham's. Friday – Dine with Lady Franklin and her brother, Sir Simpkinson, 21 Bedford Square." Like most other visiting dignitaries from "beyond the pale," he was also accorded the privilege of sitting in on a session in the House of Commons, where he witnessed a heated debate between Richard Cobden and Disraeli, and was taken to the zoo. Finally, like every self-respecting cosmopolite with the proper sensitivity for the latest European elitist fads, he joined the swelling ranks of Jenny Lind idolizers after hearing the "Swedish Nightingale" warble in a Liverpool concert hall shortly before his departure for Germany.[6]

On 19 August Copway and several hundred other delegates of the Peace Congress departed from London to Dover, where they boarded the steamer Lord Warren, bound for Calais. From Calais they proceeded by rail to Cologne, making brief stops along the way in Ghent, Liège, and Aix-la-Chapelle. Copway was only mildly impressed with Belgium: "This is a monotonous country – no hills to see. But one continual level of mud and stagnant pools of water. A very easy country to grade railroads, and a fine country for farming if it were not so level. The people seem to be very industrious. Women are as often seen in the fields as men, substantial they are too. Firm, and rugged-looking faces as round as the fat face of the moon." It is regrettable that most of Copway's descriptions of the places he saw on the European mainland were copied verbatim from contemporary British travel guides and periodicals, so that the reader is often forced to sift through a lot of boring secondhand information in order to find the scattered passages with original impressions.[7]

The delegates arrived in Cologne the next day, on 20 August. Copway was met there by August Cloos, a close friend of Freiligrath's, and the "Painter

Poet" from Philadelphia, Thomas Buchanan Read (1822–1872), who was in town to paint a portrait of his German colleague. Fortunately, Cloos wrote a detailed account of this encounter, as well as of the subsequent meeting between Copway and Freiligrath, which he later published in a Frankfurt literary newsletter. The trio stopped off at Cloos's apartment, where Copway first passed around his peace pipe for a smoke and then entertained his hosts with Ojibwa songs until late in the evening. Then they proceeded to the hotel in which Copway was to retire for the night. "But we still did not go to bed," Cloos writes, "in keeping with German drinking customs, we first emptied a few bottles of excellent Rhine wine at the hospitable Frankfurter Hof and then sat there laughing, joking and singing until way past midnight." No mention of this cheery soiree is made in Running Sketches, however. "The fatigues of yesterday rest heavily upon my eyelids," is all that Copway jotted down the following day, "and it is with difficulty that I raise them, this morning."[8]

On 21 August the delegates were brought on board two steamers, the Goethe and the Germania, which took them on a scenic tour down the Rhine River to Mainz. "The boat on which I am passenger is a long, narrow affair," Copway complains, "with no covering of any account, and is quite full if not more." The spectacular landscape, however, soon improved his spirits: "But, the scenery it is said commences at about 20 miles above Cologne. And now it is in view! Grand and lofty hills or mountains rise from the water's edge. The seven mountains are now around us. And really I am now on the Rhine. A reality, yet like a fairy dream. About this river I have heard and read a great deal. History, romance, and song, dwell along these banks. The towering cliffs frown down on the works of man." As might be expected of any ardent romantic traveler, Copway even waxes poetic at this point. "O thou river of majestic beauty, and grandeur! A tale couldst thou unfold, if but to mortal ears thy silent waters could only speak." He was obviously quite well acquainted with the subtleties of antebellum American travel literature, a genre that many of his literary acquaintances in the New World had already tried a hand at. One of its main purposes, other than entertaining its readers with glowing accounts of famous individuals and historical sites of the Old World, was to demonstrate by comparison the moral, political, and physical superiority of the New World. "I may see other countries equally beautiful and grand in scenery," he notes at the beginning of his journey, "yet let me be an enthusiast for my own dear native land."[9] So it comes as no real surprise when, in the midst of his effusive soliloquy on the Rhine, replete with ostentatious references to a long list of German historians and bards "who have all left something as a memento of their fond love for this river" and the inevitable citation from Byron's *Childe Harold*, Copway concludes: "Poetry and song. Over this river each sweet strain has exhausted itself. The Germans rightly think there is only one Rhine in the world. We give them credit for love of country, and we ask them the same, when we say it would take twenty-five or thirty such rivers to make one Mississippi! When any nation comes to boasting of rivers, we have one too that could swallow all the German rivers at once."[10] The delegates steamed past Bonn, which Copway describes summarily as an "ancient-looking place," and eventually landed at Mainz-Kastell. From here they still had to board a train to Frankfurt, where they finally arrived in the evening of 21 August after a fatiguing three-day journey.

The Third World Peace Congress convened from 22 to 24 August and was attended by approximately four hundred delegates from all over the globe – only thirty to forty Germans were represented – and several thousand spectators. Times were hardly propitious for a conference in central Europe calling for the abolishment of war, disarmament, and the creation of a special judicial body to settle disputes between states as an alternative to military force. The revolutionary movements of 1848–1849 had just been brutally crushed by professional Prussian, Austrian, and Russian armies, and countless Germans had been imprisoned, executed, or gone into exile. The Danish-German contention over Schleswig and Holstein still simmered under an uneasy truce, and armed conflict between Prussia and Austria over the question of German unity seemed imminent. The fact that the congress convened at the Paulskirche (Church of St. Paul), seat of the now moribund Nationalversammlung (General Assembly) and paramount symbol of foiled German democratic aspirations, was not entirely free of irony either. Not that long ago, in the spring of 1849, Austria and Prussia had recalled their delegates from the assembly and thus practically reinstated the old feudal order. Consequently, major European journals like the London *Times* and the Paris *Journal des Débats Politiques et Littéraires* were highly critical of the Peace Congress and tended to discredit its delegates as self-aggrandizing, starry-eyed chatterers. Those more favorably inclined, such as the majority of the local newspapers, conceded that it was a noble idea, albeit with few prospects for realization at the time. Nevertheless, even though the Peace Congress failed to produce any concrete results in an era in which Realpolitik had effectively displaced social idealism, it was still a major political event of its day covered extensively by the international media.[11]

George Copway, the only American Indian present at this dignified gathering, turned out to be the major public attraction. The somewhat skeptical Augsburg-based *Allgemeine Zeitung* reported his first appearance as follows:

The ladies no longer have eyes for the handsomely bearded men of the Left; it is the beardless Indian chieftain with the noble Roman profile and dazzling long black hair who catches their attention now. He carries a massive, mystically decorated staff, his royal scepter, and over the plain black suit he wears shiny armlets along with a colorful sash and sword-belt, his badges of distinction, just like the kings of bygone times who bore their scepters and crowns everywhere they went, even to bed. The only thing the Frankfurters regret is that he is wearing a fine, black European hat instead of a crown of feathers and leaves. This mixture of European elegance and Indian pompousness does seem somewhat ludicrous, and yet, there is still something truly unsettling about the appearance of this handsome man, who has just made the transition from the unlimited freedom of his jungle to the perpetual confines of civilization, who has traveled thousands of miles just for the sake of an ideal that must have a deep and practical meaning for him, only to discover that his own enthusiasm hardly elicits an enthusiastic response from the gaping crowds who tend to regard him as little more than a curiosity.[12]

He was accorded the honor of introducing the fifth resolution of the Congress during the third sitting on 24 August, which foreshadows Woodrow Wilson's concept of self-determination: "This Congress acknowledging the principle of non-intervention, recognizes it to be the sole right of every state to regulate its own affairs." Copway subsequently delivered a lengthy speech eulogizing the virtues of universal peace and ended it by presenting the president of the Congress, Carl Jaup (1781–1860), former member of the Nationalversammlung and Hessian minister, with an adorned catlinite peace pipe that he claimed to have been made by his own father, John Copway. His dramatic gesture drew a tremendous ovation from the audience but was viewed with mixed feelings by the press. The correspondent of the London *Times*, for instance, found little worthy of praise in Copway's presentation:

A great sensation was created by the appearance in the tribune of the Ojibbeway [sic] Chief, whose oration has, from the first opening of the Congress, been anticipated as an extraordinary *morceau*. He was dressed in a dark blue frock, with a scarf across his shoulder, after the old French Republican fashion, and the metallic plates round his arm gave a peculiar character to his costume. He began to talk something after a style which may be called "Cooper-ish," and was abundant in his allusions to the "Great Spirit" – his "pale-faced brethren," and so forth. Soon, however, he dropped the purely national style, and launched out into general morals and literature, stating how, while walking around Frankfurt, he had reflected on the miseries of war, and linking together as eminent men of mind the German poet Schiller and the American poet Longfellow. His oration was delivered in a grandiloquent style, but its effect was rather on the eye than the ear, the great point being the unwrapping of a mysterious implement which he had carried about, and which in the eyes of the peacemakers looked marvelously like a sword. When he deliberately took off the linen wrapper, and discovered something which looked rather like a cat-o'-nine-tails, and which he declared to be an Indian banner of peace, the acclamations were tremendous. This was his grand scenic effect. He should have stopped here, but he did not, and produced an anti-climax. A very wholesome regulation, published by the Congress, limits the time during which a speaker is allowed to "keep the floor" to 20 minutes, but the "stoic of the woods," luxuriating in the sound of his own voice, doubled the time. This profusion of words caused a reaction, and the venerable Dr. Jaup, the most urbane President in the world, mildly limited every future speech to a quarter of an hour.

Copway, who quoted extensively from the *Times* in his own account of the event, was undoubtedly alluding to this article as he expressed his vexation with "a fair specimen of English raillery which has been heard by us and read."[13] A similarly sarcastic commentary about the "honnêt homme d'Indienne de la tribu des Ojibeways" appeared in the Paris-based *Journal des Débats Politiques et Littéraires*, whose correspondent concluded wryly that "it was decidedly the Indian who turned out to be the real lion of the Congress; he overshadowed all the other lions of London and Paris. How is one to compete with a great chief who talks about the Great Sprit and pale-faced brothers!" Elihu Burritt dismissed Copway's talk in his diary as "a long, windy, wordy speech, extremely ungrammatical and incoherent."[14]

Copway himself was unsure of his performance on that momentous day. "The last of the Congress is about over," he notes in his journal, "and I have made my poorest speech." It appears that the pipe-wielding "Chief of the Ojibwas," who consciously acted the part of the romantic noble savage in this controversial gathering, was viewed by some critics as a tractable symbol for the illusionary position of the entire peace movement. Copway provides the following explanation in *Running Sketches*:

> For never in my life did I speak to such disadvantage. The people had already heard Girardin, the French orator, Cobden, and a host of others. The speeches of these men had given a commonplace character to the speeches which were to come after them. The people had become tired of listening, and seemed to have no desire for anything new. Besides this, no new feature could be brought forward in support of the great cause of Peace, and all the

arguments had been worn threadbare. The good speeches had preceded me, and the very best, which was to be delivered by the Rev. E. H. Chapin, of New York city, was just at my heels. In this predicament I could not look upon myself with any degree of confidence, nor as being in a very enviable situation.[15]

The enthusiastic reception accorded him by the German audience and the local press, however, for whom a flesh-and-bone Christian Indian was still a novelty, must have soothed his ruffled feathers somewhat. In Frankfurt Copway's "Cooper-ish" style of oration and exotic appearance were both appreciated. The dashed hopes for national unification and social reform caused many German intellectuals to look to the United States as a political model of democracy and, particularly, to regard its "children of nature" as the very embodiment of their own yearning for individual freedom and social harmony. Translations of American authors, especially James Fenimore Cooper and Austrian immigrant Charles Sealsfield (Carl Magnus Postl), were being widely read at the time together with the popular travel narratives by Prince Paul Wilhelm of Württemberg (1797-1860), Prince Maximilian of Wied (1782-1867), and Friedrich Gerstäcker (1816-1872). The period was, as one scholar has pointed out, also witnessing the birth of what was to become a new national genre, the "Indianerroman." While the fictitious Indian, both the noble and the rational variation, was being gradually phased out in English and French literature, in Germany he was about to rise to unprecedented popularity. Uninvolved in the more pragmatic colonial politics of North America and having been prevented from dealing with the usual ideological hangover following a bourgeois revolution, the German audience was obviously much more inclined to retain its sympathy for the "edle Rothaut." Idealistic notions of Indians would soon even be evident in the work of rational thinkers like Friedrich Engels (i.e., Der Ursprung der Familie, 1884) and finally culminate into a veritable public mania at the turn of the century under the prolific pen of Karl May.[16]

Reports of "Higaga-Bu, Häuptling der Chipawakis" in the German press were predominantly favorable, if not outright euphoric. The correspondent of the Leipzig Illustrierte Zeitung, for instance, gave a glowing account of the Ojibwa's presence at the Congress:

A truly uplifting scenario took place during the final session. Copway, the Indian Chief, takes the floor. A man in his forties, of light copper complexion, with shiny and straight black hair, nearly beardless, the eyes dark and full of compassion, his build slim and proportional. In a speech, delivered in a style of English that frequently manifests lyrical qualities, he correlates his own noble quest for peace with the peace found in God, as is taught in the Gospel. Still a wandering savage among the Indians of his tribe 15 years ago, he is now tangible evidence for the advancement of civilization. And he also mentions how he ascertained that in Frankfurt, where shady green trees now grow and children play under a canopy of flowers, there once stood embrasures, towers, ramparts and the instruments of war. From the distant West he has come, but he does not regret having sailed across the great water to present Europeans with a symbol of reconciliation from the sons of the red Cain: a pipe of peace. As he uncovers it and hands it over ceremoniously to the president as representative for all the nations here assembled, the men wave their hats, the women salute with their scarves, and the thundering ovation will not cease.[17]

Copway's impassioned speech, a translation of which was made available to the German public within two hours, and the theatrical offering of the peace pipe formed the uncontested highlight of the gathering. Newspaper reporters still find the story of "Higaga-Bu" intriguing today, and his role at the congress was recently highlighted at an exposition commemorating the city's twelve-hundredth anniversary, which opened in Frankfurt on 17 May 1994.[18] Interestingly, the most detailed summary of Copway's lengthy speech available today is found in the German minutes of the Peace Congress, which were published the following year. Less than half the space was dedicated to it in the English version of the minutes, which appeared in London simultaneously with the German edition:

Kah-ge-ga-ga-bowh, now Rev. Georg Copwah [sic], chief of the Ojibwa tribe in North America (is greeted with much applause): When I was born, the Great Spirit did not give me sufficient talent to speak here as I would like to. I can merely communicate an inspiration concerning the holy cause that has brought us together here. The words I have heard spoken here have penetrated deep into my heart. Sixteen years ago, I still did not believe that I would ever learn the language of my pale brothers this side of the great water, nor did I imagine that I would someday appear as a delegate in a country that holds such a high rank in the sciences and literature. I am the first of my race to journey all the way from America's wilderness in order to assist in establishing peace over here.

The bonds of brotherhood will someday enfold us all and extend from nation to nation, from isle to isle, from region to region. Then men of war will dedicate themselves to the tasks of peace, to the arts, to literature and science, to trade and business. To your great warriors you erect monuments that almost touch the sky, but not a few of your wonderful poets and think-ers are hardly able to keep body and soul together and suffer great privations.

Yesterday I walked through the streets and surroundings of this city for the first time; once the city and its neighborhood was formidably fortified, surrounded by ramparts and walls and mighty towers. How many times have the citizens of this city been exposed to devastating war, how many times have their women and children lamented and wailed because of it? Now I see wonderful gardens in the place of fortifications, and in their midst stands a memorial dedicated to the one who planted them. And there is yet another monument in this city, oh how it inspires me; the statue of the highly esteemed Goethe! It also reminds me of that favorite of my soul, of your Schiller, whose noble and lofty poetry has ignited a holy soul-fire on the other side of the ocean, just as it has over here. If these wonderful men had never existed and sent their spirit out into the world, then we would probably never have been blessed with a Longfellow or other like poets who now gladden our hearts.

When we arrived here, we expected all the nobles and notables to em-brace us, all the priests to teach and preach what we are striving for; but in vain. We are surrounded by prejudice on all sides, by the prejudice of gov-ernments and nations; the prejudice towers over us like hills upon hills. But the time is not far off when Italy, when Rome, the eternal city, when all nations of the world will send their representatives to us. That is impos-sible, they object. But who in the past could have imagined the wonders of the telegraph and the railroad? A man in Washington, whose wife and child were living in Baltimore, took it into his head that they were ill. He goes to the telegraph office and asks whether wife and child are well, the query flies off immediately, the answer returns just as quickly: "Yes, they are well." But the man did not believe it, he did not confide in the speed of the response and set out personally to verify it. So it is with the prejudice against us.

Once, when our parents traveled twenty, thirty miles in one day, they thought to have accomplished wonders; today we travel hundreds of miles over mountains, valleys and rivers in the same time span, and the horse that runs so fast has no need for fodder. While thousands of my fellow tribesmen still live and roam around in the wilderness, I voyage to foreign nations, come here to my pale brothers; for brothers are we all, the great star of daylight rises and sets over all of us. Long and frequently have my ancestors fought yours, the blood of my tribe and your tribe has flown and been shed in streams. With great pleasure I announce to you that a new and better spirit has come over us, inspires us, the spirit of peace. I close. As I set forth from the West to visit my European brothers, my father said to me: "Take something with you that you can present as a gift to the strange, pale nation." He gave me this. (The speaker holds it up and unwraps it.) Often as I sat down at a table, it was mistaken for a sword; but it is a calumet, the peace pipe, which we present to those with whom we wish to establish friendship. (Loud, repeated ovation.) I hand it over to the President. (The President rises and displays it – thundering ovation.)

As I traveled over mountains, across valleys and swamps, I came upon a small brook, the waters of which I could stop with my bare hands. By and by I saw how it grew, joined up with other waters, became larger and larger, wider and wider, and eventually swelled into a mighty river that finally emptied out into the Gulf of Mexico – so did Christianity once begin in Jerusalem; at first there was only one, then came more and more followers, and now it rules over half the world. Our beginning is also quiet and modest, only a few stand up for what we want and teach here, but our holy purpose will also triumph. (Great ovation.)[19]

Of course, not all German periodicals were favorably disposed toward the Peace Congress and its delegates. Die Grenzboten, an influential Leipzig-based forum for the national-liberal politics advocating a united Germany under Prussian leadership and coedited by the eminent author Gustav Freytag (1816-1895), gave a caustic evaluation of the "Farce" presented at the Paulskirche in Frankfurt by the "Crême der kosmopolitischen Romantik." Copway's presence, as well as that of the African-American delegates, was viewed with sarcasm: "Nor is there a lack of baptized Negroes who sing Lamartine's Marsellaise to the tune of Toussaint-Louverture, and to complete the picture, an Indian chief in national costume, such as we are familiar with from Catlin and Cooper, makes his appearance with a blue lizard on his chest, tri-colored tatoos on his face, dragging a lion's tail behind him, and wearing untreated buckskins on his legs: he smoked the peace-pipe for Germany in the name of his Tribes and calls himself: kagagagabauh!"[20] Even though Copway never made it to Berlin, the local satirical weekly Kladderadatsch included a front-page caricature of the "emeritierten Wilden und Menschenfressers [retired savage and cannibal] Hi Ge Ga Gah Bowh aus Otoway" in a silly roosterlike outfit offering a Bavarian-style calumet to a municipal official and promising to refrain henceforth from regarding any white man as a potential "Beefsteak." The caricature actually alludes to the Fürstenkongreß (Congress of Lords) in Berlin and its decision in late August to exclude twenty-four states that had previously withdrawn from the Prussian union plan under Austrian pressure.[21] Both references to Copway openly convey the frustration that many Germans still felt because of the failure of the reform movement and the continuing resistance against Prussian plans for a German union on the

Fig. 11. The German newspaper *Kladderadatsch* caricatures the "chief of the Chippewas":
"Your magnificence – if it is not too late – here, the peace pipe."
"It is – too late!"
"Then at least accept these twenty-five peace cigars."
"But what for?"
"Twenty-four for the gentlemen over there, and one for you."
Kladderadatsch 3, no. 35, 1 September 1850. Courtesy, Institut für Stadtgeschichte, Frankfurt am Main.

part of Austria, which called together a rival assembly in Frankfurt shortly after the Peace Congress adjourned, on 1 September. Other observers, such as the reporter for the *Allgemeine Zeitung*, had somewhat more ambivalent feelings about the issue: "Critical people refer to this Peace Congress as a comedy; yes, it was a comedy, but an imposing one. I can't make up my mind whether this Indian with his colorful trappings and peace pipe was still a child of nature, or whether he was only playing a comic role for us, but at least I do know this, that we ourselves did not play a comic role when, in those sparse moments and in the presence of brothers from all regions, we allowed our sentiments for an eternal humanitarian idea to well up."[22]

There can be little doubt, however, that Copway fascinated the general public. Frankfurt's most renowned sculptor, Eduard Schmidt von der Launitz (1797-1869), cast Copway's noble Indian features in bronze, while another ardent Frankfurt admirer set about translating "his" epic poem, *Ojibway Conquest*, for immediate publication.[23] German dignitaries were obviously also as keen to make his acquaintance as their British counterparts had been. In the evening following the third session Copway attended a soirée sponsored by a local patron and apparently enchanted the distinguished guests gathered there with his "fantastically colorful national costume."[24] A cryptic entry in Copway's account reads: "The Prince Frederick desired I should see him this morning at 7 o'clock, masonically.... He is a fine-looking man, and as stately in his bearing as General [Winfield] Scott, of the United States." The reference is to Friedrich Wilhelm Ludwig (1797-1888), Prince of Prussia and future Kaiser Wilhelm I. He was functioning as military governor of the Rhineland and Westphalia at the time and had come to Frankfurt in order to inspect the Prussian occupation forces under his command. Copway reports: "As I was passing through the Parade Grounds the Prince was having a review of the soldiers. Ten thousand soldiers in arms! The sight was an imposing one. Their burnished weapons and splendid equipage glittered before the sun, and the tall plume of the Prince, who was conspicuous on the field, waved before us as we passed. These soldiers make a brilliant and formidable appearance, but such things are altogether repugnant to my feelings since my warrior's creed has been changed to a harmless one."[25] No mention was made in the local press of this intriguing tête-à-tête between a Christian Indian peace delegate and one of Europe's most powerful military men. The Prince of Prussia, who had been instrumental in the brutal quashing of the uprising in Baden in 1849 and was quite willing to uphold by force of arms the Prussian plans for a German union (kleindeutsche Lösung), undoubtedly had little interest in exotic harbingers of pacifism. Prince Frederick Wilhelm had been protector of the Freemasons in Prussia since 1840, and Copway, like most other nineteenth- and early twentieth-century Indian writers, had a marked affinity for secret orders. Unfortunately, Copway remains secretive about the nature of their possible "masonic" connection. Perhaps he revealed to the astonished prince his own grand project for an American Indian union, as an issue of the Frankfurter Konversationsblatt mentions that he had come to Europe in order to promote this plan.[26]

After the congress adjourned, many of the American delegates were taken on brief tours to Heidelberg, Wiesbaden, Worms, Düsseldorf, and Cologne. On 26 August more than one hundred American delegates visited the University of Heidelberg – Copway supposedly having received a personal invitation from his "warm-hearted friend," the professor of theology Friedrich W. Carové (1789-1852). Here they witnessed a meeting between the renowned African-American clergymen and abolitionists, Rev. James W. C. Pennington (1809-1870) and Rev. Henry Highland Garnet (1815-1882), who had also participated in the congress, and some of the institution's theology professors. According to a report in the Allgemeine Zeitung, Copway stole the show once again and was kept quite busy signing autographs. The delegates took the opportunity to visit the university's library, where they admired a few of Martin Luther's original manuscripts, and, of course, to see Heidelberg's famous castle. Copway reports that he ascended a tower on the summit of the Königsstuhl, a hill in the vicinity of the city, from where he beheld some German women working in the fields on the other side of the Neckar River:

> The hardy race of women are in the fields performing the duties of husband-men, while their husbands, sons, and brothers are stationed at the frontier towns of the north, ready for war. These German women are short and portly and have ruddy complexions. With their sun-burnt faces they may compare to advantage, as far as redness is concerned, with any of our squaws in America; and like them they are serviceable at home and in the field. But of course there are *ladies* for the parlor in Germany as well as in every other civilized country. To grace saloons and drawing-rooms, women must be converted into butterflies, joined in the middle by a thread, ornamented with a variety of hues, formed to flutter and fly about, and to live on sickening sweets, such as their counterparts, the flowers of the boudoir, may offer. There is more heart in a German peasant woman, and more soul in a simple-minded squaw, than in a thousand toys that are formed only for ornaments and playthings. Doubtless either extreme is to be deprecated, and the noble gentlewoman is a medium between the two, free from coarseness on the one hand and from frailty on the other.[27]

Copway obviously differed markedly from some of his fellow travelers in his views about the proper occupation for women. According to the minutes of the Peace Congress, Rev. Bullard from Missouri referred to the practice of having women do heavy work in the fields as "barbarian" at a special gathering in Wiesbaden organized by the British delegates for their American colleagues; and a reporter for the *Nonconformist*, who also spied some German women working in the fields along the Bergstraße, maintained that such abuse would never occur among "civilized" peoples.[28] Nineteenth-century American writers of travel literature, and Copway is no exception, liked to point out that Europeans were nowhere near as gallant as Americans in their relations with the fairer sex. In this case, at least, the former Methodist minister, who otherwise strongly supported the agricultural programs advocated by contemporary missionary societies and the American government, seems to be adhering to the widespread nineteenth-century "traditional" Indian view that farming was properly women's work.

Upon his return to the Frankfurt train station that afternoon, Copway also took note of the uncouth smoking habits of Germans: "When we took leave of

Frankfort this morning, we left a German with a pipe in his mouth, standing near the station, pointing the passengers to another part of the building. This afternoon he is here still, standing in the same place, and smoking the same identical pipe, though it is probable that a number of pipes full of tobacco have passed into smoke since morning. In most cases useless and noxious things, however much they may be favorites of the public, end in smoke. This is a fair specimen of the smoking propensity of the Germans." The following day, on 27 August, he journeyed to Wiesbaden, where he observed as some ladies and gentlemen "with faces as hard as marble, and hearts still harder, no doubt" tried their luck at the casino. The scenic walks along the city's picturesque parks, however, were obviously more in line with the expectations of the astute American tourist. "This city is the prettiest I have seen in this country," he surmises, "without any exception."[29]

On 28 August Copway boarded the *Schiller* and steamed down the Rhine River to Cologne. The following morning he met up once again with August Cloos, who accompanied the Ojibwa to Düsseldorf for his scheduled appointment with Hermann Ferdinand Freiligrath (1810–1876). Cloos notes that Copway told him several times along the way that he would willingly run for many miles for a chance to meet the famous German poet and revolutionary. The encounter had been arranged by Henry Wadsworth Longfellow, whom Copway had met and befriended in Boston early in 1849.[30] "Let me have the great pleasure of introducing to you my friend Kah-ge-ga-gah-bowh," Longfellow had written in a letter of recommendation addressed to Freiligrath, "an American Indian Chief of the Ojibway nation, whose English name is George Copway. You will rejoice to take him by the hand, and to talk with him of the grand forests of his native land. I shall make him promise to sing you some of the mournful musical songs of his nation. In return you shall show him the Cathedral and the skulls of the Eleven thousand Virgins of Cologne, and all the remains of Melchior, Gaspar and Balthasar." In a humorous and, as it soon turned out, prophetic postscript he had added: "You send me Anarchy (Annecke) and I send you Kopfweh! (Copway)."[31]

According to Cloos, Copway and Freiligrath first met in the latter's Düsseldorf apartment, where they talked for some time over a glass of wine or two, and then returned to Cologne in the company of two other gentlemen. Back in Cologne they rented a room at a local resort and continued to socialize until the early hours of the morning. Copway and Freiligrath talked about various subjects, such as the pleasing sounds of the Ojibwa language (Copway claimed to be familiar with all major dialects) and the wild American landscape. As the evening progressed and more wine flowed, they also shared a few poems and songs. Copway no longer had a peace pipe to pass around, much to Cloos's regret, but he did ceremoniously present his ornamented hickory "scepter" as a gift to Freiligrath. The German poet was obviously captivated by his Indian visitor. "It was indeed a great satisfaction to me to receive a red man under my roof," he reported back to Longfellow, "and moreover: to see a red man, full of talents and intellectual power, burning and struggling for that civilization, which we men of the old world almost loathe and consider to be one of the sources of many of those evils which harass us." In fact, the disenchanted forty-eighter was so inspired by Copway's presence that he even requested him to stand godfather to his youngest son:

> I liked Kah-ge-ga-gah-bowh exceedingly; we passed a happy afternoon at Düsseldorf and a merry night at Cologne, and he was kind enough to accept my invitation to stand Godfather to my youngest son: George Karl Otto. Is not that capital: A chief of the Ojibways Godfather to the boy of a German Poet? The barbarian name of Kah-ge-ga-gah-bowh sounding, like a war-whoop, through the tame parish-register of Düsseldorf? Strange things happen and stranger things will happen. When the dusky brow of the Indian was stooping to the white face of the Teutonic baby, it was – as it were – a symbol to me of the fraternity of all nations, of the peace and the happiness to come after all the struggles and the battles of these our wonder-working times.

Although Copway was not able to keep his promise to return to Cologne for the actual baptism of Freiligrath's son, George Karl Otto was henceforth jokingly referred to as Kah-ge-ga-gah-bowh in family circles.[32]

For some reason, Copway has very little to say about the meeting with Freiligrath in his *Running Sketches*. He does describe the "merry night" in Cologne, which Longfellow later presumed to have been "the great and prominent feature of his Tour on the Continent, not excepting the scene at Frankfort when he handed the Calumet of peace to the President of the Peace Convention."[33] In his version of the affair, however, the convivial Germans try in vain to induce him to drink with them:

> About half a dozen of us spend the evening together and endeavour to amuse each other. Students from Bonn arrived about 12 o'clock. My friends have been trying very hard to make me drink. Though this is a very strange way of showing their friendship, they are nevertheless friends – such inconsistencies do the customs of society subject us to!
>   To their *cordial* solicitations I said "no," but finding they "would not take *no* for an answer," I left the company rather unceremoniously, about

2 o'clock in the morning. At an early hour I found they had been hunting for me through the crooked and coffin-like streets of Cologne until 4 o'clock, or daylight. They thought, I suppose, that an *Indian* could not find his way home.

For a literary and scientific people these Germans are a strange set. Their recreations are in proportion to their soundness and laboriousness as scholars. Among other things which they learn they will find that when I say *yes* I mean *yes,* and when I say *no* I mean *no*—according to the scripture injunction, "Let your ye be yea and your nay nay."

Both accounts agree as far as the twilight search for him is concerned. Copway wanted to leave the party at some point, maintaining he had plenty of work to do the next day, and was accompanied to his quarters by Cloos. His German friend noticed that he had forgotten something and asked Copway to wait for him by a lantern while he went back to the resort to retrieve it. Upon his return, he was consternated to find that his Ojibwa companion had disappeared. Freiligrath and Cloos looked all over town for him and even alarmed the constable. Much to their astonishment, they finally found the runaway quite safe and snug in bed. Copway's other merry friends apparently continued to celebrate without him. "They had agreed to meet and accompany me to the station for Calais, at 6:00 o'clock," he demurs, "but only one [most likely Cloos] was present to bid me farewell."[34]

On 29 August Copway journeyed back to Albion. He subsequently delivered dozens of speeches on temperance and other Indian-related topics throughout England and Scotland, also taking every opportunity to promote his "Kah-ge-ga" scheme, until finally setting sail for America from Liverpool on 7 December. Copway's European tour was undoubtedly the apex of his cometlike career, which began to fade rapidly after his return to the United States. In spite of the great popularity of Longfellow's *Hiawatha* (1855), the American public had also grown bored with "noble savages" by this time.[35] Copway continued to lecture on various subjects for a few years, including the Peace Congress in Frankfurt, but eventually found himself having to find other means of making a living, at times on the fringes of legality. He sought to enlist the support of the radical American Party for his "Kah-ge-gah" project, but this, too, proved to be of little avail. He then tried various scurrilous schemes that got him in trouble with the law, such as selling homemade cure-alls as Dr. Copway or collecting bounties for each Canadian Indian he could convince to volunteer for the Union army. At one point he drew the ire of the Senecas for having disinterred the remains of Red Jacket without their permission, supposedly to prevent them from being desecrated by white pilferers. Just before his death in Canada, on 17 January 1869, Kah-ge-ga-gah-bowh, alias George Copway, tried to find solace in Roman Catholicism and changed his name to Joseph Antoine.[36]

Particularly tragic for Copway, other than the permanent separation from his wife and only surviving child in 1858, was the fact that many of his literary "friends" eventually scorned him as well after his return from Europe, primarily because of his permanent solicitations for money. Freiligrath, who had thought so well of Copway, apparently changed his mind by 1853. In a letter responding to Longfellow's complaint that Copway had failed to deliver certain books and manuscripts that the German poet had entrusted him with, he commented sardonically: "Speaking of that worthy [Kah-ge-ga-gah-bowh], I was very vexed indeed to hear, that he had never delivered to you the books and music I had entrusted to his care. Tell me if the war-whoop you intended to raise has frightened him and brought into your hands the volumes in question? If not so, I shall be happy to make up the loss, – swearing, of course, at the same time most awfully at the inexactitude of that red vagabond and peacemonger."[37] Even Longfellow eventually became disgruntled with Copway. In 1858 he answered Freiligrath's enquiry as to the whereabouts of his son's godfather with a brief but telling statement: "Kahgegahgabow [sic] is still extant. But I fear he is developing the Pau-Puk-Keewis element rather strongly."[38]

It appears that Copway also developed a drinking habit at this time of despair. In a beseeching letter addressed to Erastus Corning, president of the New York Central Railway, he assured his hoped-for benefactor that he had ceased taking "firewater." He also complained that his domestic troubles had almost driven him to ruin and that he needed to borrow the sum of one hundred dollars for six weeks in order to return to England, where he thought he could earn money lecturing. From there he planned to visit the Holy Land, a popular destination for contemporary American writers of travel literature, an indication that he perhaps had another publication in mind. Curiously enough, he named Freiligrath, who was in England then, as his creditor. "Fred Freilegrath [sic] Esqr a Poet and the Presedent [sic] of the Swiss Bank No 2 Royal Exchange London," he assured Corning, "is to be the kind man who will supply me with all the money I may want – he has been writing to me several times and has sent word by his friends for me to come – for when I saw him in Germany he named his only son after my Indian name."[39] Ironically, as thousands of Germans looked to America for a new beginning, Copway hoped for a better day in the Old World.

Bernd Peyer

Notes

This is a revised and expanded version of the account included in my chapter on Copway in Peyer, *Tutor'd Mind*, 224–77.

1. The primary sources on Copway are his own publications: *Life, History, and Travels of Kah-ge-ga-gah-bowh; Organization of a New Indian Territory; Traditional History;* and *Running Sketches.* "His" poem, *Ojibway Conquest,* is said to have been written by Julius Taylor Clark. For background information on Copway, see D. B. Smith, "Kahgegagahbowh," 419–21; id., "Life of George Copway," 5–38. Further information on Copway is available in D. B. Smith *Sacred Feathers.* Copway's autobiography is analyzed in Ruoff, "George Copway," 6–17; and id., "Three Nineteenth-Century American Indian Autobiographers," 251–69. Vizenor comments briefly on Copway's life and works in his "Three Anishinaabeg Writers," 56–74. His relationship with Longfellow is detailed in Moyne, "Longfellow and Kahga-ga-gah-bowh," 48–52. Copway's reliability as historian is discussed in Eid, "Ojibwa-Iroquois War," 297–324; and MacLeod, "Anishinabeg Point of View," 194–210. His relations with the American nativistic movement is covered in Knobel, "Know-Nothings and Indians," 175–98. For shorter and not always accurate biographical sketches, see Dockstader, *Great North American Indians,* 59; Genzmer, "Copway, George," 433; and W. Jones, "Copway, George," 347.

2. For background on Burritt and the World Peace Congress, see Burritt, *Learned Blacksmith,* 28–89, and id., *Elihu Burritt,* 101–8.

3. See Dickason, *Myth of the Savage,* 203–29; A. Forbes, *Some Indian Events of New England,* 26–64; J. T. Forbes, *Africans and Native Americans,* 26–64; Foreman, *Indians Abroad;* Prins, "To the Land of the Mistigoches," 175–95. Jack Forbes even contends that Indians traveled to Europe and Africa long before the Europeans came to America. See J. T. Forbes, *Africans and Native Americans,* 6–25.

4. See the fictive account by the Iroquois sachem "King Sa Ga Tean Qua Rash Tow" written by Addison in *The Spectator.* See also Anthony Pagden, "The Savage Critic," 32–45.

5. Maungwudaus, *Account of the Chippewa Indians.* It was first published in England as *Remarks Concerning the Ojibway Indians.* The Boston edition is reprinted in Peyer, *Elders Wrote,* 66–74. A second English edition, *Account of the North American Indians,* seems to imply that Maungwudaus was not the author. However, a letter George Henry wrote to his half-brother Peter Jones (1802–1856) from France is very similar in style and contains some of the same episodes mentioned in the pamphlet. See P. Jones, *History of the Ojebway Indians,* 219–20. In the context of early Indian travel literature, see also Samson Occom's (1723–1792) journal of his tour to England, Scotland, and Ireland in 1765–66, which has been reproduced in Occum, "Journal," 81–87, 100–9, and P. Jones's notes on his three voyages to England in

1831-1832, 1837-1838, and 1844-1846 in his *Life and Journals of Ka-ke-wa-quo-na-by*, 294–346, 392–408, 410–11.

6. Copway, *Running Sketches*, 55, 98–113, 122–26, 148–52. The typical description of his appearance is taken from an article in the *Liverpool Standard*, which Copway quoted in the same publication on p. 54.

7. Copway, *Running Sketches*, 168. Approximately fifty pages of his text were quoted directly from the widely used English travel guides put out by publishers Adam Black and Charles Black. These and the numerous poetic citations included in the text may have been selected with the help of his wife, Elizabeth Howell, who accompanied him on part of the journey.

8. Cloos, "Indianerhäuptling; Copway, *Running Sketches*, 186–87, 193.

9. See Spiller, *American in England*.

10. Copway, *Running Sketches*, 198–207.

11. See Valentin, "Erste Internationale Friedenskongreß," 27–37 (Copway is mentioned on 34–35).

12. *Allgemeine Zeitung* (Augsburg), 27 August 1850, p. 1, col. 1-2; p. 2, col. 1.

13. "The Peace Congress," *Times* (London), 28 August 1850, p. 5, col. 2, 3; Copway, *Running Sketches*, 249, 252. Copway describes the Peace Congress in some detail in *Running Sketches*, 208–53. Much of his information, however, was taken directly from the London *Times* and the minutes of the Congress, the latter of which were published in English, German, and French after the event. See *Report of the Proceedings* and *Verhandlungen des dritten allgemeinen Friedenscongresses*.

14. *Journal des Débats Politiques et Littéraires*, p. 1, col. 1, 2. The Burritt statement is from a diary entry dated 24 August 1850 (Burritt's Diaries, New Britain Public Library, Connecticut); quoted in D. B. Smith, "Life of George Copway," 24.

15. Copway, *Running Sketches*, 221. The references are to Émile de Girardin (1806–1881), eminent French journalist; Richard Cobden (1804–1865), British statesman and champion of the British Anti-Corn Law League; and Rev. Edwin Hubbell Chapin (1814–1880), American Universalist clergyman and noted orator.

16. See Barba, *Cooper in Germany*; Billington, *Land of Savagery*, 29–104; Lutz, "Indianer" und "Native Americans," 244–446; Plischke, *Von Cooper bis Karl May*, 85–124.

17. *Illustrierte Zeitung* (Leipzig) 21 September 1850, 183–84. Other positive reviews of his talk are found in: *Frankfurter Oberpostamts-Zeitung*, 24 August 1850, p. 2, col. 1, 2, 3; *Frankfurter Konversationsblatt*, 27 August 1850, p. 4, col. 2; *Frankfurter Journal*, Dritte Beilage, 24 August 1850, p. 1, col. 1; *Journal de Francfort*, 27 August 1850, p. 3, col. 2; *Allgemeine Zeitung* (Augsburg), 27 August 1850, p. 1, col. 1; and *Nassauische Allgemeine Zeitung* (Wiesbaden), 27 August 1850, p. 1, col. 2-3; p. 2, col. 1.

18. See Gall, FFM 1200, 228; Häussler, "Mit der Friedenspfeife," 41. The whereabouts of the peace pipe is unknown to me.

19. "From Greenland's Icy Mountains," by Reginald Weber, 1819. Original text in *Report of the Proceedings of the Third General Peace Congress*, 42; *Verhandlungen des*

Bernd Peyer

dritten allgemeinen Friedenscongresses, 41-43. The appendix to the German publication provides additional news about Copway and clarifies the fallacy behind the title of "Chief" in the local press (97-98). The following version, which concludes with Copway's quotation of Weber's hymn, appeared in the English minutes of the congress:

> "When I look at this assembly I am astonished – astonished at its success; when I consider the state of Europe, and the difficulties to have been overcome, difficulties which rise up like hills and mountains in the way of civilization – and by being thus astonished – who need wonder if I predict that the time must soon come when all the courts of Europe will send its representatives to this Congress, even from Rome itself? You may say this is not possible. It is possible: as much so as the existence of those mighty machineries which your forefathers would have called miraculous. When I left my country in the West, my aged father came to me and said, "Here, my son, take this" – (unrolling the Indian pipe of peace) – yes, when I took my seat at this table, many persons seemed afraid to sit near me, as if I had arms in my hand; but Mr. President, it is not a weapon of war, it is a weapon of peace, which, in the name of my countrymen, I present to you – it is our calumet. And I will add, of this great quest of Peace –

Waft, waft, ye winds, the story,
And you, ye waters roll;
Till, like a sea of glory,

20. "Friedenscongreß zu Frankfurt," 365-67.
21. *Kladderadatsch,* 3, no. 35 (1 September 1850): 1. The caricature was made with reference to the decision by the Fürstenkongreß in Berlin in late August to exclude twenty-four states that had previously withdrawn from the Prussian union plan under Austrian pressure.
22. *Allgemeine Zeitung* (Augsburg), 242, 29 August 1850, p. 1, col. 1-2; p. 2, col. 1-2.
23. The bronze bust was probably destroyed during World War II, but a black-and-white photograph of the plaster mold is still found in the Frankfurt archives (Nachlass Launitz, S 1/80, Box 1-4, Stadtarchiv Frankfurt). See I. Schmidt, *Eduard Schmidt von der Launitz 1797-1869,* 140-43, 206, 253. The translation was made by R. Adler, *Die Besiegung der Odschibwäh.* August Cloos also planned to translate the poem, but I have not been able to determine whether it was ever published. The translations are mentioned in *Verhandlungen des dritten allgemeinen Friedenscongresses,* 98. See also Cloos, "Indianerhäuptling, v. 222, p. 3, col. 1; Ferdinand Freiligrath to Henry Wadsworth Longfellow, 19 June 1851, in Hatfield, "Longfellow-Freiligrath Correspondence," 1268.
24. *Verhandlungen des dritten allgemeinen Friedenscongresses,* 98.

25. Copway, *Running Sketches*, 254. There is some discrepancy in the dates given by Copway. According to the *Frankfurter Journal* (26 August 1850) and the *Nassauische Allgemeine Zeitung* (29 August 1850), the Prince of Prussia arrived in Frankfurt on the evening of the twenty-sixth and reviewed a parade early the next morning. Copway, however, claims to have met him on Saturday after the congress was over, which would have been 31 August, but he and the other Peace Congress delegates left Frankfurt by 29 August. If the meeting took place at all, it must have been in the morning before his trip to Wiesbaden, on 27 August.

26. *Frankfurter Konversationsblatt*, 27 August 1850, p. 4, col. 2. See Börner, *Wilhelm I*, 51. Copway became a member of the New York chapter of the Order of United Americans early in 1852. See Smith, "Life of George Copway," 24. There is no record of this meeting at the Geheimes Staatsarchiv Preussischer Kulturbesitz in Berlin, where much of the German imperial records are kept. Thanks to Dr. Letkemann for this information. On Indian Freemasonry, see Hertzberg, *Search for an American Indian Identity*, 213–236; Parker, *American Indian Freemasonry*.

27. Copway, *Running Sketches*, 256–57, 264–65. Copway's presence among the delegates in Heidelberg was noted in the *Allgemeine Zeitung* (Augsburg), 242, 30 August 1850, p. 2, col. 1–2.

28. *Verhandlungen des dritten allgemeinen Friedenscongresses*, 95–96.

29. Copway, *Running Sketches*, 165–66, 265–66.

30. See S. Longfellow, *Life of Henry Wadsworth Longfellow*, 2:135. Copway's relationship with Longfellow is discussed in Moyne, "Longfellow and Kah-ge-ga-gah-bowh," 48–52. Freiligrath, who later translated Longfellow's *The Song of Hiawatha* (*Der Sang von Hiawatha*), was a representative of an informal literary group known as "Das Neue Deutschland" (ca. 1830–1850), who actively participated in the reform movements of 1848–1849. He went into exile in England in 1851 and did not return to Germany until 1868. The meeting is described in detail in Cloos, "Indianerhäuptling," Part 2, p. 2, col. 1–2; p. 3, col. 1.

31. Longfellow to Freiligrath, 12 June 1850, in H. W. Longfellow, *Letters*, 258–59; also reproduced in Hatfield, "Longfellow-Freiligrath Correspondence," 1268. Quoted in Moyne, "Longfellow and Kah-ge-ga-gah-bowh" 49. Longfellow's pun on Anarchy is in reference to a revolutionary Prussian officer, Fritz Anneke, who had previously immigrated to the United States.

32. Freiligrath to Longfellow, 19 June 1851, in Hatfield, "Longfellow-Freiligrath Correspondence," 1269–73; cited in Moyne, "Longfellow and Kah-ge-ga-gah-bowh," 49. Reference to George Karl Otto's nickname is made in Ferdinand Freiligrath to Karl Etze, 1 May 1859, in Buchner, *Ferdinand Freiligrath: Ein Dichterleben in Briefen*, 2:320–21; and Gottfried Keller to Ferdinand Freiligrath, 22 September 1850, in Keller, *Gottfried Kellers Briefe und Tagebücher*, 245–50.

33. Longfellow to Freiligrath, 16 July 1851. In Hatfield, "Longfellow-Freiligrath Correspondence," 1273–74; and H. W. Longfellow, *Letters*, 3:302–4.

Bernd Peyer

34. Copway, *Running Sketches*, 268–69, 274.

35. See Berkhofer, *White Man's Indian*, 95; Sollors, *Beyond Ethnicity*, 131–41.

36. William C. Bryant to Ely S. Parker, 25 June 1884, in Parker, *Life of General Ely S. Parker*, 204–6. Bryant thought the perpetrators "should be acquitted of any intentions to do wrong" and mentioned that the articles buried with the body were found intact. Red Jacket's (1810–1876) remains were reburied ceremonially that same year with the assistance of Bryant and the Buffalo Historical Society. Copway mentions a lecture on the Peace Congress in a letter addressed to J. W. Thornton, 22 January 1851, Ayer N. A. Ms. 184, no. 3, Newberry Library, Chicago. See D. B. Smith, "Life of George Copway," 25–28.

37. Freiligrath to Longfellow, 25 September 1853. Cited in Moyne, "Longfellow and Kah-ge-ga-gah-bowh," 50. On 16 July 1851, Longfellow had written: "But the precious books you sent he has not yet delivered. I have written to him lately about them, and if they are not forth-coming, I shall raise such a war-whoop, that it will frighten him. If they are lost, I shall never forgive him." Copway called on Longfellow on 29 August 1851 and, not finding him at home, first helped himself to one of Longfellow's cigars and then wrote him a note complimenting him on his nice domicile and blaming his wife for not having brought the books from London. He promised that he would send for all his trunks and deliver the books as soon as they arrived. Apparently he never did so. See Longfellow to Freiligrath, 12 June 1851, in Hatfield, "Longfellow-Freiligrath Correspondence," 1273–74; also in H. W. Longfellow, *Letters*, 302–4; and Moyne, "Longfellow and Kah-ge-ga-gah-bowh," 50.

38. Longfellow to Freiligrath, 14 December 1858. In H. W. Longfellow, *Letters*, 4: 108–9. Pau-Puk-Keewis is the mischief-maker in his *Song of Hiawatha*. Quoted in Moyne, "Longfellow and Kah-ge-ga-gah-bowh," 50.

39. George Copway to the Honorable Erastus Corning, 24 January 1860 (Autograph Collection of Simon Gratz, Historical Society of Pennsylvania). Mentioned in Moyne, "Longfellow and Kah-ge-ga-gah-bowh," 52, n. 24. During his exile, in 1856, Freiligrath acted as president of the General Bank of Switzerland in London.

Part 3: Projections and Performances

German Indianthusiasm

A Socially Constructed German National(ist) Myth

HARTMUT LUTZ

As a German born in 1945, I have always been intrigued by the fact that a nation steeped so deeply in racism like Germany should romanticize Indians while, at the same time, committing systematic genocide against Jews. I have been convinced that the two extremes are locked in a peculiar dialectic that transcends mere stereotyping or othering. The romantic infatuation with North American Indians and annihilatory anti-Semitism, I have felt, must be charged by related, culturally transmitted psychological energies; they seem connected like the flip sides of the same coin. But how? Which collective political and psychological processes glued together those two sides of a German "ideology"?

Over the past twenty-five years I have pondered the German obsession with *Indianer* again and again. I have tried to describe the phenomenon and trace its historical origins. I have looked at American history, literature, and film, as well as at German cultural productions. I have studied children's literature and given questionnaires to pupils in the United States and Germany to find out what they knew about Indians and how they felt about them. So, in the course of time, I have gained an extensive, complex, and often contradictory impression of Indian stereotyping and the phenomenon I call *deutsche Indianertümelei* – German Indianthusiasm.[1] However, for me the main question has remained unanswered, namely how *Indianertümelei* is related to anti-Semitism, aggressive ethnocentrism, or explicit racism.[2]

There are some more general social and psychological phenomena that indicate why it is possible to romanticize and demonize at the same time. First, there is the historical context. We know from American Romanticism that it was easy for Eastern urbanites to romanticize Indians while, at the same time in the West, politicians, militiamen, and the military were busy dispossessing and relocating Native American nations. Bogardus and Lewis have shown that the closer the historical and geographical contacts between ethnic groups, the more likely the conflicts, and the further the groups are removed from each other, the easier it is to idealize. Germany as a nation never had any dealings with the indigenous nations of North America except for scattered individual contacts, so it was easy for Germans to idealize them. By contrast, Jewish Germans lived "right there." In the eighteenth and nineteenth centuries, in their state of social and political oppression and in their geographic and national fragmentation, Germans often felt, with Johann Wolfgang von Goethe, that "Amerika, du hast es besser" ("America, you are better off").[3] In this historical context, indigenous Americans became romanticized objects of colonial desire and escapist fantasies. This longing was intensified by Romantic notions of "the primitive," the "unspoiled," and "the folk" that gained currency with increasing industrialization and urbanization.

Also, there is the psychology of perception. It seems true in general that in a process of "othering" ethnic groups, our perceptional frames tend to dichotomize them into extremes of good and bad at the exclusion of a center of commonality. German perceptions of "others" seem to have followed and often still follow this general dichotomizing tendency. However, the historical or cognitive explanations for the extremity of German reactions to Jews and/or Indians as ethnic others provide no answers to what chemistry glues together the two extremes.

In the current process of so-called *Wiedervereinigung,* or "German reunification," renewed urgency and attention are given to the questions of German national identity and the construction of the German nation. Reflections on the social constructedness of (German) ethnicity and nationhood may help us identify some of the ideological components of this "glue." It appears that both anti-Semitism and *Indianertümelei* are fed by the same political and cultural processes that went into the construction of the German nation state. In the following discussion, I outline some of these processes, but I do so merely as an interested amateur, because, as a teacher of North American literature and culture, I am neither trained in nor qualified to analyze German literature or the history of ideas.

German Indianthusiasm

In my understanding, the term *Indianertümelei* signifies a yearning for all things Indian, a fascination with American Indians, a romanticizing about a supposed Indian essence, or, for want of a better translation that catches the ironic ambiguities of the German term, an "Indianthusiasm." I deliberately use the English term "Indian" and its derivatives, or the German "Indianer," whenever I am referring to the image or ideological construct conceived by European Americans and Europeans about North American aboriginal peoples. When talking about actual persons of indigenous descent in North America, I use "Native American" or other, more appropriate, terms.[4]

German "Indianthusiasm" is racialized in that it refers to Indianness (*Indianertum*) as an essentializing bioracial and, concomitantly, cultural ethnic identity that ossifies into stereotype. It tends to historicize Indians as figures of the past, and it assumes that anybody "truly Indian" will follow cultural practices and resemble in clothing and physiognomy First Nations people before or during first contact. Relatively seldom does *Indianertümelei* focus on contemporary Native American realities.

For over two hundred years, Germans have found *Indianer* so fascinating that even today an Indian iconography is used in advertising. The most popular image of the *Indianer* is provided by Karl May's (1842-1912) fictional Apache chief Winnetou and his impersonators, the Yugoslav actor Gojko Mitic (in former East Germany) and the French actor Pierre Brice (in former West Germany; see Gerd Gemünden's contribution to this volume). Indian lore is profitable and marketable, as some Native Americans traveling to Germany may attest and many would-be Indians would second. Members of many *Indianistik* clubs in East and West Germany create Native American artifacts in their spare time or spend their holidays in Indian camps, with tepees numbering in the hundreds. They regularly dance and compete in regional and national powwows. There is a marked Indian presence in German everyday culture, even down to the linguistic level, where sentences like "ein Indianer weint nicht!" (an Indian doesn't cry), "ein Indianer kennt keinen Schmerz" (an Indian braves pain), or figures such as "der letzte Mohikaner" (the last of the Mohicans) have become part of everyday speech.

Indianthusiasm and Indian hobbyism seem to provide a safety valve in a highly regulated, competitive capitalist society. Furthermore, for Germans, aware of the nation's racist history, casting themselves as the friends of Indians and feeling empathetic to Native American political causes provides an ahistorical and guilt-free ideological realm, far removed from the more depressing aspects of German reality past and present. Moreover, it allows Germans to identify with the victims of history, rather than with the victimizers.[5]

For a century, German writers have postulated a special affinity, even brotherhood, between themselves and Indians. Few Native Americans are aware of this supposedly special relationship between Indians and Germans. Those who do know about it often express their amusement in literature and the arts; some cash in on it; some use the possibilities of networking in scholarship and politics this "affinity" offers. For Germans, it is an affinity that is intimately tied to the construction of the German nation and to German national myths.

Nation-Building between Enlightenment and Romanticism

Germany as a nation state is younger than the United States or Canada. The German Reich was founded under Prussian hegemony in 1871, at the end of the Franco-Prussian War. While the idea of an ethnically defined German nation originated in the Renaissance, the Holy Roman Empire of the German Nation, which collapsed in 1806, had never been a nation state.[6] In fact, toward the end of the eighteenth century the territory of today's Germany was fragmented into over three hundred small principalities and independent townships. Under the impact of Enlightenment thought and the powerful example of the French Revolution, German intellectuals began campaigning for a united German nation state to overcome, first, absolutism and then the political and geographic fragmentation, the *Kleinstaaterei*. Later, during Napoleonic occupation, the call for national liberation gained momentum. For a brief moment in history, the liberal and emancipatory desires of the bourgeoisie and the anti-Napoleonic restorative interests of the feudal aristocracy were united under a nationalist banner.

Scholars agree that in the beginning, nation-building attempts were triggered by the ideas of the French Revolution, and there was no question that in that new German state Jews would be emancipated *citoyens* with full civil rights, as, indeed, they were in some of the more liberal German principalities. After Napoleon's defeat, however, the Restoration reinstated most of the *status-quo-ante*, thwarting attempts to create a liberal and unified Germany. The dream of an enlightened German state had to wait, but it gained momentum and found expression in rebellions throughout the century, notably in 1848. While some of the traditional Christian anti-Judaism survived in Germany as in other countries, the Enlightenment's push toward secularization temporarily curbed anti-Jewish tendencies.[7] Jews used the openings provided by liberalism, and many became a vital part of the German intelligentsia, forming part of a fully secularized, liberal, socialist, or even communist intellectual avant-garde. It was not until after 1870 that the concept of a secular but racialized anti-Semitism gained ground.[8]

This biological anti-Semitism was rooted in another, exclusionary strain in the movement toward national unity. In the course of the nineteenth century, the idea of Germanness became increasingly ethnicized and ethnophobic.

The Romantics' search for a German identity based on a shared culture, language, descent, history, and territoriality assigned an essential and a priori antiquity to what the nationalists were only about to construct.[9] While it seemed relatively easy to follow early linguists and identify language as a collective property, other criteria proved to be less conclusive, given the continuous movement of peoples throughout Europe, especially during the fifth century. The assumption of a common culture thus rested on brittle grounds, leaving room for creativity and much wishful thinking.

Instead of pushing for a liberal and enlightened state, some members of the Romantic Movement, like the brothers Grimm, turned to folk traditions, mythology, and the past to create a German nation of the mind, based on *das deutsche Wesen*, an essential national character supposedly shared by all persons of German descent. Instead of focusing on the intellectual clarity and skepticism of enlightened reasoning, they withdrew into a collective emotional realm; some even wallowed in self-pitying dreams about the lost grandeur of a German nation they fervently hoped to resurrect. In hindsight it looks as if for some of Romanticism's intellectuals, forming the German nation became primarily an exercise in the ideological construction of ethnic identity and less a rational and political push for a liberal state.[10] It is important to trace this ethnic construction in order to assert the role Indians played within German self-perceptions.

Assembling a German Ethnopoesis

According to Werner Sollors, "the typical features which romanticism dictated a nation" ideally included "folk and fairy tales, costumes, the vernacular, people's superstitions, an epic tradition ... as the nourishing ground for high art and peoplehood."[11] Distinct local or regional cultures in Germany possessed, and often continue to possess, some of these features, which, however, are not universally present on the national level. "The invention of ethnicity," as Sollors argues, rests to a large degree on defining a body "of traditional narratives."[12] But "the Germans" did not possess such a body of texts, nor was there a unifying German national epic with which all regions could identify. Klaus von See also argues that Germans lack a cohesive ethnopoesis, a "founding myth" on which the nation's cultural identity could rely and from which it might draw its strength. Indeed, Germans have no sagas like the Icelanders, nor historical or legendary figures like Jeanne d'Arc or Wilhelm Tell, neither a Mayflower compact nor a myth of Quetzalcoatl. In their quest for common cultural roots in the folk, the brothers Grimm therefore collected their tales, while other bourgeois intellectuals searched for older historical texts to lend *origo* (common descent) and *vetustas* (antiquity) to a German nation's identity. They identified as a "new" national hero Arminius (or Hermann), the Cheruscan chief who in A.D. 8 had outwitted three Roman legions on the southern rim of the North German plains, "defeated" the *imperium romanum*, and, in the eyes of nationalists almost nineteen hundred years later, liberated a "Germany" that did not even exist. In the mythological figure of an ancient and remote Tuisco, they saw the forefather of all Germans, hence the name "Deutsch."[13] In their quest for embodiments of the German nation, the Romantics furthermore relied heavily on a text by a Roman historian and on a medieval courtly epic of uncertain authorship: the *Germania* (A.D. 98) by Publius Cornelius Tacitus (c. A.D. 55-117) and the *Nibelungenlied*, the Middle High German saga of Siegfried the Dragonslayer. Both texts had been neglected or even lost for centuries until the new interest dug them up. And both not only fabricated a German "tribal" ethnicity, but prepared the ground for the German-Indian identification.

Tacitus's Germanic Tribespeople

In their search for common ethnic roots, German nationalist intellectuals abandoned the humanist classicist tradition. Instead of referring to Greece or Rome as European cultural antecedents, they resorted to a Renaissance discourse of the 1480s that located the origins of German ethnicity in the cultures of Germanic tribes described by Tacitus.[14] Tacitus's *Germania*, the most important ethnographic document about the Germanic peoples, the Teutons, had been lost in a German monastery until it was rediscovered by Renaissance scholars.[15] It was "reappropriated" by German Romantics in the nineteenth century, who constructed the Teutons, along with their military leader Arminius, as the "(ab)original Germans," thus lending an element of *indigena* (indigenity) to *origo* and *vetustas*.[16] Tacitus depicted Teutons as wild forest dwellers, *silvatici*, the Latin term that forms the root of the French *sauvage* and the English *sa(l)vage*. Seeing the Roman Empire and its virtues on the decline, Tacitus cast the barbarians to the north and east of the Roman limes – an early frontier between "civilization and savagery" – as primitive barbarians or noble savages who supposedly possessed the unspoiled virtues and unrefined vices that the "decadent" Romans had already lost.

In his simultaneous barbarization and idealization of Germanic tribes, Tacitus followed a well-established ethnotopological pattern that had originated in Greek antiquity around 500 B.C. It constructed ethnicity within a hierarchical perceptional frame, allocating civilization to the viewer and an ambivalent, dualistic primitivism to the viewed.[17] Going back to Hekataios and Herodotus, this ethnographic genre semanticized as (stereo)typically barbarian those traits that Germans often cherish as "typically German." Tacitus assigned Teutons tough blue eyes and reddish blond hair (*truces et caerulei oculi, rutilae comae*), traits that Herodotus had already listed as typical for the Scythians, and Plinius the Elder for the Ceylonese. Using Teutons to define Rome *ex negativo*, Tacitus projected into them virtues that were eagerly picked up by the Romantics eighteen hundred years later: honesty; unflinching, even self-destructive loyalty to family, clan, tribe, and tribal leaders; utter fearlessness in battle; respect for women; physical hardiness; and stoicism in the face of adversity. Tacitus praised their freedom from the restraints of civilized society, their closeness to nature, spirit of independence, and honesty. At the same time, he described Teutons as cruel, inclined to overindulge in drinking and gambling, and prone to go berserk in battle. In short, centuries before Rousseau's *bon sauvage*, Tacitus assigned to the Germanic tribesmen the dual stereotype of the noble yet bloodthirsty savage, a cliché that was consistently reapplied to ethnic groups outside Hellenism or Christianity. It is the same topological and rhetorical cluster from which Romantics later created the stereotype of the Nordic Viking seafarer and conqueror pillaging European Christendom, and it is this conceptual reservoir from which German Romantics, and not just Germans, constructed the dual stereotype of the Indian as a "red gentleman" and a "bloodthirsty red devil."

Another figure portrayed by Tacitus and eagerly taken up as a national hero was the aforementioned Arminius. After Prussian and other German troops had defeated the French in 1871, they erected a huge copper and steel statue of Arminius at a spot where they believed the historical battle had taken place in Teutoburg Forest. There he watches out, blind-eyed and hollow, holding up his sword and facing the west, a monument commemorating the Germans' victory over "Romans" throughout the centuries. Since 1987, we know that the monument is actually in the wrong place.[18]

Siegfried, Germanic Superman

Tacitus had written his book about the Germanic barbarians in Latin. His was an outsider's, even a colonizer's perspective. When it comes to early texts in German, there is scant material for a body of traditional narratives. Apart from a few fragments from pre-Christian times, written in Old High German, all pagan written documents were destroyed systematically in the often violent process of Christianizing Germanic peoples in the early Middle Ages. A text from the late Middle Ages, the Nibelungenlied, was therefore called upon to serve as a foundational fiction. Recorded around 1200 and rediscovered in at least two versions in 1757 and 1782, it is the saga of Siegfried the Dragon-slayer, who was treacherously killed by Hagen von Tronje. Hagen, the pagan, had learned through cunning the hero's one vulnerable spot under his shoulder blade, where a fallen leaf had stopped the coating of dragon's blood that had made Siegfried invincible. Hagen's literal backstabbing of the Germanic hero, the widow's rampage for revenge, and the many subplots about loyalty and battle provided Germans with at least one ethnopoesis, albeit, again, a regional one. In the figure of Siegfried some nineteenth-century nationalists found, in retrospect, the virtues they projected, in an essentializing gesture, onto a national subjectivity: honesty, unwavering and selfless loyalty, courage, self-restraint, and reliability. George L. Mosse has noted that these national virtues are very much those of the nineteenth-century German bourgeoisie.[19] The fate of Siegfried, with its strain of tragedy and betrayal, was incorporated into the construction of the German nation's collective karma. Siegfried's murder by Hagen was read as symbolizing the "death" of the German nation, which would rise again – and there are similar myths that prophesied the resurrection of the medieval German Kaiserreich.[20]

With the Germania and the Nibelungenlied, German nationalists had identified two constituent texts for a somewhat heteroglossic ethnopoesis, which could then be used to construct a "German(ic) ideology," or better, a deutsches Wesen, an essentialist German character. In addition to such ancient sources, nineteenth-century nationalist scholars as well as artists like Richard Wagner turned to Nordic mythology, that is, the Icelandic sagas and the various versions of the Edda, the old myth of creation and the struggle, downfall, and possible resurrection of the Nordic gods, who had been worshipped in (Northern) Germany before Christianity.[21] In a gesture similar to British Romanticism's flirt with Ossianism, they turned "Nordicity" into an essential ingredient of Germanness. Nationalists have since cherished "German Nordicity" from the nineteenth century through Nazi times right up to today's neo-Nazi skinhead scene and its White Aryan Resistance sister organizations.

This fabrication of a "national character" and a national "fate" served nationalists in their increasingly racialized construction of a German folk ethnicity. By racializing the German nation they paved the way for later definitions of German nationality that favor descent (ius sanguinis) over territoriality (ius solis) and provided the ideological basis for excluding Jewish Germans from participating in the "Nation."[22] These ideologues found in Tacitus's

Germanic tribesmen, in the heroes of the Nordic sagas, and even in Siegfried the racial qualities that composed the Aryan racist ideal. The German ideology based on Tacitus's ethnography thus became an ideological basis for the racist fascism of the Third Reich.[23] The self-aggrandizing tendencies within this construct only thinly veil a deep and dangerous insecurity felt by the fledgling German nation in relation to other European nations, especially the successful colonial powers England and France. This self-aggrandizement combined with insecurity not only underlies anti-Semitism but ties it to Indianthusiasm.

Tribal Brotherhood

At the Berlin Conference of 1884, when the major European powers carved up Africa, for the first time Germans, too, sat at the international table to receive "their" part of the "cake" and secure their "place in the sun."[24] But how would they succeed as colonists? Were they equal to others as colonial rulers, or even superior? I believe that this point is where Karl May's novels come in as ideological props for German imperialism and for the self-representation of Germans as both superior tribespeople and superior colonizers. Karl May, the most widely read German author of all times, provided the national reading public with a hero, Old Shatterhand (in America) or Kara Ben Nemsi (in the Orient), who was more courageous, steadfast, strong, just, benevolent, and learned than his competitors. This modern Siegfried rode the frontiers of the so-called civilized world together with an indigenous sidekick named Winnetou, supposedly a Mescalero Apache chief. Karl May showed his readers that, given the opportunity, even a book-educated German lower middle-class adventurer and would-be pioneer could become a powerful colonialist.[25] As such, Karl May's Germanized imitations of American "frontier romances" constitute a "neo-tradition" in Sollors's definition, one of the many "colonial fantasies" produced by a German "imperialist imagination."[26] Old Shatterhand's adventures have boosted German ethnocentrism and nationalism, from the *Kaiserreich* via Nazi times until today. This fictional national hero demonstrated in a nationally self-aggrandizing manner those characteristics that, as we saw above, were identified by Mosse as constitutive of the German bourgeois ideal.

In our context, the most important aspect of May's works is the special relationship between Old Shatterhand and his "Apatsche" friend Winnetou. This German version of Indian-white male bonding fits into the tradition of such archetypal couples in American literature as described by Leslie Fiedler.

Even the Indian protagonist Winnetou is remarkably bourgeois and "German" in character. This comes as no surprise since Karl May casts him as having received a thoroughly humanist education from one Klekhi-petra, a German immigrant and former revolutionary who piously repented his role as a socialist agitator in the rebellions of 1848 and turned into a transcultural exile among the "Apatschen." He appears as the teacher of Winnetou and dies conveniently early in the novel, thus clearing an ideological and emotional space for the bonding between German and *Indianer*, Old Shatterhand and Winnetou. The Indian recognizes the German's outstanding qualities, and, as a real apple-Indian, accepts the manifest destiny of white (German, Saxon) superiority: he even helps Old Shatterhand to stake out claims for a projected railroad through Apache territory. Thus, the two act out one of the most complacent colonialist myths, that is, the welcoming of the colonizer by the colonized and the latter's voluntary acceptance of colonial rule, based on a recognition of and love for the colonizer's cultural, intellectual, moral, and even physical superiority. Even today, the ritual in which Winnetou and Old Shatterhand become blood-brothers is cheered enthusiastically by the thousands of spectators who attend annual summer performances of Karl May's Winnetou novels in the open-air theater (a former Nazi-arena) of Bad Segeberg.[27]

Unlike the Pocahontas myth in the United States or the Malinche myth in Mexico, in May's novel the welcoming aspect of America is not first and foremost incarnated by a alluring indigenous female but by an alluring male.[28] There is also Winnetou's beautiful sister, Nscho-tschi, who, of course, falls in love with Old Shatterhand. But her beauty is measured in terms of Winnetou's, and her brother tells her that as an Indian woman, she cannot hope to ever marry the German.[29] The hermaphrodite beauty of Winnetou, in turn, renders this figure open to multiple desires and identifications, not only in terms of erotic attraction, but also as incorporating everything an imperialist may hope for in a colonial subject. Instead of succumbing to brute force, Winnetou falls in love with the German's exemplary prowess, honesty, self-restraint, and charm. As a fictional character, Old Shatterhand is the innocent bourgeois incarnation of an ideal German "colonizer," both pious and guiltless—quite in contrast to the actual policies employed, for example, during the so-called Herero uprising of 1904, in the notorious genocide against the indigenous people of what was then misnamed "German" Southwest Africa.[30]

In a discussion of German Indianthusiasm it seems particularly significant that this most popular neo-tradition creates not only a modern Siegfried-like super hero, Old Shatterhand, but that this ultra-German is loved and admired by his Indian blood-brother precisely *because* he is a German. Moreover, the Indians whom Old Shatterhand encounters are a bit like the Teutons described by Tacitus: both savage and noble, ferocious and free. May's *Winnetou* novels thus constitute a vital part of a German nationalist ideology in the form of a neo-tradition. In connection with the Siegfried and Arminius myths, they substantiate "politically motivated feelings of peoplehood."[31] The superhero, it seems, needs his Indian blood brother as a foil to excel and to love himself.

The Führer Loves Winnetou

Karl May was a self-avowed pacifist and anticolonialist.[32] Later readers, however, clearly understood his importance as a national mythmaker. In May's works, German nationalist mythologizing became overcoded with Indianthusiasm, both as expressive of love for all things Indian and, more importantly, for all things German.

German imperialist daydreaming incorporated a highly emotional, peaceful, empathetic Indian-German exceptionalism that transcended, in a fictional land of liberty, the borders of gender and sexuality, of race and nationality, and even class. Conservative nationalist military officers during World War I would functionalize Indianthusiastic fantasies when going into battle.[33] Indianthusiasm had to veil racism directed at other ethnicities. When the German translation of the "autobiography" of Buffalo Child Long Lance (a.k.a. Sylvester Long) was published in Germany in 1929, the translator and editor, Dr. Hans Rudolf Rieder, for example, wrote the following in his introduction: "The Indian is closer to the German than to any other European. This is perhaps due to our partiality to the world of nature. Negroes, Eskimos, peoples of the South Seas do not possess the human qualities necessary to win our friendship and arouse our sympathy. As young lads, however, we find in the Indian an example and a brother; later he remains one of our favorite memories and images of those years."[34] Rieder's comments sum up the irrational German belief in a German-Indian brotherhood. While this affinity exists in ideology only, that is, between *Indianer* and *Germanen*, and not between Native Americans and citizens of a German state, the ideological construct of a Germanic-Indian ethnocultural relatedness was consciously utilized in the so-called Third Reich for propagandistic purposes. Nazi children's literature stressed the affinity between Germans and Indians and its connection to the Arminius myth by reading Native American resistance to European encroachment as a reenactment of Arminius's fight against the Romans, or as a *Schicksalskampf*, a fateful struggle to maintain the "purity" of both races. Hitler himself was an admirer of Karl May's Winnetou, whom he saw as an excellent military tactician and a role model for German youth, as Nazi architect Albert Speer recalls in his memoirs:

> Karl May was proof that it is not necessary to travel in order to get to know the world. The character of Winnetou, for example, as created by Karl May, had always impressed him [Hitler] deeply as a tactician by his flexibility and foresight. In Winnetou he saw embodied the ideal qualities of a *Kompanieführer* [company commander]. When faced with seemingly hopeless situations, in his nightly reading hours he would turn to these narratives; he would be mentally uplifted by them, as other people might be uplifted by philosophical texts or older people by the Bible; besides, Winnetou had always incorporated the ideal of a truly noble person. It would be necessary, of course, through a heroic figure, to teach youth the proper ideas about nobility; young people needed heroes like daily bread. In this lay the great importance of Karl May. But instead, those idiots of teachers were hammering the works of Goethe or Schiller into the heads of their pitiable pupils![35]

After 1933 there was a brief but heated debate about the "political correctness" of Karl May and what was called "softie enthusiasm for colored people" (*weichliche Farbigenschwärmerei*).[36] However, given the ideological approval of May's works from the Führer, it is no surprise that only a year or two later the NS-Lehrerverband (Nazi Teachers' Association), the NS-Jugendschriftenwarte (literally, the National-Socialist Guardian Agency for Books for Adolescents), and the NS-Schriftstellerverband (the Nazi Writers' Association), agreed on using—and proceeded to use—Indian books to propagate Nazi ideals like Führerkult (cult of the Führer/leadership), Rassenlehre (race theory), and Wehrertüchtigung (fostering of military fitness).

In addition to various re-editions of May's works, there appeared a host of Indian books for the young, written by fascist authors like Fritz Steuben (pseudonym for Erhard Wittek) and Franz Schauwecker, extolling Nazi "virtues" and projecting them onto their fictional Indians. As Barbara Haible has shown in her study of *Indianer* literature under Nazism, historical figures like Sitting Bull, Pontiac, and, most prominently, Tecumseh, became fascist Führer figures involved in a racialized *Schicksalskampf*, a battle for blood, soil, language, culture, and the independence of the "red race" from foreign rule. Often, these characters would be sidekicks to an understanding and honest German pioneer who despised French treachery, British hypocrisy, and American ruthlessness, but loved the heroism and "Germanic" qualities of his Indian neighbors, as he might regret their racial "inferiority" as non-Aryans.

In several of these books there are gruesome scenes of "Indian cruelties," of torture, and even of deliberate genocide committed against Indian nations. As in Nazi ideology in general, hate was celebrated in these books as a powerful incentive, and boys were warned not to soften when performing the "craft of killing."[37] Such ideologized books, ostensibly about Indian history, were used to mentally prepare young people for the war to establish a Greater Germany, a Grossdeutsches Reich, and even for systematic genocide against "inferior" races. Curiously, unlike *Winnetou*, with its Christian anti-Judaism, the *Indianer* books of the Nazi period do not contain anti-Semitic references.

In view of the enormous impact of Karl May's works, which seem to have fulfilled sociopsychological needs, it is not surprising that *Indianertümelei* prevails even today. Stripped of its more blatant fascist contents, the Indian provides a figure of escape from the limitations of everyday life. In the seventies, AIM support groups sprouted in both East and West Germany, converting *Indianertümelei* into well-meant but often puerile and patronizing solidarity with Native Americans. In the eighties, the Green Party and Peace Movement activists in West Germany received support from Native American activists against nuclear armament and the uses of nuclear power. In the nineties, a less openly politicized and yet highly political postmodern esoteric approach has been functionalizing Indian philosophy, medicine, arts, and music for various commodified interests related to New Age culture. To this day, *Indianer* remain deeply implicated in German popular culture.

From today's perspective, Indianthusiasm appears as part of an antimodernist, essentially anti-Enlightenment ideologeme, created in a cultural context that constructed ethnicity as blood based, that is interested in escapist folk traditions, and favors genetic-essentialist approaches toward nation-building. Indianthusiasm was defined to a large degree by the popular products of a mediocre petit-bourgeois author, Karl May, at a time when German nationalism searched for "authentic" national traditions and aimed to define itself against others. In focusing on indigenity and descent, Indianthusiasm became another vehicle for exclusionary racism during the brief Nazi period. In casting Indians as brothers and as wonderful, exemplary people who love "us" because we are German, it propagated the myth of hereditary German greatness, even if and when Germans are misunderstood by other nations. The function, then, of German *Indianertümelei* is compensatory self-aggrandizement.

By contrast, or in confirmation of the above, anti-Semitism, as another antimodernist, anti-Enlightenment construct, is based on the racist assumptions that blood, folk, soil, indigenity, extended territorial occupancy, language, and a common religious belief are exclusionary paradigms that give cohesion to the people of a nation state. As a modernist, a clever radical, or a religious outsider, whose indigenity goes back to nomadic desert dwellers and who, just like about 50 percent of the German population, does not often share the "barbaric" features of *caerulei oculi, rutilae comae,* the Jew became the internal ethnic "other." In their long and often enforced tradition of religious and civil dissent and territorial migrations, Jews were constructed as the quintessential non-Germans. Ethnophobic in the extreme, many Germans shunned real contact with "the other" and destroyed those who were so close. They could not or would not see Jews as potential allies in a movement toward a liberal democracy based on the idea of an enlightened and emancipated *citoyen,* regardless of blood quantities. With those lethal and bourgeois virtues of unquestioned loyalty, obedience, and discipline praised by the admirers of Tacitus, Siegfried, and Old Shatterhand, Nazi Germans and their allies, in the darkest and most unenlightened collective act in history, asserted German "superiority" by killing those whose critical and complementary potential they could not understand and whom they had constructed as antagonistic instead. The *Indianer* as the external other who, from a safe distance, loves the self would compensate and cover up for the internal other whom the self could then hate and annihilate.

Notes

I dedicate this article to Hans Hauge of Aarhus, Denmark, and Bernie Selinger of Regina, Saskatchewan, Canada

1. See Lutz, "Sitting Bull," "Images of Indians," *"Indianer" und "Native Americans,"* "Indians and Native Americans in the Movies," and "Nations Within."

2. In the process of questioning the ideological premises of my own approach to Native American Studies, as always in such cross-cultural encounters, I began learning more about being German than if I had stayed within the confines of Germany. I came to accept the depressing truth that the relatively short period of self-imposed Nazi rule in Germany presents the most decisive period in our history. The destruction of human lives leaves a pain that will not go away for generations. German Nazism has also profoundly altered German culture within Germany itself. Academically, the destruction or the enforced exodus of our whole critical intelligentsia has resulted in a brain drain from which German intellectual culture has not yet recovered, and probably never will. Aspects of German folk traditions, everyday culture, and even the language itself have "lost their innocence." A folk song like "Hoch auf dem gelben Wagen" was sung

by German soldiers marching into Poland. Beethoven concertos were played in concentration camps as preludes to mass murder. Even pre-Christian Nordic mythology was functionalized ideologically to sanction Nazi politics. Harmless technologies like the Reichsbahn's entire railway system were utilized in the logistics of systematic genocide. All of these aspects of German culture can no longer be used in a naïve way, although fifty-five years later the majority of Germans may claim "normality." The very language is implicated, as George Steiner observed as early as 1969 (*Sprache und Schweigen*, 69). There are terms incorporated from Yiddish into Modern German, and there are words that have become over-coded with Holocaust connotations, like *vergasen* (gassing) and even *abholen* (pick up), *Kleiderkammer* (clothes room) or *Verladerampe* (ramp). The commonly accepted (West-)German term for driver's license, *Führerschein* (literally "conductor's certificate") must ring peculiar to outsiders— the more considerate East German term *Fahrerlaubnis* has fallen by the wayside in the process of reunification.

3. Goethe, "To America."

4. The use of adequate ethnic terms presents a semantic minefield. In my usage, I follow Berkhofer (*White Man's Indian*) so as to differentiate each time between signifier and signified. For want of an appropriate translation, I use the same terminology in German, "*Indianer*" and "Native American" (see "*Indianer*" and "*Native Americans*"). I am fully aware that "Indian" is still or again used widely by persons of indigenous descent both in the United States and Canada, much the same as I would be comfortable with the generic term European. In an age of heightened multicultural ethnic awareness, European Americans often stress the fact that they, too, are native Americans, and they demand the use of their proper European national terms: Irish-American, Italian-American, and so on. While I sympathize with and respect this European-American desire for ethnic identification, I am aware of the historical irony that these demands are expressed in diasporic cultures at a time when in Europe national boundaries are being deconstructed and we might well witness a reshuffling of ethnic and regional identities independent of former national boundaries. Besides, I wonder where parallel demands by African-Americans, whose African national identities were deliberately destroyed during and immediately after the middle passage, would lead. While some reconstruction seems possible, it would probably leave the majority as "African Americans" without a more specific ethnic identifier. Similarly, Native American identities were deliberately destroyed by the ethnocidal practices of residential schools on either side of the forty-ninth. Moreover, in Canada the terms "Aboriginal," "Indigenous," and, in the case of Indians, "First Nations" are in use, alongside the more encompassing "Native," which seems to be made obsolete by governmental measures. The matter is more complicated when "Métis" are included under "Aboriginal" but not under "First Nations," which has been jealously guarded by some who were formerly grouped as "Indian." In the case

of the "Métis," those of Aboriginal and British descent feel uncomfortable with the French term and often prefer "mixed-blood" or "half-breed" (Adams, *Tortured People*; see also Adams, *Prison of Grass*; Campbell, *Halfbreed*; Jo-Ann Thom, personal communication). In view of these complex and conflicted semantic choices, I shall continue to use "Indian" for the image and any other more appropriate term for the real people. I do so in the hope of respecting the dignity and identity of individuals and groups. Any misuses are not intentional and should be attributed to ignorance, insensitivity, or a naïve European approach, not to disrespect or any malign motives on my part.

5. This feeling was forcefully expressed by one of my East German colleagues in 1991, when she presented a paper in West Germany in which she described the situation of Native Americans under the BIA and compared it to the situation of East Germans after reunification under the economic control of the Treuhand, the government trust agency in charge of the assets left by the socialist state. While I am far from denying the parallels in internal colonialism, her comparison sidesteps the issues of racism, the (absence) of military invasion, the enthusiastic reactions about the fall of the wall, and so on. What seems significant in our context, however, is the identification with Indians as the helpless and morally unblemished victims of historical processes supposedly beyond their control, guilt-free and at the mercy of the greed of the "others" (West Germans) on whom the blame is liberally bestowed.

6. See Münkler and Grünberger, "Nationale Identität."

7. See Dunk, "Antisemitismus," 65-91.

8. Dunk, "Antisemitismus," 70.

9. See Alter, Bärsch, Berghoff, *Konstruktion der Nation*, 7.

10. Thanks to Lawrence Buck and Andreas Mielke at Widener University, Chester, Penn., for alerting me to some of the semantic intricacies involved in using the term "romantic" and its derivatives, here, as referring to at least three semantic fields: (a) "Romanticism" (as Romantic Movement), (b) "romanticism" as an offshoot of a part of the Renaissance's concern with an ethnically defined German nation (e.g., Ulrich von Hutten's concern with the *Germania* and the Tuisco myth), and (c) "romantic" in the vernacular, everyday usage, akin to "romance" or "how romantic!"

11. Sollors, *Invention of Ethnicity*, xiii.

12. See also Berding, *Nationales Bewußtsein*.

13. Münkler and Grünberger, "Nationale Identität," 237-48.

14. Münkler and Grünberger, "Nationale Identität," 237-48.

15. Krapf, *Germanenmythus*, 19-20.

16. See Münkler and Grünberger, "Nationale Identität.

17. For the following, see See, *Barbar, Germane, Arier*, 31-60.

18. In 1987, after persistent individual searches with a metal detector, a British

officer, Tony Clunn, stationed in Osnabrück, Germany, found at Kalkriese, 15 miles northwest of that city, Roman coins dating no later than the year before the battle and stamped with the sign of Varus, the Roman commander who led the legions routed by Arminius and his men. Subsequent digs have established beyond doubt that Clunn has actually found part of the two-thousand-year-old battlefield, which extends for miles on a sandy stretch between the former swamps of the North German plains and the foothills of the middle range. Today, Kalkriese is the biggest and most exciting archeological dig in Germany (Schlüter, *Römer, Kalkriese;* Clunn, *Auf der Suche*).

19. Mosse, "Die Juden," 20.

20. The idea of being backstabbed and betrayed, either by traitors inside or by other overpowering forces from the outside, is a persistent theme in German ideologizing about failures and defeats in history: accordingly, the surrender of the German troops in World War I is interpreted as having been brought about, not by the enemy, but by backstabbing (communist) soldiers, sailors, and workers who rebelled at home in November 1918 (*Dolchstosslegende*). After liberation from their own Nazi government, many Germans cast themselves as the betrayed and helpless victims of the Führer's machinations. There are similar victim positions occupied by some East Germans after reunification, who feel backstabbed by their former government and betrayed by the new.

21. It seems undisputed that the old German(ic) gods Wotan and Donar are, indeed, identical with the Nordic gods Odin and Thor, but the identification of Germanic tribes of Roman times with Scandinavian Vikings a millennium later appears somewhat far-fetched.

22. Dunk, "Antisemitismus," 71–72.

23. Lund, *Germanenmythologie*.

24. Zantop, *Colonial Fantasies*, 1.

25. See also Lutz, *"Indianer" und "Native Americans*," 318–56.

26. Barnett (*Ignoble Savage*) coined the term "frontier romance" for American novels dealing with the "frontier" between 1790 and 1890, but I think it is justified to use the term here for Karl May, because his epigonal Western novels share generic and topological characteristics with the texts analyzed by Barnett: there is the high adventure aspect; the multiple captivity stories, focusing on the liberators rather than on the captors; and, as in Cooper, the most realistic parts of his romances are the extensive descriptions of often idealized landscapes. See also Sollors, *Invention*, xii–xiii; Zantop, *Colonial Fantasies;* and Friedrichsmeyer et al., *Imperialist Imagination*.

27. Sieg, "Ethnic Drag," 300.

28. See Kolodny, *Lay of the Land*.

29. On her trip to the East to learn the refined skills of a white lady, she is killed by the villain Santer and thus dies, like so many of her "dark sisters" in

film and fiction, before the novel can transgress the implicit rules of apartheid. For a reading of the Winnetou novels as gay literature, see A. Schmidt, *Sitara.*

30. Christadler, "Zwischen Gartenlaube."

31. Sollors, *Invention of Ethnicity,* xii–xiii.

32. For May's positions on colonialism and his instrumentalization for colonialist purposes, see Berman, "Orientalism, Imperialism."

33. Theweleit, *Männerphantasien,* 2:67.

34. Rieder, *Häuptling,* 7; my translation.

35. Speer, *Spandauer Tagebücher,* 259; my translation.

36. For the following, I am indebted to Haible, *Indianer,* 54.

37. See Lutz, *"Indianer" und "Native Americans,"* 345 and 378–79.

Nineteenth-Century German Representations of Indians from Experience

JEFFREY L. SAMMONS

Before commenting briefly on specific examples, I should like to venture a generalization. It seems to me that the attitude toward Indians of German writers experienced with and knowledgeable about America did not notably differ from the consensus of Americans themselves. That is, there may have been a sense of sympathy, sometimes of a tragic sensitivity to the Indian fate, along with feelings of impatience or hostility, but, however these were distributed, there was a shared conviction that nothing could be done, that the cause of the Indians was doomed, a verdict of history that no imaginable force could reverse. The pattern has been summed up in the formula of Roy Harvey Pearce: "Pity and censure would be, in the long run, the price of civilization over savagism."[1] Thus Friedrich Gerstäcker, about whom there will be more to say farther along, commented in the 1850s that all conflicts with the Indians were the fault of the Americans, but, he continued, "these are sad – and useless – observations. They are going the way of all savage peoples, some slowly, others more rapidly, but all ineluctably to their certain doom."[2] A few years earlier he had commented bitterly that the Indian dies as the world is being civilized, but "savage life must yield to culture, raw strength to the higher spirit, and the bones of the Indian, along with the forest that was once his home, fertilize the white man's field."[3] This feeling of inevitability is fairly universal in the materials with which I am acquainted; the passage I have just cited almost parallels one from an American travel book of 1843: "The Indians' bones must enrich the soil, before the plough of civilized man can open it."[4] One might associate the attitude in the German texts with nineteenth-century philosophies of history, but I think it was just a product of observation. American views have been summarized quite similarly: "Even humanitarians agreed that the passing of the aboriginal culture was fundamentally just. . . . But wherever the noble savage was remembered, his demise was regretted. . . . The justice accorded to the Indian was entirely poetic; the necessary destinies of the two opposing peoples had been made all too manifest."[5] This view had already begun to take shape in the eighteenth century.[6]

"Charles Sealsfield" was the assumed identity of Carl Postl, an escaped Moravian monk who first came to the southern United States in 1823 and, between 1829 and 1844, produced a remarkable series of novels of American life, most of them written in Switzerland. One of his several peculiarities is that he is the only European German-language writer of my acquaintance who placed himself firmly within an American partisan political context: the Jacksonian movement in its originary Southern and Southwestern configuration. This allegiance logically makes of Sealsfield's narrators and protagonists adherents of the Indian removal policy of Andrew Jackson, who, it has recently been remarked, "stands as one of the premier villains in American Indian history."[7] Sealsfield's first novel was an extended adaptation of the Indian captivity tale, written in a facsimile of English and published in Philadelphia as Tokeah; or the White Rose and in London as The Indian Chief; or Tokeah and the White Rose, both in 1829; the main action takes place just prior to Jackson's victory at the Battle of New Orleans in January 1815. The Indian chief Tokeah and the actual hero, a young Englishman, are to some degree reconciled toward the end, but Tokeah himself is killed in an attack by another tribe.

In 1833 Sealsfield rewrote the novel in German, considerably revising it, under the title of Der Legitime und die Republikaner (The legitimate one and the republicans). The interesting thing about the transposition into his native German is that the novel became more Jacksonian and therefore more American.[8] This is quite clear in the treatment of Tokeah, who has become less conciliatory and more diminished in heroic stature. He is both noble and savage, but now neither is a positive attribute. That he is denominated as "legitimate" parallels him to the obsolescent monarchical tyrants of contemporary Europe; the day of legitimacy is done.[9] Tokeah is castigated by other Indians, Creeks in Alabama, for persisting in futile war against the whites. Historically, these Alabama Indians, who appear in the novel to be in the right, were turncoats who had negotiated a land giveaway with Jackson and were subsequently driven out anyway.[10] Toward the end of the novel, Jackson himself lectures Tokeah with material Sealsfield has drawn from Jackson's "Second Annual Message" of December 1830 and his "Message on Indian Affairs" of February 1831: "The Great Spirit has made the earth for the white and red men, that they might plow and plant it and live from its fruits; but he did not make it for a hunting ground in order that a few hundred red men in their lazy existence might take over a space in which millions might live happily and thrive."[11]

Sealsfield is here replicating a Jacksonian public position in favor of agricultural settlement that modern historians regard as a hypocritical mask for a policy of removal.[12] The alleged author of a probably fictive letter prefacing the novel states that, while removal may be painful for the Indians, they must for their own welfare be separated from the evils of civilization.[13] This is an argument regularly met with at the time: "Humanitarians and officials sympathetic to the natives thought removal was the only solution in light of their worsening treatment by immigrants and by the states."[14] In any case, Indians rarely appear in the rest of Sealsfield's novels. It looks as though Jackson's policy of removal was effective on Sealsfield's own fictional space. However that may be, whenever one compares Sealsfield, who constantly insisted that he was an American writer, with the environmental discourse of antebellum America, his fidelity to it is virtually seamless, and so it is in the matter of nobility and savagery, as summarized by Pearce: "American experience and understanding had been directed towards destroying just such a conception [of the noble savage] and replacing it with the conception of a savage in whom nobility was one with ignobility. Certainly, as doomed noble savage the Indian could be pitied; and American literary men, sensitive to the feeling of their readers, cultivated such pity. But he also had to be properly censured, and his nobility to be denied or so qualified as to be shown not really to be nobility; and American literary men, insofar as they were to be American, could not avoid such censure, denial, and qualification."[15]

Balduin Möllhausen took off for America in 1849 or 1850; among his various experiences, a formative one was his abandonment, in the winter of 1851–1852, on a wintry plain in the Nebraska Territory, during which he was obliged to ambush and kill a pair of marauding Indians and subsequently was rescued and nursed by other Indians, evading an offer from them of two wives. This experience, which proved him competent, strong, and fortunate, radiated through his entire life. He took part in one expedition for nine months in 1853–1854 from Arkansas across the Southwest and the Rocky Mountains to Los Angeles to explore one of the possible routes of the transcontinental railroad and in another for eight months in 1857–1858 to determine the navigability of the Colorado River, making him one of the first explorers of the Grand Canyon; he published handsomely printed reports on both expeditions.[16] After returning to Germany, he wrote a series of Western novels for which the term "mediocre" would be a euphemism.

As a skilled outdoorsman, Möllhausen was a useful member of the expeditions, but his assigned role was that of illustrator. His drawings and watercolors, many of them of Indians, are preserved in numerous museums, including the Smithsonian.[17] Möllhausen has been given a good deal of credit for tolerance and for opposing American racial prejudice.[18] In truth, he was, on the whole, a tolerant and easy-going observer, in dramatic contrast to Sealsfield, but his mind and habits of perception were conspicuously conventional. Like his contemporaries, he distributed types of Indians along a scale of virtue. He best appreciated those who appeared to approach his own standards of civilization; thus he admired the Choctaws and Cherokees because they had adapted to agriculture and the Hopis and Zunis because their way of life appeared civic, but he represented the Plains Indians as primitive and savage.[19] He took over James Fenimore Cooper's plot-generating device of dividing Indians into good and evil tribes. Unreflectively he employed blood as a metonomy for race: in his first novel, The Halfbreed, the protagonist has two kinds of blood that get into confusion with one another. Sometimes he acts red when he should be white and vice versa; when bad Indians mount an assault, his "Indian blood boiled at the treacherous attack."[20] Möllhausen was basically a simple soul who was the least thoughtful or creative of my examples and therefore may be regarded as typical of a widespread dominant discourse.

More differentiated representations can be found in the writings of Friedrich Gerstäcker, who first came to America in 1837 and remained there for six years, spending much of his time as a backwoodsman in Arkansas. In 1849, during a three-year voyage around the world, he arrived at the California gold rush and remained for over a year; in 1867 he again spent several months in the United States on his way to Latin America. He did not bring with him much of an armature of cultural philosophy, and although, like anyone else, he had preestablished images and opinions drawn from reading, he soon became skeptical of them and devoted much of his writing, especially the large part of it directed toward prospective emigrants, to countering such notions. Altogether, he may have had more direct experience of Indians than any other German fiction writer.[21] As a backwoodsman he lived and hunted with them, and in 1867 he traveled by railroad with General Sherman to a meeting with Indian chiefs.[22] In consequence, his representations are quite various. He remarks that, when he first encountered Indians, they spoke better English than he did, and he tells of an Indian expertly resetting his dislocated shoulder.[23] In a variant of the captivity tale, "Civilisation und Wildniß" (Civilization and Wilderness), a white man raised as an Indian brave is reunited with his family but decides to return to his life with the tribe; this is a version of a pattern that may be recalled, for example, from Catherine Maria Sedgwick's Hope Leslie of 1827, where the captive sister of the heroine determines to remain with the tribe.[24] However, the motif may go back to the eighteenth century, when a boy captured by the Shawnees remained with the tribe and became a companion of Tecumseh for many years.[25] Gerstäcker's Indians can be subversive: in one of his stories, "Jazede," a slave revolt is aided by an Indian whose comic, ingratiating manner masks a rage against white oppressors.[26] In another, "Der Osage" (The Osage), the Indian cadges drinks by agreeing with the whites that he is a "damned rascal," then outwits them when they try to doctor his gun in a turkey shoot.[27]

Elsewhere there are more traditional scenes of Indian hostility, such as the story "In der Prärie" (In the prairie), which contains an episode of an Indian attack on a railroad train subsequently "intertextualized" by Karl May in *Winnetou III*.[28] But the hostility can run the other way. In a story that may have been drawn from a real event, "Die Rache des weißen Mannes" (The vengeance of the white man), a captured Indian is exposed to smallpox and returned to infect his whole tribe.[29] While it is not certain that such things occurred, the motif had been in circulation since the middle of the eighteenth century.[30] Scenes in Gerstäcker's novel *Gold!* (1858) of the denial of minimal justice to Indians in California appear to correspond with the historical record.[31] Sometimes he follows a conventional observation with a twist in a subordinate clause: he commented that the Indian men make their women do all the work and lie around waiting to be called to eat, adding, "just like in Germany."[32] He reproduced Indian songs and speeches, but these are likely to have come from published sources.[33]

In contrast to Möllhausen's enthusiasm for civilizing Indians, Gerstäcker personally seems to have preferred them in their native condition. The more they are in contact with whites, the more they are portrayed as alcoholic, disorderly, greedy, and parasitical, as many Americans at the time saw them.[34] The Plains Indians at Sherman's conference Gerstäcker depicts as dirty, treacherous, and manipulative.[35] He particularly found mixed Native and white Western dress incongruous when worn by Indians.[36] He reacted the same way to blacks: he made fun of them for dressing up in party finery or taking genteel names, including some that one might think understandable in the circumstances: "Washington, Jefferson, Franklin, Lincoln, Grant, Sherman."[37] He seems to have held an essentialist view of ethnic identity, perhaps an instinctive aversion to race mixing.

Gerstäcker consistently blames the degeneracy of the Indians on white aggression, removal, and destruction of culture. He recurrently rages against exploitative missionaries, a breed of men he regarded with passionate contempt, and became persuaded that federal Indian agents were corrupt.[38] He could rise to a high dudgeon about American hypocrisy:

Jeffrey L. Sammons

How often, how appallingly often have the Indians really been treated most contemptibly by people who knew nothing sacred in the world and openly stated that they would be as pleased to shoot an Indian as a wolf – and never has the law of the whites, despite all its fluttering flags of liberty, boastful orations, and eloquently named courthouses, offered them the least protection. And then they call these poor devils "murdering scoundrels" when, having been driven to despair and chased from their hunting grounds, robbed of every means of subsistence, the bleeding corpses of their kin before them, they for once exercise the right of retaliation and, according to their laws and with perfect justice before God, seek to kill individuals from among those who have brought death and destruction to their tribes.[39]

Nevertheless, as I indicated at the beginning of this discussion, Gerstäcker was persuaded that all this atrocity and grief was historically inevitable. The hunting grounds are being occupied, and, as for turning Indians into agriculturalists, he remarked that it was as though one of us were given a bow and arrow and told to make a living with it.[40] He was a realist in the most elementary meaning of the term, perhaps even a kind of naturalist in the Lukácsian sense. What he observed, or thought he observed, he replicated; what he could not see, he did not pretend to envision.

Karl May, of course, lies outside my category of authors who wrote of America out of direct experience. He drew his information from books, including those of Sealsfield, Möllhausen, and Gerstäcker.[41] I shall restrict myself to three comments about him. First, May reverses the movement of some of his predecessors away from the model of Cooper. This movement is quite evident in the revision of Sealsfield's first novel, with its diminishment of the stature of the Indian chief and in other features, such as the virtual disappearance out of the denouement of Rosa, the quondam heroine of the captivity tale; in time Sealsfield became quite hostile to Cooper.[42] Naturally Cooper was an early and influential reading experience for Gerstäcker, but once he got past his first couple of Westerns, in which there is an Indian chief who seems descended from Chingachgook or Uncas, he grew quite skeptical of Cooper's relevance and, as he became increasingly concerned about the occupation of German consciousness by misleading images, he more consistently if implicitly combated the seductively poeticized representations of Cooper and other writers. But May clearly reverts to Cooper in characterization, especially of his noble Indian Winnetou, and in plot devices.[43] Possibly this reversal of emancipation of the apprehending consciousness from the dominance of the imaginary reflects, unwittingly and on a subliterary level, an epochal movement of modernism away from realism and toward a texture of internally related fictional components.

Second, although May is sometimes credited with modeling interracial tolerance and respect by means of the partnerships in his exotic milieus, especially the bond between Old Shatterhand and Winnetou, a closer look will show that full equality with the other is not presumed. It is true that Germans and Indians together form a moral bulwark against the Yankees. In *Winnetou III*, Old Shatterhand tells the Comanches: "The warriors of the Germani are friends and brothers of the red men," and as late as *Ardistan and Djinnistan* it is proclaimed: "The present-day Yankee will disappear, so that a new man will form in his place, whose soul is Germanic-Indian."[44] But, in the first place, a consistent idealization of the Indian is impeded by the appropriation of Cooper's division of the Indians into good tribes, associated with the virtuous white protagonists, and bad tribes: May's Apaches and Kiowas correspond to Cooper's Delawares and "Mingos." Furthermore, Old Shatterhand is often a better Indian than the Indians themselves, applying superior skills of shooting, riding, surveying, trapping, scouting, and stalking that he has learned from German books at home, presumably May's own. A number of passages postulate the superiority of white men over Indians.[45] It has frequently been noted that Winnetou and other positively valued Indians have Caucasian features.[46] More importantly, it emerges that Old Shatterhand's Christian culture is superior to the natural religion of Winnetou, who is made to admit: "The faith of red men teaches hatred and death. The faith of the white men teaches love and life." He is converted to Christianity on his death bed to the accompaniment of an *Ave Maria*, composed, naturally, by Old Shatterhand himself.[47]

Third, and on the other hand, it is not altogether clear how relevant such ideological observations are to the amazing reception history of May's works. The critical reader will easily detect a deeply conservative discourse – nationalistic, monarchist, counterrevolutionary, anti-Socialist, sometimes obscurantist. But May's German spokesmen, who bear these values, do not seem to have captured the German imagination as much as his iconic Indian has. When the German president Roman Herzog was asked what film role he would have most liked to play, he replied without hesitation: "Winnetou."[48] A German obsession with Indians has been notorious for decades; the adventures of Old Shatterhand and Winnetou are reenacted in summer festivals, and adult Germans camp in tepees while wearing feathered headdresses, along with other manifestations of the madness of crowds. There seems to be a longing to act out an exotic, utopian identity, relieved of modern alienation and unburdened by the complicities of culture and civilization. Perhaps Germany's Indians have been entirely absorbed by fictionality, as Newtown suggests: "Indians are like fairies or genies; no one really believes in them any more."[49] But questions of this kind exceed my competence.

Notes

1. Pearce, *Savages*, 53.
2. Gerstäcker, *Reisen*, 2:317.
3. Gerstäcker, *Amerikanische Wald- und Strombilder*, 1:187.
4. Pearce, *Savages*, 65.
5. Newtown, "Images," 11.
6. See Pearce, *Savages*, 48-49.
7. P. M. Marks, *In a Barren Land*, 54.
8. For details see Sammons, *Ideology*, 23-36.
9. On Europeans' mistaken attribution of monarchy to Indians, see Newtown, "Images," 113-14.
10. Sellers, *Market Revolution*, 90; P. M. Marks, *In a Barren Land*, 76-78.
11. See Emmel, "Recht oder Unrecht," 80; Grünzweig, *Das demokratische Kanaan*, 160-62. Sealsfield, *Sämtliche Werke*, 7: pt. 3, 39-40; cf. Sammons, *Ideology*, 32-33.
12. Pessen, *Jacksonian America*, 296-98; Sellers, *Market Revolution*, 308-12; Ward, *Andrew Jackson*, 41.
13. Sealsfield, *Sämtliche Werke*, 6: pt. 1, 2-3.
14. Marks, *In a Barren Land*, 64; cf. 72.
15. Pearce, *Savages*, 169-70.
16. See Sammons, *Ideology*, 91-95.
17. For examples, see Hartmann, *George Catlin*; Wickham, "Oil and Water"; on the Colorado expedition and Möllhausen's art work, see Huseman, *Wild River*, with reproductions of forty-seven recently discovered watercolors, and Pyne, *How the Canyon Became Grand*, 35-55.
18. See, for example, Huseman, *Wild River*, 11, 43.
19. Regarding the Cherokees and Choctaws, see Möllhausen, *Diary*, 1:16-18. Regarding the Hopi and Zunis, see Möllhausen, *Reisen in die Felsengebirge*, 2:200. For attitudes toward the Plains Indians, see Möllhausen, *Halbindianer*, 3:29-31; *Mayordomo*, 1:12.
20. Möllhausen, *Halbindianer*, 1:57; 3:197.
21. See Di Maio, "Borders of Culture."
22. See Sammons, *Ideology*, 136-50.
23. Gerstäcker, *Streif- und Jagdzüge*, 1:156-57; 2:232-33.
24. Gerstäcker, *Aus zwei Welttheilen*, 2:229-98.
25. Sugden, *Tecumseh*, 34-35.

26. Gerstäcker, Aus zwei Welttheilen, 3:1–74.

27. Gerstäcker, Mississippi-Bilder, 1:177.

28. Gerstäcker, Kleine Erzählungen, 1:535–79; see May, Freiburger Erstausgaben, 9: 354–96.

29. Gerstäcker, Mississippi-Bilder, 3:165–208.

30. P. M. Marks, In a Barren Land, 24–25; see Utley, Indian Frontier, 51–52.

31. See P. M. Marks, In a Barren Land, 133–38; see Sammons, Ideology, 190.

32. Gerstäcker, Reisen, 2:334.

33. Newtown, "Images," 181–85.

34. Pearce, Savages, 59.

35. Gerstäcker, Neue Reisen, 1:156–57.

36. For example, Gerstäcker, Mississippi-Bilder, 3:364.

37. Gerstäcker, In Amerika, 1:111–14, 126, 205–6.

38. Gerstäcker, Neue Reisen, 1:200–1; for an example, see P. M. Marks, In a Barren Land, 75.

39. Gerstäcker, Reisen, 2:344–45.

40. Gerstäcker, Neue Reisen, 1:200.

41. See Lowsky, Karl May, 57–62.

42. Sealsfield, Sämtliche Werke, 10: pt. 1, 15.

43. See Rossbacher, Lederstrumpf, 52; Sammons, Ideology, 230–31.

44. May, Freiburger Erstausgaben, 9:237; 31:19.

45. See Sammons, Ideology, 238.

46. For example, Newtown, "Images," 210.

47. May, Freiburger Erstausgaben, 9:427–28, 473–74.

48. Augstein, "Weiter Weg," 130.

49. Newtown, "Images," 29.

Indians Playing, Indians Praying

Native Americans in Wild West Shows and Catholic Missions

KARL MARKUS KREIS

Show Indians in Germany — Mission Indians in America

On the eve of the First World War, in July 1914, the German Circus Sarrasani was touring Germany's industrial heartland, the Ruhr region. In its advertisements, "Sarrasanis Wild-West-Schau," as the circus was called at the time, promised to present episodes of America's Wild West "true to nature [and] authentic." The Indians in the show were advertised as people who were not actors but "were living in their reservation territories a life of wild and free nomads, unrestrained by any law except the law of blood vengeance!"[1] At the end of July, the leader of the group of Sioux Indians in the circus, Chief Edward Two-Two, suddenly died in the city of Essen. He has become famous in Germany mainly through his wish to be buried in Dresden (the circus's home town), where even today his grave is the destination of many a pilgrim. On the occasion of his death, the newspapers in Essen revealed some interesting details about his personality that contrasted sharply with his image as the leader of a band of bloodthirsty, vengeful savages: Two-Two's funeral ceremonies were celebrated in the circus by the local Catholic clergy because he and his family were members of that church. Two of his sons, in fact, worked as catechists ("missionaries," the papers called them) among the Indians.[2]

But this was not the end of the Indian stories in Essen. A few days later, when the war broke out, a short note appeared in a newspaper describing how one of Sarrasani's Indians had been harassed and beaten by a mob of "hundreds of people" who took him for a Russian spy. As the newspaper explained, "since he was not familiar with our ways he was of course thinking he was going to be lynched."[3] The rampant "spy hysteria" affected local citizens also, as the paper notes and deplores. After his return to the United States, the Indian, Edward Jacobs, told reporters that he had tried to induce the others in his group to "start home with me, but they refused because none of us had anything to show that we were Americans." So he left them in Essen,

Fig. 12. Chief Two-Two, with Hagenbeck's Show, Hamburg-Stellingen. Postcard, 1910.

but he was taken for a Russian spy again and was arrested three times before reaching Holland.[4] This report also reveals that the group to which Jacobs belonged, and who had performed as "Indians from the Land of the Prairie," were, in fact, Onondagas from central New York State. The mistreatment he and his fellows experienced was cited some years later when the Onondagas, following the U.S. government, declared war on the German Reich.[5] When the circus war paint of show Indians was wiped off, other identities became visible, and other stories were revealed.

Sarrasani's Wild West Show marks the peak in a development that had started decades earlier: the conquest of Germany – or at least of most of its show lots, many of its bookshelves, and lots of its young hearts – by American Indians. The information in the newspaper about Chief Two-Two's religious affiliation was a very rare instance in that it referred to two aspects of Indian life that normally were strictly separated in their presentation: the Indian playing in the Wild West show (the Show Indian, "Indian as Savage") and the Indian praying in the mission church (the Mission Indian, "Indian as Christian").

On both the Indians playing and the Indians praying, the sources written in German are particularly important for the period around 1890, when parallel encounters of Germans and Indians took place in Germany and America, all of which involved Lakotas from South Dakota. In 1886, German missionaries founded St. Francis Mission on the Rosebud Reservation. In 1888, a young Lakota from Pine Ridge, Black Elk, and a few companions who had come to England with Buffalo Bill's Wild West were touring Germany and other European countries after having missed the Wild West's boat for the trip home; in that same year, German-speaking missionaries were establishing the Holy Rosary Mission at Pine Ridge. Two years later, in early December of 1890, at the height of the ghost dance "troubles," one of the Jesuits from this mission tried to mediate between the Lakotas and the U.S. Army, meeting with Kicking Bear and Short Bull, the two ghost-dance leaders who would tour Germany with Buffalo Bill's Wild West only a few months later.

The primary purpose of this paper is to offer a first look at reports published in Germany on those encounters, sources that so far have not been explored systematically. I will briefly sketch the images of Indians that they presented to their readers and that at first glance strongly resemble the familiar images: Indians are most often described as culturally "other," exotic people whose "inferior" civilization is doomed to give way to the "superior" white and Christian civilization, either by force, as demonstrated in Wild West show fights between representatives of "savagery" and "civilization," or through education and conversion, as the missionaries understood their labors among the "heathen Indians." However, a closer look at these sources reveals inconsistencies in the stereotypical depiction of "savages" and "pagans." The most significant of these inconsistencies is that under certain circumstances show Indians are seen by the German audience as dignified human beings, and the Mission Indians regarded as having similar spiritual pleasures and political problems as German Catholics. Thus, the Indian stereotype is ambiguous in both its versions: it possesses a countercurrent that makes the exotic "Others" sometimes surprisingly close to "us" and even offers ways of identifying with them, by "playing Indian" and by "praying with the Indians." As I will show, both ways of identifying with Native Americans are still prevalent today.

Indians in Buffalo Bill's Wild West Show

American writers have described Wild West shows touring Europe without engaging in an in-depth analysis of their impact on the popular imagination.[6] For German-speaking countries this subject matter has been addressed mainly by focusing on the image of "the Indian," on specific Native American groups in the show business industry, on German traveling show firms, or, as an exotic subject of local history, on Buffalo Bill's performances in various cities.[7] A comprehensive study of the influence of Buffalo Bill's Wild West Show and other early shows on popular perceptions in Germany of Indians and of America in general is still lacking. This is particularly unfortunate since discussions of the image of "the Indian" among Germans too often center around Karl May and other literary sources, neglecting the influence of the various shows, not only on their mass audience, but also on Karl May himself.[8] For my own research I used Bill Cody's scrapbooks at the Buffalo Bill Historical Center, which contain hundreds of clippings from German papers from the 1890-1891 tour, plus the newspaper archives of my home city of Dortmund. I concentrated on three German cities that seemed to be most relevant: Berlin (the German capital), Leipzig (a major trade center), and Dresden (where Karl May saw these shows).

The Indians: Terrifying in the Show, Well-Mannered Outside

Almost every newspaper gave a detailed description of the show's program, which was essentially the same as in the United States. The following quotation gives an idea of the tone of these reports and the impressions of the performers that they were trying to convey: "Howling, swinging their lances, the Indians in full martial attire . . . and the cowboys came dashing forward, thus greeting the audience in a truly backwoodsman-like manner. Horses and horsemen seem to be grown together, men and animals alike are exhibiting muscular strength and endurance. . . . In a sudden surge and wild race the flocks of Indians appeared, the cowboys dashed in to help the attacked, and with savage howling and cracking guns and rifles the fighting develops – scenes that are extremely graphic and true to life."[9]

The account contains some of the elements that are common to all reports on the Wild West: first of all, it stresses the Indians' closeness to nature (in the double meaning of the German word "wild"), symbolized by their affinity with their animals, the horses. Often, this particular wildness is shared with the cowboys who appear together with the Indians and are perceived as equally superb horsemen. However, what makes the Indians "really" savage are the attributes and actions that distinguish them from the "white savages." Their bodies are described as (almost) naked, their clothing coming "only from the paint box."[10] In fact, the Indians' body paint is depicted as being as impressive and frightening as their war cries and howls. The dances and songs are described as grotesque and often in condescending terms, and are again compared to animal sounds and movements: "green-clad dancers hopped in froglike movements."[11] In short: "The wild war attire of the Indians, their long hair decorated with feathers, their lances adorned with trophies, create a truly terrifying impression."[12] The visits to the Indian camp that were regularly offered to journalists during the first days of a stay normally did not modify this general picture. Nor did the regular reference to Indian novels, notably James Fenimore Cooper's, cause any substantial diversion from this simplistic imagery.

The Indians were certainly a major part, probably the central part, of the program. But one also must also take into consideration the setting that Buffalo Bill's Wild West Show presented, which was different from that of his predecessors (e.g., Doc Carver's "Wild America"). As impressive, indeed sometimes more impressive than the Indians and the cowboys, were the markswomen in the show, above all "Little Sure Shot" Annie Oakley. For German reporters, another new (or "modern") feature of the show was the demonstration of modern weaponry and the show effects that accompanied them. Reporters were also impressed by the perfect organization involved in transporting hundreds of people with animals and equipment, building and taking down with amazing speed the show lot with seats for several thousands and an Indian camp, and setting up a restaurant. Equally impressive was the breathtaking live action, which was attributed to Cody's genius. All this, plus the advertisement that accompanied the tour, made the Wild West appear "typically American," and Cody himself, the center of the program and the enterprise, the typical American hero. Cody's show presented "the West as America," but in the European sense of America as Europe's utopia, a continent to which, at that time, thousands of Germans emigrated every year. The feelings that the show evoked were not patriotic as in the United States but were another variant of European or German longings and projections.[13] Therefore, the Indians in the show were perceived, not as representing a present threat (heroes like Bill Cody had contained the threat), but as an integral part of a tableau showing an exotic, faraway world populated by human beings who represented various degrees of savagery and civilization, with the Indians at one extreme and Buffalo Bill at the other.

However, informal encounters between Indians and – literally – people in the streets offered windows in this tableau that allowed the public to look behind the staged scenery and get a glimpse of the "real people." These staged encounters took place wherever ordinary people went for sightseeing, shopping, entertaining. The best-known picture from such events shows Indians in Venice in a gondola, but they also attended Ronacher's vaudeville theater in Vienna, and in Leipzig they went shopping and bought blankets "thereby developing a strikingly good taste by refusing glaring red and colored designs. They did not speak French nor English but by using signs they could make themselves understood very well.... Their behavior was dignified and firm."[14] One shop owner wrote to the newspaper: "All the manners of these people are exceedingly unpretentious and in any case it is extraordinarily instructive to encounter them face to face."[15] In Dortmund, Cody sent the Indians on what the papers called a "beer trip" on the street that connected the show lot with the city center: "The public thought at first they were on the war path. They were, however, not thirsting for blood, but for beer. In other words: they were on the 'beer' path. Prosit!"[16] None of the newspapers mentioned any problems with alcohol.

Even Cody himself, in several interviews, tried to correct the stereotypical image of the savage Indians that his own program suggested: "In my opinion the Indian character is the most amiable and respectable in the world. . . . I never saw an Indian hit or scold his child. . . . [The Indians] have been betrayed. They are the original Americans, the land belonged to them." These statements made the interviewer wonder at Cody's enthusiasm for the virtues of the Indians, which Cody emphatically affirmed: "Indians never lie, never swear."[17] It is unlikely that these statements reached all the people who were so enthralled by what they saw in the show, but they raise the question to what extent the staged images were taken seriously, not just by Cody, but also by the audience and the actors, who knew best what this all was about.

The Show's Legacy: Playing Indian, with Feathers and War Whoops

As elsewhere, the visual image of the Indian was shaped by Buffalo Bill's Sioux. The war-bonnet stereotype was omnipresent, as illustrated by this story: In 1910 the Onondaga Reservation Brass Band toured Germany and Central Europe under the heading "WORLD TOUR of the Only Authentic North American Indian Concert Band in the World." Their tour was a failure, although they seem to have tried to compensate for their "un-Indian" music by presenting themselves in gorgeous war bonnets that demonstrated their Indianness. Some time later, one of the band's members is reported to have shown to his audience near Onondaga "a beautiful head dress made of eagle feathers that he succeeded in obtaining in Europe."[18] It seemed that Native Americans had to go to Germany if they were to become real Indians.

As in the United States, one immediate effect of Buffalo Bill's Wild West performances was that children imitated in their play what they had seen at the show. In Berlin, boys improvised a camp of Indians and cowboys that a reporter called " 'Wild-West' on a reduced scale," and in Leipzig and Vienna similar activities caused the parents concern.[19] Previous shows had had the same effect, even though the troupes had been much smaller, for instance, the group of Indians in the Dresden Zoo in 1879.[20] Although "Leatherstockings," according to newspaper reports, were also part of children's play, the

WELT-REISE der einzigen echten Nord-Amerikanischen Indianer-Konzert-Kapelle in der Welt. Manager: CARL WAHLER. Dirigent: D. RUSSELL HILL, Häuptling der Onondagas

Fig. 13. "World Tour of the only authentic North American Indian Concert Orchestra." German postcard, 1910

Wild West show stimulated "playing cowboy and Indian" by performing it in live action right in front of their eyes. The experience of seeing "real Indians" fighting must have had a tremendous impact on the imagination of children and adolescents. The stereotypical structure of the program and the simple roles and actions of the participants made it easy for children to integrate into their play what they saw, and to combine it with elements from other sources, such as the torture stake. Other imitations quickly followed: When Buffalo Bill returned to Germany in 1906, German circuses had already integrated the Wild West into their performances. In the case of Sarrasani, a quarter century later, the image and program of the Wild West show was thus firmly established. In Munich in 1913, adults (who might well have been among the children playing Indians and cowboys during the first tour of Buffalo Bill's Wild West Show in 1890-1891) founded the first known "Cowboy Club," which soon after World War I was followed by others in Germany, as well as throughout Europe.[21] Among the first films produced in Germany at that period were Westerns with cowboys and Indians.[22] All these imitations and reproductions in circuses, shows, and films reinforced existing patterns and images that had been presented by Buffalo Bill's Wild West Show. During his first tour in Germany, Cody had already peddled other genres, such as a booklet with drawings of the show by Carl Henckel. During the second tour, picture postcards were a mass souvenir, and dime novels about Buffalo Bill's adventures sold in large numbers. Others developed this multimedia com-

Fig. 14. "Life in the Prairies." German Circus Corty Althoff postcard, 1898

modification further: Hagenbeck, for example, sold artifacts made by show Indians and displayed "ethnological" objects for sale.

The main effect of Buffalo Bill's Wild West Show and all the shows that imitated his schema was to make Indians, like cowboys, a role one could play and which was fun to play. It was easy: just get some feathers, a surrogate horse, bow and arrows, some blankets or whatever to make a tepee, decide whether you want to be a cowboy or an Indian, and start with your imagination from what you saw others play at the show or on the screen. The shows, their live action, simple plot, and utopian setting all contributed to their attractiveness to children, adolescents, and many adults, by making the Indian someone or something you can play. This stereotype quickly became part of an emerging entertainment industry that reinforced it in many ways and made it suitable for mass consumption.

Further proof of the success of the show Indian image can be found in Germany's quintessential *Indianer*, the one created by Karl May. It is intriguing to see how Karl May reacted to and was influenced by the Wild West shows. On the one hand, his success as an author was undoubtedly partly caused by their popularity: the Winnetou volumes were published in 1893, shortly after Buffalo Bill had toured Germany for the first time. On the other hand, every comment May made about Buffalo Bill was negative, and he accused the Indians in the shows of being traitors to their people. The image of his ideal Indian, Winnetou, differed – at least in his head gear – from the Plains Indians of Buffalo Bill's Wild West Show. As Jeffrey Sammons pointed out,

Fig. 15. Klara May and Patty Frank with Indians and cowboys from the Sarrasani Circus in front of Karl May's log cabin. Radebeul postcard, 1928.

May's Indians were the ones he knew from books, not the real persons in the shows; his clichés were not "American" but "German."[23] Indeed, reading Karl May, one is reminded of the simple structure of the German fairy tale with its clear distinctions between good and evil, the "good" hero often being viewed a weakling by his enemies but turning out to be invincible, and always being saved in the end. But the main reason for May's hatred of Cody and his show may well have been rivalry: by embodying what Old Shatterhand pretended to be, Buffalo Bill Cody challenged May more than any other popular figure, even more so since both were blending fact and fiction in their creations.[24] Nonetheless, May's legacy in Radebeul was preserved and cultivated by an ex-member of Buffalo Bill's troupe, Patty Frank (alias Ernst Tobis), and he and May's widow, Klara, kept close contact with Sarrasani's Indians in Dresden, for instance, in many joint public relations actions staged by the circus and the Karl-May-Museum.[25] It comes as no surprise that the popularity of May's figures today among young people owes more to their adaptations in the show tradition, that is, in films and in reenactments, than to his books.

Indians in the Jesuit Missions of South Dakota

Let us now turn to those reports in German periodicals that conveyed a picture of Native Americans that was strikingly different from the one presented in the developing show business: well-mannered Indians praying and singing in mission churches.

Karl Markus Kreis

In 1886, German Jesuits founded St. Francis Mission on the Rosebud Reservation and, in 1888, Holy Rosary Mission on the Pine Ridge Reservation. From the beginning, they were assisted in their work by Franciscan nuns who also came from a German background, either, like the priests, from German-speaking countries in Europe or from the German Catholic community of Buffalo, New York. This city belonged to the German province of the Jesuits and served as their American base for the next twenty years. The priests and nuns sent reports to Germany, some of which were published by the Jesuit monthly Die katholischen Missionen. These and other missionary reports written in German are important sources for the early history of the missions and therefore are increasingly used by German-speaking scholars, but they seem not to have been accessible to American historians.[26] A compilation of the reports in Die katholischen Missionen for the years 1886-1900, together with reports originally published for internal use by the Franciscan nuns, is now available.[27]

"Our Indians": Harmless, Friendly, and Oppressed by Protestants

A report on the bishop's reception at the Third Catholic Sioux Congress held at St. Francis in 1893 describes how the ceremony finished with a powerful song "intoned by several hundred Dakotas ... a kind of battle song, reminiscent of a storm in autumn. Yes, deep down the old, savage Indian nature still burrows. . . . This is how the Teutons must have been singing when Tacitus heard them for the first time." By the end of the congress, the report says, "a formerly wild horde of Indians has become a troop of fighters for Christ" who are manifesting their enthusiasm, "supported by the sound of trumpets and trombones, [singing] 'Großer Gott wir loben dich.'"[28] This song, "Holy Lord, we praise Thy name," was and is very popular among German Catholics and usually marks the culmination and finale of their most festive ceremonies. These "fighters for Christ," a missionary wrote on the occasion of the First Catholic Sioux Congress held at Standing Rock in 1891, liked to sing hymns, not only "in the Sioux language," but also in Latin.[29] According to a report from Holy Rosary, this enthusiasm for singing was not surprising; as the writer asked rhetorically, "Who would not like the heartfelt melodies of our German hymns?"[30]

The image of the Indian underlying the work and the paternalistic attitude of the priests and nuns presupposed a fundamental equality between the white missionary and the heathen savage as human beings, since the latter had the ability and the opportunity to accept Christian religion and thereby be "saved." In practice, the missionaries perceived and described the stages of this process of change in terms of their specific Catholic culture and the general white American culture, thus making the process of "Christianizing" the Indians largely identical with that of "civilizing" them. When the nuns saw the Indians for the first time, they were most impressed, not unlike the visitors to the Wild West shows, by their strange ways of painting their faces and doing their hair: They "hardly could refrain from laughing" when they saw a chief's strange hairdo.[31] On another occasion one describes the Indians' face paint as so shiny that "you think you are looking into the setting sun when such a face suddenly appears at the door."[32] The image developed of strange, exotic people could nevertheless change, and they could become like whites by becoming Christians. Special attention was given to the children at school: A few of their skills, such as riding on horseback, were admired, but every effort was made to draw them away from their heathen habits. The transformation of the children was carried out by washing and clothing them and by cutting their hair and braids. The report from the Third Catholic Sioux Congress at St. Francis, quoted above, made extensive reference to the new appearance of the adults: the women wore light blue scarves and head shawls, the men red embroidered scarves and hats with a red feather, "Dakota dress was not tolerated." Cutting one's hair "means breaking with savagery, but is a hard sacrifice for the Dakota."[33] According to an early report by a nun, Catholic adornment was also welcome, albeit for different reasons by the missionaries and the children. The sister claimed that the children are made "quite happy" when given rosaries, "the longer the better, which even the older ones keep wearing around their necks, and medals with colored ribbons," and, "with rings and beads." She also referred to the learning of Catholic rituals: "It is quite moving to see how the seventeen- to eighteen-year-old boys are making efforts to learn the sign of the cross and to say the 'Our Father' and the 'Hail Mary.'"[34] Their trouble learning how to kneel — supervised by an Indian policeman — was described in detail and made the sister smile.[35]

The reports described "our Indians" as "a harmless, friendly (little) people" ("ein harmloses, freundliches Völkchen") who "have a very compassionate heart and who share with each other what food they get without being asked."[36] The Indians are never described as frightening, except during the fight at Holy Rosary Mission after the Wounded Knee massacre, and even then, the missionaries soon discovered, the Indians never intended to harm them.[37] The "little savages" are characterized as causing "on the whole, less trouble than some white children; their main faults are laziness, mendaciousness, and a ravenous hunger. . . . In spite of all the difficulties, in this short time we had mainly comfort and joy with our wild pupils, and we are truly feeling homesick for them as we wait for school to start again."[38] Indian children were described as peaceful, obedient, good-tempered, not spoiled: "Our children don't cause one tenth of the trouble white children make in European schools."[39] Their greatest vice, according to the missionaries, was their alleged inability and/or unwillingness to work, usually meaning work as farmers. This complaint was voiced again and again, however, with varying emphasis. The longer the missionaries were involved with the Indians and knew their situation on the reservations, the more they cited political reasons for their inability to work as farmers, for instance, that nobody taught them, that they were given the wrong equipment, that the soil was unsuitable for farming, that they had been betrayed too often by white agents to cooperate with them, and so on.

In short, the Indians are described as victims of government policy and of corrupt Indian agents. The missionaries in their reports even provided understanding, if not sympathetic views of the ghost dancers and the hostile Indians, blaming Washington for their plight and, like Father Jutz, trying to mediate between the Army and the hostiles.[40] The only Indians definitely excluded were the medicine men, the missionaries' spiritual rivals. Especially in matters involving their schools, the missionaries took sides with the Indians or with what they perceived to be the Indians' best interest, for example, in the joint resolutions of the Catholic Sioux congresses. These resolutions protested cuts in subsidies or denounced the general Indian policy as made by Protestants against the interests of Indians, and against those of Catholic Indians in particular. "Protestant politicians" in Washington and their allies on the reservations were said to be the main enemies of the Indians.[41] The ghost dance, which Father Jutz witnessed several times, was interpreted to be the result of Mormon influence on the Indians in Utah.[42] Repeatedly, Red Cloud and Spotted Tail, who had called in the Jesuits, and, according to Bishop M. Marty, even Sitting Bull were claimed as friends of the "blackrobes," thus implying that they appreciated the Catholic priests as their true allies.[43]

Occasionally the missionaries also voiced their opinion on Wild West shows. One report deplored the hesitation of some Indians to have their braids cut off and named the shows and their "follies" as the reason why the Indians wanted to keep their long hair.[44] Another report referred explicitly to Buffalo Bill in Europe and lamented that the shows were presenting a false image to the German public.[45] However, the German editors of Die katholischen Missionen could not always refrain from also delivering some of the imports of the

Wild West shows, thus implicitly acknowledging their popularity. In addition to pictures showing the "successes" of missionary work – schoolchildren in uniforms looking sad or bored, with nuns and priests looking severe and pious – are illustrations displaying a more romantic, even "wild" scenery: a tepee camp, Indians attacking a stagecoach, and a long-haired Sioux chief. So, similar to the windows in the tableaux of the Wild West show, there is a window in the missionary church to the "wild" world outside.

The Jesuit Tradition: Heroic Missionaries, Catholic Solidarity

The journal Die katholischen Missionen was published monthly for the Verein der Glaubensverbreitung, the German branch of the missionary organization of the Catholic Church. It aimed at "educated readers," and although the published statistics do not include membership figures, those given for funds raised by the various missionary organizations show the Verein der Glaubensverbreitung in a leading position.[46] Through their influence on priests and teachers, Die katholischen Missionen could also claim, with some justification, to be a leading intellectual force in shaping the missionary ideas and ideals of German Catholics.[47] Each issue contained articles of varying length on Catholic missions in every part of the world, and on activities (fund-raising, etc.) in German-speaking countries. The publishing house was Herder in Freiburg im Breisgau, which also had a branch in the United States. Reports on the Sioux missions appeared several times a year, plus long articles, sometimes stretching over several issues, on topics such as the causes for the "Indian troubles," the Catholic Sioux congress at St. Francis, missionary work, and the history of the Sioux missions.[48]

These reports and the images they promoted also left their traces, though they are not as ubiquitous as those of Buffalo Bill's Wild West Show. Die katholischen Missionen regularly had a supplement with stories for young readers, which covered the same range of themes as the journal itself. Some of them were published separately by Herder throughout the next decades: a list from 1926 contains thirty-one titles in the series "Aus fernen Landen" (From distant lands), three of which refer explicitly to the North American missions.[49] A survey taken in the early 1930s reveals that this series was the most popular reading among ten- to fourteen-year-olds; at that time the series had grown to forty volumes and more than a million printed copies.[50] Given the structure of German Catholicism with its libraries in parishes, associations, and so on, this is not a small readership. During these years, Franz X. Weiser, an Austrian-born Jesuit and – up to the 1950s – very popular author, began writing mission novels for young readers, at least six of which, in one way or another, refer to Jesuit missionary heroes such as F. Brébeuf and F. de Smet and Indian converts such as Kateri Tekakwitha; two of them (*Der Sohn des Weißen Häuptlings* (The son of the white chief) and *Das Mädchen der Mohawks* (The Mohawk girl) are still in print today.[51]

Putting the missionary (and the convert) in the center is a trait that missionary novels by and about the Jesuits share with the huge bulk of books by other missionary organizations. But there are also some specific characteristics, particularly for missionaries among the Sioux, that structured German readers' perceptions: The missionaries were, first of all, Jesuits; this meant their missionary efforts had a long tradition that predated and therefore was not flatly identical with European imperialism and colonialism. Second, they were Germans or from German-speaking countries, a fact that the reports liked to stress every so often and in two different respects. One was cultural, as the references to German hymns have shown: they were designed to inspire the readers' sympathy for the Indians singing the same melodies as German Catholics. The other was political and was also made explicit whenever the Jesuits complained about government harassment as "a Kulturkampf": the readers could draw parallels to the political situation of Catholics in the Bismarck Reich Kulturkampf, and also to the countermeasures of German Catholicism, that is, rallying the faithful in big gatherings to create mutual trust and strength.[52] In fact, these congresses, called *Katholikentage*, were cited as a model for the Catholic Sioux congresses.[53] In short, the missionaries – intentionally or not – used a channel of reception that was based on the idea that German Catholics and Sioux Catholics shared not only the same belief but also the same threat of oppression by their respective protestant governments. Unlike the show Indian image, this reception to some degree seems to have contributed to a generally critical attitude toward American politics, that is, the politics of the federal government in Washington, that can be found among Germans since the nineteenth century and that has often been labeled "anti-Americanism."

Indians Playing, Indians Praying – Who Is Paying?

Summarizing the results of our brief look at two seemingly very different sources of the image of the Indian in German media a hundred years ago, it can be said that "the Indian playing in the show lot" and "the Indian praying in the mission church" are, roughly speaking, two sides of the same coin. This may come as a surprise, but only if we take for granted the strict separation of the two versions of the Indian image in the mass media. When we consider the whole picture that is conveyed in each version of this image, we find more or less hidden cross references. Naturally so, because the people who play and pray most often are the same individuals, as we have seen in the example of Chief Two-Two.[54]

Yet despite implicit cross references, a distinction remains between the two images of Indians in Germany. The prevalent one is that of entertainment in the show tradition. The fun of "playing Indian" continues to dominate many segments of popular culture's Indian lore, not only in the "Indianerclubs," which offer opportunities for "living like Indians" on weekends, but also in the Karl May reenactments and festivals, which attract hundreds of thousands of visitors every year. The industry that uses and exploits this popular fun is powerful, reaching from public and private TV stations to theme parks to toy manufacturers. Sharing and following these popular attractions are the numerous pedagogical "Indian" projects in kindergartens and summer camps that try to attract children by offering opportunities to "play Indian" and that also use the traditional, in the show's sense, elements, sometimes with some well-intentioned environmentalist concerns.

But what about the paternalistic solidarity promoted by the missionaries? I dare say that if you take away the Catholic element you can find many, if not all, of its ingredients in those people and media that proclaim some kind of abstract, pseudopolitical solidarity with "the Indians." I explicitly exclude those who have personal and long-standing direct contact (and mutual learning experiences) with Native Americans and are involved in practical or political cooperation. But the more widespread attitude that distances itself emphatically from all show aspects of the Indian image mentioned above and pretends to be political (or politically correct) very often reminds one of the missionary context and the image it produced. Indians are viewed as "good," simple, peaceful, close to nature, "like us" or rather "like we ought to be," and therefore we know what is good for them (e.g., being environmentalists and/or being radical) and bad (alcohol, casinos). Anything negative in the lives of the Indians is, in this view, owing to the bad politicians in Washington, the Indian agents, or American capitalism/imperialism, thus reinforcing the so-called anti-American attitude. One can find this image in many of the educational materials using "serious" Indian themes for teaching history or social science in German schools. But religious references are also made, particularly in the popular literature for the spiritual edification of readers (often adorned with photographs by Edward S. Curtis) that jams the shelves of the "Indian corners" of our bookstores – not to speak of the posters showing those same or similar photographs with "An Indian Prayer," "Ten Indian Commandments," or some "Indian wisdom" added. The drawbacks of this idolization are obvious: While the groups and individuals who espouse this kind of imagery would reject the show Indian stereotype as unpolitical and exploitative, they, too, often follow their own kind of (anti)stereotype, using elements taken from the show imagery for defining a "real Indian": long hair, warrior mystique, and, above all, closeness to nature. Thus, they share the image of the Indian as the romanticized "Other." This view often leads to disappointment and misunderstandings when German "friends of the Indians" meet Native Americans for the first time: only then do they realize that they, too, were trapped in preconceived images. The reason for the dominance of these preconceived notions is their omnipresence in the popular mass culture I have described. Hardly anyone can escape the image of Indians fashioned to the needs of the entertainment industry, which makes a profit from the peddling of these images.

So, if we explore the meaning of Indians playing or Indians praying, we may well look at who is paying and at what price: The consumers of mass culture, including those who try to escape it, are lured into buying images that seem to become ever more simple and stereotypical—the price they are paying is self-delusion. The Native Americans who are identified with those images by their audiences have to choose whether to give in to popular expectations or to try to destroy those very images. This latter choice would imply an uphill battle against the overwhelming power of the entertainment industry.

Notes

Thanks to Christian Feest, Diane Krumrey, and my wife, Josi, for their helpful comments.

Newspaper clippings were obtained from the following repositories: Buffalo Bill Historical Center, Cody, Wyo.; Onondaga Historical Association, Syracuse, N.Y.; Stadtarchiv, Essen; Institut für Zeitungsforschung, Dortmund; *Die katholischen Missionen*: Institut für Missionswissenschaft, Universität Münster.

1. *Essener General-Anzeiger*, 24 July 1914; all translations are mine.
2. *Essener Volks-Zeitung*, 29 July 1914.
3. *Arbeiter-Zeitung* (Essen), 4 August 1914.
4. *The Syracuse (New York) Post Standard*, 2 September 1914.
5. *The Syracuse (New York) Post Standard*, 3 August 1918.
6. Most recently Moses, *Wild West Shows*; Reddin, *Wild West Shows*.
7. On the image of "the Indian," see Lutz, "*Indianer.*" On specific Native Ameri-

can groups in shows, see Feest, *Indians and Europe* and "Buffalo Bill"; Lindner, "Bull and Bill." On Sarrasani, see Günther, *Sarrasani*; on Hagenbeck, see Thode-Arora, *Für fünfzig Pfennig.* On Buffalo Bill's shows, see Spiegel, *"Buffalo Bill"*; Conrad, "Mutual Fascination"; Riegler, " 'Tame Europeans' "; Hoffmann, "Circensische Völkerschauen"; Kreis, *Die wilden Indianer;* Homann, "Ein paar Mokassins"; Juen, "Buffalo Bills Wild West Show."

8. An exception is Hoffmann, "Circensische Völkerschauen."

9. *Nachrichten* (Leipzig), 18 June 1890.

10. *Das kleine Journal* (Berlin), 24 July 1890.

11. *Die Post* (Berlin), 25 July 1890.

12. *General Anzeiger* (Leipzig), 18 June 1890.

13. Bieder, "Marketing."

14. On the Vienna experiences, see Riegler, " 'Tame Europeans' "; Juen, "Buffalo Bills Wild West Show." On the Leipzig excursion, see *Stadt und Dorf-Anzeiger* (Leipzig), 22 June 1890.

15. *Tageblatt und Anzeiger* (Leipzig), 19 June 1890.

16. *General-Anzeiger* (Dortmund), 16 May 1891.

17. *Die katholischen Missionen,* abbreviated hereinafter as KM.

18. *Marcellus (New York) Observer,* 27 August 1915.

19. *Das kleine Journal* (Berlin), 9 August 1890; *Nachrichten* (Leipzig), 22 June 1890.

20. Hoffmann, "Circensische Völkerschauen," 70–71.

21. Boger, *Western-Hobby,* 25.

22. Göktürk, *Künstler,* 174–99.

23. Sammons, *Ideology,* 246–56.

24. Lutz, "Indianer," 360.

25. Seifert, *Patty Frank.*

26. For German scholarship, see Feest, "Buffalo Bill"; Mohr, "Unmögliche Mission?" For American historical scholarship, see Peterson, "Challenging"; A. G. Green, "German Missionary Participation"; Enochs, *Jesuit Mission;* Galler, "History"; Thiel, "Catholic Sodalities"; Vecsey, *Where the Two Roads Meet.*

27. See Kreis, *Rothäute.*

28. KM 1893, 226, 230.

29. KM 1892, 17–18.

30. KM 1894, 118.

31. KM 1886, 199.

32. KM 1887, 22.

33. KM 1893, 226.

34. KM 1887, 66–67.

35. KM 1887, 22.

36. KM 1887, 66; KM 1887, 22.

37. KM 1891, 189–91.

Karl Markus Kreis

38. KM 1887, 66–67.

39. KM 1888, 258.

40. KM 1891, 186–89.

41. For Example, KM 1897, 115–17; KM 1900/1901, 207–10; see Feest, *Beseelte Welten*, 188.

42. KM 1891, 158–59.

43. KM 1891, 65.

44. KM 1897/1898, 92.

45. KM 1900/1901, 207.

46. Arens, *Handbuch*, 323. In size of membership, the Verein der Glaubensverbreitung was second only to the Kindheit-Jesu-Verein in 1899/1900: KM 1900/1901, 166.

47. Arens, *Jesuitenorden*, 67.

48. KM 1891, 157–59, 186–91; KM 1893, 225–30; KM 1895, 49–55; KM 1897/1898, 150–54, 177–80, 199–203, 220–23.

49. Baumgartner, *Drei Indianergeschichten*, appendix.

50. Arens, *Jesuitenorden*, 70–71.

51. Arens, *Jesuitenorden*, 72.

52. KM 1896, 259.

53. KM 1892, 16.

54. The question of how these individuals perceived their roles in shows and churches is a different subject. Most recent books on Wild West shows and on Catholic missions discuss it broadly (in the wording of this paper's title, omitting the comma: Are they playing when praying? Or vice versa?) See Moses, *Wild West Shows*; Vecsey, *Where the Two Roads Meet*.

Germans Playing Indian

MARTA CARLSON

"German?" he asked in surprise, and suddenly began talking that language. "As a fellow countryman, let me bid you welcome. That must have been the reason I immediately was attracted to you. – A German who became an Apache. Doesn't that strike you as strange?" – May, *Winnetou*

Dominant cultures often have the privilege and freedom to appropriate and incorporate cultural practices of the "Other," and these appropriations serve various purposes. The fact that some Germans imagine themselves as weekend Indians and take on as a hobby the cultural symbols, dress, ritual, and language of American Plains Indians illuminates particular mechanisms of hegemony.

Continuing a long and deeply problematic historical progression, German hobbyists are appropriating American Indian culture and spirituality through their club practices. I went to Germany in the spring of 1999 to investigate and expose the troubling and dangerous aspects of these practices, in the hope that my ethnographic fieldwork will in some way lead to greater awareness of how these practices function as mechanisms of cultural appropriation.

I believed that the German *Indianer* groups would be similar in their beliefs about and practices of their common hobby. What I discovered were two different approaches to their exotic hobby. West and East Germans played Indian with dissimilar values. One of my first meetings with an East German *Indianer* club surprised me. I had expected to enter a room and see the club's members in full Indian regalia. But what I encountered was a group of ordinary-looking people dressed in street clothes from diverse educational and economic backgrounds. I was impressed with this particular group's academic approach to the study of American Indians and their involvement with contemporary Native American issues. My first contact with a West German *Indianer* group was not as positive. They told me of the tepee they had pitched in their backyard and claimed that one of their members was a sacred pipe carrier. They also told me of their being adopted into a Canadian Indian tribe. I was eager to meet with this group, but as our interview date grew nearer, they would postpone the meeting, until eventually they decided to cancel, their reason being that I would in some way ridicule their beliefs. This kind of response was a frequent occurrence among the clubs in the West. Many of the East German *Indianer* clubs were helpful to me and to my research and are actively involved in the political struggle of contemporary Native American peoples. I found the groups from the East very respectful of Native American philosophies, whereas the West Germans were primarily concerned with acquiring cultural material. They regarded me with suspicion and avoided me unless I was selling authentic Indian merchandise or cultural knowledge. Their lack of cooperation was very revealing. I felt that they were arrogant and selfish and that my presence was an affront and threat to their Indian illusion.

Naturally, I gravitated to the East Germans. Coming from the United States, a country that denigrates the American Indian, to a country that reveres our image can be quite an intoxicating experience. At first, I was reeling in confusion from the instant status and admiration I had attained. In a warped way, I can empathize with the Native American men who choose to live in Europe, permanently selling our cultural practices and spirituality to the willing hobbyist consumer. I do not condone what they do, but I understand how they arrived at their choice of career. In my mind I began to make correlations between East German and American Indian cultures. I felt that they, too, had in a sense lost their identity and communities to the tide of Western capitalist expansion. I had empathy for their new status or lack thereof in a newly reunited Germany. But, even with my East German subjects/collaborators/friends, I was still uneasy. My experiences made me more and more confused and in denial of the main ideas of my fieldwork.

I found myself wondering if they were feigning reverence for the culture. If you really revere the culture, why do you try to be it? And what is it doing for you? How dare you even revere the culture without being willing to articulate what it is doing for you? And if you are not revering it for yourself or you have that illusion, then for whom are you doing it?

In thinking about these questions, I considered German and North American histories and used the lens of whiteness theory to do so. Whiteness theory posits that racial consumption is a form of white hegemony. When white dominant culture caricatures nonwhite groups, they are acting in a way that diminishes the subordinate groups' power and identity. Germans are former colonists, and Germany has a history of racial oppression. Germany colonized foreign countries and was responsible for the Jewish Holocaust. The United

States colonized within its own borders and is responsible for its continued genocide of Native Americans and people of color. And in this way Germany shares its legacy of oppression and whiteness with the people of European descent in the United States. But Germany's history is unlike the mix of colonialism and racial oppression in the United States.

Why are Germans not appropriating from their own colonial past? Why are they turning to the United States? What is it about the U.S. colonial past that is more romantic for them than their own colonial past?

These questions deal with forms of consumption, of racial consumption. In a sense this form of racial consumption is equal to Nazi domination. What is not clear is why a culture that produced Nazism, an ideology that proposed a pure Aryan race, also uses "racial inferiors" from the United States as a group model. How does this come about? There is more here than Hitler's fascination with the romanticized images of Indians that Karl May fabricated in his novels. The identity struggle that the people of East Germany face with the reunification of Germany distinguishes them and their motives for playing Indian from those of the West German hobbyists. That struggle still does not excuse what they do for a hobby. What all of these hobbyists are doing is making entertainment out of genocide. And whereas in the United States the tendency is to museumize Native American culture, in Germany people want to revitalize the Native American demise by a racial reembodiment.

This racial embodiment is an appropriation of exoticized colonized peoples. Germans are engaged in two forms of racial consumption, one of which is pure appropriation of the West; for instance, some West German *Indianer* groups replicate spiritual practices and claim these practices as their own. The other form of consumption is less appropriative and is upheld as appreciative, such as duplication of clothing and crafts. But it is still appreciative in the museum sense. They are getting the pleasure, the racial pleasure of reembodying something that their whiteness has participated in destroying.

So in my journey to Germany I also traveled through the cultural structures of my own colonial state. I had to come to terms with my confusion over the questionable admiration of my culture and try to remain focused on what was really being played out on this cultural stage by these actors. I find it questionable that both East and West German *Indianer* clubs are clueless as to the racial implications of their activities. If these groups had a true appreciation and respect for Native Americans, they would cease their appropriation of Native American culture altogether. Even though I was temporarily bedazzled and flattered by the authenticity of the skill and craftsmanship displayed by the

Germans in the replication of Native American arts and culture, I equate their hobby with the American usage of Indians as team mascots. Americans and Germans are playing the same white hegemony game but with different sets of rules. They have no idea how their use of the Native American image affects Native Americans themselves.

Indian Impersonation as Historical Surrogation

KATRIN SIEG

In the early 1990s, activist and writer Ward Churchill traveled through Germany as part of a Native American delegation. He was astonished to find there large numbers of people in Indian garb attending the group's presentations, who, he discovered, consider themselves to be Indians: "These 'Indians of Europe,'" Churchill observed,

> were uniformly quite candid as to why they felt this way. Bluntly put – and the majority were precisely this harsh in their own articulations – they absolutely hate the idea of being Europeans, especially Germans. Abundant mention was made of their collective revulsion to the European heritage of colonization and genocide, particularly the ravages of nazism. Some went deeper, addressing what they felt to be the intrinsically unacceptable character of European civilization's relationship to the natural order in its entirety. Their response, as a group, was to try and disassociate themselves from what it was/is they object to by announcing their personal identities in terms as diametrically opposed to it as they could conceive. "Becoming" American Indians in their own minds apparently fulfilled this deep-seated need in the most gratifying fashion.[1]

He goes on to ridicule this "weekend warrior" endeavor, scolds hobbyists for replacing political activism with cultural escapism, and concludes that, in fact, their leisure activity allows them more effectively to fulfill the social roles they symbolically reject. The heated arguments between Churchill's group and the hobbyists that he describes typify the struggle for cultural authority and ownership that ensues every time contemporary Indians face the power of metaphorical Indianness: while the Germans underscore their distance from a European history of colonization, Churchill interprets hobbyism as its postcolonial continuation by cultural and spiritual means. While hobbyists are quick to cite a long history of German-Indian contact as the foundation of Germans' interest in and knowledge about Native American cultures, Churchill's insistence on the ideological function of contemporary

217

Germans' identification with Indians seems justified. I hope to show, however, that hobbyist styles are more disparate than he allows and should not be collapsed into a single meaning.[2]

Similar to Philip Deloria, who underscores the changing meanings of the Indian in the American imagination in the course of the twentieth century, I perceive great differences among German hobbyists' attitudes toward Native Americans. These differences are generational, underscoring the changes in hobbyism over time; they are regional, pointing to a number of local performance traditions with which hobbyism has shared space; and they are ideological, in the sense that the antimodernism that Churchill stresses in his description challenges Nazi racism and imperialism in some instances, while in others it is directed against social features specific to socialism, democracy, and capitalism. Even within the small sample of hobbyists that I interviewed and on whose testimony this article is based, these differences resulted in very different views of their practice and interpretations of its social and political meanings. Some (primarily within the younger generation) identify with American Indians as a way of practicing an alternative, "green" lifestyle marked by ecological awareness and a rejection of the trappings of consumer culture and the class distinctions it fosters. By contrast, others (who first took up hobbyism in the postwar years) appear to have been impelled by a sense of victimization, national defeat, and emasculation feelings that they were able to symbolically redress through the ritual of ethnic masquerade. While Germans' choice of the Indian as a model of heroic manliness and anti-imperialist defiance probably resulted from the popularity of Karl May's Wild West novels, such cross-cultural identification was complicated by the Cold War. Some of the West German men who joined or founded hobbyist clubs after the war, who shaped these clubs' direction and now occupy leadership positions within the national umbrella organizations, felt that they, like Indians, were oppressed by white Americans – but they also met Native Americans who served as soldiers in the occupying forces and attended hobbyist meetings in U.S. Army uniforms. In order to research Native American history, they had to learn English, enter army base stores to purchase hobbyist periodicals like *American Indian Hobbyist*, and visit libraries maintained by the American forces. Hobbyists in the German Democratic Republic (who called themselves "Indianists") were encouraged by the socialist state to develop an understanding of and solidarity with Indians as emblems of anti-imperialist oppression and resistance. As Birgit Turski shows, however, some East German Indianists perceived themselves as antisocialist resisters instead, rejecting communism as a form of alien domination. Questions such as the following therefore seem appropriate: Did hobbyism in East and West Germany fit within the ideological identifications and enmities set up by the Cold War, or did it subvert them? Is all German hobbyism fueled by antifascism, as Ward Churchill suggests? And if so, does Indian impersonation correlate with progressive, antiracist endeavors in general; in other words, does it entail solidarity with all oppressed peoples, as Yolanda Broyles-González maintains in one of the very few extant scholarly essays about hobbyism? Or does the merely symbolic rejection of "European civilization," as opposed to activist opposition, in fact bolster the very ideological structures hobbyists lament, as Churchill contends? Finally, can hobbyism be a model for imagining the sharing of power and authority by Germans and Native Americans? Is the hobbyists' revision of biological concepts of "race" (based on impermeable and unbridgeable boundaries between people) in favor of what I call "ethnic competence" (based on knowledge and performance) a welcome step toward overcoming racism? Or does the transformation of Native American identities into cultural roles that can be donned by white Europeans continue the history of cultural theft and ethnic chauvinism?

In the following discussion, I will first outline in greater detail the generational, regional, and ideological differences among practitioners, before proceeding to assess the social meanings of hobbyism in the crucible of the Cold War. Finally, I will consider its political consequences for intercultural relations, both between Native Americans and Germans and between Germans and other ethnic minorities. Before I do so, however, let me briefly describe the conception and objective of my project. In the summer of 1993, I watched a stage adaptation of Karl May's Wild West novel *Der Schatz im Silbersee* (The treasure in Silver Lake) at the festival held annually in Bad Segeberg and walked through the adjacent theme park named "Indian Village."[3] During that visit, I met and spoke with some members of the local Indian club, who had handcrafted some of the artifacts on display in the museum that is located in the theme park. I was struck by the variety of professional, amateur, and ethnological styles of Indian impersonation by the white actors portraying Indians on stage, by the families who had dressed up as Indians to attend the show and visit the theme park, and by the hobbyists who stressed authenticity in their costumes and activities. Each of these distinct forms of what I came to call "ethnic drag" suggested an identification with oppressed peoples portrayed as victims and heroes in the racial struggle of the American frontier. Yet I was baffled by the contrast between the massive outpouring of

Katrin Sieg

sympathy for Native Americans and the arson of a hostel of asylum seekers in nearby Hamburg that same summer, which was one in a long string of racist incidents since German reunification.[4] The image of German crowds cheering white aggressors in one instance and the resisters against such aggression in the other raised the question in my mind whether there was any connection between these two displays of enthusiasm.

That question prompted me to undertake a longer study of ethnic drag in postwar German theater and performance. In my book Ethnic Drag: Performing Race, Nation, Sexuality in West Germany, I examine what theater scholar Joseph Roach terms "surrogation," namely, the "three-sided relationship of memory, performance, and substitution. . . . In the life of a community, the process of surrogation does not begin or end but continues as actual or perceived vacancies occur in the network of relations that constitutes the social fabric. Into the cavities created by loss through death or other forms of departure, I hypothesize, survivors attempt to fit satisfactory alternates. Because collective memory works selectively, imaginatively, and often perversely, surrogation rarely if ever succeeds. The process requires many trials and at least as many errors. The fit cannot be exact."[5] Roach's concept of surrogation encompasses both the work of remembering loss, that is, it facilitates what psychoanalysts have called "the labor of mourning," but also the work of repression, disavowal, and historical revisionism. Ethnic drag, I hypothesized, provided Germans with a way both to mourn the vacancies left by the Holocaust and to refuse the role of perpetrator in racial aggression. Indian impersonation thus facilitated the work of restitution, by allowing Germans to explore alternative notions of ethnic differences and to reject learned concepts of Aryan supremacy. Their identification with the victims of foreign invasion reflected (and displaced) the historical experience of Allied occupation, but it also constituted a form of historical denial. The contradictory functions of surrogation might therefore explain the simultaneous expressions of xenophilia and xenophobia that I observed in the summer of 1993.

Because in the book my attention, as a theater scholar, was trained on the way in which specific cultural venues (film, theater, journalism, clubs), genres (ritual, classical drama, comedy), and culture styles (high, mass, popular, avant-garde) shaped Germans' imagined and actual interaction with other ethnic subjects, my research about hobbyism as well was initially determined by the performance genres that, I speculated, had given rise to it, namely, the circus, the Völkerschau (ethnic show), the carnival, and the Karl May theatricals. After I had already met the hobbyists in Bad Segeberg (the

Fig. 16. The Präriefreunde Köln (Friends of the Prairie, Cologne) are a self-described group of hobbyists who study the customs, culture, and history of North American tribes. Founded in 1951, the club has thirty-four members. Reprinted from Petra Hartmann, Stephan Schmitz, and Matthias Heiner, *Kölner Stämme* (Cologne: Vista Point, 1991). Courtesy, Petra Hartmann and Stephan Schmitz.

site of the largest Karl May festival in western Germany), I therefore sought out clubs in Cologne, which had been featured in a book of photographs titled *Kölner Stämme* (Cologne tribes) and presented as avid participants in the carnival, a custom prevalent in the Catholic regions of Germany. In addition, I was curious whether Broyles-González's thesis about hobbyism as a way of coping with modernization processes and the loss of local, rural, oral traditions would also be confirmed by urban hobbyists. Since I usually stay in Berlin when I visit Germany, I contacted two groups, one in the western and the other in the eastern part of the formerly divided city. In the summers of 1998 and 1999 I conducted interviews with members of four different Indian clubs in Germany: the Interessengruppe der Plains Indianer (Interest Group Plains Indians) in Bad Segeberg, the Präriefreunde Köln (Friends of the Prairie, Cologne), the Interessengruppe Nordamerikanische Völkerkunde (Interest Group North American Ethnology) from West Berlin, and Indianer heute (Indians Today) from East Berlin (fig. 16).[6] In addition, I draw on Birgit Turski's study *Die Indianistikgruppen der DDR* (The Indianist groups of the

Katrin Sieg

GDR), a sociological study written by a practitioner, and an essay titled "Cheyennes in the Black Forest: A Social Drama" by Yolanda Broyles-González, which is based on twelve years of participant-observation of one club in the Black Forest region in southwestern Germany.

In the course of my research, I discovered that the differences in hobbyist styles resulting from local performance traditions were less significant than those created by age and by political leanings. My sample is too small to be representative of even the main variants of hobbyism—for instance, I was unable to interview any of the so-called Öko-Indianer (eco-Indians), for whom hobbyism is an integral part of ecological activism, or any of the East German groups affiliated with the Indianistikbund (discussed later in this essay). The people who shared their experiences, memories, and insights with me happened to be mostly men between fifty and sixty years of age; hence my focus on the postwar years, when these particular men first became interested in Indians. During our meetings, I encouraged them to tell me about their fascination with Native American culture in their own words, describe the orientation and composition of their club, and speculate about the reasons for Germans' love of Indians in general. Since several of them were meticulous archivists of their club's records, they composed detailed and opinionated amateur histories of hobbyism. My work consists of a close reading of the stories they told me, which meant listening to both what they said and what they kept silent about; sometimes I call attention to contradictions and disagreements between speakers, and sometimes I elaborate on what they say by placing their remarks in historical context. Although it is important to me to faithfully convey speakers' intentions or the flavor of their statements, on occasion reproducing lengthy passages, I also want to distance myself from their views rather than subordinate myself to them. I am not a hobbyist delivering an insider's account, but a scholar, who has to balance her respect for these individuals with her commitment (and right) to a critical analysis of their controversial practice. I am as dedicated to revealing what Germans find appealing in hobbyism as I am to clarifying why many aspects of it are painful and objectionable to Native Americans. Although many clubs have documented their own development, a comprehensive, historical overview of this subculture remains to be written. I hope that this project, despite its shortcomings and limitations, can help readers understand through specific examples how cultural "exchange" in a context defined by unequal power and authority can potentially renegotiate social hierarchies—or why it fails to do so.

Institutional Genealogies, Personal Biographies: Origins

Hobbyists trace the birth of Indian clubs from the spirit of Karl May through three narratives of origin. These three narratives track the process by which the carnival, the circus (including the Wild West shows by Buffalo Bill, Billy Jenkins, and a train of successors), and the ethnic show created widespread interest in and fascination with Indians and produced groups of amateur and specialist performers for whom casual interest or professional training increasingly turned into a serious commitment, even a lifestyle.[7] While some clubs had existed during the 1910s and 1920s, club foundings rose steeply after World War II.[8] The largest cluster of clubs can be found in the southern and southwestern states of North Rhine-Westphalia and Baden-Württemberg and in eastern Germany in the cities of Dresden (twelve clubs) and Leipzig (six clubs), locations associated with the carnival, the *Völkerschau*, and Karl May, respectively.[9] Despite the perception of shared roots, hobbyism developed quite differently in East and West Germany. Today, two umbrella organizations exist, one in each part of the formerly divided Germany: the Western-bund (Western Association) in the old Federal Republic and the Indianistik-bund (Indianist Union) in the erstwhile German Democratic Republic. In 1998 the Western Association had a membership of 156 clubs, while 53 clubs are affiliated with the Indianist Union. The main difference between the Western Association and the Indianist Union is the exclusive focus on Indian cultures in the latter, whereas the former comprises a wide range of identifications with anything Western – including scouts, mountain men, military (both Union and Confederate soldiers), and cowboys.[10]

Another reason why there is so little overlap between the two organizations may be the fiercely competitive atmosphere prevailing at the annual meetings, when individuals, clubs, and associations immerse themselves in the Western/Indian experience, dress up, and participate in a diverse program of activities for children and adults, which includes singing, dancing, story-telling, and handicrafts. More ethnologically oriented clubs use the annual meetings to offer slide presentations or to display and discuss their collections of artifacts. While the emphasis is on the affirmation of shared interests, the members I interviewed are also intensely critical of the many shortcomings and errors in accuracy they perceive among their fellow practitioners. The Bad Segeberg group criticized the tyranny of authenticity prevailing at the annual meeting, which creates hierarchies and divisions. Several interviewees commented on the fact that GDR hobbyists were disadvantaged because they had fewer resources and less access to purveyors of authentic materials. Perhaps for this reason, the East-West separation continues to hold. Both umbrella organizations hold annual meetings of seven to fourteen days, when clubs recreate frontier life. The first Indian Council took place in West Germany in 1951. In the mid-1980s, the Western Association purchased grounds in the Westerwald Forest (near Koblenz) that were large enough to accommodate all attendees (two to three thousand) and provided storage room for the 250 to 350 tepees. In contrast, the location of the annual meeting changed from year to year in the former East Germany and continues to do so today. At their meetings, the German clubs are joined by practitioners from almost every other European country. Apart from these summer meetings, numerous Western and/or Indian camps are organized throughout the year by individual or regional associations, where members have the opportunity to live in tepees, dress in authentic costumes, and participate in a host of activities.

The narrative of West and East German hobbyism's evolution from "low" entertainment to quasi-scientific endeavor is repeated on the individual level by the practitioner's development from enthusiast to expert. The teleological narrative of each hobbyist career constructs a development: from superficial fascination to scholarly earnestness, from playful mimicking to creative, respectful, and historically correct emulation. The Bad Segeberg group's evolution from extras to experts, one Cologne hobbyist's transformation from carnivalistic Winnetou-fan to Lakota emulator, and the West Berliner's metamorphosis from cowboy-stuntman to Oglala ethnologist exemplify rhetorical strategies of demonstrating expertise, seriousness, and mimetic competence.[11]

All four (groups of) individuals that I interviewed repeatedly used the term *serious* to underscore their ethnological aspirations and expertise. "Seriousness" has a range of connotations concerning the hobbyists' self-characterization: it signals respect for Native Americans, as opposed to the "foolery" of carnival Indians, artistes, or Karl May fans. Moreover, seriousness connotes scholarly accuracy, as opposed to the casual, often faulty reproductions of many hobbyists. It means hard work, as opposed to the laziness of those who would buy their gear rather than make it with their own hands. Finally, "seriousness" indicates a commitment to "substance" rather than to surface, an important though difficult distinction given the preoccupation with the material culture of the Indians. For most hobbyists, seriousness has both an aspirational function, illuminating the long, unremitting effort, the exertion, and the obstacles overcome in their striving for expertise, and a differentiating function in setting the serious expert apart from the majority of "casual" Indian hobbyists.[12] Even when an expert has, in his own view, reached the pinnacles of expertdom, he is still caught in a nerve-racking battle against the ignorance and indifference of his own brethren, who give in all too easily to the temptations of relaxation, laziness, and commercialization. The continued necessity of distinguishing "serious" mimesis from inauthentic masquerade constitutes a central dimension of the hobbyists' struggle for expertise. Yet hobbyists' insistence on the "truthfulness" of their performance, their claim to mimesis, predictably creates crises of authority in the encounter with real Indians.

Mimesis, Masquerade, and Mastery in the Contact Zone

John Paskievich's documentary If Only I Were an Indian (1995), which records a visit by a trio of Native Americans to a Czechoslovakian hobbyist camp, superbly dramatizes the hopes and anxieties that attend especially the hobbyists' first encounter with the living objects of their admiration. Whereas that particular group was enormously relieved that they apparently passed muster in the eyes of their guests, some of my interlocutors' encounter stories revealed an abiding ambivalence, since facing the "originals" would logically require hobbyists to demur to the subordinate status of imitation – something that conflicted with their sense of expertise and mastery. All hobbyists I interviewed narrated stories of encounter as epiphanies, moments when they gained sudden, deep insights into their own identity/role and their relationship to Indians, which prompted them to revise or modify their representational practice. Out of a particular view of German-Indian history, narrators constructed quasi-familial relationships between the two peoples, epitomized by the trope of interracial adoption, which would literally insert German sons into Indian families and tribes. As I will argue, the harmonizing intent of the filial metaphor in some cases cloaks a deep ambiguity in the adopted sons' relationship to their Indian fathers, whose position they want to both emulate and usurp.

The hobbyists I interviewed were acutely aware of the oppression, persecution, and near-genocide of indigenous North Americans. The Cologne group and the hobbyist from West Berlin especially stressed that Native Americans' forced relocation to reservations, the loss of their possessions, the interruption of oral traditions by the separation of children from their families all contributed to a situation in which Indians were cut off from their homes, their material culture, and their linguistic/oral traditions. Yet in their stories, these hobbyists depicted Germans as bystanders, arbitrators, and avengers of white aggression, rather than its perpetrators – much like Karl May's Old

Katrin Sieg

Shatterhand.[13] They regarded the activity of nineteenth-century travelers and collectors such as Prince Maximilian zu Wied as fortunate, because, given the vicissitudes of Indian history, these collections now provide some of the most complete, accurate, and best-preserved links to the past from which Indians have been cut off. While hobbyists respond to the Indians' loss with sympathy and regret, their construction of the history of German-Indian relations illuminates the rhetorical functions of competence/expertise in relation to cultural authority. The interruption of a history that could no longer be passed down through family and bloodlines, to their minds, created a sort of "equal opportunity" for Indians and German hobbyists, both of whom had to (re)learn Indian culture. Wolfgang Wettstein, a practitioner from Cologne, claims that "the Indian does not have the answers to the hobbyist's questions. Because the Indian doesn't write down things." In short, Indians are not experts. In view of this lacuna, the Germans' vast collections of Indian artifacts and their dedication to recreating the past constitute a repository of historical memory. Several accounts stress the admiration of real Indians when first confronted with the Germans' expertise. Wettstein describes the moment when a Blackfoot Indian from Canada first participated in a German council:

> He was baffled. Sure, he's an Indian, and suddenly he sees his culture, which for him is over and done with, it's mostly lost. It's history. And there he could see it all again just the way he himself – he's over seventy – the way he himself had remembered it in part, or at least how his parents and grandparents had told him about it, buffalo hunts, and so on, and so on, and so on. Sure, we don't hunt buffalo, that's true, but we all live in tepees, and he walked into a tepee and was astonished. Today in the U.S.A., if you go to a powwow you can walk into a tepee, but it's not furnished the way it was 150 years back. But that's what we try to do.

Scenes like this, in which Indians are supposedly awed by German re-creations of their own past, are important in establishing the Germans' expertise, as well as conferring on them a valid function for the Indians. The Blackfoot Indian can only remember "in part," his past is lost, and suddenly it is brought to life again "just the way" it had been, now wrested from oblivion. The German reenactments provide the missing link in an interrupted history, literally restoring the experience of the grandfathers, whose knowledge had been lost to the anglicized, bereft Indian child. The hobbyists cast themselves as ethnographers, salvagers of a culture the Indians had thought they had forfeited and which the Germans now generously share with them. To this gift they can only respond with admiration and gratitude. Although I would not impute such motives or intentions to all hobbyists, I want to point out that such a reconfiguration of cultural access can potentially reassign the roles of model and copy, teacher and student, amateur and expert in a way that privileges the knowledgeable and generous German hobbyist over the dispossessed (and ignorant) Indian.

The following anecdote related by Curt-Dietrich Asten, a hobbyist from West Berlin, about an encounter with another Blackfoot performer illustrates the struggle for authority between Indian and German that is masked by the trope of the generous German safekeeper. It shows, furthermore, how the postwar discourse of cultural relativism revised prior notions of racial supremacy but nevertheless allowed for a notion of *cultural* supremacy. Asten had a loud public argument at a powwow with a Blackfoot Indian, whose narration of his history provoked the German's scorn. When Asten told the Native American that the Blackfoot elders (whose names he rattled off) would turn in their graves and kick him out of the tribe if they could hear his story, his counterpart exploded and told him in no uncertain terms that no white man would tell him what his own history was; Asten only shook his head in exasperation at the Indian's "racism." The German hobbyist views of Indian history, which I noted earlier, explain how in this particular encounter a German could perceive himself as having special access to Indian culture. In this instance, the evacuation of an organic notion of race, usually regarded as an ideologically progressive move, undermines Indian cultural authority and ownership. Asten's accusation of racism against the furious Indian is interesting for the contrasting notions of cultural authority and ownership it reveals: one (which he attributes to the Indian) based on entitlement by blood, the other one on familiarity, effort, and expertise.[14] For a man born in 1933, who as a self-labeled half-Jew was himself victimized by the racial nomenclature of the Nazi race laws, sensitivity to bloodline-definitions of race is not surprising, and his concept of ethnic competence might indeed be interpreted as a welcome alternative to biological racism. Yet the condescending tone of his story suggests that ethnic competence does not preclude cultural arrogance. Invoking a long list of tribal elders, Asten made a claim to authority that rested on his personal as well as his scholarly knowledge of the Blackfoot and the assertion that "many Indians don't know their own history any longer."

Asten described his sense of profound affinity with Indians as a religious or spiritual affirmation of a mutual bond. Significantly, he articulated this feeling after I had asked him about his Jewish background and family history of ostracization and punishment, which, he surmised, "might have opened a door in my soul to the Indian." Asten's father, and his father's side of the family, were all killed in the Nazi concentration camps of Theresienstadt, Auschwitz, and Bergen-Belsen. This childhood experience was compounded with the memory of the horror of "Operation Gomorrah," when Hamburg was attacked by Allied bombers from 23 July to 3 August 1943. Asten was ten years old at the time. Asten asserted a mystical, cross-cultural kinship based on his general "openness" to the Indians, as well as their special openness to him. To be called "brother" by one Indian, and one he scarcely knew, was, to his mind, equally significant as a formal adoption or even superior to a formal and hence external rite of acceptance.[15] The sacredness of that connection led him to question the masquerade character of Indian club culture as caught up in externals, so that he considered giving up Indian dress altogether. He resolved this crisis by integrating his sense of inner kinship as a category of differentiation in the hobbyist hierarchy, affording him a sense of mastery within it, rather than opposing his practice to hobbyism per se. As his stand-off with the Blackfoot Indian illustrates, however, his self-representation as the Indians' "brother" appears less able to ensure Indian authority and cultural ownership against appropriation – on the contrary, he rejects such efforts as racist.

The ritual of white hobbyists' adoption into Indian families and tribes makes literal the trope of familial insertion by which Germans insinuate themselves into Indian history and traditions. Moreover, these adopted sons (I heard of only one female adoptee) potentially take up an oedipal relationship to their new families. Such a filial position accounts for the vacillation between respect and servitude, on the one hand, and authority and mastery, on the other. Adoption ceremonies are initiated either by a family or by a tribe; they are celebrated with elaborate rites and confer on the adoptee visiting and residency rights on a reservation. Among the interviewees, Wolfgang Wettstein was the only one who had been adopted by a Blackfoot family. Wettstein, who often used the terms *originalgetreu* (authentic) and *stilgerecht* (in keeping with the style) in his description of the hobby, nevertheless developed a complex notion of *emulation* that allowed him to conceptualize the relationship between himself and Indians as one exceeding copying and imitating, striving instead for creative autonomy and artistic maturity. Clearly, he and his group see themselves as artists in their own right, inspired by rather than duplicating another people's art. This notion of emulation, which allows both for cultural distance, difference, and respect and for expertise and mastery across cultural lines, goes right to the heart of the problem of appropriation.

Wettstein himself delivered an eloquent analysis of this problem, and phrased it at the same time as a collective epiphany. His narration of that epiphany came at the very end of the interview, after I had asked him if I could use a photograph of him in a rare, antique bear mask:

> (Groaned. Paused.) It could be that Indians object – not that they haven't seen it [my bear mask] before, I've shown it to them. In the beginning, when we first came in contact with Indians and showed them pictures from Germany, they had very different reactions. They were very suspicious and objected right away. They said: "Look, what kind of tepee decoration is this? That's the tepee decoration of my grandfather. That's the tepee decoration of my uncle. How can you copy that, you don't have the right. Who gave you the right?" Because we, myself included at that time . . . in the meantime we've completely rethought that. For instance, let's take my tepee, I used a design that doesn't exist in Indian society. It's inspired by Blackfoot design, but otherwise it's an ornament that I designed. I've never seen a picture or anything else where I could say: "I copied that." I made my own tepee decoration. Right? The way the Indians did it through dreams, through visions and so on. In the meantime, more of our hobbyists go and say, wait a minute, either you ask an Indian: "May I?" Or they don't use it anymore, because they realize, it has a significance, a religious, mythical significance: "I may not use that because he hasn't given me the right, it's not my property." That's what happened. In the old days, the first years, one saw the book – copied it. That's idiotic, if you think about it, it's idiotic. We had to go through this learning process.

The slippage between the refusal to cross the boundary marked by religion and myth, on the one hand, and the reference to the spiritual process (dream, vision quest) that precedes the hobbyist's creative practice, on the other, indicates a deep-seated ambiguity between emulation and usurpation. The passage is remarkable because it articulates rather than represses this slippage, spelling out the crucial distinction between expertise as a thorough, rigorous, and scrupulous emulation of Indian material culture and a notion of identification based on inner, spiritual sameness. Apparently, Wettstein's recognition of Indian spirituality as an inalienable, untranslatable cultural good that should not be appropriated enabled him to shift his entire perception of his hobby. By referring to specific designs belonging to grandfathers and uncles, he questions the trope of familial commonality and articulates a materialist critique that clearly denounces cultural copying as theft. This is indeed an important insight. It throws into sharp relief the commonalities as well as the differences of Indian and hobbyist and establishes a conceptual and pragmatic boundary against appropriation while conceding the possibility of achieving mastery at certain crafts. In short, it combines (albeit unstably) the notion of authority with that of distance and respect. What emerges is a "middle ground," in which hobbyists are no longer either "simply" German whites or Blackfoot but something else: friends of the prairie.

Contacts with real Indians, while often inspiring awe and romantic admiration, create a predicament for hobbyists, who must reconcile their claims to authenticity and mastery with a practice perceived as imitative. While some resolve this dilemma by constructing hierarchical intercultural relations modeled on the patriarchal family, others strive for collaboration, aiming to disperse talent, expertise, and authority across ethnic lines. The fantasy of the German safekeeper of the Indian past inverts the Platonic taxonomy of original and copy, teacher and student, in order to grant Germans authority, but it also subverts this taxonomy through such notions as emulation. In the context of postwar efforts to change racial ideologies and interactions, some hobbyists' revision of ethnic or cultural identity in terms of competence rather than biology might still be seen as an important corrective to what Nazi teachers had taught them when they were boys. Still, the question persists whether a hobbyist who identifies with Indians necessarily feels herself or himself to be in solidarity with other marginalized groups as well, specifically Germany's resident minorities. In other words, are there any political, moral, or social imperatives that grow out of hobbyism?

Counteracting Modernity

To most hobbyists Indians embody an intact social order in harmony with nature – an essentially antimodern fantasy. Yolanda Broyles-González's study of the "Black Forest Cheyenne," a hobbyist club in southern Germany, argues that Indian impersonation allowed club members to express fear of modernization, grief over geographical and social displacement, and mourning of lost indigenous traditions, but also to validate and celebrate a past marked by rural artisan lifeways and a primarily oral culture. What interests me here is Broyles-González's conclusion that club members translate their feeling of alienation into a felt commonality with other groups who "share" their "underdog position" such as "so-called 'Gastarbeiter' (foreign workers) or the Sinti, or so-called 'gypsies.'"[16] Likewise, Kubat and Rühmann's organization Indianer heute, whose focus on endangered peoples is not limited to indigenous populations in faraway places, actively supports the struggles of Vietnamese asylum seekers or the Sinti and Roma in Germany. Yet they were the only group in my sample whose practice translated into a more generally applicable ethos of solidarity with marginalized people, including ethnic minorities living in Germany. Given that hobbyists often imagine German-Indian relations as unique and exceptional, I doubted whether the stance of either Broyles-González's hobbyists or of Kubat and Rühmann was exemplary of hobbyism overall. To begin with, I found that "modernity" means very different things to different groups and individuals: while for some, the opposition to modernity entails a quest for nonalienated, communal lifeways approximating a "green" philosophy, others associate modernity with the democratic erosion of social hierarchies and contrast it with the stability of a patriarchal order in which women, foreigners, and ethnic minorities still "knew their place." GDR Indianists first identified modernity with the "techno-scientific" socialist state that regimented their practice and, around the time of reunification, with the catastrophic modernization processes launched by Western capitalism's eastward expansion. How does hobbyists' understanding of modernity shape their antimodern surrogations, and what are the political consequences of such views?

The Interest Group Plains Indians in Bad Segeberg articulated their critique of modernity as a felt distance to commodity culture, which alienates humans from nature and creates artificial social hierarchies. Their hobby entails a temporary renunciation of civilization's amenities, which Turski also notes in her analysis of East German groups, particularly younger ones. When I raised this topic, the otherwise rather quiet interview partners in the group, the nineteen-year-old Ingrid Bartsch and the sixty-three-year-old Conny Schamborski, suddenly jumped into the discussion. The older woman explained: "When we go to our grounds for the weekend, the moment we get there, we are no longer. . . ." "We have no telephone, no television, no radio," added Ingrid, "just like the Indians," Schamborski nodded, and Inge Bartsch, Ingrid's mother, concluded: "One leaves everything behind and is outside, in nature, for the weekend." They stressed their admiration for the Indians as people who do not buy ready-made objects but make what they need from the natural resources around them, without producing a lot of waste or creating inessential items. With this view, they approximate a "green" perspective on Indians as environmentally conscious people, although they distance themselves from what they perceive as the "public hullabaloo" created by groups such as Greenpeace or the Green Party: "We prefer to withdraw into the private sphere." All club members experienced the club grounds as an extended private sphere offering a refuge from the anxieties, hierarchies, and rivalries that mark "civilized" human interaction. They praised the camaraderie in the club, the sense of neighborliness, support, and respect epitomized in the collective preparation and consumption of meals, to which everyone contributed according to her or his abilities and received according to her or his needs. Their vision of community crystallized in the story of a backyard barbecue, in which German and Native American participants shared food, music, and stories and in which individuals' special talents did not create hierarchies but a greater sense of trust and mutual respect. One might object that this anecdote evokes the cliché of multiculturalism as a "smorgasbord" of cultural differences. The question it raises is whether such utopian communing in the privacy of the backyard or the campgrounds can be seen as a rehearsal for social transformation, or whether the segregation of the private sphere from the social divisions in the public realm upholds the very hierarchies the hobbyists privately subvert.

Asten's view of the perils of modernity is almost diametrically opposed to the antimodernism of the Bad Segeberg "Plains Indians." Whereas they associate "civilization" with the erection of artificial boundaries of class, ability, and ethnicity, he objects precisely to the blurring of the division between natives and foreigners, men and women, competent and incompetent he sees as characteristic of modern democracy. He articulates his antimodernism as a fear of foreign domination and social alienation:

> Germany, or the territory where the German-speaking peoples lived, has for centuries been the battlefield of many, many . . let's call them foreign rulers. There were the English, there were the Swedes, there were the Russians, there were the French, there were the Italians, there was the Pope, and so on, and so on, and so on. And over and over again he [the German] had to obey foreign rule. Over and over again he was put under the yoke. But somewhere in these stories about the Indians, there was a hint of freedom, there was a hint of pride, of indestructible pride and self-confidence. No German was conscious of that while he read [the Wild West novels]. And then: [the Indians] were the last ones who tried till the end to defend their lives, their culture, everything that made them special, against the evil immigrants, although they had never been a nation, had never been a state. . . . Who defended themselves against all of that but in the end were vanquished, had to adapt, and still persist! Isn't that exactly the same as what has happened in Germany ever since the first occupation by the Romans? Or the Slavs, or whoever else ravaged this country?

He portrays Germans as the victims, not only of outside invaders, but also of their own rulers whose machinations threaten to extinguish German culture – just like white invaders destroyed Indian cultures. In contrast to the alienated, self-destructive, and emasculated Germans of today, historical Indian society, Asten claims, was healthy (if somewhat brutal), without *Randgruppen* (marginal groups) or the kind of gender crisis typical of a degenerate civilization.[17] Impersonating Indians, then, appears as a form of surrogated German patriotism. The hobbyist who identifies with the Indian warrior gains a temporary respite from and compensation for the "wrongness" of things as they presently are in Germany.[18] Although Asten's narrative of German victimization spanned two millennia, he interpreted current conditions within this frame as well, reserving special criticism for Turkish residents' refusal to forswear their Islamic faith as the prerequisite for assimilation into German society. As a German who feels dejected in the face of foreign "domination" and abandoned by his own government, Asten's identification with Indians serves to ennoble his sense of defeat and isolation by fantasizing himself as the last warrior of his race. Moreover, Asten connects the fear of *Überfremdung* (literally, saturation with foreigners) with that of classic *Entfremdung* (alienation):

> I think, the pride of the Indians, whether actually true or idealized by the novels (and hence even more effective because it works subliminally) resonates with something in the reader. Against the hegemony that threatens to break me. Whether that is my country or my life, if that's so instrumentalized that I have to work at the assembly line and have to perform the same gesture all day long. Or I am an important guy in the company and things fall apart the minute I'm sick, but nobody thanks me! I'm not promoted and I won't get more money, I'm always the little guy, and the one up there in the big office who does nothing, really, he gets 10,000 DM a month more, well... so that deep down I say: these [Indians] are still real men! And when I get into my loincloth with only my stone axe in my hand and a feather in my hair: then I'm a real man too!

Getting into drag helps him recover his masculinity: the fantasy of getting into a loincloth, gripping a stone axe, and adorning himself with a feather allows him symbolic mastery over modernity's perils. Asten's image of the lone warrior reveals the Indian to be a kind of idealized (Ger)man, allowing him to act out what Germans could be if only they stood up to the tyranny of foreigners and incompetents, rather than meekly accepting it. His extended lamentation about Turkish residents, asylum seekers, and other foreigners demonstrates that the perception of victimization, which elsewhere or earlier might have produced the solidarity with other oppressed groups (as Broyles-González contends), can also fuel white rage and xenophobia as an increasingly acceptable public sentiment and political discourse in the mid-1990s.

Asten furthermore contrasts an "intact" social order, in which "all know their place and are honored for their natural role," with what he perceives to be a confusing blurring of gender roles today. The fact that men have not honored women in their role as mothers/rebuilders of the nation has caused women to "run around like men" in a misguided effort toward liberation. Conversely, men are so effeminized that "you walk down the street and see someone from behind, you think, man, what a sexy woman, then he turns around and has a long beard!" The specter of inversion, with its attendant threat of homosexual seduction, appears in its traditional role as a figure of degeneracy and decline. Even as hobbyism requires its practitioners to transgress and reassemble German gender codes in their emulation of Indian masculinity – all men sew and embroider their own costumes, for example – Asten conceptualizes the variability of culturally specific (historical and fictional) gender systems as a decline from "natural" to degenerate. Nor does men's proficiency in traditionally female skills result in egalitarian gender relations in the German clubs. In Asten's estimation, most women hobbyists join clubs to oblige their husbands or partners and were, until fairly recently, rarely if ever elected into leadership positions in the West German clubs.[19] "The Indian woman belongs in the tepee and does the domestic work. . . . If I want to portray the Indian around 1850 with historical accuracy, then the woman who lives in my tepee would have to make sure that there is food on the . . . in the pot at all times. That this is no longer possible today is a different matter." How can the roles of emancipated (German) woman and Indian woman be reconciled? "Not at all," Asten maintained. Yet the modern gender order of self-confident female breadwinners also prevails in his household, and he appeared eminently comfortable with being a househusband. While his hobby allows him to express nostalgia for the golden days of yore when men were warriors and women the nurturers as well as the obedient servants, he seemed to welcome the benefits of having a working wife who is also a critical interlocutor, and he appeared untroubled by performing domestic tasks. While the views he expressed in reference to his hobby would suggest the demeanor of a blustering patriarch, the divergence between his Indian fantasy and his social role points to the compensatory, stabilizing function of hobbyist reenactments. To be sure, Asten provided the most puzzling instance of a man whose patriarchal symbolic practice, while seemingly opposed to democratic principles, did not prevent him from welcoming its everyday benefits. Nor did it cause this highly articulate man to experience the divergence between the symbolic and the social in his own life as a contradiction: women's changing social status is simply "a different matter." Yet are we to conclude from Asten's case, to phrase it pointedly, that patriarchal fantasies make men fit for feminism? Perhaps even that, analogously, racist reenactments prepare whites for multiculturalism? The GDR, where Indianism was couched in the explicitly political terms of international solidarity, offers a privileged example for further examining the connection of symbolic and social practices in hobbyism.

The official language Indianists used to legitimate themselves in the eyes of the socialist state appealed to the GDR state because it seemed to share its anti-imperialist vision, its international solidarity with the oppressed, and its adversarial stance toward the United States. These rhetorical appeals are exemplified by the statement of purpose adopted in the early 1980s by individual clubs in order to ensure municipal toleration and support. Local bureaucrats sometimes mistrusted Indian clubs, possibly because of their American (class enemy) orientation, and subjected them to *Unbedenklichkeitsprüfungen* (tests of ideological correctness). The Indianists' official statement promised to connect the groups' interest in Native American history with "contemporary Indians' fight for their human rights. Thus they contribute to the intensification of the humanist idea of friendship between peoples and hence to the keeping of lasting peace on earth." Their professed dedication to the "creation and development of well-rounded socialist personalities" rested on the integration of past and present, culture and politics, the symbolic and the social.[20]

Yet Turski's book demonstrates how the antimodern critique split into an official discourse, and a covert, in-group discourse about Indianism. In contrast to the manifest content of the Indianists' statement of purpose, the main portion of her study denies the consonance of the (Cold War–inspired) socialist mission and Indianist self-definition, instead casting the socialist bureaucracy itself as the feature of modern life that Indianists opposed. According to Turski, the Indianists' antimodernism, which she portrays as a form of cultural resistance, ran deeper than their antisocialism. She describes one incident around the time of reunification that illustrates a change in the symbols that practitioners used to signal their relationship to dominant ideology, while maintaining a critical stance vis-à-vis, first, the socialist state and, later, the new, Western regime. Turski relates how in the past the emissaries to the annual chiefs' meeting would appear wearing Indian jewelry and Stetson hats, a piece of clothing that, in her view, signaled their commonality and "expressed a certain playful opposition to everyday life around them," namely the socialist state's habitual denigration and suppression of all things American.[21] However, at the first chiefs' meeting after the opening of the Berlin Wall in March 1990, only one member appeared in a Stetson hat, whereas others, especially young people, appeared wearing Palestinian scarves. "Without prior agreement, this sign [of opposition] changed as soon as social transformations caused the Stetson hat to lose its propensity for provocation, while the Palestinian headdress came from a different social context, was not specific to the hobby, and did not symbolize their commonality."[22] Turski hints that the symbolic identification of the GDR youth with an ethnic minority struggling for recognition, autonomy, and statehood reflected their own situation as citizens of a vanishing state. Her interpretation of the Palestinian scarf suggests that the Indianists' self-perception as persecuted yet defiant is the common denominator of their practice before and after the fall of the Wall, despite a change in props and despite the fact that their dramatization of the GDR as an annexed state presupposes an identification they had previously rejected. Despite the official mandate of political solidarity among the opponents of capitalist imperialism, it appears that the unofficial practice of GDR Indianism did not correspond to the ideological prescription of a "red brotherhood" uniting Indians and socialists. On the contrary, Indianists viewed the state's politicization of social relations as a symptom of the modernity they rejected in their practice.

Kubat and Rühmann's group, Indianer heute, severely criticized GDR Indianists like Turski for their self-representation as cultural resisters, who want to have it both ways: Indianer heute refutes the claim that Indianists "resisted" state socialism and are angered by present-day Indianists' capitalizing on a GDR "mystique." In their eyes, the decentering of white authority in German-Indian relations has pragmatic consequences: they have long advocated the repatriation of Native American artifacts, in addition to supporting Native American cultural and political institutions materially and ideologically. They maintained close relationships with the leaders of the American Indian Movement, protested the U.S. government's punitive actions against them, and hosted Native American delegates traveling in Europe.[23] Their involvement in repatriation efforts has prompted them to understand colonialism, not only as the literal appropriation of non-European resources and artifacts, but as a figurative system shaping, for instance, the way museums display "exotic" objects for the visual pleasure of the spectators. The exhibition of Native American artifacts is particularly offensive because of the sacred significance of many of these objects. Hence, in order to call attention to the alignment of visual consumption with colonial possession, they suggest a museum pedagogy in which the placement of scrims would impede or partially block sight, signaling to museum visitors the need to question Germans' material and visual access to artifacts. Those artifacts not yet returned to their rightful owners would thus be put "under erasure," marking a history of theft and a commitment to change. They view Native American spirituality as the cultural good most in need of protection. Although their American visitors had on occasion invited Kubat and Rühmann to join them in traditional Native American rituals, their search for community and spiritual fulfillment did not confine them in the past, nor did it preclude their tenacious, risky struggle with state bureaucrats in the GDR or the reunified Germany. I find it significant that Indianer heute does not take up an antimodernist stance and resists the nostalgic reenactment of a "golden age" prior to white people's domination of the North American continent. Its focus on the present and dedication to practical intervention along with, but not confined to, symbolic redress refuses two central elements of hobbyism. On the one hand, its members reject white people's romantic identification with the victims of white aggression, which leaves the equation of whiteness with domination itself intact. On the other, their refusal to separate symbolic and political practice stems from the recognition that primitivist rituals stabilize, rather than transform, modern society. Can members of Indianer heute be called "hobbyists" at all? Their focus on the material culture of indigenous populations would warrant the label of "object hobbyism," according to Philip Deloria, in contrast to the "people hobbyism" practiced in the other groups discussed here. Indianer heute does not uphold the symbolic opposition of oppressive European modernity versus wholesome non-European primitivism that prevents Europeans from exploring remedies to alienation from within modern societies while also continuing to exclude non-Europeans from the benefits of modernity. In my estimation, they offer a promising prospect of connecting an intense, lifelong engagement for ethnic minorities, indigenous cultures, and spiritual wholeness with the endeavor to transform European whiteness into a practice that is symbolic *and* explicitly political.

In my discussion, I have emphasized the historical specificity of hobbyism in order to assess its social meanings and political implications. My emphasis on the historical and biographical determinants of hobbyist styles questions the assertions of their practitioners that there exists a transhistorical, mystical bond between Indians and Germans. I underscore instead the uniqueness of hobbyists' response to the end of the Third Reich, postwar reconstruction, the Allied occupation, and the division of Germany into a socialist and a capitalist state. To two of the older men in my sample, who recalled the terror of Allied bombing raids, Indian impersonation seems to have provided the symbolic means to cope with their sense of national humiliation, shame, and emasculation, producing in one case an identification with strongly antidemocratic overtones. The recuperation of a warrior-like masculinity through Indian drag, too, appears reactionary when compared to official discourses, which encouraged a demilitarized, paternal masculinity during the reconstruction period.[24] Yet hobbyism should by no means be equated with submerged fascist tendencies in general. Even the acting out of bellicose, patriarchal fantasies does not automatically translate into an antifeminist social practice. Moreover, the notion of "ethnic competence" appears progressive when compared to the racial ideologies to which these practitioners were exposed in Nazi schools. One might even see hobbyism as a popular, theatrical equivalent to antiracist anthropological insights into the social construction of ethnicity. Although fascist ideologies of race and Germany's defeat and reeducation by Allied forces form the crucible of meaning in which many postwar hobbyists forged their practice (and which continues to impel some of its aspects, as Ward Churchill found in the early 1990s), Nazism should not be seen as the only or the chief determining force against which hobbyists define themselves. German hobbyism predates the Third Reich, although, unfortunately, the motives of earlier practitioners can no longer be ascertained because they are no longer alive to offer accounts of their activity. Nor should modernity be equated with late capitalism: in East Germany, Indianists created a refuge from the bureaucratic reach of the socialist state, resisting its command to politicize intercultural relations. A small minority developed a critique of real existing socialism but embraced communist appeals to international solidarity with the oppressed. For many among the younger generation of hobbyists East and West, hobbyism offers a zone outside and opposed to capitalist commodity culture and the materialist mentality with which some grew up but which others see as imposed by the Western victors of the Cold War. To some, such an exploration of a nonalienated, simple life is also connected with the search for spiritual fulfillment left unsatisfied by organized Christian religions or political ideologies.

Further research is needed to ascertain whether some of the features I have discussed here also apply to other hobbyist communities in Europe. John Paskievich's documentary as well as Christian Feest's comparative research on representations of Indians in other European literatures indicate that the myth of the Noble Savage, which continues to inspire romanticized views of Indians today, is shared across European cultures. The yearning for a nonalienated, pre- or antimodern world that hobbyists express appears to be eminently adaptable to local conditions, whether they are communist or postcommunist Czechoslovakia (which has since separated into the Czech Republic and Slovakia) or the occupied, divided, and now unified Germany. In addition, future scholarship might take its cue from the documentary *Das Pow-wow* by Native American anthropologist Marta Carlson, who, similar to the "counter-anthropology" developed by the performance artist Guillermo Gómez-Peña, turns the anthropological gaze around to investigate those who have historically held the power to describe, catalog, and interpret their "exotic" subjects.[25] The dialogue that Carlson initiates from behind the camera stages the anxiety around referentiality that continues to haunt hobbyists in every encounter with "real Indians," requiring them to negotiate their desire for recognition as kindred spirits and their fear of being exposed, at best, as imitators and, at worst, as modern-day cultural colonizers.

Notes

1. Churchill, *Fantasies*, 224.

2. Unfortunately, Churchill does not speculate about the motivations of other western and eastern European hobbyists. Indian clubs exist in many European countries that quite obviously have a different relationship to fascism and where the kinds of enacted historical revisionism I discuss in this article would play no part in practitioners' identification with Native Americans. Although I have no firsthand evidence, I would speculate that the motivations of many hobbyists in other European countries are informed by the generally antimodern, "green," and pacifist impulses that also characterize the practice of younger German hobbyists. An excellent discussion of the changing meanings of "playing Indian" across the generations in North America can be found in P. Deloria, *Playing Indian*; some of his suppositions, I believe, also pertain to the European context. See also Christian Feest's contribution to this volume.

3. I have described the performance and the setting in my article " 'Wigwams on the Rhine': Race and Nationality on the German Stage."

4. I decided to call these forms of cross-racial masquerade "ethnic drag," because I have been inspired by feminist and queer scholarship on theater and performance, as well as by American scholarship on the minstrel show (e.g., Eric Lott's *Love and Theft*).

5. Roach, *Cities of the Dead*, 2.

6. I conducted a group interview with Interessengruppe der Plains Indianer members Ekkehard Bartsch, Ingeborg Bartsch, Ingrid Bartsch, and Conny Schamborski in Bad Segeberg on 23 April 1998. I interviewed Wolfgang Wettstein and Harro Hesse of Präriefreunde Köln on their club grounds (on the outskirts of Cologne) on 26 April 1998. I spoke with Kurt Dietrich "Ted" Asten, a member of

Katrin Sieg

Interessengruppe Nordamerikanische Völkerkunde, in his West Berlin apartment on 6 May 1998. I met Indianer heute members Dieter Kubat and Steffi Rühmann for an interview on 18 July 1998 in their apartment in Berlin. I also conducted a follow-up interview with them on 24 May 1999.

7. Asten stated that the first Indian clubs in Leipzig and Dresden were founded in direct response to the ethnic shows in Leipzig that Hagenbeck had organized. Regarding impact on lifestyle, Wettstein, for instance, told me that his entire apartment is a museum, in which he exhibits his collection of self-made and Indian-made artifacts. See also the brief article on his club in Hartmann and Schmitz, Kölner Stämme, 65–69.

8. In 1968, Curt-Dietrich Asten, one of my interlocutors, had written his thesis in social work about German Indian clubs. Unfortunately, no copies of it exist any longer. In it, he had included a timeline about club foundings, as well as another chart that divided clubs by state.

9. Turski counted fifty clubs in 1991, showing a slightly falling tendency when compared with the forty-seven East German clubs Asten had on his list in 1998.

10. As the association's name indicates, East German Indian clubs are devoted exclusively to Indian culture; Turski as well as some West German hobbyists interpret the shrinking and splitting of clubs since reunification in the context of the changing leisure culture in the new states, specifically the fact that the white frontier characters listed above had been unavailable for performative identification under socialism, whereas Indian culture, fostered by the GDR Kulturbund, enjoyed the status of an oppressed people and fit well within the anti-American agenda of the socialist state. Turski notes that those Western fans interested in emulating cowboys failed to legitimate their interest vis-à-vis state agencies, by portraying cowboys as "the poorest sector of the rural proletariat" (Indianistikgruppen, 27). Moreover, increasing identification with the political plight of Native Americans led younger Indianists to vilify cowboys as the imperialist/racial enemy, making it even more difficult for cowboy hobbyists to pursue their interest.

11. Wettstein and Asten in particular spent extraordinary effort and time demonstrating their ethnological knowledge, explaining particular techniques and describing artifacts during the interviews. They also engaged in repeated and repetitive list-making, enumerating names of tribes, regions, Indian individuals, artifacts, and raw materials. These lists, sometimes concluded with linguistic fillers like "and and and and and," suggested boundless, exhaustive knowledge.

12. Asten and Wettstein both displayed great exasperation at the unwillingness of the great majority of hobbyists to get better at what they do, at their contentment to play without deepening their knowledge, their resistance to criticism and self-improvement, and their resentment toward the experts.

13. Asten remarked that German settlers were probably as hostile or friendly

with Indians as other whites, but like Wettstein, he did not comment on the circumstances under which the sizeable German "collections" were amassed or entertain the possibility of returning these collections to Indians, as Kubat demands.

14. On the issue of race, Asten performed dialectical somersaults, however, and it would be impossible to construct a cohesive, noncontradictory stance in this matter. On the one hand, he claimed that there were incontrovertible "racist characteristics" such as the cruelty of Asian peoples; on the other, recent European, German, and even Berlin history showed him that under the thin veneer of civilization there lurked a savage beast in all of humanity. Philip Deloria, in his analysis of American hobbyism, observes that often, hobbyists grant Native Americans exception from generally held biologist-racist beliefs (*Playing Indian*, 146); Asten was less consistent than that.

15. In answer to my question about the phenomenon of adoption, he told the story of meeting the son of an Indian woman who was dying of cancer and in whose healing ceremony he participated, "one of the most sacred ceremonies the Blackfoot still perform." It might seem odd that he, a stranger to this family, was invited to this ceremony in which allegedly only close friends are asked to take part, but his point was precisely that he was intuitively recognized as kin even though he had just met the family.

16. Broyles-González, "Cheyennes," 74–75.

17. Regarding brutality, on the topic of "marginal social groups" he related, for instance, the Indian practice of leaving the old and infirm behind in the wilderness, so that they either faced a slow death, killed themselves, or had a close relative kill them. This practice was tough but necessary "because the survival of the group came before that of the individual" and it epitomized a healthy society in his view.

18. Richard Dyer points to a similar dynamic in reference to American muscle-men war-movies, for example, Sylvester Stallone's *Rambo* cycle, which illustrate the compensatory fantasies of disaffected, white working-class masculinity. Asten's elaborations on the Western similarly stress the combination of white men's disaffection after a lost war and the phantasmatic identification with a hero who is ennobled by his suffering and whose extermination has already become myth. Asten's perception of Germany's continual invasion, however, constructs a narrative of victimization over two millennia. It not only conflates Allied occupation forces with so-called "guestworkers" (recruited by West German companies) as well as political refugees, but also elides Germany's invasion and colonization of other European (and non-European) countries. See also Poiger on postwar masculinity and the Western in West and East Germany. Regarding the suppression in the GDR of things associated with the United States, see Turski, *Indianistikgruppen*, 63–64.

Katrin Sieg

19. Although Turski provides no information about the gender of the membership in East German clubs, her reference to "groups in which women and children participate but are not allowed to vote in membership meetings" indicates that gender indeed determined membership status and rights. Thus the thirty-five groups that participated in a census had 544 "full members" out of 776 participants (Turski, *Indianistikgruppen*, 31).

20. See Turski, *Indianistikgruppen*, 75.

21. Annual meetings in clubs affiliated with the Indianist Union were hosted in rotation by individual clubs. With rising membership and attendance, this practice caused growing logistical problems: one had to find grounds large enough to accommodate all, and, under a system of centralist planning, it was not easy to provide sufficient food for the hundreds of people attending sites in remote rural areas. This required an extra planning session called the *Chief-Treffen* (chiefs' meeting) attended by emissaries of all member clubs. This body also discussed the structure, status, and purpose of the clubs and drafted the statement of purpose adopted by individual clubs (see discussion in this essay).

22. Turski, *Indianistikgruppen*, 63–64.

23. In the 1980s, many tribes sent emissaries to enlist European support and publicity for their grievances against the U.S. government; to many of them, hobbyists appeared as logical allies, until they realized the subculture's limited political clout. As one delegate, Russel Barsh, told me in a conversation at Dartmouth on 14 May 1999, Native Americans realized in the 1990s that the United Nations would offer a more appropriate forum for appeal and consequently shifted their efforts in that direction.

24. See Moeller, " 'Last Soldiers,' " 129–46.

25. Carlson's documentary makes an important contribution to a comparative analysis of East and West German hobbyism, limited in my discussion by my inability to contact East German "people hobbyists." Gómez-Peña's counter-anthropology is exemplified by the play *Border 2000: The New World Order* (1998) (in *Dangerous Border Crosses*) and his book *The New World Border*. San Francisco: City Lights, 1996. Please also see his interactive work in cyberspace: http://www.telefonica.es/fat/egomez.htm51#pape.

Between Karl May and Karl Marx

The DEFA Indianerfilme

GERD GEMÜNDEN

Here's a scenario we're all familiar with: Gold has been discovered in the Black Hills. The lure of sudden riches attracts fortune seekers, merchants, and riff-raff. White settlers move in, building forts and reclaiming territory that had been promised to Native tribes. A deadly struggle between cowboys and Indians ensues. If this were a Hollywood Western, John Wayne would fight off the "redskins" single-handedly before riding off into a prairie sunset. But in the East German film *Die Söhne der großen Bärin* (The sons of Great Mother Bear) (1965/1966), there are some differences: the Black Hills are in Yugoslavia, the cowboys are German, the horses are Russian, and the day is saved by Gojko Mitic, who is not a cowboy but an Indian.

Die *Söhne der großen Bärin* is one of twelve films that DEFA, the centralized film studios of East Germany, produced between 1965 and 1983 and which all revolve around the struggle of North American tribes in the eighteenth and nineteenth century.[1] These *Indianerfilme*, as they were called in distinction to U.S. Westerns, were shot in the Babelsberg film studios and on location in Yugoslavia, Czechoslovakia, Rumania, Bulgaria, various parts of the Soviet Union, and even Cuba, and produced, for the most part, by the "Arbeitsgruppe Roter Kreis" (which included directors such as Josef Mach, Richard Groschopp, Gottfried Kolditz, and Konrad Petzold). Against the skepticism of state officials and to the surprise of its own makers, Die *Söhne der großen Bärin* was a hugely successful film, attracting more than ten million viewers and launching DEFA's most successful series of films made in one genre. While critics, both in the East and the West, often ridiculed poor production values, predictable plots, and clumsy acting, audiences swooned over the staunch figure of the film's newborn star, Gojko Mitic, a student of physical education turned actor. These films contain many of the ingredients that make for a good Hollywood Western: the ambush of the stagecoach, the attack on the railroad, fistfights and shootouts, swinging bar doors, Indians on the warpath attacking an army fort, and so on. And like most Hollywood Westerns, these films have a clear division of good guys and bad guys – except that

243

Fig. 17. Gojko Mitic as Osceola, the Seminole leader, in the 1971 film *Osceola*.

in the DEFA films sympathy lies exclusively with the tribe and their heroic chief (always played by Mitic) in their struggle against greedy white settlers, treaty-breaking army colonels, corrupt sheriffs, imperialist oil magnates, and plantation owners.

Made in response to the success of Harald Reinl's Karl May adaptations produced in West Germany from 1962 onward (East Germans would travel to Prague to see them) and, in fact, using some of the same Yugoslav locations, sets, and extras, the *Indianerfilme* successfully cashed in on the renewed popularity of the genre in Europe. (Similarly, the Italian spaghetti Western profited from the commercial context provided by Reinl's films and would be unthinkable without their international success.) Their ideological goal was to articulate an outspoken critique of the colonialism and racism that fueled the westward expansion of the United States. By paying more attention to historical detail, the producers and filmmakers were hoping to infuse what state officials considered a sensationalist and escapist genre with an enlightening and educative purpose, thus creating politically correct entertainment. As Dr. Günter Karl, a DEFA dramaturge, explained: "From the outset we knew full well that we had to set ourselves apart from the capitalist movies of the same genre. In doing so, we were nevertheless forced to use at least part of the elements that make this genre so effective, elements that are not totally devoid of a certain attraction and – as far as the Indians are concerned – a certain romanticism. . . . If we were to use these effective elements, we had to set ourselves off through a different content. Most importantly, we had to assume a historic-materialist perspective of history and make the focus on the historical truth the guiding theoretical principle."[2] It is not difficult to see how shifting the narrative perspective from the whites to the Indians is compatible with the GDR's official critique of imperialism: the fate of the North American Indians provided a showcase of what it means to be a victim of capitalist expansion, the consequences of which can range from unequal trade, theft, and deceit to willful starvation, random murder, and organized genocide.

Like many Hollywood Westerns, the Indianerfilme are far more revealing about the political agenda of their makers than about the subjects that they profess to portray. Not surprisingly, in the DEFA films the various responses of the Indian tribes to the ever-advancing Western frontier of the United States look like blueprints for a better socialist Germany: At the end of Die Söhne der großen Bärin, for example, chief Tokei-ihto leads his people to fertile grounds by announcing: "Ackerbau, zahme Büffel züchten, Eisen schmieden, Pflüge machen – das ist unser neuer Weg" ("farming, raising domesticated buffaloes, being blacksmiths and making plows – that's our new path"), a message that had to resonate in the country of workers and farmers, as the GDR liked to be called. Similarly, Chief Osceola's most important victory is won, not on the battlefield, but at the bargaining table as he secures fair wages for all plantation workers. In both Chingachgook, die große Schlange (Chingachgook, the great snake) (1967) and Osceola (1971), the title hero succeeds in ending warfare among rival tribes by persuading them to unite against a common enemy, following the motto "Indians of all countries, unite!"

The exclusive focus on Native Americans was at the time without parallel in film history; it allowed for a historical accuracy that most Hollywood films had always lacked. From the beginnings of studio production to the present, Hollywood had to continuously rewrite and deliberately distort historical facts to couch its films in plots acceptable for the home audience. Nevertheless, Günter Karl's belief that a more politically enlightened content can simply be poured into the same form overlooks the deeply ingrained racism and sexism of this genre. The DEFA films, too, provide us with little more than the well-known clichés of tribal life. Like most Western views of Third World, Native, aborigine, or tribal cultures, the East German Indianerfilme participate in forms of "othering" that involve strategies of domination, appropriation, and stereotyping.[3] If in most Hollywood productions the Indian was a red devil, in the DEFA films the "primitive" invariably becomes a placeholder for the noble savage. As with most Hollywood Westerns, DEFA films focused on a few selected tribes (primarily the Plains Indians and the Apaches) during the second half of the nineteenth century, thus ignoring a wide spectrum of historical and regional difference.[4] The focus is always on the interaction with whites; an autonomous Native past does not exist. We are treated to stalwart and proud warriors who excel in horseback riding, bow and arrow or tomahawk contests, who speak in short sentences (but without accent!) and mysteriously look into the distance to spy the advancing enemy. The chief's wife, if she exists, invariably has to be killed to propel dramas of revenge and reckoning. As in most Hollywood films, there is no mixing of blood as interracial marriages are always doomed (Ulzana, Blutsbrüder). Similarly, the mixed-blood character in Tödlicher Irrtum (Fatal error) (1970) has to die at the end of the film. Given the high moral ground the DEFA films claim for themselves, and also because they have been lauded in recent reviews as "anthropologically correct" or "politically correct" portrayals of Native Americans avant la lettre, it is important to point out these racist blind spots.[5] But my main point is a different one.

My interest in these films is not to unveil or ridicule the thinly disguised ideology with which their creators imbued them, nor is it to detect the perpetuation of generic clichés and racist stereotypes of Native Americans that still abound, even though the films were intended to criticize the genocide of the North American Indians. Such approaches, while valid forms of ideology critique, do not provide answers to the question why the films were so widely and surprisingly successful with East German audiences. To address this popularity, one has to analyze the ways in which the films mobilize audience identification. These modes of identification certainly involve manipulation of spectatorial expectations established by the models on which they most obviously draw – the Hollywood Westerns of the 1940s and 1950s and the West German Reinl Westerns of the early 1960s. But I would argue that the surprising success of the Indianerfilme suggests that Die Söhne der großen Bärin and its many follow-ups were also able to articulate more deeply seated processes of identification that resonated with postwar constructions of national and cultural identity; they attest to what it means to be East German in the 1960s and 1970s. The Indianerfilme thus emerge as a discursive site where meanings of national and cultural identity were negotiated and contested, paradoxically staged both as escapes from and confirmations of state-prescribed national identities – a battle, not only between Whites and Reds, but between state ideology, studio fantasy production, and spectatorial identification.

In his study *The Powers of Speech: The Politics of Culture in the* GDR, David Bathrick has argued that the GDR's ideology of progress was based on a critique of cultural modernity in both its avant-garde and mass-cultural forms, the only alternative to which was a rejuvenated national culture.[6] One would expect that in this triangle, the *Indianerfilme* as embodiment of mass culture would be undesirable, and indeed, as the production history reveals, these films could only be made against the skepticism of state officials, who considered the genre escapist and sensationalist but who had to acquiesce to the films' overwhelming success. Evidence suggests, however, that we should consider the *Indianerfilme* as part of what Bathrick calls a rejuvenated national culture: the reasons for success of the *Indianerfilme* in the 1960s and early 1970s, and for their remarkable return on German television and in fan books in recent years as part of a broad wave of "Ostalgie" (nostalgia for the East), lie, not so much in the successful appropriation of proven formulas, but rather in the way in which the films tap into broadly held notions of national identity, firmly appropriating the "other," that is, the North American Indians, as an "us."[7] Coming from a long tradition of German fascination with Native Americans, the East German *Indianerfilme* derived their success from turning alien characters into figures of a decisively *German* national culture.

The most important model for the negotiation of national identity through fiction centered around North American Indians is, of course, the oeuvre of Karl May. The differences and parallels between the *Indianerfilme* and the writings of Karl May reveal both the strong continuity of the German imaginary relation to the American West from the late nineteenth century onward as well as the particular East German inflection of this imaginary. Often considered the most popular writer in the German language, Karl May was officially held in disregard in the GDR; he was looked down upon as an inferior writer, a bourgeois or even chauvinist whose exotic tales paved the way for the ideology of blood and soil. Klaus Mann's indictment of May as "the cowboy mentor of the Führer" and Hitler's supposed order to his generals, after the debacle of Stalingrad, to read *Winnetou* to boost their morale were well known.[8]

Officially made to correct May's pulp fiction, not a single *Indianerfilm* was based on his writings. Instead, one searched among the works of contemporary East German authors; the first *Indianerfilm*, *Die Söhne der großen Bärin*, adapted a cycle of novels of the same title by Liselotte Welskopf-Henrich. An internationally renowned anthropologist, Welskopf-Henrich sees her work as a combination of literature and scholarship and a direct response to the irresponsible fabulations of Karl May.[9] And yet, May's shadow looms large. Ehrentraud Novotny described the situation at DEFA in the mid-1960s as follows: "It is indeed not easy to renew the representation of the problems of the Indians after Karl May and other bourgeois have affected generations with their creations."[10] Despite the anxiety of influence, the Indianerfilme show traces of May's powerful vision at every step. As in May, the Indians are portrayed as noble savages who rally against American materialism and greed. May's romantic anticapitalism is similar to that of the DEFA films. May dehistoricized the West to portray it outside of industrial modernity; this abstraction from the real history of the Native Americans was in fact the precondition of their internationalization.[11] The GDR films, in contrast, make it their goal to return to history; rather than seeking an international or universal appeal, the representation of Indian history is intended to mirror the history of one's own country. Thus in both May's novels and the DEFA films, the history of the Other remains subordinated to one's own agenda. If in May the master narrative is one of Christian redemption, in the DEFA films it is the struggle of a beleaguered, precapitalist minority. Furthermore, the DEFA films pair historical accuracy with unrealistic good guys versus bad guys plots and thus undermine anthropological credibility. And as in May, we find in the Indianerfilme the search for homogeneous communities and peaceful coexistence of Indians and whites, the central image of which is the "Blutsbrüderschaft" (brotherhood of blood). May's story of the bonding between Winnetou and Old Shatterhand in the Winnetou novels is recast in the DEFA film Blutsbrüder (Blood brothers) (1975); as in May's tales of the friendship of the noble Apache and the German hero, two enemies become friends for life after they have fought each other. Harmonica, like May's hero Old Shatterhand, wins the heart of the sister of his blood brother, thus fortifying family ties. Yet like Nscho-tschi in Winnetou, Rehkitz in Blutsbrüder has to die, underscoring the taboo of interracial offspring in both Karl May and the DEFA films. The DEFA film adds an additional twist to the brotherhood through the fact that Harmonica is played by Dean Reed, an American singer and songwriter of protest songs who had come to the GDR for political reasons. In the film, he deserts from the U.S. Army and joins the Indians (like the Kevin Costner character in Dances with Wolves) after having witnessed how the army massacred an Indian village – the brotherhood is, therefore, open to Americans provided they, like Harmonica, are willing to burn the American flag.

In an analysis of the 1950s West German Karl May festivals, Katrin Sieg has shown how May's Winnetou tales provided their West German audience with Wiedergutmachungsphantasien (fantasies of restitution). By offering his friendship to Old Shatterhand, Winnetou not only "forgives" him as a representative of the race who organized the genocide of the Native Americans but also alludes to the genocide that goes unnamed, namely, the Holocaust of the European Jews. "[Winnetou's allegiance with] the 'good' whites (= Germans), and his refusal to hold them responsible for the atrocities of the 'bad' whites (= the Yankees) register postwar [West] Germans' fantasies of absolution and restitution: to be forgiven for the horrors perpetrated and to render them undone."[12]

Harald Reinl's *Winnetou* trilogy from the 1960s restages these fantasies since they are central to May's novels, but the films make an effort to deflect any connections to recent German history. The two main characters of the trilogy, Old Shatterhand and Winnetou, are played by an American, Lex Barker, and a Frenchman, Pierre Brice, respectively; many of the supporting roles are filled by foreigners as well. This effort to internationalize the story is also under-scored by shooting it in Yugoslavia. While much of this is standard procedure to assure a film its largest possible audience, one can surmise that Reinl was sensitive to the fact that May's image of a patronizing German vis-à-vis an ethnic minority would echo unwanted memories of cultural superiority.[13] In a similar vein, much of the missionary enthusiasm of May's German *West-männer* is translated into mere action film.

The processes of denial and repression that propel identifications with Winne-tou in May's novel in the annual Bad Segeberg open-air festival and (to a lesser degree) in Reinl's films are also detectable in the East German films. If Winnetou offers *Wiedergutmachungsphantasien* – a most powerful fantasy offered to an audience ridden by guilt and attentive to state-prescribed philo-Semitism – the Indians played by Mitic offer a fantasy designed to resonate with the commitment to antifascism, the founding principle, or foundational fiction, of the GDR. Gojko Mitic, in his incarnations of Tecumseh, Osceola, Ulzana, Tokei-ihto, Chingachgook, Weitspähender Falke, Hard Boulder, Shave Head, White Feather, and Severino, initiates organized struggles and partisan attacks against the whites bent on the destruction of Native tribes. Refus-ing to be a powerless victim of a genocide, Mitic acts out the fantasy of the resistance fighter and antifascist, providing a role model for young citizens and relieving older ones from responsibilities they may not have been up to during the rise of Nazism and Hitler's rule.[14]

Partisan warfare is particularly important in *Apachen* (1973). After white miners have killed more than four hundred members of the Mimbrenos tribe, chief Ulzana, one of only few survivors of the massacre, vows revenge, and, of course, is victorious in the end. Similarly, in the sequel *Ulzana* (1974), the peace-loving tribe has to go on the warpath after their irrigation system, which provided their economic independence, is destroyed by local business-men. Although outnumbered, the Apaches attack Fort Craig, where Captain Burton holds Ulzana's kidnapped wife. After Burton kills her, Ulzana hunts down Burton in the mountains and throws him into a gorge. Both films were cowritten by Mitic and portray Ulzana as a peace-loving, farming chief who acts in self-defense against genocidal settlers and army officials. According to DEFA ideology, the impetus of the films was to dispel the image of the Apache as war-mongering tribe presented in many Hollywood films; Mitic's Ulzana seems to be the exact reversal of the Indian chief portrayed in Robert Aldrich's *Ulzana's Raid* (1972). In Aldrich's film Ulzana and his men escape from the reservation to go on an extremely violent rampage, only to be hunted and eventually killed by a cavalry unit. By merely reversing the stereotypes from red devil to noble savage, the DEFA films miss out on the moral ambiguity and complexity of Aldrich's film. *Ulzana's Raid* explains Indian violence as stemming from a resistance to assimilation and maltreatment on the reservation, but it also insists on a radical cultural alteriority that ultimately defies comprehension and prohibits coexistence. It is telling that in Aldrich's film Ulzana is killed, not by an army soldier, but by the scout Ke-Ni-Tai, an Apache himself; Aldrich's film suggests that if there is a future for Indians, it will be only as acculturated subjects in the service of the whites. *Apachen* and *Ulzana*, in contrast, cherish the possibility of a *Nischengesellschaft*, of survival on a remote reservation outside the parameters of U.S. imperialism.

Both the attraction and the credibility of these fantasies are based in no small measure on the acting and personal background of their star, Gojko Mitic. Born in Yugoslavia to a father who fought Hitler's army as a partisan, Mitic had moved to East Berlin in the mid-1960s after having already acted in some English and Italian productions and some of Reinl's Karl May films. Mitic was thus a highly visible exception to the westward flow of East German actors and film professionals. Director Konrad Petzold praised Mitic as a professional and an ideological role model: "It is not as if Gojko had no other choice than to portray Indians here in the East. He had, and as far as I know he continues to have, offers from the capitalist countries. It's a sign of his straightforwardness [*Geradlinigkeit*] and honesty that he chooses to work here exclusively. He is really serious about this work, and it is important to him to participate in the new discoveries and the new developments of this genre, according to our Marxist view of history."[15] Mitic's offscreen character-istics, which biographer Ehrentraud Novotny describes as "understated, dis-ciplined, modest, hard-working, reliable, sympathetic and companionable," combine with his on-screen courage, athleticism and good looks, wisdom, and leadership; just as the athlete Gojko Mitic is a convinced antialcoholic, his Indians will not be fooled by "firewater" either.[16] These qualities make him a role model for children, the dream of teenage girls, and an ideal son-in-law – a particularly Teutonic form of model Indian and model citizen. As one commentator described the reaction of fans: "When Gojko was on the scene, we had mass rallies that weren't even ordered from above."[17]

It could be argued that Mitic's star persona thus not only incorporates the Yugoslav partisan, the model German, the Native American tribal hero, and the displaced Jew, but also the American. Even if DEFA was at pains to downplay the U.S. origin of the Western genre, and even if the films' message was always anti-American, it was still articulated through a Hollywood genre, and one that, as Bazin had claimed, was quintessentially American.[18] The emulated players were Americans too – the historical Indian chiefs were indeed "First Americans" or "Native Americans" and would later by law become U.S. citizens as were the twentieth-century actors who embodied them. Indeed, an obvious association one makes when watching Mitic on screen is with the many white American men, such as Burt Lancaster, Jeff Chandler, Charles Bronson, Paul Newman, and others, who had performed the role of the Indian. The star cult that surrounded Mitic in the GDR is reminiscent of that of these famous Hollywood stars – yet another indication of how a capitalist phenomenon successfully penetrated socialist culture, even if on a much smaller scale.

One could read the Indianerfilm as a strategy of resistance where the colonized uses the language of the colonizer to turn the table. But a less heroic reading seems more plausible. Not only is the model of colonizer and colonized inaccurate in this historical context, but more importantly, except for plot reversals, DEFA did little to question established genre conventions. It would seem, therefore, that a certain degree of Americanization was willingly accepted if its employment would help gain favor with home audiences, who had begun to show less and less interest in DEFA's political fables. It is ironic, but perhaps no coincidence, that the breakthrough success of the Indianerfilme came during the year of the so-called Kaninchenfilme, when almost an entire year's production ended up on the shelves of the censors.[19] Among the twelve banned films was Frank Beyer's Spur der Steine (1965), which read the Western genre against the grain, thus doing what the Indianerfilme had not dared. Rather than enacting a costume drama in a distant place and time, Spur der Steine restages the Western on a GDR construction site where a crew

Fig. 18. Gojko Mitic attending a powwow near Seattle with Richard Restoule, actor and Ojibwa elder.

of carpenters, reminiscent in garb and demeanor of the Magnificent Seven, have assumed control.[20] Filmed in CinemaScope, the plot of the film is driven by the conflict that also propels Hollywood Westerns: a strong and singular individual asserts his power by neglecting laws and regulations he deems morally inferior. Even though the hero Balla is crushed in the end, his resistance toward the inhuman bureaucracy and petrified structures of the Party system has won him the sympathies of the audience. Where *Spur der Steine* creatively translates the U.S. genre into an allegory on what it means to be a hero under socialism, the *Indianerfilme* impose a socialist notion of community onto the genre. In contrast to Manfred Krug's Balla, Mitic's Indians are almost always team players. The leadership they provide is regulated by tribal laws that are never questioned; decisions are not made on impulse, and they are monitored by tribe elders. Conflicts arise with white settlers and the U.S. Army but seldom within the community. Whereas the *Indianerfilme* dress up

Swiss Saxony as Monument Valley, *Spur der Steine* presents genuine GDR urban cowboys.

Mitic, the "DEFA-Chefindianer" as he was called, is undeniably an East German Indian. Contemporaneous developments in West Germany show some similarities but mostly significant differences from the image presented by Mitic. In the late 1960s, tribal culture became the model of an "alternative" lifestyle in the Federal Republic. Following broad trends toward environmentalism and antitechnology, North American Indians became symbols for a precapitalist social and economic model, a fascination also clearly evident in the agrarian, simple, and easy to grasp life of Indian tribes staged in the DEFA *Indianerfilme*. In the Federal Republic, however, the Indian acquired popularity as a model for a modern rebel. "*Stadtindianer*," hut dwellers, and urban guerrillas fought airport extensions, nuclear power plants, and other evils of the White Man's society. The Göttinger *Stadtindianer* acquired fame in Germany's subculture when in a "Mescalero letter" they expressed "klammheimliche Freude" (clandestine joy) after the killing of state general attorney Siegfried Buback by terrorists in 1977. The notion of transposing the qualities of Indians onto the modern metropolis, of searching for the "Strand unter dem Pflaster" (the beach under the cobblestones), is completely absent in the DEFA *Indianerfilme*; even though they can be read as allegories of contemporary East Germany, their portrayal of Indian life is always a costume drama, a period piece from which one can learn only by implication. Nor is there any of the guerrilla rhetoric so prominent in the West or the anarchism of Herbert Achternbusch's Bavarian Comanches. As I have shown elsewhere, Achternbusch's idiosyncratic performances of Native Americans criticize rather than endorse the contemporary fascination with all things Indian; they specifically link the Germans' eagerness to identify with the victim with a displacement of their historical responsibility for the Holocaust and its legacy.[21] In striking contrast to Achternbusch's portrayals of rebels and renegades, the fantasies offered through Mitic's heroics stress responsibility for the community, fairness, openness, and willingness to reach peaceful agreements with an enemy one knows to be overpowering. Though more docile, these fantasies are equally utopian: for a people that only four years ago had experienced the building of the Berlin Wall, to watch nomadic tribes move about in wide open landscapes held an obvious attraction, and it is indeed striking how many of the films conclude with the tribe moving to a better hunting ground, the ultimate fantasy of the citizens of the GDR.

The differences between East and West German appropriations of *Indianer* only underline the fact that in both Germanys, both before and after its division into two national states, there exists a common, widespread, and existential identification with Indians that seems to surpass that of other nations. Germans seem to want to understand Indians, not only better than other people could (especially people in the United States), but also better than they themselves could. Phil Lucas, a Native American filmmaker, tells the anecdote of filming a German "Indianerklub" that had adopted the Yakima tribe: "We went to their clubhouse and it was like going to a museum. It was very impressive; they had all made it themselves. . . . They were about to have a drum blessing ceremony, and they told us that this was a holy ceremony which we couldn't film. That was very funny for us, to hear this as Indians, for this is what we usually tell others. . . . It was very impressive – to find real recognition of Native Americans, one has to go to Europe."[22]

The *Indianerfantasien* of both East and West Germany are clearly interchangeable because they both stem from the same tradition. This flexibility is also evident in Mitic's career. When the Wall fell, Mitic thought he would have to go to the eternal hunting grounds to which Karl May sends his dead protagonists; instead, the West accepted him as readily as the East, making him the successor of Pierre Brice, veteran of Karl May films, at the Bad Segeberg open-air festivals. In the 1960s and 70s, the slogan "Unser Gojko," with which Mitic was commonly greeted at the summer festival premieres of the latest DEFA *Indianerfilm*, was a sign of a double appropriation of the Yugoslav *Indianer*: as East German citizen and collector of national identity.

Notes

1. I will not consider here two films made without Gojko Mitic, *Blauvogel* (1979) and *Atkins* (1985), because even though they involve Indians, the story is not told from their perspective.

2. From a 1971 interview with *Berliner Zeitung*; quoted in Habel, *Gojko Mitic*, 12, my translation.

3. See Torgovnick, *Gone Primitive*.

4. See Ward Churchill: "To date, all claims to the contrary notwithstanding, there has not been one attempt to put out a commercial film which deals with native reality through native eyes." (*Fantasies*, 236).

5. See, for example, Richard Restoule, known from his performance in *Northern Exposure* and himself a tribal elder of the Ojibwas: "After everything that has been done to my people, also through bad films, it is good to know that already thirty years ago, people in East Germany began to think seriously how to do things dif-

ferently." (In a speech given at a screening of *Die Söhne der großen Bärin* in Seattle, October 1996. Quoted in Habel, *Gojko Mitic*, 6.)

6. Bathrick, *Power of Speech*, 178.

7. Apart from Habel's coffee-table book quoted above, there are also Gojko Mitic's memoirs, *Erinnerungen*. A Web site maintained by fans is located at http://www.wazel.org/wildeast/.

8. See Mann, "Cowboy Mentor," 217–22.

9. In their attempt to get the history "right," the producers not only based their script on Welskopf-Henrich's novel but also asked her to be a consultant on the film. She accepted the task but later complained about the many liberties the film took with her novel, often sacrificing her attention to detail and accuracy for dramatic effect.

10. Novotny, *Gojko Mitic*, 25.

11. On May's relation to U.S. history see Hohendahl, "Von der Rothaut," 229–45. See also Jeffrey Sammons's contribution to this volume.

12. Sieg, "Ethic Drag," 303. See also Sieg's contribution in this volume.

13. On Reinl's May adaptations see also Koll, "Der träumende Deutsche," 384–97. It should also be pointed out that as far as the critics – not the public – was concerned, Reinl's films fared much better abroad than in West Germany.

14. The triangulation one finds in these films is not endemic to German cinema. When the American public learned about the Holocaust in the 1950s, the portrayal of Indians in Hollywood film became somewhat more realistic and less stereotypical. Yet this development did not necessarily lead to an investigation of the role of the United States in the Holocaust of the European Jews nor in the genocide of North American Indians. Thus in John Ford's *Cheyenne Autumn* (1964), for example, the strategy of blaming a third party is also visible. The film portrays the long march of the Cheyennes, reduced by disease and starvation, from their Oklahoma reservation to North Dakota. While the Cheyenne are pursued by the U.S. Army, it is particularly the figure of Wessels, an army captain of German descent, who brutalizes the Indians. It is ironic to see that Ford, who boasted to have "killed more Indians [in his films] than Custer, Beecher, and Chivington put together" (see Bogdanovich, *John Ford*, 104), in a film that he considered his personal act of restitution toward the Native Americans is yet again deflecting the responsibility for genocide.

15. Novotny, *Gojko Mitic*, 27.

16. Novotny, *Gojko Mitic*, 14.

17. Habel, *Gojko Mitic*, 12.

18. See André Bazin, *What is Cinema?*

19. The term *Kaninchenfilme*, literally "rabbit films," refers to the banned *Das Kaninchen bin ich* (I am the rabbit) by Kurt Maetzig.

20. The film was released in 1966 and met with great interest by the public.

Gerd Gemünden

After staged protests in East Berlin and Leipzig, the film was censored. *Neues Deutschland* wrote: "This film presents a distorted view of our socialist reality, its glorious Party, and the self-sacrificing efforts of its members." (6 July 1966). It was not shown again until 1989.

21. See Gemünden, *Framed Visions*.

22. Peipp and Springer, *Edle Wilde*, 269–70. The ambiguities of German hobbyism and particularly the significance of meeting with the approval and respect of Native Americans are discussed in detail by Sieg and Marta Carlson in their contributions to this volume.

Part 4: Two-Souled Warriors
The Conjunction of Germans and Indians Revisited

"Stranger and Stranger"

The (German) Other in Canadian Indigenous Texts

RENATE EIGENBROD

In September 1995 I met for the first time Daniel David Moses, Delaware poet and coeditor of *An Anthology of Canadian Native Literature in English*. I met him in Trier, Germany, in the context of an international conference organized by the Association for the Study of the New English Literatures and talked to him on a boat that took the conference participants for a cruise on the Moselle River. Asking him for an autograph in his anthology, which I had used as a textbook in my Native literature courses since 1992, when it first came out, he wrote the following:

> for Renata [sic]
> Daniel David Moses
> in Trier '95
> "Stranger and stranger"

I remembered this play on words when I started to think about the role of the European stranger in indigenous texts. Moses's autograph makes sense on several levels. We had not known each other before and were strangers to each other. I am also a stranger to him as a nonaboriginal person and he a stranger to me as a non-German person. The "strangeness" of the situation was highlighted by the circumstances: for him to read his poetry in a strange country, for me to meet him in a place I had become estranged from as I had emigrated to Canada, and for both of us to be surrounded by German tourist guides and by the stereotypical "romantic" German landscape of villages and castles. Cross-cultural encounters were indeed becoming "stranger and stranger."

I assume that our meeting in Canada would have been different: I, the immigrant, would still be the stranger, but he, the indigenous person, would belong. However, in his conversation with Terry Goldie, which functions as a preface to his anthology, he specifically mentions that while he feels comfortable with Native groups all over the country, he may feel strange wherever

Fig. 19. While the Caribou was in Europe, the Stag asked, "Would you help me be spiritual again?" Ahmoo Angeconeb, 1998. Courtesy of the artist.

there are no Native people: "I feel that I can go to any Native events. Whereas I have lived in Toronto for many years, and there are places here I feel strange."[1] In other words, it is not so much the country or the continent as the people who evoke strangeness or estrangement. Anishinabe writer Kateri Akiwenzie-Damm states this quite categorically and emphatically: "The Native peoples of this land are *fundamentally different from anyone else. We are fundamentally different from anyone else in this land, fundamentally different from Canadians.*"[2]

   In the following essay I discuss how such "difference" is constructed in fictional and nonfictional texts by indigenous writers. In particular, I explore how they create an inclusive concept of "pan-Native similarity" in opposition to "strangers," in this case, Germans.[3] Is strangeness, I want to ask, a negative or a positive concept in Native thought? What makes someone a "stranger"? And how is ethnic (i.e., racial and cultural) difference articulated and resolved with respect to the people of a country, which, in its own past, has resorted to an annihilatory battle against anybody outside its racial-cultural "norm"?[4]

In many Native texts, "difference" or strangeness has positive connotations. Thus in one of the so-called legends passed on orally for generations among the Anishinaubae (or Anishinabe) nations, "The Spirit of Maundau-meen (Maize)," corn is "personified as a stranger" who was sent to the Anishinaubae to feed them.[5] This "migrant," as he is called in Johnston's version of the story, comes from Mexico and travels to different peoples, among them hunters and fishermen, whom he dares to "master" him. He also challenges the Anishinaubae people, who eventually overcome him in battle; through his death a new plant is born, which the people name "Maundau-meen, the seed of wonder, or the wonderful food."[6] After enjoying the abundance of food provided by the stranger for some years, the corn harvest (and other harvests as well) begin to fail because of disrespectful behavior of the people toward plants and animals. Only after they recognize their mistake and change their attitudes do they again have food in abundance. Strangers, the story tells us, bring valuable gifts. If properly integrated, they will take root and contribute to the welfare of their host culture.

Another legend raises a cautionary note. In his prophecy story, set in pre-contact time, Basil Johnston's storyteller tells of strange-looking people, "men and women with white skins," who will be fought "too late." Instead of being "domesticated" like the corn stranger, these strangers come "from the east across a great body of salt water . . . in quest for lands."[7] The plural of the word "land" signifies a quantification of land, something to be divided up among different "owners." Wanting to own lands, these strangers use their technology, not to the benefit of all, but in order to displace the indigenous people, driving them "from their homes and hunting grounds to desolate territories where game can scarce find food for their own needs and corn can bare take root."[8] Johnston's storyteller, Daebaudjimoot, compares these predatory strangers to birds: "After them [the first few] will come countless others like flocks of geese in their migratory flights. Flock after flock they will arrive."[9]

A similar confrontation between sedentary indigenous people and ravenous birds/strangers is thematized in "This Is a Story" (1990) by Jeannette Armstrong from the Okanagan First Nation. Her allegory features Kyoti, the well-known "trickster," who wanders in search of his people with whom he is out of touch because he slept too long. Instead of finding the "People" who speak the language and eat the food he is used to, he finds people who adapted their way of life to the powerful Swallows. With the help of an old woman and a young man, Kyoti sets out to destroy the dam that was built by the Swallows and to transform these "monstrous" Swallows into less destructive beings.

Kyoti's migrations parallel with and contrast to the Swallows' migratory behavior. His traveling has a purpose; he needs to get around in order to help his people by changing "the Swallows from Monsters into something that didn't destroy things," whereas the homesteading Swallows are perceived as coming and going with only their own interests in mind. The contrast, then, is not between migrant and homesteader, but between those who take care of the land and those who divide and destroy: the Swallows "took over any place and shitted all over it"; they "stole anything they could pick up for their houses."[10]

In her poem "History Lesson," Armstrong makes her point even more explicit by openly challenging the notion of civilization as conventionally linked to the settler culture.[11] After listing the "gifts" of the colonizers,

Smallpox, Seagrams
and Rice Krispies,

she adds further sarcasm:

Civilization has reached
the promised land.

According to Armstrong, the destructive forces of Western history are the consequence of a search based on wrong ("unholy") motivations. She ends her poem with the following stanza:

Somewhere among the remains
of skinless animals
is the termination
to a long journey
and unholy search
for the power
glimpsed in a garden
forever closed
forever lost.

It is the motivation of Europeans, their greedy, exploitative, materialistic dominating attitude toward the land and its people, that makes them "strangers" in paradise.

Similar to Canadian First Nations writers, Native American intellectuals and activists like Vine Deloria, Russell Means, and Winona LaDuke construct "difference" between European immigrants and indigenous peoples on the basis of different attitudes toward the land. As Anishinabe/Native American writer Winona LaDuke puts it, indigenous people of North America think of themselves as "the North American Host World, the truly landbased people" in contrast to the European (im)migrants who cut themselves off from the land.[12] She further explains that the settlers in their "arrogance" created a "synthesis" of an imported ideology with the naturally given conditions so that "a new economic order was forged *on* the land, not *with* the land."[13] Like Jeannette Armstrong she sees this "unholy" ideology as the reason for colonization and exploitation. Russell Means, Oglala Lakota actor and lecturer, who is widely known as a leader in the AIM movement, argues that "American Indians know" that the "belief that man is god" is "totally absurd. Humans are the weakest of all creatures, so weak that other creatures are willing to give up their flesh so that we may live."[14] For many indigenous writers, Europeans are, therefore, not of a different race or ethnicity but people who espouse a different mindset. European "imperialist thought," as Armstrong argues, needs to be replaced by "the relearning of co-operation and sharing."[15]

If "European" characters as allegorical figures serve to determine the boundaries between two different modes of thinking and acting, particularly vis-à-vis the land, German characters in literary texts seem to generate or entertain a somewhat more "hybrid" in-between position. As go-betweens, they problematize the European-indigenous binaries, suggesting multiple forms of border crossings. In the following discussion, I concentrate on three texts, the novels *Ravensong* (1993) by Salish/Métis author Lee Maracle, *A Quality of Light* (1997) by Anishinabe Richard Wagamese, and the short story *Compatriots* (1990) by Emma Lee Warrior (included in this volume).[16] In all three, German characters figure prominently, if differently, as emblems of successful or flawed assimilation, association, or impersonation.

Among the three texts under scrutiny, *Ravensong* most openly moves back and forth between constructions of "us" and "them," as it seeks to undermine such dichotomization. The title of the novel, which is set in the 1950s along the Pacific Northwest coast, refers to the so-called trickster figure of the West Coast First Nations, Raven, and her larger-than-human message (song) about cross-cultural communication. Raven knows that an environmental disaster can only be prevented if the European "others" will be "rooted to the soil of this land" (44). Observing from "high up" the events in a Native community, which is located in the immediate vicinity of a non-Native community, she tries to communicate her insights to Stacey, the seventeen-year-old Native high school student and human protagonist of the novel – unsuccessfully so, for instead of reaching out to others, Stacey fails, forcing Raven to send sickness as a means of bringing the two communities together.[17] The novel shows how Stacey's aptitude for becoming a boundary crosser (she "had all the advantages of Dominic's and Nora's [the Native elders'] good sense and

Renate Eigenbrod

the knowledge of the others," [44]) is hampered by her thinking in unreconcilable oppositions. The thrust of the narrative is therefore on negotiating connections, a tension that is reflected in the coexistence of the two central images of the novel, the gulf and the bridge.

Mostly seen through Stacey's eyes, the "white" community in this novel is perceived as "rootless" (39), that is, as lacking in positive lineage memory: they consider children to be "transient visitors" (26, 27) and have no strong family ties. The "lack of connectedness" (17) with biological relatives manifests itself in other ways as well. As Stacey states, "some white people had no roots in the creative process" so that if "you have only yourself as a start and end point, life becomes a pretense at continuum" (61). While Stacey's thinking about the courage of the salmon mates on their way over the falls to the spawning grounds makes her feel "rooted . . . to a sense of duty she could not explain" (61), this link with all of creation is not seen as a solution for "white folks," who apparently lack "this sensibility" (61). Because of their lack of spiritual connectedness, they suffer from a "frailty" that "did not look physical" (29), but leads to suicide and (sexual) abuse with which they eventually also infect the Native people. "The old snake [a Native wife abuser] had brought a piece of white town with him to the village. Stacey knew Shelly had been abused and discarded by a white man. It's how they are, she thought. They don't really like us. . . . Now the old snake was just like them" (149–50). Stacey uses the generalizing third-person pronoun "they" and "them" and "boundary-constructing images" such as "the outside world" (63) and "the other world" (113) to explain "the gulf" between colonizers and colonized or, in one of her comments, between masters and slaves (75).[18] Toward the end of the novel, in her last meeting with Steve, a young man from the white town who wants to be her friend, Stacey concludes that they cannot be together: "There is this gulf between us. I have no idea how deep or wide it is. I just know it's there" (185).

By constituting ethnic contrasts Stacey's voice in the novel generates "feelings of dissociative belonging," sometimes to the extent of dehumanizing the other.[19] Even more extreme than Stacey is Stacey's mother, who has only left the village once. " 'They aren't human,' she had told Stacey a while back, categorically dismissing them all" (193). The rigid dichotomies of us versus them established by Stacey and her mother create a "biased perspective."[20] However, they are contested by a series of boundary-crossing devices in the form of shifting imagery, narrative point of view, an "oral aesthetic" (Blaeser) of reader response-ability, and, in particular, by the character of "German Judy."

The gulf or chasm between the Native village and the white town is set off by the other central image of the novel, the bridge. It is on this bridge that Stacey meets with her two friends from "the other world," Carol, with whom she walks to school every morning, and Steve, whom she does not want on the bridge observing her watching the salmon swim upstream: "If she stopped for her habitual private vigil he might ask what she was doing. He might disturb the peace of the vigil, *contaminate* its peaceful nature by *disrupting* its *privacy*" (75, my emphasis). As Stacey considers the others' search for knowledge only a nuisance, an intrusion, and even a contamination of the purity of her (spiritual) experience, she does not bother to teach her friend about the source of strength for her. It is in situations such as these – symbolically located on or close to the bridge – that Stacey's limitations as a bridge builder between two cultures becomes most obvious.

Raven, the trickster, holds a less one-dimensional view of "the Europeans" than Stacey does: she sympathizes with the "uprooted" others, "poor pale creatures who had forgotten their ways centuries before. She mused over their recounting of origins from the time Jesus was murdered. Parched throat, he had perished straddling sacred cedar in a land far from their own. They borrowed his spirit, his heroism, but did so in distorted fashion" (44). In the indigenous way of "thinking in space" (Deloria) a religion that was "transplanted" (Cardinal-Schubert), such as Christianity, is considered an imitation, "borrowed."[21] While Raven is also critical of such "transplanting," his choice of words suggests a link between Christian and Native beliefs: on the one hand, the "sacred cedar" that Jesus is "straddling" refers to the crucifix made of cedar wood to which Jesus was nailed; on the other, it refers to Native beliefs in the sacredness of all beings, for cedar is sacred by simply being a tree. No wonder, then, that Cedar, besides Raven, is the other nonhuman character who tries to guide humans, in particular Stacey, and who is spiritually connected to them.

The word "straddling" also indicates a bringing together of two sides or a crossing over. Similar to the "trickster," a "pivotal and important figure" in the world of North American Indian mythology, who "straddles the consciousness of man and that of God, the Great Spirit," Christ straddles both the human and the supernatural world.[22] In short, although one layer of meaning in Raven's message clearly separates "the uprooted others" from the villagers, another layer hints at possible connections between the two groups so that her plan "to root" the others "to the soil of this land" (44) does not seem to be an impossible task.

In addition to inserting "bridge" moments that supersede Stacey's one-sided point of view, Maracle undercuts her position by introducing a polyphony of voices. Stacey's biased, self-deceptive, often confused, and hence un-reliable perspective is challenged by the voices of Raven, Cedar, and Earth, whose inner thoughts the omniscient narrator also reveals. Although Stacey dismisses Raven as "a foolish crow" (75), the narrator gives enough context for readers to understand Raven's "indignant shriek" (75) as a critical com-ment on Stacey's behavior toward Steve.[23] Raven also criticizes Stacey's mother for having missed an opportunity for teaching the "others," young men who stayed in her house during the Depression, about their ways. " 'Shame on you, Momma,' Raven now sighed from cedar's branch outside. . . . You could have taken the time to teach these men when first I brought them here" (54). The corrective voice of the trickster character Raven signifies difference *within* a Native community; it shows Native culture as a contested site.

In Maracle's own interpretation of the novel, there is differentiation in per-spectives, not only between the human and the nonhuman characters, but also among the four human storytellers identified in the epilogue: Stacey, her sister Celia, her mother, and Rena, another woman in the village, are charac-ters "who come to their culture from four different directions."[24] Although their role as storytellers is of unequal weight, since most of the attention is given to Stacey's thoughts, these four characters differing in age, edu-cational background, and sexual orientation further foreground difference against a seemingly homogeneous Native community and thus keep the reader from creating fixed images of Nativeness. The elder Dominic declares "*combined* wisdom" [my emphasis] as the Native way. Not "just one knowl-edge or another, but all knowledge should be joined" (67). It is with this philosophy of "human oneness" (67) contrapuntally set against the dualities created in the novel that I want to understand Maracle's characterization of German Judy.

The name of the character German Judy emphasizes her ethnically con-structed otherness, but she is also an Other in terms of her sexual orientation, as she lives in a lesbian relationship with Rena. One may argue that Maracle utilizes the German identity of one partner as a device to pronounce the strangeness of the situation. Although the novel conveys some of the commu-nity's discomfort and concerns with the lifestyle of the two women, German Judy is more discriminated against than Rena, the Native woman, because of her ethnically different background. German Judy is "the white woman" living "in a village that virtually ignored her. She was white. No one we know," Stacey told herself" (79). And her mother, in the context of her moral outrage over Stacey's "unchaperoned visit" with the women (121), totally dehuman-izes her when responding to Stacey's statement that they are not single: "She is white and so she don't count" (123). Rena, on the other hand, is respected despite her sexual orientation, as is shown in her status as a storyteller.

Ethnicity is understood as a significant marker of difference. Like German Judy, Madeline from the Manitoba Saulteaux, another female outsider in the native village, speaks with an accent. Her emphasized "difference" (173) draws attention to cultural variations among Native peoples and, as she is supported by the community, also to acceptance of difference. Although Madeline "was not one of them" (159), she gets help against her abusive husband (who, although a villager, is ostracized). Both strangers, Madeline and German Judy, become Stacey's teachers as they make her question judgments and assumptions about individual people and society as a whole. In fact, German Judy acquires special significance for the protagonist Stacey, as she "held the key" (81) to questions about the white world – from reasons for suicide to the role of women to registration procedures at a university. Stacey does not take full advantage of German Judy's knowledge. She does not allow "a white woman" to challenge her opinions: she only feels "a bit uneasy" (81) when German Judy tries to explain to her how gender may undermine racial binaries. While the novel grants more space to the depiction of Madeline's character than to Judy's, the inclusion of a German character still signals the novel's message of "combined wisdom" as the Native way. In her role of providing medical help to the villagers, she becomes part of Raven's design and hence an important voice in the novel's overall message of bringing together both cultures for the survival of all. Living as a non-Native person in a Native community and as a lesbian in patriarchal society, she is also a boundary crosser herself. Unlike Stacey's failed friendship with the young white man Steve, her relationship with a Native woman shows the possibilities of love as crossing the gulf of us and them. As Stacey observes: "They must really love each other . . . to have somehow climbed all the hills of complete misunderstanding" (114).

The mentioning of German Judy's accent identifies her as somebody who was not born in Canada but who came over as an adult, in this case, given the setting of the novel in the 1950s, probably shortly after World War II. This evocation of a political context connects her indirectly with another, if absent, character associated with the war and the ideology of fascism that caused it. Stacey's uncle, her mother's brother, became a naturalized Canadian when he enlisted in the war. For the longest time, her mother did not know what that term meant. When Stacey explains to her, "It means you're not an Indian anymore" (52) and that the soldiers had "to naturalize" in order to fight fascism, connections are established between geographically separated but ideologically linked political systems: In each country, rights (and lives) of a minority are taken away. Stacey's mother "burned with shame. Benny had gone half-way 'round the world to kill some boys in a fight against something that he had not been willing to fight at home" (53). The irony of this reversal is echoed in the novel's plot: A character linked through her nationality with the fascism that a Native man had fought against makes the Native community he cannot return to her home, her refuge from the past: "It dawned on Stacey that maybe her [German Judy's] segregation from the village was self-imposed and comfortable for her" (80). The figure of German Judy highlights that national and individual histories are not isolated but intertwined and overlapping. As Cathy Caruth puts it: "History, like trauma, is never simply one's own . . . history is precisely the way we are implicated in each other's traumas."[25]

Although the character of German Judy functions as a corrective to Stacey's dualistic thinking, her role remains marginalized since she is not one of the storytellers. It rests with readers who are "as much part of the story as the teller[s]" to understand the significance of her voice.[26] Coming to writing from the perspective of an orator, Maracle assumes that readers, at least readers familiar with "the principles of oratory," become responsible participants in the construction of meaning.[27] Lessons in this indigenous novel are thus not explicit but may be inferred. Native readers — according to Maracle's dualistic division of readers into "Europeans" and "us" in her often cited "Preface: You Become the Trickster" — need to understand that Stacey's point of view, although Native, is limited and must be complemented. European readers should read the novel with an understanding of colonization and its specific examples given in the text. Stacey's mother's seemingly racist views are related to and therefore explained, but not excused, by her experience of oppression; similarly, Stacey's harsh judgments are often influenced by her observations of the unfair treatment of her people during the flu epidemic in which non-Native people make no attempt to cross the bridge and help. Besides making these connections, European readers also need to accept Raven, a nonhuman, as a teacher.

In her article "Indigenous Peoples and the Cultural Politics of Knowledge," Laurie Anne Whitt emphasizes "a commitment to epistemological pluralism" as a feature of "indigenous knowledge systems": "Without glossing over the important differences in indigenous epistemologies (whose full range and richness should be stressed even if it is not here explored), we can note that many indigenous cultures place considerable significance and value on alternative ways of knowing the world, particularly on gaining access to the perspective of the other-than-human."[28] If the multiple point of view in

Ravensong is read also as an expression of a culturally embedded epistemology, Raven's alternative way of knowing the world, differing from and superseding the human characters' perspectives, may provide an interpretive framework for a nondualistic reading of the novel. The teacher Raven starts the novel by taking the reader into a space without boundaries: "The sound of Raven spiralled out from its small beginning in larger and larger concentric circles, gaining volume as it passed each successive layer of green. The song echoed the rolling motion of earth's centre, filtering itself through the last layer to reach outward to earth's shoreline above the deep" (9). The spiral movements of her song set the tone for an ethical narrative that dialectically moves back and forth between a condition that *is* – segregation, racism, prejudice, injustice – to what *"ought-to-be"*: "a combined wisdom" (67).[29]

German Judy's novel relationship with the Native culture is, to use Edward Said's distinction, one of *affiliation* rather than of *filiation*.[30] She keeps her name throughout the novel. Rather than "becoming Native," she functions as a bridge between the cultures, a link. An outsider, she joins in the many voices that make up "community."

Gloria Anzaldúa, herself a "border crosser," identifies two opposite ways of appreciating "a culture that is not your own culture": celebration and appropriation.[31] Unlike German Judy, who mediates but neither celebrates nor appropriates, the two German characters in Richard Wagamese's *A Quality of Light* and Emma Lee Warrior's "Compatriots" oscillate between these two poles, because they attempt to come to terms with what they perceive to be an identity they covet.

A Quality of Light (1997), Wagamese's second novel following his partly autobiographical bestseller *Keeper'N Me* (1994), "helped to establish him as one of Canada's major new literary talents."[32] His first novel is the story of a young man returning to his Native community from which he had been taken as a child. Raised in non-Native foster families, he is confused when he comes back into a Native environment. The elder "Keeper," who helps him (re)connect with his ethnic roots, insists that, because of unbridgeable differences between the two cultures, placing Native children into non-Native homes has disastrous effects: "Got raised up all white but still carryin' brown skin. Hmmpfh. See, us we know you can't make a beaver from a bear. Nature don't work that way. Always gotta be what the Creator made you to be" (37). In his second novel Wagamese challenges this concept of a "natural" identity. Again narrated from a first-person point of view by an Ojibwa character who grew up in a non-Native family, *A Quality of Light* looks at how identity is constructed out of multiple layers. Adopted as a baby by a devout Christian family, Josh Kane tells of his friendship with the non-Native Johnny Gebhardt, while traveling from southern Ontario to Calgary in order to bring a solution to a political standoff staged by his friend. Already in the prologue Josh highlights the significance of their relationship: "It's about Johnny and me becoming Indians together, one because he wanted to and the other because he had to. It's only now that I understand that those parts are interchangeable" (9). Rather than espousing the concept of a biologically given identity, this story suggests choices.

The non-Native character of German descent, Johnny Gebhardt, serves to question fixed racial or cultural identities. As most of the story is told from the point of view of the Native traveler who sees himself as an "emotional voyageur" (1) and a "pilgrim" (97-98) reflecting upon nomads, his "nomadic consciousness," to use Rosi Braidotti's term, informs his reflections on difference.[33] In fact, his nomadic sensibility unearths "multiple layers of signification" of what it means to be "Native" or "indigenous."

Johnny Gebhardt's family, like other homesteading families in the agricultural southern Ontario setting of the novel, is of German or, more precisely, of "German Caucasian" (301) ancestry. However, he does not grow up learning about his ancestry or his family's place in Canadian society. Rather, his upbringing is characterized by the lack of any "cultural, historical anchor" (201) and by abuse. Both predestine him to "wanna be someone else" (70, 179). Inspired by books and popular culture, his substitute or chosen identity is "Indian." In one of his letters inserted into Josh's memoirs, he explains how one summer at camp he found a book in the library "called Indians. That's all, just Indians. I opened that book and I was gone. . . . When you grow up like I did, all your dreams involve being the opposite of the way you are and the warrior thing was directly opposite from me and my life" (77). The "warrior thing" shapes his imagination so much that he is confused about "the real Indian" Josh when he first meets him, as is obvious from his conversation with Josh's parents:

Well, reading's good," he [Josh's dad] said. "Joshua reads all the time too. What do you like to read about?"
"Indians, mostly, sir."
"Indians?"
"Yessir. I like 'em."
"You know that Joshua's an Indian, don't you, John?" my mother asked.
"Yes, ma'am. But I mean real Indians. You know, warriors and stuff."
"I think there's more to Indians than just being warriors, isn't there, John?" my dad asked.

"No, sir. I read about it. They were warriors."
"Joshua is not a warrior," my mother said.
"Yes, ma'am. That's what I mean. Real Indians." (56)

This conversation humorously captures the dehumanizing, dehistoricizing power of stereotypes. It also comments on (and questions) the belief in the authority of the written word: Johnny is not to be swayed, as he "read about it." For him – as for many Germans – fantasy Indians are "the real thing." However, the dialogue does not simply cast Johnny as ignorant and carried away by his imagination against a reality that speaks for itself. The fact that Josh, the adopted Ojibwa, *looks* Indian does not necessarily make him a *real* Indian – not just in Johnny's eyes but also within the larger sociocultural context of the novel. Some Native readers will question the reality of his "Indian" identity because Josh grows up in a non-Native home without knowing his Native language and culture. Johnny, on the other hand, will become a warrior in *reality*, in *real* wars like Oka, Alcatraz Island, Wounded Knee, and Anishanabe Park.[34] And, in a further ironic reversal, Johnny, the one who learns from books about "Indians," will teach the *real* Indian Josh about his history and culture. If the boundaries between fiction and reality are blurred in this way, culture is also shown as mediated: the question of who is a *real Indian* cannot be answered simply by referring to physical appearance.

Thematic movements in the novel questioning preconceived notions of "being Indian" are supported by a narrative structure that defies any kind of fixation. Not only is most of the story told by a traveling narrator, but also past and present events overlap: the story of Josh's travel, told in the present tense, serves as a frame for his memories of the past to which are added the memories of his friend, interspersed in italics. In this way the novel is narrated by two voices, made up of two stories, each told from a first-person point of view: one by the Ojibwa narrator Josh, who is given the most space, the other by his friend Johnny. The German character thus has a corrective, complementary, critical function insofar as he questions and expands the protagonist's (and readers') assumptions.

Reading *A Quality of Light* against Wagamese's *Keeper 'N Me*, which also includes the strategy of a dual-voiced narrative point of view, we can assess the development of Wagamese's thinking on identity. In his first novel he uses italicization to highlight the oral voice of the Native elder, by many Native people considered to be the authentic voice. He leaves the more standardized written English to the Native character who had become an outsider to his culture. In *A Quality of Light*, the oral-written binary – which Métis scholar Emma LaRocque defines as "the power struggle between the oral and the written, between the native in us and the English" – is confirmed insofar as the voice of the non-Native Johnny is largely expressed through his letters.[35] However, his words are italicized, so that, if we read the two novels together, a new intertext emerges that links Johnny's letters to the "authentic" Native voice.

A duality of voices and a dialogue are also created in the novel's discussions of Native versus Christian beliefs. The relationship between the two faiths is a controversial subject in Native communities, and attitudes vary from individual to individual.[36] Wagamese questions an often established exclusionary polarity by creating a character who combines both faiths as an Ojibwa minister who practices both the sweat lodge and Christian ceremonies. The twinning of the two beliefs is shown at the beginning of the novel in Josh's father's interpretation of the parable of the prodigal son. As the discussion about this particular aspect of cultural hybridity will be a contested area for the two friends, the interpretation of a biblical story about two brothers at the welcoming party for Johnny's family may be read as an attempt to show the adaptability of Christian teachings to Native culture. In his interpretation of the parable, Josh's father contrasts Johnny's father, the "agricultural refugee" (22), with himself, who never left the farm. This link anticipates the meeting of the sons and their eventual bonding in brotherhood.

Gebhardt's life as a "refugee" made Johnny's childhood homeless. Johnny remembers his family as nomads "willing to settle anywhere" (201). As an adult he continues the nomadic life: in a literal sense, since he traveled a lot, and metaphorically, since "he wandered alone in the vacuous maze of the wilderness" (185). Josh, on the other hand, belongs to "the lucky ones" who "grow up and out of the land of our births" (89), "salvation and geography intermingled like blood" (89). He considers himself "saved" and – although searching – on a "guided tour" (185), whereas Johnny belongs to "the wounded": "nomads moving like ghosts, incorporeal, ethereal, leaving no sign on the territories they cross" (185). Wagamese problematizes the colonialist discourse on European "settlers" and Native "nomads" in this reversed juxtaposition; for now it is the German Caucasian who roams the wilderness in contrast to the settled Native who, like a tourist, goes on "guided tours." Josh's link to the land is expressed in images of hybridity that connect Native conceptualizations of the sacredness of the land with an agricultural, homesteading understanding of it. The phrase to "grow up and out of the land of our births" echoes Native understanding of rootedness to the land of the ancestors, and the mentioning of "salvation" and "saved" recalls an often-cited Native spiritual connection with the land. This double-layered language linking the experience of growing up on a farm with Native ideas about the sacredness of the land is explained by the Christian minister Josh in the prologue of the novel. Looking back on his life, the Ojibwa narrator explains how he came to love the land through his father, with whom he worked on the farm since early childhood. "It was my father who brought me the spirit of the land. He'd sink his furrowed fingers deep into it, roll its grit and promise around his palms, smell it and then rub it over the chest of his overalls like he wanted it to seep through into his heart. It did—and it seeped into mine too" (7). Unlike Lee Maracle, who in *Ravensong* pitted her Indian character against the white characters for their wearing gloves for their garden work (and hence disrupting the physical connection to the soil), Wagamese foregrounds class and occupation rather than race. He challenges an essentialist reading of indigenousness, since he substitutes a supposedly authentic indigenous relationship with the nurturing connection to the earth that any true farmer might experience. In this way Wagamese shows that respectful relationships with the land are not "genetically" Indian but are, as Russell Means explains, *acculturated* traits.[37] After all, as the Ojibwa character states, the "land is a palimpsest" (246); the different layers of this text ask for different readings. But only the wounded, nomadic character Johnny is able to help his friend decipher a text that his Christian, non-Native parents, who had never left the security of their farm, had chosen to ignore. Reading about Wounded Knee, Josh learns about the blood of massacred people seeping into the earth: "This land is a palimpsest, but it requires the eyes and ears of the enlightened to hear its songs and see its scars" (246). Because his German Caucasian friend Johnny, scarred himself, was enlightened enough to hear and see, he could teach his friend Josh to read the hidden stories of the land and, in this way, to "become Indian."

In this novel the specifically Germanic legacy of the non-Native character seems to be incidental, except for a brief dialogue between Josh and Johnny near the end of the novel, when the latter realizes that he is after all only "a whiteman" and a German to boot: " 'I'm a Germanic Caucasian male because that's what my Creator created me to be. I am not an Indian. I never can be. . . . I was created a whiteman and I need to explore that, and maybe cast it away once my exploration's over and return to the circle anyway. But I can't deny myself any longer. Can't go on living as a displaced person. Besides, I've never tasted Wiener schnitzel, never did the polka or visited the country.' 'Then I guess we'd better get busy getting out of here so we can get you on a slow boat to the Rhineland!' I said" (301). Similar to his initial learning about "Indian" culture, the uprooted nomad Johnny thinks (together with his friend) in touristic stereotypes of Germany, the country of his ancestors.[38] In order to gain a truer sense of self, he needs to explore and eventually transcend both essentialized identities.

Although Johnny understands at the end that there is another layer to his self that he needs to acknowledge, his adopted "Indian" identity helps his *real* Indian friend, who adopted a non-Indian identity, to discover the other side in himself. Ironically and again blending fiction and reality, the teaching of his friend starts in a bonding ceremony, "as seen on TV." Johnny explains to Josh that they need to keep their meetings about learning how to play baseball secret. The pledge has " 'gotta be done in blood. Blood's the most magical ingredient. . . We'll smear the blood around and promise each other to secrecy and loyalty. Blood brothers.' 'Blood brothers?' 'Yeah. Indians do this all the time. I saw it on TV' " (45). Imitating what is already a fiction, this ceremony creates the foundation of their relationship – fictional and yet very real in its implications and consequences for their lives. Hence, it constructs indigenity, *not* as "authentic" and "pure," but as mediated and hybrid and nonetheless empowering. On the plot level it is linked with the boys' learning about baseball, which initiated their friendship and which they learn from a *really* existing "epitome of how-to books, especially for hitters," namely, Ted Williams's *The Science of Hitting*, as Wagamese points out in the same prefatory note in which he comments on the reality of Native political history in his novel. However, the *real* quality of this book of instructions is fictionalized by Wagamese's changing of the publishing date "for the benefit of the story," and the categorical nature of instructions is blurred in the boys' added "inventions" of the game. The connection between learning about a culture and learning about a game, on the one hand, affirms Johnny's "how-to" approach to "becoming an Indian," but, on the other hand, it comments on the constructedness rather than the innate quality of an ethnic identity.

To a German reader the ceremony of blood brotherhood between a Native and a German evokes Karl May's fictional friendship between the Apache Winnetou and the German Old Shatterhand in the famous *Winnetou* trilogy of the 1890s.[39] Reading Wagamese's novel through this lens allows us to understand the homosexual overtones as yet another instance of subversion of a hierarchical encounter model. In a first meeting with Josh, Johnny appears "feminine," sexualized: "The hand that reached out to clasp mine was thin and meatless. Moist. Soft. Girlish, almost" (27). The narrator explains "the life force" that radiates from this boy in an even more overt feminine image, comparing it to "the feeling you get when you lay your hand upon the flank of a calving heifer" (27). In a reversal of the traditional relationship, the European is cast as the "effeminate," seductive partner who feels betrayed when the Native chooses a woman over him, and a white woman at that. A homoerotic reading of the relationship of these two boys who discover love as "the answer to baseball" (76) upsets not just the colonial power hierarchy, but any conventional racial divide.

When Johnny reflects back on their blood-brother ceremony in which Josh named him Laughing Dog (after the mangy collie of another German family!), he explains how insulted he was, but he also states that in his memory of the event he finds the empowering effect much more important than the ceremony itself. And he adds, "I was filled with light for the first time" (59). Friendship or love, "a quality of light," is more important than names or categories – for cultures, peoples, or individuals. In the satirical name for Johnny, Wagamese, on the one hand, makes fun of a "wannabee," but, on the other, he makes readers understand this character's search for a brother, his need for secrets and for an identity "other" than his own miserable life.

A much less positive set of German characters emerges in Emma Lee Warrior's short story "Compatriots" (which is reprinted in this volume). It relates the German character Hilda's daylong visit to a Blackfoot reserve for the purpose of "studying about Indians" (49). Told from a third-person point of view, the narrator privileges the perspective of the Native woman Lucy, Hilda's hostess, who tries to educate the stranger about the complex history and present-day make-up of the community. Unlike Johnny Gebhardt, however, Hilda never transcends her preconceptions about Indians that she has formed in reading the books of her compatriot Helmut Walking Eagle, a "cultural cross-dresser" who has wormed his way into the reserve.[40] At the end of the story, Hilda is still looking for "real" Indian culture. The other German, Helmut Walking Eagle, is no less problematic. Dressed for the sun-dance ceremony like Laughing Dog during the standoff so that it is "hard to believe that he's a whiteman" (Wagamese, *Quality*, 14), Helmut's name also reveals the author's critical perspective, as Hartmut Lutz explains: "For many Native cultures the eagle is a sacred bird, whose feathers are used in prayer. But the 'eagle' in the character's name is not a soaring but a 'walking' one. The bird is not closest to the sun, does not hover above a sacred Pinetree to watch over the peace of nations, as in the Haudenosaunee tradition, but rather it hobbles on the ground."[41] The choice of Helmut as a first name ironically plays with the fact that two consecutive chancellors in Germany were named Helmut – the name thus seems to imply that this character represents Germany and the German people.[42] In fact, Helmut Walking Eagle is a caricature of a German fantasy: like Old Shatterhand in the Winnetou trilogy, he knows more about Native cultures than the Indians themselves. He assumes authority as the expert on Native culture by writing books about it (selling them more cheaply to Indians) so that travelers like Hilda will want to learn from him rather than from the Blackfoot people. In other words, he instrumentalizes Native cultures for his own (mercenary/psychological) purposes. And also in his appearance he tries to represent "the culture." The omniscient narrator, who intermittently comments on the story through the thoughts of the Blackfoot character Lucy, alerts the reader in the following words: "Whenever Lucy saw him [Helmut Walking Eagle], she was reminded of the Plains Indian Museum across the line" (185), an observation that ties Helmut's impersonation to the *Völkerschau* (the exotic Wild West shows of the late nineteenth century) and to ethnic drag acts, which also favored the Plains Indians as *Indianer* per se. This German character thus represents not so much Blackfoot culture as his own culture's essentializing, authoritative way of dealing with Native peoples. Like a chancellor Helmut Walking Eagle thus "represents" his country – but with an ironic twist: as he is only a *walking* eagle, he is not aware that "most of the Indians wished Helmut would disappear" (180). The Blackfoot characters in this narrative disagree with his "cross-cultural impersonation" or "ethnic drag" act, because it appropriates, rather than celebrates, the other culture. Sieg's definition of "ethnic drag" as "the impersonation of ethnic others by a subject that stages and conceals its dominance" adequately describes this character, who lives among the Blackfoot, speaks their language, and yet defines and objectifies "their" culture for "them."[43]

Warrior utilizes the importance of naming in Native cultures as a "writing back" strategy: Helmut Walking Eagle's stereotyping of Blackfoot culture is not only ridiculed but also exposed through the connotations of his name. But there is an additional twist to this naming. As Hartmut Lutz has pointed out, "Helmut Walking Eagle . . . is only a thinly disguised/fictionalized impersonation of Adolf Hungry Wolf, the German or Swiss Blood Indian, . . . who publishes his *Good Medicine Books*."[44] The intertextual allusion to a "real" Adolf not only reflects "changes in German political leadership" but also helps us understand the reasons for Helmut Walking Eagle's desire to "become Indian," that is, to escape a problematic German identity by slipping into the accoutrements of another ethnicity.[45] In his resentment about being "undressed" by his German compatriot Hilda, who wants to talk with him about her home town, we can see an escapist attitude similar to German Judy's self-imposed segregation.

In conclusion it can be said that the German characters in the indigenous narratives analyzed here only at first impression reinforce categorical divisions between "us" and "them." Although they are the others, it is their role in the story to problematize ethnic boundaries. German Judy's character in *Ravensong* illustrates the novel's emphasis on "combined wisdom" for the sake of the survival of all, whereas the male German characters in the other two narratives challenge the resilience of boundaries through their cross-cultural impersonations. All three characters evince a nomadic identity, without an apparent sense of history or rather with a rejection of or silence about their own history. Wagamese and Warrior fictionalize this problematic of "the rootless" holding on to "the rooted," which Wendy Rose described in the following words: "The roots of colonized people are grasped firmly but blindly by the rootless in order to achieve some kind of stability, however superficial and delusional."[46] According to Rose, this rootlessness is at the heart of what she calls "whiteshamanism" – an appropriative form of border crossing similar to Sieg's concept of ethnic drag. However, Wagamese's German Caucasian character becomes, not a shaman, but an activist who devotes his life to the struggles of Natives peoples for justice and equality. Through the development of this character Wagamese shows that the "problem with 'whiteshamans' is one of integrity and intent."[47] Johnny Gebhardt is portrayed as uprooted, but he maintains his integrity on his journey toward constructing a more inclusive identity for himself. Surrounded by media that define Germans as well as Indians, he is given the ability to change from being unaware about himself *and* Indians to critically reflecting multiple identity positions.

The theme of whiteshamanism as an appropriative act of border crossing evokes different questions in Warrior's short story. In the naming of this German character, "Compatriots" ironically undercuts Helmut Walking Eagle's "ethnic drag" act. The author also reveals her criticism through the words of a Blackfoot elder character, the alcoholic Sonny: "Shit, that guy's just a phony. How could anybody turn into something else? Huh? I don't think I could turn into a white man if I tried all my life. They wouldn't let me, so how does that German think he can be an Indian. White people think they can do anything – turn into Chinese or Indian – they're crazy" (53). This statement by an elder is validated in the context of Warrior's narrative through the depiction of a sociopolitical reality that shows a state of inequality between Blackfoot people and white people; as the story makes clear, the option of ethnic drag remains open only to those with privilege and power.[48] Yet Sonny's notion of "a phony" cannot be left unquestioned – and the text suggests as much. As seen throughout my discussion, the respective indigenous authors construct their narratives on multiple levels with multiple and shifting perspectives. Therefore, the political implications of the elder's adage need to be read together with the other concern in this story: ghettoizing definitions of culture and cultural identity. The last word is given, not to the elder or to Helmut Walking Eagle, but to the editorial narrator commenting on the other stranger in the text, the German visitor Hilda. Her ironically formulated desire for a ceremony so that she may experience what is *real* Indian (at the end of her day on a reserve) overwrites the elder's comment. The problem of *crossing* cultural boundaries arises because of the *existence* of boundaries. To define means "to determine the boundary of" (OED), to reify what is in flux, othering a culture and a people. Hence, Hilda's desire for a definable culture complements Helmut Walking Eagle's ethnic drag. With an awareness of such desire the so-called ethnic writers who were discussed in this article establish an indigenous perspective in contrast to the placeless, uprooted, migratory European or German; however, they counterbalance in their own nomadic writing any kind of definition of indigenity by continuously negotiating their complex cultural sites.

Notes

1. Moses and Goldie, *Anthology*, xxvi.
2. Akiwenzie-Damm, "We Belong To This Land," 84.
3. Moses and Goldie, xxvi.
4. For a discussion of the history and present status of Germany's relationship with indigenous peoples in North America, with special emphasis on Native literature, see Hartmut Lutz's article "Nations Within as Seen from Without." See also his article in this volume.
5. Johnston, "Spirit of Maundau-meen," 103.
6. Johnston, "Spirit of Maundau-meen," 104.
7. Johnston, "Prophecy," 98.
8. Johnston, "Prophecy," 99.
9. Johnston, "Prophecy," 99.
10. Armstrong, "This Is a Story," 130, 133.
11. Armstrong, *Breath Tracks*, 28–29.
12. LaDuke, "Natural to Synthetic," vii.
13. LaDuke, "Natural to Synthetic," iii.
14. Means, "Same Old Song," 28.
15. Armstrong, "Disempowerment," 241.
16. Page numbers in the text refer to the editions quoted in the general bibliography. In two more recently published novels by Canadian Native writers, German characters feature as well. In Tomson Highway's *Kiss of the Fur Queen*, one

of the teachers in a residential school, a character who on the whole is depicted negatively, is of German ancestry, characterized by "his chilling German glare" (147). Highway also ridicules German tourists' frequent attendance of powwows, an aspect of cross-cultural encounters emphasized in Thomas King's latest novel, *Truth and Bright Water*. Critical of any touristic experience of another culture, in the overall context of this novel he still positions the "German guys dressed up as Indians" (211) between the two poles of cultural appropriation and cultural celebration and refers to Adolf Hungry Wolf, the German who "speaks good Blackfoot and lives in the woods" (202). Other instances of German allusions in indigenous text include comparisons between the genocide of indigenous peoples and the Holocaust made in a collection of poetry titled *She Said Sometimes I Hear Things*, by Michael J. Paul-Martin, and in a book of paintings and poetry paralleling the experience of Jewish people with those of the Cree people (Littlechild et al., *In Honour of Our Grandmothers*).

17. At the end of the novel, Stacey is shown as planting "the seeds of shame" (191) in Steve, a doctor's son, by making him feel guilty about the doctor's neglect of her people during the flu epidemic. Raven interprets this positively as starting a transformation in one of "the others."

18. Sollors, *Beyond Ethnicity*, 300.

19. Sollors, *Beyond Ethnicity*, 303.

20. Schneider, *"We Have a Commonality,"* 111.

21. Vine Deloria's classic work *God Is Red* examines exactly this question of the link between place and religious ceremonies. He explains how "sacred lands" are "permanent fixtures" in indigenous "cultural or religious understanding" (67) and asks, from the point of view of a religion that is "spatially determined," if "ceremonies [are] restricted to particular places" and if they "become useless in a foreign land" (71). He does not give an answer but regrets that a religion "bound to history" and preoccupied with "temporal considerations" has "never . . . critically examined" these questions.

22. Highway, *Dry Lips*, 12. See also Gloria Anzaldúa, who uses the term to describe her "new *mestiza* consciousness," the "consciousness of the Borderlands" from the perspective of a feminist of color: "Cradled in one culture, sandwiched between two cultures, straddling all three cultures and their value systems, la mestiza undergoes a struggle of flesh, a struggle of borders, an inner war" ("La conciencia," 377-78).

23. The nonrecognition of the trickster is a frequently occurring theme in Canadian Native literature. See, for example, Highway's play *The Rez Sisters* and Taylor's play *Toronto at Dreamer's Rock*.

24. Kelly, "Conversation," 86.

25. Caruth, *Unclaimed Experience*, 24.

26. Maracle, "Preface," 11.

27. Maracle, "Preface," 11.

28. Whitt, "Indigenous Peoples," 246.

29. Harpham, "Ethics," 403.

30. Said, World, 19.

31. Anzaldúa, "Border Crossings," 46.

32. Wagamese, Keeper'N Me, back cover blurb.

33. Braidotti, Nomadic Subjects, 171.

34. Wagamese acknowledges the inclusion of this political reality in his work of fiction in a brief preface to the novel.

35. LaRocque, "Preface," xx. Okanagan storyteller Harry Robinson expresses the oral-written binary as racial difference in his creation story about the twins, one of whom is the literate "white man," the other, older one, the "Indian" who does not have the "paper" ("Twins: White and Indian," in Write It on Your Heart, 40–52).

36. See, for example, a recent article in Wawatay News, a bilingual (Oji-Cree and English) newspaper published in Sioux Lookout, Northwest Ontario, by Joyce Atcheson, "Who's God? Whose God?"

37. Means, "Same Old Song," 30. But Linda Hogan, whom Kateri Akiwenzie-Damm quotes in her article on "cultural difference," asserts that although it is possible for immigrants "to have the connectedness to the land ... it's not the land all our stories took place on, the land all the myths come from, your ancestors" ("We Belong To This Land," 85).

38. Besides being stereotypical Johnny's associations with Germany hint at a European more than a specifically German culture: Wiener schnitzel is a dish originally from Austria and the polka a dance from Poland. It may be assumed that Wagamese deliberately chose non-nation-specific culture traits in order to comment indirectly on the colonial idea of an undifferentiated North American Native culture.

39. See Sieg's essay "Ethnic Drag and National Identity," in which she interprets the blood brotherhood as a Wiedergutmachungsfantasie, a fantasy of restitution, in connection with the Holocaust.

40. Fachinger, "Cross-Dressing," 40.

41. Lutz, "Confronting Cultural Imperialism," 147.

42. It may be coincidental, but the national seal displayed in the German Bundestag looks a bit like a "walking eagle."

43. Sieg, "Ethnic Drag," 297; see also her contribution to this volume.

44. Lutz, "Confronting Cultural Imperialism," 147.

45. Lutz, "Confronting Cultural Imperialism," 147.

46. Rose, "Just What's All This Fuss," 15.

47. Rose, "Just What's All This Fuss," 21.

48. For a more in-depth discussion of the "irreversibility of ethnic drag," see also Sieg's article "Ethnic Drag," 316–17.

An Introduction to Louise Erdrich's *The Antelope Wife*

UTE LISCHKE-MCNAB

One of the most prolific and respected contemporary American writers, Louise Erdrich – of Ojibwa and German descent – has written a series of works in which she interweaves stories that focus on the lives of Anishinabe (Chippewa) families. Her novels *Love Medicine* (1984, 1993), *The Beet Queen* (1986), *Tracks* (1988), *The Bingo Palace* (1994), *Tales of Burning Love* (1996), *The Antelope Wife* (1998), and *Last Report on the Miracles at Little No Horse* (2001) form an interconnected epic of contemporary Indian life. Written in a nonlinear, nonchronological, multivocal postmodern style, they relate the memories, loves, and battles of Native characters as they live and struggle alongside European immigrants on and off reservations. Erdrich has also published several volumes of poetry, and many of her short stories have appeared in periodicals such as the *New Yorker* and *Harper's Magazine*. Recently, she has also turned to writing books for children, for instance, *Grandmother's Pigeon* (1996) and *The Birchbark House* (1999). Illustrated by the author herself, the latter is an autobiographical account of growing up as a Native American. Similarly, her anthology *The Blue Jay's Dance: A Birth Year* (1995) is a collection of autobiographical essays and meditations that deal with her life as a wife, mother, and writer. Despite their profound differences, all of Erdrich's texts are, on some level, autobiographical. And all address, in one way or another, the interconnected, often conflicted relationships between Native Americans and Europeans as well as the complex relationship between "native" and "German" cultural traditions that the author herself experiences.

Questions of split identity and multiple allegiances have figured prominently in Erdrich's thinking. In an interview with John Blades for the *Chicago Tribune* in 1986, she expressed her hope that *The Beet Queen*, her second novel, would establish her as an *American* writer – not as a hyphenated American and not just as a writer about American Indians. It was her hope that she would come to be regarded as a writer of American experiences in all their diversity. In another interview with Allan and Nancy Feyl Chavkin about eight years later, Erdrich was asked if she had concerns about being labeled a Native-

American writer or a woman writer.[1] She responded that such labels have their origins in course descriptions, and that if a work of literature survived, these labels would eventually fall away, and different criteria would establish its value to its readers. Erdrich did express regret, however, that *The Beet Queen*, which is less concerned with Native American characters than are *Love Medicine* or *Tracks* and instead attests to her desire to explore the European side of her heritage and experience, does not often appear on course syllabi.

Curiously, much of the critical literature about Erdrich – while stressing her Native roots – has ignored her European, or German, connections. Critics have often characterized her as a writer of "magical realism," a characterization Erdrich herself has questioned.[2] Rather, her peculiar type of storytelling blends Chippewa/Cree traditions, where orally transmitted myths are still an integral part of the culture, with European narrative forms introduced to her by her father, an immigrant of German, Austrian Catholic, and Jewish origins.[3] Erdrich proudly acknowledges her rural European background – her German forefathers were farmers and butchers, Metzger – in *The Blue Jay's Dance*: "On my father's side, the Erdrich family was established in Pforzheim, near the Black Forest, as Metzger Meistern [sic]. 1882. They raised a Bauernhof that still stands in the Renchtal. The last of the Indian treaties were signed, opening up the West. Most of the Anishinabe were concentrated in small holdings of land in the territory west of the Great Lakes" (99). Like a signpost, the inserted date, the year 1882, immediately links the German events with occurrences on the American soil – the Indian treaties and relocation of Indian tribes that directly affected her mother's family. "All land west of the Appalachians was still Indian territory and the people from whom I am descended on my mother's side, the Ojibwa or Anishinabe, lived lightly upon it, leaving few traces of their complicated passage other than their own teeth and bones. They levered no stones from the earth. Their houses, made of sapling frames and birchbark rolls, were not meant to last" (98). On the one hand, then, we find the earthiness and rootedness of European farmers, the weight and traces of history (the farm still stands), and on the other the Natives, who "lived lightly" upon the land, leaving few traces. The dualism Erdrich fashions for herself also translates to literary traditions. In her recollections of her father, she stresses how he, a highly educated teacher, encouraged his children to write by promising them money for every story they had written. The tradition of encouraging education through "literature" and writing is contrasted with the oral traditions of her mother's peoples, who transmit experience and who teach, not through writing, but through story telling. As Erdrich suggests, her own thinking and writing has incorporated both traditions – the emphasis on history and on the written word as well as on orality, myth, and spirituality. They form a productive, although not always harmonious or easy mix.

The complications arising from different, at times warring, allegiances are stressed in an interview with Mickey Pearlman in 1989, in which Erdrich paints a much less upbeat picture of her origins and the traditions from which she draws:[4]

> I think ... that if you believe in any sort of race memory, I am getting a triple whammy from my background – in regard to place and home and space. . . . The connection that is Chippewa is a connection to a place and to a background, and to the comfort of knowing, somehow, that you are connected here before *and before* the first settler. . . . Add to that that the German part of my family is most probably converted Jews and the Jewish search for place, and you have this awful mix. A person can only end up writing – in order to resolve it. You can even throw in the French part of the background – the wanderers, the voyagers, which my people also come from. There is just no way to get away from all this, and the only way to resolve it, without going totally crazy looking for a home, is to write about it. The Germans have a word for it – *unziemliches Verlangen,* unseemly longing. . . . I feel that I am very fortunate to have some place to put these longings because otherwise they would become very destructive. (151–52)

The quote suggests that the source of Erdrich's writing is not so much the knowledge of belonging to either, or both, cultural traditions, but the longing to belong: an "unseemly" desire to belong to the peoples who populated America before the European conquerors, colonists, and settlers arrived; and an unseemly desire to find an imaginary home in and through writing. While her family history forms the point of departure, the raw material and stimulus for her writings, her ultimate aim is to expose and possibly resolve the tensions between wandering and immigrating, on the one hand, and settling or "being," on the other, between foreign and native, European and (Native) American.

Although most of Erdrich's fictions deal with this European-Native American tension, in her recent novel, *The Antelope Wife,* published in 1998, questions of multiple origin and cultural mix form the main topic and structuring device of the whole narrative. Set mostly in present-day Gakahbekong (contemporary Minneapolis), the novel interweaves Native American myth, spirituality, and traditional culture with historical and contemporary stories. Like earlier novels by Erdrich, it thematizes the ways in which the lives of contemporary mixed-blood Ojibwa Indians are affected by the history of earlier generations – and how they reconcile family patterns with the culture-sapping effects of modern urban life. It portrays the American Indian experience from a variety of narrative perspectives, bouncing back and forth in time, giving voice to characters of every age and social standing, mixing the mythical with the prosaic, the historical with the contemporary.

The actual beginning of the story – in the magic year 1882 mentioned above! – is prefaced by a kind of foundational myth: the image of twin sisters who, since the beginnings of time, have been sewing beads into an indiscernible pattern. The twins are juxtaposed: one sewing with light, one with dark thread; one attaching cut-glass white and pale beads, the other glittering deep red and blue-black indigo ones; one using an awl made of an otter's sharpened penis bone, the other that of a bear. And yet they are weaving with a single sinew thread, furiously competing with each other to set one more bead into the pattern than the competitor, thereby "trying to upset the balance of the world." They are at once different and the same, divided and united by the ambitions of their lives' work. They describe parallel paths like the Two Row Wampum of the white and the red cultures.

The image of the identical twins in furious competition is a fitting preamble for the novel's underlying preoccupation with dualisms, unity, and diversity; the beadwork of the two sisters is a metaphor for the novel's complex structure and its secret meanings. Like beads in a necklace, its different stories have a decorative-aesthetic as well as symbolic role; like the beads, the many stories in the novel are strung together by the many narrative voices, creating oneness from multiplicity, meaning from chaos.[5] Like beads, they are perfect in themselves; yet, in their composition, they create an even more perfect whole.

The novel opens in the late nineteenth century with a young U.S. Cavalry private, a Pennsylvania Quaker named Scranton Roy, who during an attack on an Indian village kills an old woman who is chasing a dog. Scranton follows the dog, which has a *tikinagun* tied to its back that encloses a child in moss and is trailing blue beads; he retrieves the child, suckles it on his own breast, and raises her as his own, until her mother, Blue Prairie Woman, comes for her. Shortly after, the newly motherless girl is sheltered by a herd of antelope that somehow sense that she is one of them. She will return again to civilization to begin a cycle of restlessness and unbelonging that afflicts her descendants and the men who love them.

From this haunting beginning, a powerful and dauntingly elliptical tale of obsession and separation evolves that moves backward and forward through time from Northern Plains Indian settlements to present-day Minneapolis.

Revolving around the complex relationship between the Roy and Shawano families, the novel's striking characters include: Sweetheart Calico, silent and wrathful, as the "antelope wife" of the title, named for the fabric that ties her to Klaus Shawano, the man who abducts and enchants her away from the open places where land meets sky; Klaus Shawano, who acquires "the antelope woman" but cannot keep her (one of several tales of kidnapping and captivity in the novel), as she languishes in the urban prison of Minneapolis; several sets of twin daughters, all frustratingly distant from the men who claim them; Richard Whiteheart Beads, who causes the deaths of those he loves and attempts to take his own life when his beleaguered former wife remarries; and the ghostly "windigo dog," a creature magically akin to the humans it patiently serves and protects.

Told from the perspective of these and other characters, the deft episodes often have the quality of independent short stories that are powerfully dramatized. One of them includes a wedding scene that is spectacularly disrupted by the failed suicide of the bride's uninvited former husband. The following episode, "Blitzkuchen," which occurs halfway through the novel, shares the elliptical, dreamlike storytelling found throughout the novel. In a recasting of the traditional captivity narrative, Klaus Shawano tells how he – a kidnapped German prisoner of war – is adopted into the tribe after baking a delicious "blitzkuchen." This blending/baking ritual leads ultimately to a mixing of bloods, which Cally Roy – who describes herself as "a Roy, a Whiteheart Beads, a Shawano by way of the Roy and Shawano proximity . . . a huge can of family lumped together like a can of those mixed party nuts" – feels is a particularly dangerous one: "Some bloods they go together like water – the French Ojibwas: you mix those up and it is all one person. Like me. Others are a little less predictable. You make a person from a German and an Indian, for instance, and you're creating a two-souled warrior always fighting himself" (110).

The (un-)German word "blitzkuchen," or "lightning cake," which combines allusions to warfare (blitzkrieg) with those to ritualistic feasts (sweet pastry), has, of course, multiple connotations. It connects the Germans' use of lightning air strikes during the war with the Anishinabe concept of lightning as a transforming agent.[6] The cake made in a hurry, under threat of death, has the power to magically transform the relationship between Indians and Germans into one of communication, communion, and cultural adoption, as Klaus, the baker, becomes one of the Shawano family. Yet in a subsequent story, set just after World War II, the reader hears about how young Frank Shawano's taste of the blitzkuchen pastry inspires Frank's career as a baker and his lifelong quest for the exquisite blitzkuchen recipe. It is only at his own wedding feast, when the possibility of a poisoned blitzkuchen wedding cake threatens the party guests, that Frank finally learns of its secret ingredient – fear.

Notes

1. Chavkin and Chavkin, "Interview with Louise Erdrich."
2. Chavkin and Chavkin, "Interview with Louise Erdrich," 221.
3. Foley, *Teaching Oral Traditions*, 151-61, 225-38.
4. Chavkin and Chavkin, "Interview with Louise Erdrich," 221.
5. Beads are significant in Erdrich's work and in Indian culture, as Gerald Hausman reminds us:

> "The Cherokee word for bead and the word for money are the same. The pearl necklace did not come to the Indians from Europe. It was made on Turtle Island. And from the milk tooth of the elk, the canine tooth of the bear, and from birds' beaks and talons came a multitude of lovely beads. What was the purpose of the bead? Tied into the hair, worn singly on strings, dangling from wrist, waist, and lower limb, the bead made the wearer proud. It celebrated heraldic animals; it told stories and prophesied power; it carried for the wearer an aura of symmetry, suggesting family, tribe, culture. Attractive and precious, sacred and ornamental, the bead was a wealth of things – all of them symbolizing the power of good health and excellent living. As such, the bead did not represent the material world as much as the nonmaterial one.
>
> The bead, like the basket, is round; and, like the old tribal culture, a single part of many other parts. the string of beads, the blazon of beads told a story in which the single bead was a necessary link to all the others.
>
> One and many; the meaning of the tribe. Together there is strength, unity. The tribal man or woman was as strong as the tribe from which he/she came. And the tribe, naturally, got its strength from the single bead, the pearl, the individual man or woman." (Hausman, "Turtle Island Alphabet," 8-9)

6. Erdrich, *The Blue Jay's Dance*, 98-99.

"Blitzkuchen"

An Excerpt from *The Antelope Wife*

LOUISE ERDRICH

Klaus Shawano: When the ogitchida came home from the land of the frog
people he was strange, but that is often how warriors are when they return.
1945. End of the war. So many spirits out, wandering. And, too, the ogitchida,
that is my father Shawano, had lost his cousin who in the warrior's blood
relation was more like another self and could not be adequately revenged.

"Owah," my father cried suddenly. They were sitting at his uncle's house.
"I tried. I made his mark on every German soldier that I killed!"

"Was it a deep mark?" hissed old wrinkled-up and half-unstrung Asinigwesance, whose opinion was that the proper way to deal with this thing was
for the U.S.A. to make all the Germans into slaves. Ship the whole country full
of people here and teach them to be humble. That's how they would have done
it in the old days. He couldn't get over how he had heard our government
sent them money, help, Red Cross boxes of food and soap.

My father was a slim and handsome boy when he left, but his look when
he returned was reeling and deathly. His face was puffed up and his eyes, they
were like pits in his face. He had a thousand-year-old stare.

"He took a stomach wound," said Shawano. "I had to stuff my cousin's
guts and loops back into his body, and all the time he kept his eyes on me.
He couldn't look down. When I had them back in, his teeth were clicking
together and he got these words out. 'You sure you got them back in the right
order?' I said I did my best. 'Because I don't wanna be pissing out my ears,' he
said. His voice was real serious and I answered, 'I checked. Your pisser made it.
No damage, cousin.' He seemed real happy with that statement. The ground
shook around us. Close one landed. I lost my hold and they all poured out of
him again."

Shawano was exhausted and they got my Mama, Regina, to come in where
the men were and put him to sleep. She was big with her child, that is, myself.
Calming. To her, my dad would always listen. Before he slept, though, he gave
Asinigwesance a funny look and repeated himself, "Old man, I did what you

told me. I sent as many as I could with him after that to be his slaves in the land of spirits. It didn't help."

Old Asin looked at him long, deeply, watching.

"Maybe," said Asinigwesance at last, "you need to do the next thing."

"Which is what?"

Asinigwesance hunched into his gnarled body and then tapped a leathery bone finger on the pocket of his shirt just over his heart.

"Replace your cousin with a slave brother."

Shawano mulled this one, took it in slow.

"Where do I get one, a German?" he wondered, at last.

"Oh, they're all over the place here," Asinigwesance said, sweeping at the air side to side with the flat of his hand. "All over here like frogs."

Why we call them Omakakayininiwug I don't really know, unless it was because they popped out of nowhere. In the beginning, there were whole village tribes of them, we heard, shipped over here from Omakakayakeeng to tear up our land. They took it over. They killed it. Most of the land is now half dead. Plowed up. Still, we had no ill feeling versus any one individual. Even the Germans who made the war.

And lost it, too. As they tell it, there was a whole bunch of prisoners shipped over in the beginning who wanted to stay in this country now. They moved up north and worked the timber, two on a cross-end saw. Ditched timber roads. Learned only swear English. Walked along piercing the earth with pointed iron bars, tamping in seedlings with their shoes. It was only a short while before Shawano would get word of them. Waiting for D.D. status, they were living inside the fence of the state work farm. Yes, they slaved away, they worked, but none of them belonged to anyone personally. Someone should have told that to Shawano. Before anyone could give him the information, though, he listened to Asin. Overcome with the proximity of Germans, the old warrior encouraged my dad to fetch him one. A moonless night, then, Shawano clipped a hole in the wire fence, sneaked into the work camp.

The men were summoned the next morning to his house.

"Of course, I stole the German at night," said Shawano, explaining. "I crept right up to the barracks without detection."

"Without detection." Asinigwesance gloated. He was excited by this ancient working out of the old-way vengeance, pleased young Shawano had taken his advice. He nodded all around at the other men, grinning. "I remember the old man's teeth were little black stubs – all except for the gold one. That tooth glinted with a slightly mad sheen."

"I dropped the gunnysack over the Kraut's head when he came outside to take a leak," Shawano went on. "Bound his arms behind him. Goose-stepped him. Got him right back through the fence and from there, here."

Silent, they looked at the figure sitting bound in the corner. Barefooted. Wearing a baggy shirt and pants of no particular color. And the man, his head covered by the gunnysack, was quiet with a peculiar stillness that was not exactly fear. Nor was it sleep. He was awake in there. The men could feel him straining to see through the loose weave over his face.

My uncle, Pugweyan, got spooked by the way the guy composed himself, and suddenly he couldn't stand it one more minute. He went over and ripped away the gunnysack hood. Maybe some expected to see a crazy eagle – how they stare mad into the air from their warrior hearts of ice – but they did not see an eagle. Instead, blinking out at us from spike tufts of hair, a chubby boy face, round-cheeked, warm and sparkling brown eyes. The men all reared back at the unexpected sense of warmth and goodwill from the German's pleasant smile.

"Owah!" Expectation was something more impressive than a porcupine man! His hands were chubby, his skin almost as brown as ours. Around his circle eyes his stubby hair poked out like a quill headdress. His smell – that came off him too now – was a raw and fearful odor like the ripe armpit stink of porcupine. He moved quite slow, like that creature, his deep eyes shining with tears, and he took us all in one by one and then cast his eyes down, bashful, as though he would rather be under the porch or inside his own burrow.

"Put the bag on him again," said Asin hurriedly.

"No," said Shawano, hurt and surprised at the meekness of his catch.

"Grüssen!" the prisoner bowed. His voice was pie sweet and calm as toast. "Was ist los? Wo sind wir?"

Nobody answered his words even though he next made known by signs – an imaginary scoop to his mouth, a washing motion on his rounded stomach – his meaning.

"Haben Sie hunger?" he asked hopefully. "Ich bin sehr gut Küchenchef."[1]

"Mashkimood, mashkimood." Asin's attitude was close to panic. He wanted to put the bag over the boy's head. Because he had once been known as a careful and judicious old man, the others had to wonder if there was something in the situation they just hadn't figured yet. The kitchen, a window shedding frail light on an old wooden table, the stove in the background of the room, the prisoner blinking.

"Skimood!" Asin cried again, and Shawano picked up the gunnysack uncertainly, ready to lower it back onto the porcupine man's head.

"Hit him! Hit him!" Asin now spoke in a low and threatful tone. At his command, everyone fell silent, considering. Yet it was apparent, also, that the old man was behaving in an extreme and uncharacteristic fashion.

"Why should we do that?" asked Pugweyan.

"It is the only way to satisfy the ghosts," Asin answered.

"Haben Sie alles hunger, bitte? Wenn Sie hunger haben, ich werde für sie ein Kuchen machen. Versuch mal, bitte." The prisoner asked his question, made his offer, modestly and pleasantly, though he seemed now in his wary poise to have understood the gravity of Asin's behavior. He seemed, in fact, to know that his life hung in the balance although Asin had spoken his cruel command in the old language. Not only that, but he suddenly, with a burst of enormous energy, tried again to make good on his offer using peppy eating motions and rubbing his middle with more vigor.

One among the men, of the bear clan, those always so eager for food, finally nodded. "Why not?" said Bootch. "Let him prepare his offering. We will test it and see if his sweet cake can save his life."

He said this jokingly, but Asin's gleam and nod told that he took the baking test seriously and looked forward to the German's failure.

The porcupine man drew a tiny diagram or symbol for each thing he needed. Little oval eggs, flour in a flour sack, nuts of a rumpled shape, sugar, and so on. By now, even though the men had no money extra, they had to go along and so they all dug deep for whatever food money their we'ewug trusted – into their hands, socks, the liners of their shoes, and the rabbit fur inside their moccasins. They sent my brother Frank to the traders' for these things and he returned with his lower lip stuck out and fire in his eyes. He was just at that young age where he hated to be bossed and yet loved to be taken care of by his relatives.

The stove. The German seemed to have a problem with that. So did my mother, who refused to take on my father's name or to marry him and felt in bearing his sons and giving us her bear dodem, since Shawano's windigo family had lost his, she'd done enough. And it was true. She had picked these red berries for us, though, odaemin, the heart berry, from the clearings. So fresh and dewy and tender the red melted in your mouth. She gave her makuk full of them to the prisoner, and was surprised by the emotional way he accepted the offering. He lifted the container in his hand, inhaled the fragrance of the berries. His dark round eyes filled again and this time spilled over with tears.

"Erdbeeren," he said, softly, with mistaken and genuine sincerity. "I fuck you thank you."

The men stood there in the kitchen before the stove and looked down at their feet, at the floor, anywhere, not knowing what to say. Regina reached out, and they got in that moment a sense of her grace, another side of her. She shook the German's hand, or paw, which we saw with a certain fear had fur on the back.

"Gaween gego," she said, meaning it was nothing special.

Her kindness was a match to Asin's low fury and he flared up, insisted that Klaus had just delivered a most clever insult veiled in ignorance, fixed Klaus with a crushing stare, bared his black teeth and then just a hint of a snarl, so that the men had to step away from the clash and out the door, leaving the original Klaus, who waved the watchers away from the smoking woodstove abruptly, anyhow, to begin his efforts.

From inside the kitchen, then, where Frank had stubbornly placed himself and from where Regina, heavy as the stove herself, refused to move, they got as much of the story as they could, or maybe as I was ever supposed to know.

First, the prisoner pounded almonds to a fine paste between two lake rocks. Took the eggs, just the yellows in a little tin cup. There was, in my mother's house, a long piece of wire which he cleverly twisted into a beater of some sort. He began to work things over, the ingredients, grinding with the bottom of the iron skillet pods and beans and spices into the nuts and then adding the sugar grain by grain.

When he was finished, he took the thick syrupy batter and poured it as though it contained, as it did for him, the very secret of life. He made dark pools in four round baking pans. He bore them ceremonially and with extreme care toward the oven, which yawned, perfectly stoked beneath with coals glowing in the firebox. Bending with maternal care, he placed the pan within the dark aperture. Closed with a toweled hand the oven door. For a moment all of the men, who had slowly returned, drawn by the composed fury of his efforts, regarded the words set in raised letters upon the oven door. The Range Eternal. Then, as a body, they backed slowly away and sat down, lighting their pipes, to smoke and wait.

They paid respect to the east. In their thoughts, in their prayers. They respected the manito who guards the south. They regarded with humble pleading the direction of our dead, the west. North was last. And now you may ask, in all this time, where was Shawano, my dad, himself?

He sat with them and he sat alone. He sat in a deep embarrassment of thought. He sat wondering, he sat appalled, he sat in memory. He sat just like the rest, waiting for the next thing to happen.

My mother did not wait, of course. She was a woman. What woman sits

Louise Erdrich

waiting for something to cook in the oven? Disgusted by the male mystery and presence in her kitchen, she bustled ostentatiously. In. She bustled out. Made a lot of noise coming, going. Banged her washing board and banged pots. Banged anything she could, including the heads of her children and the chairs of the men, who jumped. Once, but just once, she banged the stove. At which point Klaus leaped high and with a scream that still shakes in our hearing, grabbed Regina by the apron strings and swung her toward the door. She flew as though shot from a bow. With as quick and lithe a bounce as some limber wildcat, Klaus poised, light on the balls of his feet, and motioned one and all to hush.

Again the men sat, now staring and caught in the grip of what the prisoner sensed happening behind the raised Range Eternal letters and the blue enamel of the oven door.

Light in the window turned subtly more golden. Klaus set pans of water into the oven like offerings. A breeze sprang up. Welcome. Leaves tapped. Nobody said a thing. Their inner souls leaned toward the stove, their outer selves didn't even smoke. Asin's eyes grew bloody. His hands trembled and the air whistled between his teeth. They sat until finally Klaus rose and, like a groom pacing tranced toward his bride, approached the oven. At the lip of the door he closed his eyes, cocked his head to the side as though listening, and then slowly and pliantly bent, hands wrapped in two thick rags. Carefully but with firm control he pulled the handle on the door until it opened and then, just for a moment, the waiting men lost their bearings as the scent of the toasted nuts and honey and vanilla and sugar and subtly united oils and flours escaped the oven box and trembled in the air.

More than delicious, the fragrance that floated. Impossible. Perhaps an Anishinabe vision word comes close and perhaps there is no way to describe the premonition they all experienced then, as he tenderly drew the pan along the rack until it rested secure between his thick, furry, rag-protected paws.

More sitting while the brown cake cooled. Eyes of Asin sunk, blackening. He made everyone uneasy now with his wild breathing and in the silence of space in which the creation cooled, the watchers remembered things they'd rather have forgotten: how Asinigwesance had suffered from time to time with nameless angers, which now had assumed a name and form in the person of the porcupine man. Klaus.

The original Klaus. My namesake.

Air poured in the screen door, cooling and healing. Dusk air. Pure air. Moved onto Shawano. Pugweyan took his fan, the wing of an eagle, and with immense care he swept the air toward Asin, whose face now worked in and out like a poisoned mud puppy's, and who said, hissing, fixing us with eyes crossed from behind, a strict power in his gaze:

"Let us deliver him to the west. We are Ojibwa men – the name has a warrior's meaning. We roast our enemies until they pucker! Once, we were feared. Our men brought sorrow. What have we here? Chimookoman? Women? Our enemy is in our hands and we do not make him suffer to console the spirits of our brothers. We let him cook our food. It is this . . . Klaus," he scoured the name off his tongue, "whom we should burn to death!"

In the space of quiet that followed on his words, then, each man realized and understood Asinigwesance was lost.

They were talking to the old man's bitter ghost.

"Ohhh, ishte, my grandfather," Pugweyan said, drawing the wing of the eagle through the air in a soothing and powerful fashion. "Good thing you've told us this." Looking at the rest of us meaningfully, he said to Asinigwesance in a calm tone, "We respect your wishes, grandfather. However" – and now Pugweyan held the wing of the eagle stiffly pointed toward the cake – "would we be honorable men if we did not keep our promise even to our enemy? Before we roast the prisoner, let us try his offering. . . ."

And Klaus, whose intuition of their meaning just barely kept him horrified, then took from his pile of ingredients a tiny packet of white sweet powder and, with a gravity equal to Pugweyan's, coated the top of the cake with the magical dust and then motioned to the men to cup their hands, each one of them, Asin, too, as he cut the cake into a piece for everyone, including Regina and my Shawano brother, Frank, who jostled into the circle. When they all had the cake in hand, they looked at it hungrily and waited for the elder to taste. Asin, however, was too slow and my brother too tempted. Frank bit into the cake. Before he chewed, he gave a startled and extraordinary squeak and his eyes went wide. It was too much for the rest of them. They all bit. Or nibbled. Tasted. And every one emitted, according to my mother's memory, some particular and undiluted sound. There was not a one who'd ever tasted the taste of this thing or come into the rare vicinity of such a quietly extreme sensation on the tongue.

We are people of simple food straight from the earthen earth and from the lakes and from the woods. Manomin. Weyass. Baloney. A little maple sugar now and then. Suddenly this: a powerful sweetness that opened the ear to sound. Embrace of roasted nut-meats and a tickling sensation of grief. A berry tartness. Joy. Klaus had inserted jam in thinspread layers. And pockets of spices that have no origin in our language and no experience on our part or in the Zhaginash tongue and so, too, there was no explanation for what happened next.

Together, they sat, swallowed the last crumbs, pressed up the powdery sweetness with their fingers. When they had licked every grain into themselves, they sat numb with pleasant feelings and then, over the group, there stole a sweet poignance. Some saw in the lowering light the shadows of loved ones who went before us on the road, whose spirits they had fed as well as they could, food of the dead. Curious, they doubled back. Others heard the sharp violin string played in the woods, the song of the white-throated sparrow. Regina spoke to me, knew my name, and I believe I heard her voice. Some saw their mother's hands plunge in and out of flour and some tasted on their faces the hot sun and breathed warm thick berry summer odor and the low sigh of the moving dancing white grass that grows all along the road to the other world.

They breathed together. They thought like one person. They had for a long unbending moment the same heartbeat, same blood in their veins, the same taste in their mouth. How, when they were all one being, kill the German? How, in sharing this sweet intensity of life, deny its substance in even their enemies? And when there is an end of things, and when I all so sudden fade into the random scheme and design, I believe I will taste the true and the same taste, mercy on the tongue. And I will laugh the same way they all did, at once, in surprise and at the same sweet joke, even old Asin.

So that is how the German was adopted into the Shawano clan, how Frank got fixed on duplicating that sweet hour, and how I got my name.

Note

1. We decided to keep the German as it appears in the original, without improving on its spelling or grammar. Eds.

Bibliography
Primary Literature & Secondary Literature

Primary Literature

Adams, Howard. *Prison of Grass*. 1975. Saskatoon, Sask.: Fifth House, 1989.

Addison, Joseph. "King Sa Ga Tean Qua Rash Tow." In *The Spectator*, edited by Donald F. Bond, 211-21, 236-40. Oxford: Clarendon Press, 1965. First published in *The Spectator*, 1, no. 50, (27 April 1711); no. 56, (4 May 1711).

Adelung, Johann Christoph. "Proben der Dichtung ungebildeter Völker." In vol. 1 of *Erholungen*, edited by W. G. Becker, 194-208. Leipzig: 1799.

Adelung, Johann Christoph, [continued by] Johann Severin Vater. *Mithridates oder allgemeine Sprachenkunde mit dem Vater Unser als Sprachprobe*. 4 vols. Berlin: Voss, 1806-1817.

Adler, R. *Die Besiegung der Odschibwäh*. Frankfurt: Brönner, 1851.

Aimard, Gustave. *The Indian Scout: A Sequel to "The Prairie Flower."* Philadelphia: Peterson, 1878.

———. *Les trappeurs de l'Arkansas*. 4th ed. Paris: Amyot, 1858.

Anderson, Gary Clayton, and Alan R. Woolworth, eds. *Through Dakota Eyes: Narrative Accounts of the Minnesota Indian War of 1862*. St. Paul: Minnesota Historical Society Press, 1988.

Armstrong, Jeannette. *Breath Tracks*. Stratford, Ont.: Williams-Wallace; Vancouver, B.C.: Theytus Books, 1991.

———. "This Is a Story." In *All My Relations*, edited by Thomas King, 129-35. Toronto: McClelland & Stewart, 1990.

Baurmeister, General. *Revolution in America: Confidential Letters and Journals, 1776-1784 of Adjutant General Baurmeister of the Hessian Forces*. Edited and translated by Bernard A. Uhlendorf. Reprint, Westport, Conn.: Greenwood, 1973.

Boas, Franz. *Anthropological Essays Presented to Frederic Ward Putnam in Honor of His Seventieth Birthday, April 16, 1909, by His Friends and Associates*. New York: G. E. Stechert, 1909.

———. *Anthropology and Modern Life*. New York: Norton, 1928.

———. *Aryans and Non-Aryans*. New York: Information and Service Associates, 1934.

———. *Beiträge zur Geschichte und Völkerkunde*. 2 vols. Frankfurt am Main: Rütten & Loening, 1885-1886.

———. *The Ethnography of Franz Boas*. Compiled and edited by Ronald Rohner.

With an introduction by Ronald P. Rohner and Evelyn C. Rohner. Translated by Hedy Parker. Chicago: U of Chicago P, 1969.

————, ed. *General Anthropology*. With contributions by Ruth Benedict, Franz Boas, Ruth Bunzel et al. Boston, New York: D. C. Heath, 1938.

Bogaert, Harmen Meyndertsz van den. *A Journey into Mohawk and Oneida Country, 1634-1635: The Journal of Harmen Meyndertsz van den Bogaert*. Translated and edited by Charles T. Gehring and William A. Starna, with a word list and linguistic notes by Gunther Michelson. Syracuse, N.Y.: Syracuse UP, 1988.

Boyd, Julian P., ed. *Indian Treaties Printed by Benjamin Franklin, 1736-1762*. Philadelphia: Historical Society of Pennsylvania, 1938.

Brave Bird, Mary, with Richard Erdoes. *Ohitika Woman*. New York: Grove Press, 1993.

Burritt, Elihu. *Elihu Burritt: A Memorial Volume Containing a Sketch of his Life and Labors, with Selections from His Writings and Lectures, and Extracts from His Private Journals in Europe and America*. Edited by Chas Northend. New York: D. Appleton, 1879.

————. *The Learned Blacksmith: The Letters and Journals of Elihu Burritt*. Edited by Merle Curti. New York: Wilson-Erickson, 1937.

Campbell, Maria. *Halfbreed*. Lincoln: U of Nebraska P, 1973.

Census Office. *Statistics of the Population of the United States at the Tenth Census (June 1, 1880)*. Vol. 1. Washington, D.C.: Government Printing Office, 1883.

Chamisso, Adalbert von. *Reise um die Welt: mit der romanzoffischen Entdeckungs-Expedition in den Jahren 1815-1818 auf der Brigg Rurik, Kapitän Otto von Kotzebue*. Leipzig: Bibliographisches Institut, [183?].

————. *A Voyage around the World with the Romanzov Exploring Expedition in the Years 1815-1818 in the Brig Rurik, Captain Otto von Kotzebue, by Adelbert von Chamisso*. Translated and edited by Henry Kratz. Honolulu: U of Hawaii P, 1986.

Chateaubriand, François René de. *Atala ou Les amours de deux sauvages dans le désert*. Paris: Migneret, 1801.

Claus, Christian Daniel. *The Journals of Christian Daniel Claus and Conrad Weiser: a Journey to Onondaga, 1750*. Translated and edited by Helga Doblin and William A. Starna. Philadelphia: American Philosophical Society, 1994.

Cloos, August. "Der Indianerhäuptling Kah-ge-ga-ga-bowh in Köln und Düsseldorf." Parts 1-2. *Didaskalia*, 221 (16 September 1850): p. 2, col. 2; p. 3, col. 1-2; 222 (17 September 1850): p. 2, col. 1-2; p. 3, col. 1.

Copway, George. *The Life, History, and Travels of Kah-ge-ga-gah-bowh (George Copway), a Convert to the Christian Faith, and a Missionary to His People for Twelve years; With a Sketch of the Present State of the Ojebwa Nation, in Regard to Christianity and Their Future Prospects*. Albany, N.Y.: Weed & Parsons, 1847. Reprint, Lincoln: U of Nebraska P, 1997.

———. *Ojibway Conquest: A Tale of the Northwest.* New York: George B. Putnam, 1850.

———. *Organization of A New Indian Territory, East of the Missouri River. Arguments and Reasons Submitted to the Honorable Members of the Senate and House of Representatives of the 31st Congress of the United States: By the Indian Chief Kah-ge-ga-gah-bowh, or Geo. Copway.* New York: S. W. Benedict, 1850.

———. *Running Sketches of Men and Places, in England, France, Germany, Belgium, and Scotland.* New York: J. C. Riker, 1851.

———. *The Traditional History and Characteristic Sketches of the Ojibway Nation.* London: C. Gilpin, 1850. Reprint, New York: AMS Press, 1978.

Cronau, Rudolf. *Im Lande der Sioux.* Leipzig: Weigel, 1886.

———. "My Visit Among the Hostile Dakota Indians and How They Became My Friends." *South Dakota Historical Collections* 22 (1946): 410–25.

Crow Dog, Mary, with Richard Erdoes. *Lakota Woman.* New York: HarperCollins, 1990.

Deloria, Vine, and Raymond J. DeMallie, eds. *Documents of American Indian Diplomacy: Treaties, Agreements, and Conventions, 1775–1979.* 2 vols. Norman: U of Oklahoma P, 1999.

De Schweinitz, Edward. *The Life and Times of David Zeisberger.* 1870. Reprint, New York Times and Arno Press, 1971.

———. *The Moravian Manual.* Bethlehem, Penn.: A. C. & H. T. Clauder, 1869.

Erdrich, Louise. *The Antelope Wife.* New York: HarperCollins, 1998.

———. *The Birchbark House.* New York: Hyperion, 1999.

———. *The Blue Jay's Dance: A Birth Year.* New York: HarperCollins, 1995.

Ewald, Johann. *Diary of the American War, a Hessian Journal: Captain Johann Ewald, Field Jager Corps.* Edited by Joseph P. Tustin. New Haven, Conn.: Yale UP, 1979.

Faull, Katherine M., trans. *Moravian Women's Memoirs: Their Related Lives, 1750–1820.* Syracuse, N.Y.: Syracuse UP, 1997.

Ferry, Gabriel. *An Adventure with the Apaches.* New York, Cincinnati: Benzinger Bros., 1901.

———. *Le coureur des bois; ou, Les chercheurs d'or.* 4th ed. Paris: Hachette, 1856.

Finerty, John. *War-Path and Bivouac: The Big Horn and Yellowstone Expedition.* Edited by Milo M. Quaife. Chicago: R. R. Donnelley & Sons, 1955.

Foehse, Ludwig. *Der letzte Sitting Bull. Indianererzählung aus dem Jahre 1890.* Münchner Volksbücher 43. Munich: Münchner Verlagsinstitut, 1891.

Franklin, Benjamin. *Observations Concerning the Increase of Mankind.* 1755. Reprinted in *The Papers of Benjamin Franklin,* vol. 4, edited by Leonard W. Labaree. New Haven, Conn.: Yale UP, 1959.

———. *The Papers of Benjamin Franklin.* 35 vols. Edited by Leonard W. Larrabee et al. New Haven, Conn.: Yale UP, 1959–1999.

Frey, W. *Büffelauge, der Sohn des Dakota Häuptlings Sitting Bull. Kleine Volkserzählungen.* Mülheim, Germany: J. Bagel, 1891.

"Der Friedenscongreß in Frankfurt. In *Die Grenzboten,* edited by Gustav Freytag and Julian Schmidt, 365-67. Leipzig: Verlag von Friedrich Ludwig Hubig, 1850.

Fries, Adelaide L., ed. and trans. *Records of the Moravians in North Carolina.* 11 vols. Raleigh: North Carolina Historical Commission, 1922-1968.

Gerstäcker, Friedrich. *Amerikanische Wald- und Strombilder.* 2 vols. Dresden: Arnold, 1849.

———. *Aus zwei Welttheilen.* 2 vols. Leipzig: Arnold, 1854.

———. *Each for Himself, or, the Two Adventurers.* London: Routledge, 1859.

———. *In Amerika. Amerikanisches Lebensbild aus neuerer Zeit.* 3rd ed. 2 vols. Jena: Costenoble, 1878.

———. *Kleine Erzählungen und nachgelassene Schriften.* 2 vols. Jena: Costenoble, 1879.

———. *Mississippi-Bilder.* 3 vols. Dresden: Arnold, 1847.

———. *Narrative of a Journey round the World. Comprising a Winter-passage across the Andes to Chili; with a Visit to the Gold Regions of California and Australia, the South Sea Islands, Java, and c.* New York: Harper & Brothers, 1853.

———. *Neue Reisen durch die Vereinigten Staaten, Mexiko, Ecuador, Westindien und Venezuela.* 2d ed. 3 vols. Jena: Costenoble, 1876.

———. *Reisen.* 5 vols. Stuttgart: Cotta, 1853-1854.

———. *Streif- und Jagdzüge durch die vereinigten Staaten Nord-Amerikas.* 2 vols. Dresden: Arnold, 1844.

Gillett, James G. *Six Years with the Texas Rangers, 1875-1881.* Edited by Milo M. Quaife. Lincoln: U of Nebraska P, 1976.

Goethe, Johann Wolfgang von. "To America." Translated by Stephen Spender. In *The Permanent Goethe,* edited by Thomas Mann, 655. New York: Dial, 1948.

———. *Werke.* Hamburger Ausgabe. 14 vols. Hamburg: Deutscher Taschenbuch Verlag, 1982.

Gómez-Peña, Guillermo. *Dangerous Border Crosses: The Artist Talks Back.* New York: Routledge, 2000.

———. *The New World Border: Prophecies, Poems, and Loqueras for the End of the Century.* San Francisco: City Lights, 1996.

Graffenried, Christoph von. *Christoph von Graffenried's Account of the Founding of New Bern.* Edited by Vincent H. Todd. Raleigh, N. C.: State Printers, 1920. Facsimile reprint, New Bern, N.C.: Joh. P. Shermann, 2000.

Gymir, Gerda. *Der Sontschem: Ein Volk kämpft für Freiheit und Ehre gegen Puritaner.* Cologne: Schröder, 1940.

Hackett, Charles W., ed. *Pichardo's Treatise on the Limits of Louisiana and Texas.* 4 vols. Austin: U of Texas P, 1931-1946.

Hammond, George P., and Agapito Rey, eds. *Narratives of the Coronado Expedition, 1540-1542.* Albuquerque: U of New Mexico P, 1940.

Hawley, Gideon. "An account of the number of Indian houses in Mashpee, July 1, 1793." Manuscript, autograph file. Houghton Library, Harvard U.

Heckewelder, John. *A Correspondence between the Rev. John Heckewelder . . . and Peter S. Duponceau. Esq. . . . Respecting the Languages of the American Indians.* Special Collections. Dartmouth College Baker Library.

———. *History, Manners, and Customs of the Indian Nations Who Once Inhabited Pennsylvania and the Neighboring States.* 1876. Reprint, Arno Press and New York Times, 1971.

———. *A Narrative of the Mission of the United Brethren among the Delaware and Mohegan Indians: from its Commencement, in the Year 1740, to the Close of the Year 1808; Comprising all the Remarkable Incidents which Took Place at Their Missionary Stations during that Period.* Philadelphia: McCarty & Davis, 1820.

Herold, Heinrich. *Sitting Bull, oder Der Todeskampf der Indianer.* Unterhaltungsbibliothek 1118. Reutlingen, Germany: Ensslin & Laiblin, 1892.

Highway, Tomson. *Dry Lips Oughta Move to Kapuskasin.* Saskatoon, Sask.: Fifth House, 1989.

———. *Kiss of the Fur Queen.* Toronto: Doubleday Canada, 1998.

———. *The Rez Sisters.* Saskatoon, Sask.: Fifth House, 1988.

Holmes, John Beck. *Historical Sketches of the Missions of the United Brethren for Propagating the Gospel among the Heathen, from their Commencement to the Present Time.* Dublin: Napper, 1818.

Im Lande der Rothäute: Der Letzte der Mohikaner von J.F. Cooper; Der Waldläufer von Gabriel Ferry. Mülheim an der Ruhr, Germany: Julius Bagel, 1900.

Jacobsen, Johan Adrian. *Capitain Jacobsen's Reise an der Nordwestküste Amerikas, 1881–1883.* Edited by A. Woldt. Leipzig: Max Spohr, 1884.

Johnson, William. *The Papers of Sir William Johnson.* Edited by James Sullivan, Alexander Flick et al. 15 vols. Albany: State U of New York P, 1921–1965.

Johnston, Basil. "The Prophecy." In *An Anthology of Canadian Native Literature in English,* edited by Daniel David Moses and Terry Goldie. Toronto: Oxford UP, 1992.

———. "The Spirit of Maundau-meen (Maize)." In *The Manitous,* 103-4. Toronto: Key Porter Books, 1995.

Jones, Peter. *History of the Ojebway Indians; With Especial Reference to Their Conversion to Christianity.* London: A. W. Bennett, 1861.

———. *Life and Journals of Ka-ke-wa-quo-na-by (Rev. Peter Jones), Wesleyan Missionary.* Toronto: Anson Green, 1860.

Journal des Débats Politiques et Littéraires, Paris 1850.

Journey to Onondaga in 1743 by John Bartram, Lewis Evans, and Conrad Weiser, A. Barre, Mass.: Imprint Society, 1973.

Keller, Gottfried. *Gottfried Kellers Briefe und Tagebücher 1830-1861.* Edited by Emil Ermatinger. Stuttgart: Cotta'sche Buchhandlung Nachfolger, 1916.

Kelly, Jennifer. "A Conversation with Lee Maracle." Ariel 25, no. 1 (Jan. 1994): 73–88.

King, Thomas. Truth and Bright Water. Toronto: Harper Collins, 1999.

Kohl, Johann Georg. Kitchi-Gami: Wanderings Round Lake Superior. London: Chapman & Hall, 1860. Reprinted as Kitchi-Gami: Life Among the Lake Superior Ojibway, St. Paul: Minnesota Historical Society Press, 1985.

Kolben, Peter. The Present State of the Cape of Good-Hope. 2 vols. London: 1731.

Kotzebue, Otto von. A Voyage of Discovery, into the South Sea and Bering's Straits, for the Purpose of Exploring a North-east Passage, Undertaken in the Years 1815-1818, at the Expense of His Highness . . . Count Romanzoff, in the Ship Rurick, under the Command of the Lieutenant in the Russian Imperial Navy, Otto von Kotzebue. London: Longman, Hurst, Rees, Orme, & Brown, 1821.

Krause, Aurel. The Tlingit Indians: Results of a Trip to the Northwest Coast of America and the Bering Straits by Aurel Krause. Translated by Erna Gunther. Seattle: Published for the American Ethnological Society by the U of Washington P, 1956.

———. To the Chukchi Peninsula and to the Tlingit Indians, 1881/1882: Journals and letters by Aurel and Arthur Krause. Translated by Margot Krause McCaffrey. Faibanks: U of Alaska P, 1993

Kurz, Rudolph Friedrich. "Journal of Rudolph Friedrich Kurz: An Account of His Experiences Among Fur Traders and American Indians on the Mississippi and the Upper Missouri Rivers During the Years 1846 to 1852." Edited by J. N. B. Hewitt. Translated by Myrtis Jarrell. Bureau of American Ethnology Bulletin no. 115. Washington, D.C.: 1937.

Langsdorff, G. H. von. Voyages and Travels in Various Parts of the World during the Years 1803-1807. 2 vols. London: Henry Colburn, 1813.

Lederer, John. The Discoveries of John Lederer, in Three Several Marches from Virginia, to the West of Carolina, and Other Parts of the Continent: Begun in March 1669, and Ended in September 1670. Together with a General Map of the Whole Territory which he Traversed. Coll. and trans. out of Latine form his discourse and writings, by Sir William Talbot, baronet. London: Heyrick, 1672.

———. The Discoveries of John Lederer, with Unpublished Letters by and about Lederer to Governor John Whinthrop, J., and an Essay on the Indians of Lederer's Discoveries by Douglas L. Rights and William P. Cumming. Edited with notes by William P. Cumming. Charlottesville: U of Virginia P, 1958.

Lehmann, Hermann. Herman Lehmann, Nine Years Among the Indians. Edited by J. Marvin Hunter. 1927. Reprint, Albuquerque: U of New Mexico P, 1993.

Linderholm, Helmer. De roda kampar: fjarde delen av berattelsen om den svenske indianen Amisko (Lars Bure). Stockholm: Tiden, 1975.

Littlechild, George, Linda Spaner Dayan Frimer, Reisa Smiley Schneider, and Garry Gottfriedson. In Honour Of Our Grandmothers. Penticton, B.C.: Theytus Books, 1994.

Loher, Franz von. *Aussichten für gebildete Deutsche in Nordamerika*. Berlin: Julius Springer, 1853. Microform.

———. *Beiträge zur Geschichte und Völkerkunde*. 2 vols. Frankfurt am Main: Rütten & Loening, 1885–1886.

———. *Geschichte and Zustände der Deutschen in Amerika*. Cincinnati: Eggers & Wulkop, 1847. 2nd. ed. Göttingen: Wigand, 1855.

———. *Land und Leute in der alten und neuen Welt: Reiseskizzen*. Göttingen: Wigand; New York: L. W. Schmidt, 1855–1858.

———. *Ueber Deutschlands Weltstellung*. Munich: Königl. Akademie, 1874. Microform.

Longfellow, Henry Wordsworth. *The Letters of Henry Wordsworth Longfellow*. Edited by Andrew Hilen. Cambridge, Mass.: Belknap P of Harvard UP, 1972.

Longfellow, Samuel, ed. *Life of Henry Wadsworth Longfellow with Extracts from his Journals and Correspondence*, 2 vols. Boston: Ticknor & Company, 1886.

Loskiel, George Henry. *History of the Mission to the United Brethren Among the Indians of North America*. Translated by C. I. La Trobe. London: Brethren's Society, 1794.

Lucier, Armand Francis, comp. *Pontiac's Conspiracy and Other Indian Affairs: Notices Abstracted from Colonial Newspapers, 1763–1765*. Bowie, Md.: Heritage Books, 2000.

Lurie, Nancy O. *Mountain Wolf Woman: The Autobiography of a Winnebago Woman*. Ann Arbor: U of Michigan P, 1961.

Magnusson, Magnus, and Hermann Pálsson, trans. and eds. *The Vinland Sagas; the Norse Discovery of America*. New York: New York UP, 1966.

Manhart, Paul, ed. *Eugene Buechel: A Dictionary of the Teton Dakota Sioux Language; Lakota-English, English-Lakota, with considerations given to Yankton and Santee. Oie wowapi wan Lakota-Ieska, Ieska-Lakota*. In cooperation with the Institute of Indian Studies, University of South Dakota, Vermillion. Pine Ridge, S.D.: Red Cloud Indian School, Holy Rosary Mission, 1970.

Maracle, Lee. *Ravensong*. Vancouver, B.C.: Press Gang Publishers, 1993.

———. "Preface: You Become the Trickster." In *Sojourner's Truth and Other Stories*, 11–13. Vancouver, B.C.: Press Gang Publishers, 1990.

Maungwudaus. *An Account of the Chippewa Indians, Who Have Been Travelling in the United States, England, Ireland, Scotland, France, and Belgium; with Very Interesting Incidents in Relation to the General Characteristics of the English, Irish, Scotch, French, and Americans, with Regard to Their Hospitality, Peculiarities, etc*. Boston: by the author, 1848.

———. *An Account of the North American Indians, Written for Maungwudaus, a Chief of the Ojibway Indians Who Has Been Travelling in England, France, Belgium, Ireland, and Scotland*. Leicester, England: T. Cook, 1848.

———. *Remarks Concerning the Ojibway Indians, by One of Themselves Called Maungwudaus, Who Has Been Travelling in England, France, Belgium, Ireland, and Scotland*. Leeds: C. A. Wilson, 1847.

May, Karl. *Djinnistan.* New York: Seabury Press, 1977.

———. *Freiburger Erstausgaben.* 33 vols. Edited by Roland Schmidt. Bamberg, Germany: Karl-May-Verlag, 1982–1984.

———. *Der Schatz im Silbersee.* 1894. Bamberg, Germany: Karl-May-Verlag, 1951.

———. *Winnetou: Reiseerzählung.* 3 vols. 1983. Bamberg, Germany: Karl-May-Verlag, 1951.

———. *Winnetou and Ardistan.* New York: Seabury Press, 1977.

McMichael, James. "Diary of Lieutenant James McMichael of the Pennsylvania Line, 1776–1778." Reprinted in *Pennsylvania Archives,* edited by Samuel Hazard, et al. Harrisburg, Penn.: State P of Pennsylvania, 1838–1935.

Medicine Crow, Joseph. *From the Heart of Crow Country: The Crow Indians' Own Stories.* New York: Crown, 1992.

"Minutes of the Committee of Observation and Inspection of Northampton County, Pennsylvania, 1774–1777." Reprinted in *Two Hundred Years of Life in Northampton County, Pennsylvania.* Easton, Penn.: Northampton County Bicentennial Commission, 1976.

Minutes of Conferences Held at Easton in August 1761. Philadelphia: Franklin & Hall, 1761,

Minutes of Conferences Held at Easton in October 1758. Philadelphia: Franklin & Hall, 1758.

Minutes of the Provincial Council of Pennsylvania. Harrisburg, Penn.: Penn & Company, 1852.

Möllhausen, Balduin. *Balduin Möllhausen: Ein Preusse bei den Indianern: Aquarelle für Friedrich Wilhelm IV.* Berlin-Brandenburg: Stiftung Preussische Schlösser und Gärten Berlin-Brandenburg, 1995.

———. *Diary of a Journey from the Mississippi to the Coast of the Pacific with a United States Government Expedition.* 2 vols. London, 1858.

———. *Der Halbindianer.* 4 vols. Leipzig: Costenoble, 1861.

———. *Der Mayordomo.* 4 vols. Leipzig: Costenoble, 1863.

———. *Reisen in die Felsengebirge Nord-Amerikas bis zum Hoch-Plateau von Neu-Mexico.* 2 vols. Leipzig: Kurfürst, 1861.

———. *Tagebuch einer Reise vom Mississippi nach den Küsten der Südsee.* Leipzig: Mendelssohn, 1858.

———. *Wanderungen durch die Prairien und Wüsten des westlichen Nordamerika vom Mississippi nach den Küsten der Südsee, im Gefolge der von der Regierung der Vereinigten Staaten unter Lieutenant Whipple ausgesandten Expedition.* Introduction by Alexander von Humboldt. 2d. ed., with a lithographic map drawn by Henry Lange. Leipzig: Herman Mendelssohn, 1860.

Moses, Daniel David, and Terry Goldie, eds. *An Anthology of Canadian Native Literature in English.* 2d ed. Toronto: Oxford UP, 1998.

Occom, Samuel. "Journal." In *An Indian Preacher in England*, edited by Leon B. Richardson. Hanover, N.H.: Dartmouth College Publications, 1933.

Paul-Martin, Michael J. *She Said Sometimes I Hear Things*. Toronto, Ont.: 7th Generation Books, 1996.

Pennsylvania Archives, 1st series. Philadelphia, 1853.

Peyer, Bernd C., ed. *The Elders Wrote: An Anthology of Early Prose by North American Indians 1768–1931*. Berlin: Dietrich Reimer Verlag, 1982.

———. *The Singing Spirit: Early Short Stories by North American Indians*. Tucson: U of Arizona P, 1989.

Pistorius, Franz. *Der Aufstand der Dakotahs*. Mülheim, Germany: J. Bagel, 1891.

Post, Christian Frederick. *Journal of Christian Frederick Post, from Philadelphia to the Ohio*. In vol. 1 of *Early Western Travels, 1748–1846*, edited by Reuben G. Thwaites, 175–291. Cleveland: Arthur H. Clark, 1904–1907.

Pouchot, Pierre. *Memoirs on the Late War in North America Between France and England by Pierre Pouchot*. Edited by Brian Leigh Dunnigan. Translated by Michael Cardy. Youngstown, N.Y.: Old Fort Niagara Association, 1994.

Proposals for Propagating Christianity among the Native Indians of North America. Ca. 1750. Manuscript. Lambeth Palace Library, London.

Reck, Baron von. "A Short Report on Georgia and the Indians There." In vol 2. of *Detailed Reports on the Salzburger Emigrants Who Settled in America . . .* Edited by Samuel Urlsperger, edited by George Fenwick Jones, 135–48. Athens: U of Georgia P, 1968–1976.

Records of the Moravian Mission among the Indians of North America. From original materials at the Archives of the Moravian Church, Bethlehem, Pa. New Haven, Conn. Microfilm, 40 reels.

Report of the Proceedings of the Third General Peace Congress, held in Frankfort, on the 22nd, 23rd, and 24th August, 1850. London: C. Gilpin, 1851.

Rieder, Hans Rudolf. *Lagerfeuer im Indianerland*. Essen: Essener Verlagsanstalt, 1939.

———, trans. and ed. *Häuptling Büffelkind Langspeer erzählt sein Leben*. 1929. Reprint, Munich: List, 1958.

Rimius, Heinrich. *A candid narrative of the rise and progress of the Herrnhuters, commonly called Moravians, or, Unitas Fratrium: with a short account of their doctrines, drawn from their own writings . . .* 2d ed. London: A. Linde, 1753.

Robinson, Harry. *Nature Power: In the Spirit of an Okanagan Storyteller*. Compiled and edited by Wendy Wickwire. Vancouver, B.C.: Douglas & McIntyre; Seattle: U of Washington P, 1992.

———. *Write It On Your Heart: The Epic World of an Okanagan Storyteller*. Compiled and edited by Wendy Wickwire. Vancouver, B.C.: Talon Books, Theytus, 1989.

Rowland, Dunbar, A. G. Sanders, and Patricia Kay Galloway, eds., *Mississippi Pro-*

vincial *Archives, French Dominion*. Vol. 5, 1749–1763. Baton Rouge: Louisiana State UP, 1984.

Sealsfield, Charles. *Sämtliche Werke*. 24 vols. Edited by Karl J. R. Arndt et al. Hildesheim, Germany: Olms, 1972–1991.

Shute, Samuel M. "Journal of Lieutenant Samuel M. Shute." Reprinted in *Journals of the Military Expedition of Major General John Sullivan*, edited by Frederick Cook. Auburn, N.Y.: Knapp, Peck, & Thompson, 1887.

Sitting Bull. *The Works of Sitting Bull, in the Original French and Latin*. 2d ed. Edited by Robert Dunlap Clarke. Chicago: Knight & Leonard, 1878.

Sitting Bull, Sioux-Indianers Siste Höfding. Stockholm: Svithiod, 1908.

Smith, John. *Travels and Works of Captain John Smith*. 2 vols. Edited by Edward Arber and A. G. Bradley. Edinburgh: John Grant, 1910.

Smith, William. *A Brief State of the Province of Pennsylvania*. London, 1755.

Snow, Dean R., Charles T. Gehring, and William A. Starna, eds. *In Mohawk Country: Early Narratives about a Native People*. Syracuse, N.Y.: Syracuse UP, 1996.

Spangenberg, A. G. *An Account of the Manner in Which the United Brethren Preach the Gospel and Carry on Their Missions Among the Heathens*. Translated. London: H. Trapp, 1788.

"Statistical Census for the District of Cape Girardeau." In *The Spanish Regime in Missouri*, 2 vols., edited by Louis Houck. Chicago: R. R. Donnelley & Sons, 1909.

Steller, Georg Wilhelm. *Journal of a Voyage with Bering, 1741–1742*. Edited and with an introduction by O. W. Frost. Translated by Margritt A. Engel and O. W. Frost. Stanford, Calif.: Stanford UP, 1988.

Steuben, Fritz. *Tecumseh, strahlender Stern: eine Erzählung vom Kampf des roten Mannes*. 1956. Stuttgart: W. Keller, 1972.

Tacitus, Publius Cornelius. *Germania/Bericht über Germanien*. Translated and edited by J. Lindauer. Munich: DTV, 1975.

Tarble, Helen M. "The Story of My Capture and Escape during the Minnesota Indian Massacre of 1862, with Historical Notes, Descriptions of Pioneer Life, and Sketches and Incidents of the Great Outbreak of the Sioux or Dakota Indians as I Saw Them." In vol. 105 of *The Garland Library of Narratives of North American Indian Captivities*, edited by Wilcomb E. Washburn. New York: Garland, 1976.

Taylor, Drew Hayden. *Toronto at Dreamer's Rock*. Saskatoon, Sask.: Fifth House.

"Texas: Die deutschen Ansiedler und die Comanches." *Magazin für die Literatur des Auslands* 31, no. 104 (August 1847): 415–16.

Thwaites, Reuben Gold, ed. *The Jesuit Relations and Allied Documents: Travels and Explorations of the Jesuit Missionaries in New France 1610–1791*. 73 vols. Cleveland, Ohio: Burrows Brothers, 1896–1901.

Tolzmann, Don Heinrich, ed. *The Sioux Uprising in Minnesota, 1862: Jacob Nix's*

Eyewitness History. Indianapolis: Max Kade German-American Center & Indian German Heritage Society, 1994.

Verhandlungen des dritten allgemeinen Friedenscongresses, gehalten in der Paulskirche zu Frankfurt a/M., am 22., 23., und 24. August 1850. Frankfurt am Main.: J. D. Sauerländer's Verlag, 1851.

Vizenor, Gerald, *Fugitive Poses: Native American Indian Scenes of Absence and Presence.* Lincoln: U of Nebraska P, 1998.

———. "Three Anishinaabeg Writers." In *The People Named the Chippewa,* 56-74. Minneapolis: U of Minnesota P, 1984.

Wagamese, Richard. *Keeper'N Me.* Toronto: Doubleday Canada, 1994.

———. *A Quality of Light.* Toronto: Doubleday, 1997.

Welskopf-Henrich, Liselotte. *Die Söhne der großen Bärin.* Berlin: Altberliner Verlag, 1962.

Wied-Neuwied, Maximilian Alexander Philipp, Prinz von. *People of the first man: life among the Plains Indians in their final days of glory: the firsthand account of Prince Maximilian's expedition up the Missouri River, 1833-34.* Edited and designed by Davis Thomas and Karin Ronnefeldt, with watercolors by Karl Bodmer. New York: Dutton, 1976.

———. "Travels in the Interior of North America, 1832-1834." In vols. 22-25 of *Early Western Travels, 1748-1846,* edited by Reuben Gold Thwaites. Cleveland: A. H. Clark, 1904-1907.

Winfrey, Dorman H., James M. Day, et al, eds. *Texas Indian Papers, 1825-1916, edited from the original manuscript copies in the Texas State Archive.* 4 vols. Austin: Texas State Library, 1960-1961.

Withers, Alexander Scott. *Chronicles of Border Warfare: or a History of the Settlement by the Whites of north-western Virginia; and of the Indian wars and massacres in that section of the state; with reflections, anecdotes, and c.* Clarksburg, Va.: Joseph Israel, 1831.

Württemberg, Paul Wilhelm, Graf von. *Paul Wilhelm, Duke of Württemberg: Travels in North America 1822-1824.* Edited by Savoie Lottinville. Translated by Robert Nitske. Norman: U of Oklahoma P, 1973.

Secondary Literature

Adams, Howard. *A Tortured People.* Penticton, B. C.: Theytus Books, 1994.

Akiwenzie-Damm, Kateri. "We Belong To This Land: A View of 'Cultural Difference.'" In *Literary Pluralities,* edited by Christl Verduyn, 84-91. Peterborough, England: Broadview Press, 1998.

Alter, Peter, Claus-Ekkehard Bärsch, and Peter Berghoff, eds. *Die Konstruktion der Nation gegen die Juden.* Munich: Fink, 1999.

Bibliography

Ames, Eric. "Where the Wild Things Are: Locating the Exotic in German Modernity." Ph.D. diss., U California at Berkeley, 2000.

Anders, Ferdinand, et al. Lukas Vischer (1789–1840): Reisender-Künstler-Maler. Völkerkundliche Abhandlungen 2. Hannover, 1967.

Anderson, Gary Clayton. Kinsmen of Another Kind: Dakota-White Relations in the Upper Mississippi Valley, 1650–1862. Lincoln: U of Nebraska P, 1984.

———. Little Crow: Spokesman for the Sioux. St. Paul: Minnesota Historical Society Press, 1986.

Anderson, John Alvin. Sioux of the Rosebud: A History in Pictures. Norman, Okla.: U of Oklahoma P, 1971.

Andreas, Christoph. Adolf Hoeffler. Frankfurt am Main: Verlag von J. P. Schneider jr., 1998.

Anzaldúa, Gloria. "Border Crossings." Trivia (spring 1989): 46–52.

———. "La conciencia de la mestiza: Towards a New Consciousness." In Making Face, Making Soul, 377–89. San Francisco: aunt lute books, 1990.

Arens, B. Handbuch der katholischen Missionen. Freiburg im Breisgau, Germany: Herder, 1920.

———. Jesuitenorden und Weltmission. Regensburg, Germany: Pustet, 1937.

Armstrong, Jeannette. "The Disempowerment of First North American Native Peoples and Empowerment Through Their Writing." In An Anthology of Canadian Native Literature in English, 2d ed., edited by Daniel David Moses and Terry Goldie, 239–42. Toronto: Oxford UP, 1998.

Arndt, Wibke. Rote Wolke, Blaues Pferd: Bilder aus dem Leben der Sioux. Hamburg: Christians Verlag, 1997.

Atcheson, Joyce. "Who's God? Whose God?" Wawatay News 7 (October 1999).

Augstein, Rudolf. "Weiter Weg zu Winnetou." Der Spiegel 49, no. 18 (1 May 1995): 130–35, 138, 140–42, 144.

Auth, Stephen F. The Ten Years' War: Indian-White Relations in Pennsylvania, 1755–1765. New York: Garland, 1989.

Axtell, J. The Invasion Within. New York: Oxford UP, 1985.

Bailyn, Bernard, and Philip D. Morgan, eds. Strangers Within the Realm: Cultural Margins of the First British Empire. Chapel Hill: U of North Carolina P, 1991.

Bankmann, Ulf. "The 'Esquimaux-Indians' in Berlin, 1824–1825: Drawings and Prints." European Review of Native American Studies 11, no. 2 (1997): 21–26.

Barba, Preston A. Cooper in Germany. Bloomington: Indiana UP, 1914.

Barnett, Louise K. The Ignoble Savage: American Literary Racism 1790–1890. Westport, Conn.: Greenwood, 1975.

Barsh, Russel L. "American Indians in the Great War." Ethnohistory 38 (1991): 276–303.

———. "'Colored' Seamen in the New England Whaling Industry: An Afro-Indian Consortium." In Confounding the Color Line: Indian-Black Relations in

Multidisciplinary Perspective, edited by James F. Brooks and Gary Dunham. Lincoln: U of Nebraska P, forthcoming.

———. "Puget Sound Indian Demography, 1900–1920: Migration and Economic Integration." *Ethnohistory* 43 (1996):65–97.

Barsh, Russel L., and James Youngblood Henderson. *The Road: Indian Tribes and Political Liberty.* Berkeley: U of California P, 1980.

Barth, John. *The Sot-Weed Factor.* London: Panther Books, 1965.

Barthel-Winkler, Lisa. "Das Drama des sterbenden Volkes." *Karl-May-Jahrbuch* 7 (1924): 338–43.

Barwin, L. F. *Pontiac.* Heidenau, Germany: Langer, 1943.

———. *Das vergessene Volk.* Darmstadt, Germany: Büchner, 1956.

Baskauskas, Liucija, and Bea Medicine. *"Speaking the Spirit": Plains Indians in Russia.* Santa Monica, Calif.: Warrior Women Inc. 1998. Videotape.

Bathrick, David. *The Power of Speech: The Politics of Culture in the* GDR. Lincoln: Nebraska UP, 1995.

Baumgartner, A., et al. *Drei Indianergeschichten.* Freiburg im Breisgau, Germany: Herder, 1926.

Bazin, André. *What is Cinema?* 2 vols. Translated by Hugh Gray. Berkeley: U of California P, 1967.

Beidler, Peter G., and Gay Barton. *A Reader's Guide to the Novels of Louise Erdrich.* Columbia: U of Missouri P, 1999.

Bemelmans, Ludwig. *My War with the United States.* New York: Viking Press, 1937.

Berding, Helmut, ed. *Nationales Bewußtsein und kollektive Identität.* Frankfurt am Main.: Suhrkamp, 1994.

Berkhofer, Robert F., Jr. *The White Man's Indian: Images of the American Indian from Columbus to the Present.* New York: Alfred A. Knopf, 1978.

Berman, Nina. "Orientalism, Imperialism, and Nationalism: Karl May's Orient-zyklus." In *The Imperialist Imagination*, edited by Sara Friedrichsmeyer et al. Ann Arbor: U of Michigan P, 51–68.

Bernstein, Alison R. *American Indians and World War II: Toward a New Era in Indian Affairs.* Norman: U of Oklahoma P, 1991.

Berthrong, Donald J. *The Southern Cheyennes.* Norman: U of Oklahoma P, 1963.

Bhabha, Homi K. *The Location of Culture.* London: Routledge, 1994.

Bieder, Robert E. Introduction to *Kitchi-Gami: Life Among the Lake Superior Ojibway*, by Johann George Kohl. St. Paul: Minnesota Historical Society Press, 1985.

———."Marketing the American Indian in Europe. In *Cultural Transmissions and Receptions*, edited by Rob Kroes, R. W. Rydell, and D. F. J. Bosscher, 15–23. Amsterdam: VU UP, 1993.

Biesele, R. L. "The Relations between the German Settlers and Indians in Texas, 1844–1860." *Southwestern Historical Quarterly* 31 (1927): 116–29.

Billington, Ray Allen. *Land of Savagery — Land of Promise: The European Image of the American Frontier in the Nineteenth Century*. New York: W. W. Norton, 1981.

Blades, John. "Louise Erdrich Taps a Slightly Lighter Vein in Quest to Shed Labeling." *Chicago Tribune*, 31 August 1986, Book section: 14, 30.

Blaeser, Kimberly. "Writing Voices Speaking: Native Authors and an Oral Aesthetic." Paper presented at the Talking on the Page Conference. University of Toronto, 15–16 November 1996.

Bogardus, Emory Stephen, and Robert H. Lewis. *Social Life and Personality*. New York: Burdett, 1938.

Bogdanovich, Peter. *John Ford*. Berkeley: U of California P, 1978.

Boger, J. *Western-Hobby heute*. Stuttgart: Motorbuch, 1990.

Bolz, Peter. "Indianer und Deutsche: eine klischeebeladene Beziehung." In *Indianer Nordamerikas: Die Sammlungen des Ethnologischen Museums Berlin*, edited by P. Bolz and H.-U. Sanner. Berlin: Ethnologisches Museum, 1999.

———. "Life among the 'Hunkpapas': A Case Study of German Indian Lore." In *Indians and Europe: An Interdisciplinary Collection of Essays*, edited by Christian F. Feest, 475–90. Aachen: Rader, 1987. Reprint, Lincoln: U of Nebraska P, 1999.

Bonomi, Patricia. *The Lord Cornbury Scandal: The Politics of Reputation in British America*. Chapel Hill: U of North Carolina P, 1998.

Börner, Karl Heinz. *Wilhelm I. Deutscher Kaiser und König von Preußen*. Cologne: Pahl-Rugenstein Verlag, 1984.

Borsányi, László. "An Emerging Dual Image of Native North Americans During the Second Half of the 19th Century." In *Indians and Europe: An Interdisciplinary Collection of Essays*, edited by Christian F. Feest, 287–96. Aachen: Rader Verlag, 1987. Reprint, Lincoln: U Nebraska P, 1999.

Bournichon, Joseph. *Sitting Bull, le héros du désert: Scènes de la guerre indienne aux États-Unis*. Tours: Cattiers, 1897.

Brackert, Helmut, ed. *Das Nibelungenlied: Mittelhochdeutscher Text und Übertragung*. Frankfurt am Main: Fischer, 1991.

Bragdon, K. J. *Native People of Southern New England, 1500–1650*. Norman: U of Oklahoma P, 1996.

Braidotti, Rosi. *Nomadic Subjects: Embodiment and Sexual Difference in Contemporary Feminist Theory*. New York: Columbia UP, 1994.

Brenner, Peter J. *Reisen in die Neue Welt: Die Erfahrung Nordamerikas in deutschen Reise- und Auswandererberichten des 19. Jahrhunderts*. Tübingen: Niemeyer, 1991.

Britten, Thomas A. *American Indians in World War I*. Albuquerque: U of New Mexico P, 1997.

Brown Francis J., and Joseph Slabey Roucek, eds. *Our National and Racial Minorities: Their History, Contributions, and Present Problems*. New York: Prentice-Hall, 1937.

Broyles-González, Yolanda. "Cheyennes in the Black Forest: A Social Drama." In

The Americanization of the Global Village: Essays in Comparative Popular Culture, 70-86. Bowling Green, Ken.: Bowling Green State U Popular P 1989.

Buchner, Wilhelm, ed. *Ferdinand Freiligrath: Ein Dichterleben in Briefen*. 2 vols. Lahr, Germany: Druck und Verlag von Moritz Schanenburg, 1882.

Buechel, Eugene. *Rosebud and Pine Ridge Photographs, 1922-1942*. El Cajon, Calif.: Grossmont College, 1974.

Burgert, Annette Kunselman. *Eighteenth-Century Emigrants from German-Speaking Lands to North America*. Vol. 2, *The Western Palatinate*. Birdsboro, Penn.: Pennsylvania German Society, 1985.

Busatta, Flavia, and Emilio Salgari. "A Writer for Armchair Travelers." *European Review of Native American Studies* 14, no. 1 (2000).

Calloway, Colin G. *The American Revolution in Indian Country: Crisis and Diversity in Native American Communities*. New York: Cambridge UP, 1995.

———. *New Worlds for All: Indians, Europeans, and the Remaking of Early America*. Baltimore: Johns Hopkins UP, 1997.

Campisi, Jack. "Fur Trade and Factionalism of the Eighteenth-Century Oneida Indian." In *Studies on Iroquoian Culture*, edited by N. Bonvillain. Man in the Northeast, Occasional Papers in Northeastern Anthropology 6, 1980.

———. *The Mashpee Indians: Tribe on Trial*. Syracuse, N.Y.: Syracuse UP, 1991.

———. "Oneida." In *Northeast*, edited by B. G. Trigger, vol. 15 of the *Handbook of North American Indians*, edited by W. C. Sturtevant. Washington, D.C.: Smithsonian Institution, 1978.

Cardinal-Schubert, Joanne. "In the red." *Fuse* 13, nos. 1-2 (fall 1989): 20-28.

Carlson, Alvar W. "German-Russian Houses in Western North Dakota." *Pioneer America*, 13, no. 2 (Sept. 1981): 49-60.

Carlson, Marta. *Das Pow-wow*. University of Massachusetts, 1999. Videotape.

Caruth, Cathy. *Unclaimed Experience: Trauma, Narrative, and History*. Baltimore: Johns Hopkins UP, 1996.

Champion, Walter T., Jr. "Christian Frederick Post and the Winning of the West," *Pennsylvania Magazine of History and Biography* 104 (1980): 308-25.

Chavkin, Allan, ed. *The Chippewa Landscape of Louise Erdrich*. Tuscaloosa: U of Alabama P, 1999.

Chavkin, Allan, and Nancy Feyl Chavkin, eds. "An Interview with Louise Erdrich" In *Conversations with Louise Erdrich and Michael Dorris*, 220-53. Jackson: UP of Mississippi, 1994.

Chidsey, A. D., Jr. *A Frontier Village: Pre-Revolutionary Easton*. Easton, Penn.: Northampton County Historical and Genealogical Society, 1940.

Chinard, Gabriel. *L'Amérique et le rêve exotique dans la littérature française au XVIIe et au XVIIIe siècle*. Paris: Librairie E. Droz, 1934.

———. *L'Éxotisme américain dans la littérature française au XVIe siècle*. Paris: Librairie Hachette, 1911.

Christadler, Marieluise. "Jungdeutschland und Afrika: Imperialistische Erziehung durch das Jugendbuch, 1880-1940." In Die "Dritte Welt" im deutschen Kinderbuch 1967-1977, edited by Jörg Becker and Rosmarie Rauter, 36-75. Wiesbaden: Akademische Verlagsgesellschaft, 1978.

———. "Zwischen Gartenlaube und Genozid: Kolonialistische Jugendbücher im Kaiserreich." In Die Menschen sind arm, weil sie arm sind, edited by Jörg Becker and Charlotte Oberfeld, 61-98. Frankfurt am Main: Haag & Herchen, 1977.

Churchill, Ward. Fantasies of the Master Race. Monroe, Me.: Common Courage, 1992.

———. Indians Are Us? Culture and Genocide in Native North America. Monroe, Me.: Common Courage, 1994.

———. "Indians 'R' Us? Reflections on the 'Men's Movement.'" In From A Native Son: Selected Essays on Indigenism, 1985-1995, 367-408. Boston: South End Press, 1996.

Clunn, Tony. Auf der Suche nach den verlorenen Legionen. Translated by Karsten Igel. Bramsche, Germany: Rasch, 1998.

Cobb, Clay. "Taming the Wild West: American Popular Culture and the Cold War Battles over East and West German Identities, 1949-1961." Ph.D. diss., History Dept., Brown University, 1995.

———. "Taming the Wild Wild West: Transforming a Cult TV Show into a Summer Event Movie." Creative Screenwriting 6, no. 4 (July-Aug. 1999): 72-73.

Codignola, Luca. "The Battle is Over: Campeau's Monumenta vs. Thwaites's Jesuit Relations, 1602-1650." European Review of Native American Studies 10, no. 2 (1997): 3-10.

Cole, Douglas. Captured Heritage: The Scramble for Northwest Coast Artifacts. Seattle: U of Washington P, 1985.

Colee, P. S. "The Housatonic-Stockbridge Indians: 1734-1749." Ph.D. diss., State U of New York, Albany, 1977.

Colley, Linda. Britons: Forging the Nation, 1707-1837. New Haven, Conn.: Yale, 1992.

Conkey, L. E., E. Boissevain, and I. Goddard. 1978. "Indians of Southern New England: Late Period." In Northeast, edited by B. G. Trigger, vol. 15 of Handbook of North American Indians, edited by W. C. Sturtevant. Washington, D.C.: Smithsonian Institution, 1978.

Conrad, Rudolf. "Mutual Fascination: Indians in Dresden and Leipzig." In Indians and Europe: An Interdisciplinary Collection of Essays, edited by Christian F. Feest, 455-73. Aachen: Rader Verlag, 1987. Reprint, Lincoln: U Nebraska P, 1999.

Coutancier, Benoît, ed. Peaux-Rouges: Autour de la collection anthropologique du prince Roland Bonaparte. Thonon-les-Bains, France: Éditions de l'Albaron, 1992.

Cronon, William. Changes in the Land: Indians, Colonists, and the Ecology of New England. New York: Hill & Wang, 1983.

Daumann, Rudolf. *Sitting Bull: Großer Häuptling der Sioux—Der Untergang der Dakota.* 2 vols. Berlin: Verlag Neues Leben, 1957-1958.

De Forest, J. W. *History of the Indians of Connecticut from the Earliest Known Period to 1850.* Hartford, Conn.: W. J. Hamersley, 1851.

Deloria, Philip J. *Playing Indian.* New Haven, Conn.: Yale UP, 1998.

Deloria, Vine. *God Is Red.* 1973. Golden, Colo.: Fulcrum Publishing, 1994.

Dickason, Olive P. *The Myth of the Savage and the Beginnings of French Colonialism in the Americas.* Edmonton: U of Alberta P, 1984.

Di Maio, Irene S. "Borders of Culture: The Native American in Friedrich Gerstäcker's North American Narratives." *Yearbook of German-American Studies* 28 (1993): 53-75.

Dockstader, Frederick. *Great North American Indians: Profiles in Life and Leadership.* New York: Van Nostrand Reinhold, 1977.

Dowd, Gregory Evans. *A Spirited Resistance: The North American Indian Struggle for Unity, 1745-1815.* Baltimore: Johns Hopkins UP, 1992.

Dubois, Daniel. "Indianism in France." *European Review of Native American Studies* 7, no. 1 (1993): 27-36.

Dunk, Hermann von der. "Antisemitismus zur Zeit der Reichsgründung – Unterschiede und Gemeinsamkeiten: Ein Inventar." In *Die Konstruktion der Nation gegen die Juden,* edited by Peter Alter, Claus-Ekkehard Bärsch, and Peter Berghoff, 65-91. Munich: Fink, 1999.

Dunn, Mary Maples. "Saints and Sisters: Congregational and Quaker Women in the Early Colonial Period." In *Women in American Religion,* edited by Janet Wilson James, 27-46. Philadelphia: U of Pennsylvania P, 1980.

Egmond, Florike, and Peter Mason. *The Mammoth and the Mouse: Microhistory and Morphology.* Baltimore: Johns Hopkins UP, 1997.

Eid, Leroy V. "The Ojibwa-Iroquois War: The War the Five Nations Did Not Win." *Ethnohistory,* 26, no. 4 (fall 1979): 297-324.

Emmel, Hildegard. "Recht oder Unrecht in der Neuen Welt. Zu Charles Sealsfields Roman 'Der Legitime und die Republikaner.'" In *Amerika in der deutschen Literatur: Neue Welt—Nord Amerika—U.S.A.,* edited by Sigrid Bauschinger, Horst Denkler, and Wilfried Malsch. Stuttgart: Kohlhammer, 1975.

Enochs, R. A. *The Jesuit Mission to the Lakota Sioux.* Kansas City, Mo.: Sheed & Ward, 1995.

Enter, Hans, and Hartmut Lutz. "'Compatriots': Eine Short Story, vorgestellt für die Behandlung im Englischunterricht der Sekundarstufe II." *fsu* 42, no. 51 (1998): 86-94.

Fachinger, Petra. "Cross-Dressing as Appropriation in the Short Stories of Emma Lee Warrior." *Studies in American Indian Literatures,* 8, no. 3 (fall 1996): 36-48.

Fanon, Frantz. *Black Skin, White Masks.* (1952). New York: Grove, 1967.

Feest, Christian F. *The Art of War.* New York: Thames & Hudson, 1980.

———. *Beseelte Welten: Die Religionen der Amerikaner Nordamerikas.* Freiburg im Breisgau, Germany: Herder, 1998.

———. "Buffalo Bill und sein 'Wild West.' " In *Lakol Wokiksuye*, edited by H. Lomosits and P. Harbaugh. Vienna: Jugend & Volk, 1990.

———. "Die Entdeckung des edlen Wilden. Maximilian Prinz zu Wied (1782–1867) und Karl Bodmer (1809–1893) reisen an den oberen Missouri." In *Nachbar Amerika: Verwandte — Feinde — Freunde — in drei Jahrhunderten*, edited by G. Schäfer, 117–46. Landau in der Pfalz, Germany: Knecht Verlag. 1996.

———. *Gold und Macht: Spanien in der Neuen Welt: eine Ausstellung anläßlich des 500. Jahrestages der Entdeckung Amerikas.* Cologne: Rosenheimer, 1987.

———. *Indians and a Changing Frontier: The Art of George Winter.* Compiled by Sarah E. Cooke and Rachel B. Ramadhyani. Indianapolis: Indiana Historical Society, in cooperation with the Tippecanoe County Historical Association, 1993.

———. "Indians and Europe? Editor's Postscript." In *Indians and Europe: An Interdisciplinary Collection of Essays*, edited by Christian F. Feest, 609–28. Aachen: Rader Verlag, 1987. Reprint, Lincoln, Nebr.: U of Nebraska P, 1999.

———. "The Indian in Non-English Literature." In *History of Indian-White Relations*, edited by Wilcomb E. Washburn, vol. 4 of *Handbook of North American Indians*, edited by W. C. Sturtevant, 582–86, 665–66. Washington D.C.: Smithsonian Institution, 1988.

———. *Indians of Northeastern North America.* Leiden: E. J. Brill, 1986.

———. "Johann Baptist Wengler: A Portfolio of Drawings, 1850/1." *European Review of Native American Studies* 2, no. 1:41–48.

———. *Native Arts of North America.* New York: Oxford UP, 1980. Revised ed., New York: Thames & Hudson, 1992.

———. "Österreicher und Indianer." In *Österreich und die Neue Welt*, edited by Elisabeth Zeilinger, 33–44. Vienna: Österreichische Nationalbibliothek, 1993.

———. "The Polish Movement Friends of the American Indians." In *Indians and Europe: An Interdisciplinary Collection of Essays*, edited by Christian Feest, 599–608. Aachen: Rader Verlag, 1987. Reprint, Lincoln: U of Nebraska P, 1999.

———. "Pride and Prejudice: The Pocahontas Myth and the Pamunkey." *European Review of Native American Studies* 1, no. 1: 5–12.

———. " 'Travestie der Lebensformen' oder 'kulturelle Konversion'? Zur Geschichte des kulturellen Überläufertums." In *Abwehr und Verlangen: zur Geschichte der Ethnologie*, edited by K.-H. Kohl, 7–38. Berlin: Qumran, 1987.

———. "The Virginia Indian in Pictures, 1612–1624." *The Smithsonian Journal of History* 2, no. 1 (1967): 1–30.

———, ed. *Indians and Europe: An Interdisciplinary Collection of Essays.* Aachen: Rader Verlag, 1987. Reprint, Lincoln: U Nebraska P, 1999.

————, ed. *Sitting Bull: "Der letzte Indianer."* Darmstadt: Hessisches Landesmuseum, 1999.

Fertig, George. "Transatlantic Migrations from the German-Speaking Parts of Central Europe, 1600–1800: Proportions, Structures, and Explanations." In *Europeans on the Move: Studies on European Migration, 1500–1800,* edited by Nicholas Canny, 192–235. Oxford: Clarendon Press, 1994.

Fiedler, Leslie. *The Return of the Vanishing American.* New York: Stein & Day, 1968.

Fiorentino, Daniele. " 'Those Red-Brick Faces': European Press Reactions to the Indians of Buffalo Bill's Wild West Show." In *Indians and Europe: An Interdisciplinary Collection of Essays,* edited by Christian F. Feest. Aachen: Rader Verlag, 1987. Reprint, Lincoln, Nebr.: U of Nebraska P, 1999.

Fogleman, Aaron Spenser. *Hopeful Journeys: German Immigration, Settlement, and Political Culture in Colonial America, 1717–1775.* Philadelphia: U of Pennsylvania P, 1996.

Foley, John Miles, ed. *Teaching Oral Traditions.* New York: MLA, 1998.

Forbes, Allan. *Some Indian Events of New England.* Boston: State Street Trust, 1934.

Forbes, Jack T. *Africans and Native Americans: The Language of Race and the Evolution of Red-Black,* 26–64. Urbana: U of Illinois P, 1993.

Foreman, Carolyn T. *Indians Abroad, 1493–1938.* Norman: U of Oklahoma P, 1944.

Fowler, Don D. *The Western Photographs of John K. Hillers: "myself in the water."* Washington, D.C.: Smithsonian Institution, 1989.

Frazier, P. *The Mohicans of Stockbridge.* Lincoln: U of Nebraska P, 1992.

Friedrichs, Michael. "Tecumseh's Fabulous Career in German Fiction." *European Review of Native American Studies* 11, no. 2 (1997): 47–52.

Friedrichsmeyer, Sara, Sara Lennox, and Susanne Zantop, eds. *The Imperialist Imagination: German Colonialism and Its Legacy.* Ann Arbor: U of Michigan P, 1998.

Fries, Adelaide L. *The Moravians in Georgia, 1735–1740.* 1905. Reprinted Baltimore: Genealogical Publishing, 1967.

Fron, Alicia. "Polish Indianist Movements – Myth and Reality." *Ad Americam* 1 (2000): 97–112.

Gall, Lother, ed. *FFM 1200: Traditionen und Perspektiven einer Stadt.* Sigmaringen: Jan Thorbecke Verlag, 1994.

Galler, R. W. "A History of Red Cloud Indian School." Ph.D. diss., University of South Dakota, 1994.

————. "A Triad of Alliances." *South Dakota History* 3 (1998): 144–60.

Galtung, Johan. *Strukturelle Gewalt: Beiträge zur Friedens- und Konfliktforschung.* Reinbek, Germany: Rowohlt, 1975.

Gemünden, Gerd. *Framed Visions: Popular Culture, Americanization, and the Contemporary German and Austrian Imagination.* Ann Arbor: U of Michigan P, 1998.

Bibliography

Genzmer, George Harvey. "Copway, George." In vol. 4 of *Dictionary of American Biography*, 433. New York: Charles Scribner's Sons, 1930.

Giordano, Fedora. *Gli Indiani d'America e l'Italia*. Turin: Edizioni dell'Orso. 1997.

Gipson, Henry. *The British Empire Before the American Revolution*. Rev. ed. New York: Knopf, 1958–1970.

Gipson, L. H., ed. *The Moravian Indian Mission on White River*. Indianapolis: Indiana Historical Bureau, 1938.

Goddard, Ives. "Delaware." In *Northeast*, edited by B. G. Trigger, vol. 15 of *Handbook of North American Indians*, edited by W. C. Sturtevant. Washington, D.C.: Smithsonian Institution, 1978.

———. "Eastern Algonquian Languages." In *Northeast*, edited by B. G. Trigger, vol. 15 of *Handbook of North American Indians*, edited by W. C. Sturtevant. Washington, D.C.: Smithsonian Institution, 1978.

———, ed. *Languages*. Vol. 17 of *Handbook of North American Indians*, edited by W. C. Sturtevant. Washington, D.C.: Smithsonian Institution Press, 1996.

Goetzmann, William H. et al. *Karl Bodmer's America*. Introduction by William H. Goetzmann. Annotated by David C. Hunt and Marsha V. Gallagher. Artist's biography by William J. Orr. Omaha: Joslyn Art Museum; Lincoln: U of Nebraska P, 1984.

Göktürk, Deniz. *Künstler, Cowboys, Ingenieure*. Munich: Fink, 1998.

Goll, Georg. *Der Untergang der Dakota*. Leipzig: Gustav Weise, 1929.

Gomez, Michael. *Exchanging Our Country Marks: The Transformation of African Identities in the Colonial and Antebellum South*. Chapel Hill: U of North Carolina P, 1998.

Gray, E. E., and L. R. Gray. *Wilderness Christians*. Ithaca: Cornell UP, 1956.

Graymont, Barbara. *The Iroquois in the American Revolution*. Syracuse, New York: Syracuse UP, 1972.

Green, A. G. "German Missionary Participation During the Ghost Dance of 1890." *European Review of Native American Studies* 1 (1992): 31–34.

Green, Michael K., ed. *Issues in Native American Cultural Identity*. New York: Peter Lang, 1995.

Grubb, Farley. "German Immigration to Pennsylvania, 1709 to 1820." *Journal of Interdisciplinary History* 20 (1989–1990): 417–36.

Grünzweig, Walter. *Das demokratische Kanaan. Charles Sealsfields Amerika im Kontext amerikanischer Literatur und Ideologie*. Munich: Fink, 1987.

Grytz, Gerhard. " 'Old Shatterhand and Winnetou in Arizona?': Myth and Reality of German-American Indian Relations in Nineteenth-Century Arizona." Paper presented at the Deutsche und Indianer Conference, Dartmouth College, May 1999.

Guidi, Benedetta Cestelli, and Nicholas Mann, eds. *Photographs at the Frontier: Aby*

Warburg in America 1895–1896. London: Merrell Holberton and the Warburg Institute, 1998.

Günther, E. *Sarrasani wie er wirklich war*. Berlin: Henschel, 1984.

Habel, Frank-Burkhard. *Gojko Mitic, Mustangs, Marterpfähle: Die DEFA-Indianerfilme*. Berlin: Schwarzkopf & Schwarzkopf, 1997.

Haberland, Wolfgang. *"Ich, Dakota": Pine Ridge Reservation 1909. Photographien von Frederick Weygold*. Berlin: Dietrich Reimer, 1886.

————. "Nine Bella Coolas in Germany." In *Indians and Europe: An Interdisciplinary Collection of Essays*, edited by Christian F. Feest, 337–74. Aachen: Rader Verlag, 1987. Reprint, Lincoln: U Nebraska P, 1999.

Haible, Barbara. *Indianer im Dienste der NS-Ideologie*. Hamburg: Kovacs, 1998.

Hallowell, A. Irving. "American Indians, White and Black: The Phenomenon of Transculturalization." *Current Anthropology* 4 (1963): 519–31.

Hämäläinen, Pekka. "The Western Comanche Trade Center: Rethinking the Plains Indian Trade System." *Western Historical Quarterly* 29 (1998): 485–513

Hämäläinen, Riku. " 'We Are the Mystic Warriors of Finland': Finnish Indianism." *European Review of Native American Studies* 12, no. 1 (1998): 13–19.

Hamilton, Henry W. et al. *Sioux of the Rosebud: A History in Pictures*. Norman: U Oklahoma P., 1981.

Hamilton, J. T., and K. G. Hamilton. *History of the Moravian Church*. Bethlehem, Penn.: Moravian Church in America, 1967.

Harpham, Geoffrey Galt. "Ethics." In *Critical Terms for Literary Study*, edited by Frank Lentricchia and Thomas McLaughlin, 387–405. 2d. ed. Chicago: U of Chicago P, 1995.

Hartmann, Horst. *George Catlin und Balduin Möllhausen: Interpreten der Indianer und des Alten Westens*. Berlin: Reiner, 1963.

Hartmann, Petra, and Stephan Schmitz. *Kölner Stämme: Menschen, Mythen, Maskenspiel*. Cologne: Vista Point, 1991.

Hatfield, James Taft. "The Longfellow-Freiligrath Correspondence." *Publications of the Modern Language Association* 48, no. 4 (1933): 1268.

Hausman, Gerald. "Turtle Island Alphabet." In *A Lexicon of Native American Symbols and Culture*. New York: St. Martin's Press, 1992.

Häussler, Bernd. "Mit der Friedenspfeife über das große Wasser nach Frankfurt." *Frankfurter Allgemeine Zeitung*, 3 December 1986: 41.

Hendricks, Gordon. *Albert Bierstadt: Painter of the American West*. New York: H. N. Abrams 1974, 1988.

Hertzberg, Hazel W. *The Search for an American Indian Identity: Modern Pan-Indian Movements*. Syracuse, N.Y.: Syracuse UP, 1971.

Heyden, Ulrich van der. "Die Native American Studies und ihre Rezeption in der DDR." In *Amerikanistik in der DDR: Geschichte — Analysen — Zeitzeugenberichte*, edited by Rainer Schnoor, 123–51. Berlin: Trafo-Verlag, 1999.

Hoerig, Karl A. "The Relationship between German Immigrants and the Native Peoples in Western Texas." *Southwestern Historical Quarterly* 97 (1994): 423-31.

Hoffman, Gerhard, ed. *Indianische Kunst im 20. Jahrhundert: Malerei, Keramik und Kachinafiguren indianischer Künstler in den U.S.A.* Munich: Prestel-Verlag, 1985.

Hoffmann, K. "Circensische Völkerschauen und exotische Abenteuerliteratur in Dresden." *Dresdner Hefte* 5 (1989): 68-76.

Hohendahl, Peter Uwe. "Von der Rothaut zum Edelmenschen: Karl Mays Amerikaromane." In *Amerika in der deutschen Literatur*, edited by Sigrid Bauschinger, Horst Denkler, and Wilfried Malsch, 229-45. Stuttgart: Kohlhammer, 1975.

Hölz, Karl. *Das Fremde, das Eigene, das Andere: Die Inszenierung kultureller und geschlechtlicher Identität in Lateinamerika.* Berlin: E. Schmidt, 1998.

Homann, W. "Ein Paar Mokassins blieb zurück." *Magazin für Amerikanistik* 1 (1995): 10-14.

Honour, Hugh. *The New Golden Land: European Images of America from the Discoveries to the Present Time.* London: Allen Lane, 1975.

Horton, James Oliver, and Hartmut Keil. "African Americans and Germans in Mid-Nineteenth Century Buffalo." In *Free People of Color: Inside the African American Community*, edited by Oliver Horton, 17-183. Washington, D.C.: Smithsonian Institution Press, 1993.

Hovens, Pieter. *Herman F. C. ten Kate jr. (1858-1931) en de antropologie der noordamerikaanse indianen.* Meppel, Netherlands: Krips Repro, 1989.

Hulme, Peter. *Colonial Encounters: Europe and the Native Caribbean 1492-1797.* New York: Routledge, 1989

Hunter, William A. "Documented Subdivisions of the Delaware Indians." *Bulletin of the Archaeological Society of New Jersey* 20 (1978): 20-40

———. "Moses (Tunda) Tatamy, Delaware Indian Diplomat." In *A Delaware Indian Symposium*, edited by Herbert C. Kraft, 71-88. Harrisburg, Penn.: Pennsylvania Historical and Museum Commission, 1974.

Huseman, Ben W. *Wild River, Timeless Canyons: Balduin Möllhausen's Watercolors of the Colorado.* Fort Worth: Amon Carter Museum, 1995.

"Ich bin ein Cowboy." *The Economist*, 26 May 2001:124.

Ireland, Owen S. *Religion, Ethnicity, and Politics: Ratifying the Constitution in Pennsylvania.* University Park: Pennsylvania State UP, 1995.

Isernhagen, Hartwig. "(Un)Translatable? Constructions of the Indian and the Discourse(s) of Criticism." *European Review of Native American Studies* 11, no. 1 (1997) 11-17.

Israel, Heinz. "Johann Gottfried Schadow and His Inuit Portraits." In *Indians and Europe: An Interdisciplinary Collection of Essays*, edited by Christian F. Feest, 235-41. Aachen: Rader Verlag, 1987. Reprint, Lincoln: U Nebraska P, 1999.

Jacobson, Matthew Frye. *Whiteness of a Different Color: European Immigrants and the Alchemy of Race.* Cambridge, Mass.: Harvard UP, 1998.

Jacquin, Philippe. *Les Indiens Blancs: Français et Indiens en Amérique du Nord* (XVIe-XVIIIe siècle). Paris: Payot, 1987.

Jahner, Elaine. *Spaces of Mind: Narrative and Community.* Unpublished manuscript.

Jennings, Francis. *The Ambiguous Iroquois Empire: The Covenant Chain Confederation of Indian Tribes with English Colonies from its Beginnings to the Lancaster Treaty of 1744.* New York: Norton & Company, 1984.

———. *The Invasion of America.* Chapel Hill: U of North Carolina P, 1975.

———, ed. *The History and Culture of Iroquois Diplomacy.* Syracuse, N. Y.: Syracuse UP, 1985.

Jones, George Fenwick. *The Georgia Dutch: From the Rhine and Danube to the Savannah, 1733-1783.* Athens: U of Georgia P, 1992

Jones, Gwyn. *The Norse Atlantic Saga: Being the Norse Discovery and Settlement to Iceland, Greenland and North America.* New York: Oxford UP, 1986.

Jones, Maldwyn Allen. *American Immigration.* Chicago: U of Chicago P, 1960.

Jones, William. "Copway, George." In *Handbook of American Indians North of Mexico,* edited by F. W. Hodge, 347. Bureau of American Ethnology Bulletin 30. Washington, D.C.: Government Printing Office, 1907-1910.

Jones-Lamb, Karen. *Native American Wives of San Juan Settlers.* Seattle: Bryn Tirion Publishing, 1994.

Jordan, Terry G. *German Seed in Texas Soil: Immigrant Farmers in Nineteenth-Century Texas.* Austin: U of Texas P, 1966.

Jordan, Terry G., and Matti Kaups. *The American Backwoods Frontier: An Ethnic and Ecological Interpretation.* Baltimore: Johns Hopkins UP, 1989.

Juen, M. "Buffalo Bills Wild West Show 1890 im Wiener Prater." Ph.D. diss., University of Vienna, 1996.

Karrer, Wolfgang, and Hartmut Lutz, eds. *Minority Literatures in North America: Contemporary Perspectives.* Frankfurt am Main: Peter Lang, 1990.

Kasprycki, Sylvia S. "Matters of Faith: Notes on Missionaries and Material Culture." *European Review of Native American Studies* 10, no. 2 (1997): 45-50.

Kavanagh, Thomas S. *The Comanches: A History 1706-1875.* Lincoln: U of Nebraska P, 1996.

Kidwell, Clara Sue. "Every Last Dishcloth: The Prodigious Collecting of George Gustav Heye." In *Collecting Native America, 1870-1960,* edited by Shepard Krech III and Barbara A. Hail, 105-38, 232-58. Washington, D. C.: Smithsonian Institution Press, 1999.

King, Irene Marshall. *John O. Meusebach, German Colonizer in Texas.* Austin: U of Texas P, 1967.

Kittlitz, Hans-Wernher von. "Karl Bodmer. A Biographical and Bibliographical Survey." *European Review of Native American Studies* 12, no. 1 (1998): 19-34.

Kläy, Ernst J., and Hans Läng. *Das romantische Leben der Indianer malerisch dar-*

zustellen . . . Leben und Werk von Rudolf Friedrich Kurz (1818-1871). Solothurn, Switzerland: Aare, 1984.

Klotzbach, Kurt. *Die Solms-Papiere: Dokumente zur deutschen Kolonisation von Texas.* Wyk auf Foehr, Germany: Verlag für Amerikanistik, 1990.

Knobel, Dale T. "Know-Nothings and Indians: Strange Bedfellows?" *Western Historical Quarterly* 15 (April 1984): 175-98.

Kohl, Karl-Heinz. " 'Travestie der Lebensformen' oder 'kulturelle Konversion'? Zur Geschichte des kulturellen Überläufertums." In *Abwehr und Verlangen: Zur Geschichte der Ethnologie,* edited by K.-H. Kohl, 7-38. Berlin: Qumran, 1987.

Koll, Horst Peter. "Der träumende Deutsche: Die Winnetou-Filmtrilogie." In *Idole des deutschen Films: Eine Galerie von Schlüsselfiguren,* edited by Thomas Koebner, 384-97. Munich: Text & Kritik, 1997.

Kolodny, Annette. *The Lay of the Land: Metaphor as Experience and History in American Life and Letters.* Chapel Hill: U of North Carolina P, 1975.

Korniss, Péter. *In the Land of Red Cloud: Among North-America's Indians.* Budapest: Corvina Kiadó, 1982.

Krapf, Ludwig. *Germanenmythus und Reichsideologie: Frühhumanistische Rezeptionsweisen der taciteischen "Germania."* Tübingen: Niemeyer, 1979.

Krech, Shepard, III. *Passionate Hobby: Rudolf Frederick Haffenreffer and the King Philip Museum.* Providence, R.I.: Haffenrefer Museum of Anthropology, Brown U, 1994.

Kreis, K. M. *Die wilden Indianer in ihrem bunten Geflitter.* Dortmund: Fachhochschule, 1993.

———. *Rothäute, Schwarzröcke und heilige Frauen: Deutsche Berichte aus den Indianer-Missionen in South Dakota, 1886-1900.* Bochum, Germany: Project Verlag, 2000.

Kuhlenbeck, L. *Der Occultismus der nordamerikanischen Indianer.* Supplement to *Der Occultismus des Altertums,* by K. Kiesewetter. Leipzig: Wilhelm Friedrich, 1895.

LaDuke, Winona. "Natural To Synthetic and Back Again." In *Marxism and Native Americans,* edited by Ward Churchill. Boston: South End Press, 1983.

Lamar, Howard R. ed., *The New Encyclopedia of the American West.* New Haven, Conn.: Yale UP, 1998.

Landsman, Ned C. *Scotland and Its First American Colony 1683-1765.* Princeton, N.J.: Princeton UP, 1985.

Langton, E. *History of the Moravian Church.* London: Allen & Unwin, 1956.

Laniel-Le François, Marie-Elizabeth. "Les Hopi." In *Kachina: Poupées rituelles des Indiens Hopi et Zuni,* 51-77. Marseille: Musées de Marseille, 1994.

LaRocque, Emma. "Preface or Here Are Our Voices — Who Will Hear?" In *Writing the Circle,* edited by Jeanne Perreault and Sylvia Vance, xv-xxx. Edmonton, Alba.: NeWest, 1990.

Levy, Barry. *Quakers and the American Family: British Settlement in the Delaware Valley.* New York: Oxford UP, 1988.

Liebersohn, Harry. *Aristocratic Encounters: European Travelers and North American Indians.* Cambridge, England: Cambridge UP, 1998.

Lindner, M. "Bull und Bill: eine späte Freundschaft." In *Sitting Bull: Der letzte Indianer,* edited by Christian F. Feest, 22-25. Darmstadt: Hessisches Landesmuseum, 1999.

Lott, Eric. *Love and Theft: Blackface, Minstrelsy and the American Working Class.* New York: Oxford UP, 1993.

Lowsky, Martin. *Karl May.* Stuttgart: Metzler, 1987.

Luebke, Frederick C. *Germans in the New World: Essays in the History of Immigration.* Urbana: U of Illinois P, 1990.

Lund, Allan A. *Germanenmythologie im Nationalsozialismus: Zur Rezeption der "Germania" des Tacitus im "Dritten Reich."* Heidelberg: Winter, 1995.

Lutz, Hartmut. "Confronting Cultural Imperialism: First Nations People Are Combating Continued Cultural Theft." In *Multiculturalism in North America and Europe: Social Practices — Literary Visions,* edited by Hans Braun and Wolfgang Klooss, 132-51. Trier, Germany: Wissenschaftlicher Verlag Trier, 1995.

———. *Contemporary Challenges: Conversations with Canadian Native Authors.* Saskatoon, Sask.: Fifth House, 1991.

———. "Images of Indians in German Children's Books." In *The Slant of the Pen,* edited by Roy Preiswerk. Geneva: World Council of Churches, Program to Combat Racism, 1980.

———. *"Indianer" und "Native Americans": Zur sozial- und literaturhistorischen Vermittlung eines Stereotyps.* Hildesheim, Germany: Olms-Verlag, 1985.

———. "'Indians' and Native Americans in the Movies: A History of Stereotypes, Distortions, and Displacements." *Journal of Visual Anthropology* 3 (1990): 31-48.

———. "Nations Within as Seen from Without: Ten Theses on German Perspectives on the Literature of Canada's First Nations." In *Native North America,* edited by Renee Hulan, 83-108. Toronto: ECW Press, 1999.

———. "Sitting Bull and Siegfried: Some Thoughts about Recent Trends in German Books on American Indians." *Kritikon Litterarum* 4 (1975): 175-86.

MacLeod, D. Peter. "The Anishinabeg Point of View: The History of the Great Lakes Region to 1800 in Nineteenth-Century Mississauga, Odawa, and Ojibwa Historiography." *Canadian Historical Review* 73, no. 2 (June 1992): 194-210.

Maligne, Olivier. "Cheval Debout, un Indien de France?" *Recherches amérindiennes au Québec* 29, no. 3 (1999): 53-65.

Mancall, Peter C. *Deadly Medicine.* Ithaca, N.Y.: Cornell UP, 1995.

———. *Valley of Opportunity: Economic Culture along the Upper Susquehanna, 1700-1800.* Ithaca, N.Y.: Cornell UP, 1991.

Mandell, Daniel R. *Behind the Frontier: Indians in Eighteenth-Century Eastern Massachusetts.* Lincoln: U of Nebraska P, 1996.

Mann, Klaus. "Cowboy Mentor of the Führer." *The Living Age* 359 (1940/1941): 217-22.

Marietta, Jack D. *The Reformation of American Quakerism, 1748-1783.* Philadelphia: U of Pennsylvania P, 1984.

Marino, Cesare. "Carlo Gentile, il fotografo italiano che adottò Carlos Montezuma." In *Gli Indiani d'America e l'Italia,* edited by F. Giordano, 129-37. Turin: Edizioni dell'Orso, 1997.

Marks, M. L. *Jews among the Indians: Tales of Adventure and Conflict in the Old West.* Chicago: Benison Books, 1992.

Marks, Paula Mitchell. *In a Barren Land: American Indian Dispossession and Survival.* New York: William Morrow, 1998.

McConnell, Michael N. *A Country Between: The Upper Ohio Valley and Its Peoples, 1724-1774.* Lincoln: U of Nebraska P, 1992.

McCoy, Ingeborg Rubert. "Tales of the Grandmothers: Women as Purveyors of German-Texan Culture." In *Eagle in the New World: German Immigration to Texas and America,* edited by Theodore Gish and Richard Spuler. College Station: Texas A & M UP, 1986.

McGregor, Robert K. "Cultural Adaptation in Colonial New York: The Palatine Germans of the Mohawk." *New York History* 69 (1988): 6-34.

McGuire, James Patrick. "Observations on German Artists in Texas." In *Eagle in the New World: German Immigration to Texas and America,* edited by Theodore Gish and Richard Spuler, 190-93. College Station: Texas A & M UP, 1986.

McLoughlin, William G. *Cherokee Renascence in the New Republic.* Princeton, N.J.: Princeton UP, 1986

McMullen, Ann. " 'The Heart Interest': Native Americans at Mount Hope and the King Philip Museum." In *Passionate Hobby: Rudolf Frederick Haffenreffer and the King Philip Museum,* edited by Shepard Krech III, 167-85. Providence, R.I.: Haffenrefer Museum of Anthropology, Brown U, 1994.

Means, Russell. "The Same Old Song." In *Marxism and Native Americans,* edited by Ward Churchill. Boston: South End Press, 1983.

Meinig, D. W. *Atlantic America, 1492-1800.* Vol. 1 of *The Shaping of America: A Geographical Perspective on 500 Years of History.* New Haven, Conn.: Yale UP, 1986.

Merrell, James H. *Into the American Woods: Negotiators on the Pennsylvania Frontier.* New York: Norton & Company, 1999.

———. "Shamokin, 'the very seat of the Prince of darkness': Unsettling the Early American Frontier." In *Contact Points: American Frontiers from the Mohawk Valley to the Mississippi, 1750-1830,* edited by Andrew R. L. Clayton and Frederika J. Teute, 16-59. Chapel Hill: U of North Carolina P, 1998.

———. "Shickellamy, A Person of Consequence." In *Northeastern Indian Lives, 1632-1816,* edited by Robert S. Grumet. Amherst: U of Massachusetts P, 1996.

Merritt, Jane T. "Dreaming of the Savior's Blood: Moravians and the Indian Great Awakening in Pennsylvania." *William and Mary Quarterly* 54 (1997): 723–46.

———. "Kinship, Community, and Practicing Culture: Indians and the Colonial Encounter in Pennsylvania, 1700–1763." Ph.D. diss., University of Washington, 1995.

Meynen, Emil. *Bibliographie des Deutschtums der kolonialzeitlichen Einwanderung in Nordamerika.* Leipzig: Harrassowitz, 1937.

Moeller, Robert. " 'The Last Soldiers of the Great War' and Tales of Family Reunions in the Federal Republic of Germany." *Signs: A Journal of Women in Culture and Society* 24, no. 1 (autumn 1998): 129–46.

Mohr, K. H. "Unmögliche Mission? Das Christentum, Sitting Bull und die Lakota." In *Sitting Bull: Der letzte Indianer,* edited by Christian F. Feest, 62–65. Darmstadt: Hessisches Landesmuseum, 1999.

Moses, L. G. *Wild West Shows and the Images of American Indians 1883–1933.* Albuquerque: U of New Mexico P, 1996.

Mosse, George L. "Die Juden im Zeitalter des modernen Nationalismus." In *Die Konstruktion der Nation gegen die Juden,* edited by Peter Alter, Claus-Ekkehard Bärsch, and Peter Berghoff, 15–25. Munich: Fink, 1999.

Moyne, Ernest J. "Longfellow and Kah-ga-ga-gah-bowh" In *Henry W. Longfellow Reconsidered: A Symposium,* edited by J. Chesley Mathews, 48–52. Hartford, Conn.: Transcendental Books, 1970.

Müller, Johann Georg. *Geschichte der Amerikanischen Urreligionen.* Basel: Schweighauser, 1855.

Münkler, Herfried, and Hans Grünberger. "Nationale Identität im Diskurs der Deutschen Humanisten." In *Nationales Bewusstsein und kollektive Identität,* edited by Helmut Berding, 211–48. Frankfurt am Main: Suhrkamp, 1994.

Murrin, John M. "English Rights as Ethnic Aggression." In *Authority and Resistance in Early New York,* edited by William Pencak and Conrad Edick Wright, 56–94. New York: New York Historical Society, 1988.

N., N. "Indianism in Hungary." *European Review of Native American Studies* 7, no. 1 (1993): 37–42.

Napier, Rita. "Across the Big Water: American Indians' Perceptions of Europe and Europeans, 1887–1906." In *Indians and Europe: An Interdisciplinary Collection of Essays,* edited by Christian F. Feest, 383–401. Aachen: Rader, 1987. Reprint, Lincoln: U of Nebraska P, 1999.

Nash, Gary B. *Red, White, and Black: The Peoples of Early North America.* 4th ed. Englewood Cliffs, N.J.: Prentice Hall, 2000.

Newcomb, W. W., Jr. "German Immigrants and Texas Indians." In *German Artist on the Texas Frontier: Friedrich Richard Petri,* 47–63. Austin: U of Texas P, 1978.

Newtown, George Allyn. "Images of the American Indian in French and German Novels of the Nineteenth Century." Ph.D. diss., Yale University, 1979.

Novotny, Ehrentraud. *Gojko Mitic.* Berlin: Henschel, 1976.

Nowicka, Ewa. "The Polish Movement Friends of the American Indian." In *Indians and Europe: An Interdisciplinary Collection of Essays,* edited by Christian F. Feest, 599–608. Aachen: Rader, 1987. Reprint, Lincoln: U of Nebraska P, 1999.

Olmstead, Earl P. *Blackcoats among the Delaware: David Zeisberger on the Ohio Frontier.* Kent, Ohio: Kent State UP, 1991.

———. *David Zeisberger: A Life among the Indians.* Kent, Ohio: Kent State UP, 1997.

Orcutt, S. *The Indians of the Housatonic and Naugatuck Valleys.* Hartford, Conn.: Case, Lockwood, & Brainard, 1882.

Owen, Nicholas. *British Remains: or, a Collection of Antiquities Relating to the Britons.* London: J. Bew, 1777.

Pagdon, Anthony. "The Savage Critic: Some European Images of the Primitive." *Yearbook of English Studies* 13 (1983): 32–45.

Pardoe, Elizabeth Lewis. "The Many Worlds of Conrad Weiser: Mystic Diplomat." Paper presented at the McNeil Center for Early American Studies Seminar, 9 October 1998.

Parker, Arthur C. *American Indian Freemasonry.* Albany, N.Y.: Buffalo Consistory, 1919.

———. *The Life of General Ely S. Parker.* Buffalo, N.Y.: Buffalo Historical Society, 1919.

Paskievich, John, director. *If only I were an Indian.* Canada, 1995. Videocassette.

Pearce, Roy Harvey. *The Savages of America: A Study of the Indian and the Idea of Civilization.* Rev. ed. Baltimore: Johns Hopkins UP, 1965.

Peipp, Matthias, and Berhard Springer. *Edle Wilde, rote Teufel: Indianer im Film.* Munich: Heyne, 1997.

Perkins, Elizabeth A. *Border Life: Experience and Memory in the Revolutionary Ohio Valley.* Chapel Hill: U of North Carolina P, 1998.

———. "Distinctions and Partitions amongst Us: Identity and Interaction in the Revolutionary Ohio Valley." In *Contact Points: American Frontiers from the Mohawk Valley to the Mississippi, 1750–1830,* edited by Andrew R. L. Clayton and Fredrika J. Teute. Chapel Hill: U of North Carolina P, 1998.

Pessen, Edward. *Jacksonian America: Society, Personality, and Politics.* Urbana: U of Illinois P, 1978.

Peterson, Jacqueline, and Jennifer S. H. Brown, eds. *The New Peoples: Being and Becoming Métis in North America.* Lincoln: U of Nebraska P, 1985.

Peterson, S. C. "Challenging the Stereotypes." *Upper Midwest History* (1984): 1–10.

Peyer, Bernd C. *The Tutor'd Mind: Indian Missionary-Writers in Antebellum America.* Amherst: U of Massachusetts P, 1997.

———. "Who Is Afraid of AIM?" In *Indians and Europe: An Interdisciplinary Collection of Essays,* edited by Christian F. Feest, 551–61. Aachen: Rader, 1987. Reprint, Lincoln: U of Nebraska P, 1999.

Pierson, William D. Black Yankees; The Development of an Afro-American Subculture in Eighteenth-Century New England. Amherst: U of Massachusetts P, 1988

Plischke, Hans. Von Cooper bis Karl May: Eine Geschichte des völkerkundlichen Reise- und Abenteuerromans. Düsseldorf: Droste Verlag, 1951.

Poiger, Uta. "A New, 'Western' Hero? Reconstructing German Masculinity in the 1950s." Signs: Journal of Women in Culture and Society 24, no. 1 (1998): 147–62.

Powers, William K. Beyond the Vision: Essays on American Indian Culture. Norman: U of Oklahoma P, 1987.

———. "The Indian Hobbyist Movement in North America." In Indian-White Relations, edited by W. E. Washburn, vol. 4 of Handbook of North American Indians, edited by W. C. Sturtevant, 557–61. Washington, D.C.: Smithsonian Institution, 1988.

———. Yuwipi, Vision and Experience in Oglala Ritual. Lincoln: U of Nebraska P, 1982.

Pratt, Mary Louise. Imperial Eyes: Travel Writing and Transculturation. New York: Routledge, 1992.

Price, R. Alabi's World. Baltimore: Johns Hopkins UP, 1990.

Prins, Harald E. L. "To the Land of the Mistigoches: American Indians Traveling to Europe in the Sage of Exploration." American Indian Culture and Research Journal 17, no. 1 (1993), 175–95.

Pyne, Stephen J. How the Canyon Became Grand: A Short History. New York: Viking, 1998.

Reddin, P. Wild West Shows. Urbana: U of Illinois P, 1999.

Reichel, W. C. A Memorial of the Dedication of Monuments Erected by the Moravian Historical Society. Philadelphia: J. B. Lippincott, 1860.

Reiss, Winold. Winold Reiss: Plains Portraits. Exhibition 4–28 October 1972.

Renaud, Chantal. "Le Far West Made in France." Châtelaine (August 1987): 35–42.

Richter, Daniel K. "Cultural Brokers and Intercultural Politics." Journal of American History 75 (1988): 40–67.

———. The Ordeal of the Longhouse: The Peoples of the Iroquois League in the Era of European Colonization. Chapel Hill: U of North Carolina P, 1992.

Rickard, Jolene. "Alterity, Mimicry and German Indians." In Bavarian by Law— German Indians, edited by A. Robbins and M. Becher, 30–31. Syracuse, N.Y.: Light Works, 1998.

Riegler, J. "'Tame Europeans' and the 'Mysteries of Wild America.'" European Review of Native American Studies 1 (1988): 17–20.

Roach, Joseph. Cities of the Dead: Circum-Atlantic Performance. New York: Columbia UP, 1996.

Roeber, A. G. "'The Origin of Whatever Is Not English among Us:' The Dutch-speaking and the German-speaking Peoples of Colonial British America." In Strangers Within the Realm: Cultural Margins of the First British Empire, edited by

Bernard Bailyn and Philip D. Morgan, 220-83. Chapel Hill: U of North Carolina P, 1991.

———. *Palatines, Liberty, and Property: German Lutherans in Colonial British America.* Baltimore: Johns Hopkins UP, 1993.

Roediger, David. *Wages of Whiteness: Race and the Making of the American Working Class.* New York: Verso, 1991.

Rose, Wendy. "Just What's All This Fuss About Whiteshamanism Anyway?" In *Coyote Was Here: Essays on Contemporary Native American Literary and Political Mobilization,* 13-24. Aarhus, Denmark: Seklos, 1984.

Rossbacher, Karl Heinz. *Lederstrumpf in Deutschland: Zur Rezeption James Fenimore Coopers beim Leser der Restaurationszeit.* Munich: Fink, 1972.

Rothermund, Dietmar. "The German Problem of Colonial Pennsylvania." *Pennsylvania Magazine of History and Biography* 84 (1960): 3-21

———. *The Layman's Progress: Religious and Political Experience in Colonial Pennsylvania.* Philadelphia: U of Pennsylvania P, 1961.

Ruoff, A. LaVonne Brown. "George Copway: Nineteenth-Century American Autobiographer." *Auto/Biography* 2, no. 1 (1987): 6-17.

———. "Three Nineteenth-Century American Indian Autobiographers." In *Redefining American Literary History,* edited by A. LaVonne Ruoff Brown and Jerry W. War, 251-69. New York: MLA, 1990.

Rusinowa, Izabella. "Indians in the Reports of Polish Travelers of the Second Half of the 19th Century." In: *Indians and Europe: An Interdisciplinary Collection of Essays,* edited by Christian F. Feest, 297-306. Aachen: Rader, 1987; reprint, Lincoln: U of Nebraska P. 1999.

Ryerson, Richard Alan. "Portrait of a Colonial Oligarchy: The Quaker Elite in the Pennsylvania Assembly, 1729-1776. In *Power and Status: Officeholding in Colonial America,* edited by Bruce C. Daniels, 75-105. Middletown, Conn.: Wesleyan UP, 1986.

Sadovszky, Otto von. *The Discovery of California: A Cal-Ugrian Comparative Study.* Istor Books 3. Budapest: Akadémiai Kiadó, 1996.

Said, Edward W. *Orientalism.* New York: Random House, 1978.

———. *The World, the Text, and the Critic.* Cambridge, Mass.: Harvard UP, 1983.

Salisbury, N. *Manitou and Providence.* New York: Oxford UP, 1982.

Salwen, B. "Indians of Southern New England and Long Island: Early Period." In *Northeast,* edited by B. G. Trigger, vol. 15 of *Handbook of North American Indians,* edited by W. C. Sturtevant. Washington, D.C.: Smithsonian Institution, 1978.

Sammons, Jeffrey L. "An Austrian Jacksonian: Charles Sealsfield's Political Evolution, 1829-1833." In *Gender and Politics in Austrian Fiction,* edited by Ritchie Robertson and Edward Timmss. Edinburgh: Edinburgh UP, 1996.

———. "Charles Sealsfield: A Case of Non-Canonicity." In *Autoren damals und heute:*

Literaturgeschichtliche Beispiele veränderter Wirkungshorizonte, edited by Gerhard Knapp, 155-72. Amsterdam: Rodopi, 1991.

———. "Charles Sealsfield's Images of Life from Both Hemispheres: A New Acquisition." *Yale University Library Gazette 64*, no. 1-2 (Oct. 1989): 66-72.

———. "Friedrich Gerstäcker: German Realist of the American West." *Yale University Library Gazette 70*, no. 1-2 (Oct. 1995): 39-46.

———. *Ideology, Mimesis, Fantasy: Charles Sealsfield, Friedrich Gerstäcker, Karl May, and Other German Novelists of America*. Chapel Hill: U of North Carolina P, 1998.

Sanner, Hans-Ulrich. "Karl von den Steinen in Oraibi, 1898. A Collection of Hopi Indian Photographs in Perspective." *Baessler-Archiv*, N.F. *44*, no. 2 (1996): 243-93.

Schlüter, Wolfgang. *Römer im Osnabrücker Land: Die Ausgrabungen in Kalkriese*. Bramsche, Germany: Rasch, 1991.

———, ed. *Kalkriese—Römer im Osnabrücker Land: Archäologische Forschungen zur Varusschlacht*. Bramsche, Germany: Rasch, 1993.

Schmidt, Arno. *Sitara und der Weg dorthin: Eine Studie über Wesen, Werk und Wirkung Karl Mays*. Karlsruhe: Stahlberg, 1963. Reprint, Frankfurt am Main: Fischer, 1969.

Schmidt, Emil. *Vorgeschichte Nordamerikas im Gebiet der Vereinigten Staaten*. Braunschweig, Germany: Vieweg, 1894.

Schmidt, Isolde. *Eduard Schmidt von der Launitz 1797-1869: Ein Beitrag zur Skulptur des 19. Jahrhunderts in Frankfurt am Main*. Frankfurt am Main: Kramer, 1992.

Schneider, Isabella. *"We Have a Commonality and a Common Dream:" The Indigenous North American Novel in the 1990*. Frankfurt am Main: Peter Lang, 1998.

Scholer, Bo, ed. *Coyote Was Here: Essays on Contemporary Native American Literary and Political Mobilization*. Aarhus, Denmark: SEKLOS, 1984.

Scott, Douglas D., P. Willey, and Melissa A. Connor. *They Died With Custer: Soldiers' Bones from the Battle of the Little Bighorn*. Norman: U of Oklahoma P, 1998.

See, Klaus von. *Barbar, Germane, Arier: Die Suche nach der Identität der Deutschen*. Heidelberg: Winter, 1994.

Seifert, W. *Patty Frank*. Bamberg, Germany: Karl-May-Verlag, 1998.

Sellers, Charles. *The Market Revolution: Jacksonian America, 1815-1846*. New York: Oxford UP, 1991.

Sheehan, Bernhard. *Savagism and Civility: Indians and Englishmen in Colonial Virginia*. Cambridge, England: Cambridge UP, 1980.

Shoemaker, Nancy. "An Alliance between Men: Gender Metaphors in Eighteenth-Century American Indian Diplomacy East of the Mississippi." *Ethnohistory 46* (1999): 239-63.

Sieg, Katrin. "Ethnic Drag and National Identity: Multicultural Crises, Crossings, and Interventions." In *The Imperialist Imagination: German Colonialism and Its Legacy*, edited by Sara Friedrichsmeyer et al., 295-319. Ann Arbor: U of Michigan P, 1998.

Bibliography

————. *Ethnic Drag: Performing Race, Nation, Sexuality in Postwar Germany*. Durham, N.C.: Duke UP, forthcoming.

————. "Wigwams on the Rhine: Race and Nationality on the German Stage." *TheatreForum* 6 (winter/spring 1995): 12–19.

Slobodin, Richard. *Métis of the MacKenzie District*. Ottawa: Canadian Research Centre for Anthropology, St. Paul U, 1966.

Smaby, Beverly Prior. *The Transformation of Moravian Bethlehem: From Communal Mission to Family Economy*. Philadelphia: U of Pennsylvania P, 1988.

Smith, Donald B. *From the Land of Shadows: The Making of Grey Owl*. Saskatoon, Sask.: Western Producer Prairie Books, 1990.

————. "Kahgegagahbowh." In vol. 9 of *Dictionary of Canadian Biography*, 419–21. Toronto: U of Toronto P, 1976.

————. "The Life of George Copway or Kah-ge-ga-gah-bowh (1818–1869) – and a review of his writings." *Journal of Canadian Studies* 23, no. 3 (autumn 1988): 5–38.

————. *Sacred Feathers: The Reverend Peter Jones (Kahkewaquonaby) and the Mississauga Indians*. Lincoln: U of Nebraska P, 1987.

Sollors, Werner. *Beyond Ethnicity: Consent and Descent in American Culture*. New York: Oxford UP, 1986.

————. "Ethnicity." In *Critical Terms for Literary Study*, edited by Frank Lentricchia and Thomas Mclaughlin. 2d. ed. Chicago: U of Chicago P, 1995.

————, ed. *The Invention of Ethnicity*. New York: Oxford UP, 1989.

Speer, Albert. *Spandauer Tagebücher*. Frankfurt am Main: Ullstein, 1982.

Spiegel, S. " 'Buffalo Bill" und die Wild-West-Show in München." Ph.D. diss., University of Munich, 1983.

Spiller, Robert E. *The American in England During the First Half Century of Independence*. 1926. Reprint, Chicago: Porcupine Press, 1976.

Spitzer, Leo. *Hotel Bolivia: The Culture of Memory in a Refuge from Nazism*. New York: Hill & Wang, 1998.

Splitter, Wolfgang. "The Germans in Pennsylvania Politics, 1758–1790." *Pennsylvania Magazine of History and Biography* 122 (1998): 39–76.

Stamps, Quanah Crossland. "Germany: Market for Native American Goods." *American Indian Report* (April 2000): 21–22.

Steiner, George. *Sprache und Schweigen*. Translated by A. Kaun. Frankfurt am Main: Suhrkamp, 1969.

Steltzer, Ulli. *Indian Artists at Work*. Vancouver, B.C.: Douglas & McIntyre, 1976.

Stenholt, Lars A. *Sitting Bull, billeder fra den sidste indianerkrig*. Minneapolis, Minn.: W. Kriedt, 1891.

Stewart, Jeffrey C. *Winold Reiss: An Illustrated Checklist of His Portraits*. Washington, D.C.: Smithsonian Institution Press for the National Portrait Gallery, 1990.

Stewart, Rick, Joseph D. Ketner II, and Angela L. Miller. *Carl Wimar: Chronicler of the Missouri River Frontier*. Fort Worth: Amon Carter Museum, 1991.

Stocking, George, ed. *Volksgeist as Method and Ethic: Essays on Boasian Ethnography and the German Anthropological Tradition*. Madison: U of Wisconsin P, 1996.

Sturtevant, William C., and David Beers Quinn. "This New Prey: Eskimos in Europe in 1567, 1576, and 1577." In *Indians and Europe: An Interdisciplinary Collection of Essays*, edited by Christian F. Feest, 61–65. Aachen: Rader, 1987. Reprint, Lincoln: U of Nebraska P, 1999.

Sugden, John. *Tecumseh: A Life*. New York: Holt, 1998.

Surratt, Jerry L. *Gottlieb Schober of Salem: Discipleship and Ecumenical Vision in an Early Moravian Town*. Macon, Ga.: Mercer UP, 1983.

Suttles, Wayne, and Barbara Lane. "Southern Coast Salish." In *Northwest Coast*, edited by Wayne Suttles, vol. 7 of *Handbook of North American Indians*, edited by W. C. Sturtevant, 485–502. Washington D.C.: Smithsonian Institution Press, 1990.

Swiggers, Pierre. "C. C. Uhlenbeck (1886–1951) and the Scientific Study of Algonquian Languages." *European Review of Native American Studies* 2, no. 1:7–8.

Tanner, Helen Hornbeck, ed. *The Settling of North America: The Atlas of the Great Migrations into North America from the Ice Age to the Present*. New York: Macmillan, 1995.

Taylor, Colin. "The Indian Hobbyism Movement in Europe." In *Indian-White Relations*, edited by W. E. Washburn, vol. 4 of *Handbook of North American Indians*, edited by W. C. Sturtevant, 562–69. Washington, D.C.: Smithsonian Institution, 1988).

Teiwes, Helga, and Wolfgang Lindig. *Navajo*. Zürich: Bär Verlag, 1991.

Theisz, R. D. "The Bad Speakers and the Long Braids: References to Foreign Enemies in Lakota Song Texts." In: *Indians and Europe: An Interdisciplinary Collection of Essays*, edited by Christian F. Feest, 427–34. Aachen: Rader, 1987. Reprint, Lincoln: U of Nebraska P, 1999.

Theweleit, Klaus. *Männerphantasien*. 2 vols. Reinbek, Germany: Rowohlt, 1980.

Thiel, M. "Catholic Sodalities Among the Sioux, 1882–1910." *U.S. Catholic Historian* 2 (1998): 56–77.

Thode-Arora, H. *Für fünfzig Pfennig um die Welt*. Frankfurt am Main: Campus, 1989.

Thorp, Daniel B. *The Moravian Community in Colonial North Carolina: Pluralism on the Southern Frontier*. Knoxville: U of Tennessee P, 1989.

Tiro, Karim M. "James Dean on the Early American Frontier." Unpublished paper, 22 April 1996.

Todorov, Tzvetan. *The Conquest of America: The Question of the Other*. New York: Harper & Row, 1984. Originally published as *La conquête de l'Amérique: La question de l'autre* (Paris: Editions du Seuil, 1982).

Torgovnick, Marianna. *Gone Primitive: Savage Intellects, Modern Lives*. Chicago: Chicago UP, 1990.

Tower, Beeke Sell. *Envisioning America: Prints, Drawings, and Photographs by George*

Grosz and his Contemporaries, 1915–1933. With an essay by John Czaplicka. Cambridge, Mass.: Busch-Reisinger Museum, Harvard U, 1990.

Tully, Alan. *Forming American Politics: Ideals, Interests, and Institutions in Colonial New York and Pennsylvania*. Baltimore: Johns Hopkins UP, 1994.

———. "Quaker Party and Proprietary Policies: The Dynamics of Politics in Pre-Revoluntionary Pennsylvania, 1730–1775." In *Power and Status: Officeholding in Colonial America*, edited by Bruce C. Daniels, 106–35. Middletown, Conn.: Wesleyan UP, 1986.

Turnauer, Christine. *Portraits*. Calgary, Alba.: PAS Publishing, 1992.

Turski, Birgit. *Die Indianistikgruppen in der DDR: Entwicklung, Probleme, Aussichten*. Idstein/Taunus, Germany: Baum, 1994.

———. "The Indianist Groups in the GDR: Development, Problems, Prospects." *European Review of Native American Studies* 7, no. 1 (1993): 43–48.

Usner, Daniel H. *Indians, Settlers, and Slaves in a Frontier Exchange Economy: The Lower Mississippi Valley Before 1783*. Chapel Hill: U of North Carolina P, 1992.

Utley, Robert M. *The Indian Frontier of the American West 1846–1890*. Albuquerque: U of New Mexico P, 1984.

Valentin, Veit. "Der Erste Internationale Friedenskongreß auf Deutschen Boden 1850." In *Veit Valentin: Von Bismark zur Weimarer Republik: Sieben Beiträge zur deutschen Politik*, edited by Hans-Ulrich Webler, 27–37. Cologne: Kiepenheuer & Witsch, 1979.

Vecsey, Christopher. *Where the Two Roads Meet*. Notre Dame, Ind.: U of Notre Dame P, 1999.

Vecsey, Christopher, and William A. Starna, eds. *Iroquois Land Claims*. Syracuse, N.Y.: Syracuse UP, 1988.

Vermeulen, H. F. "The Emergence of 'Ethnography' ca. 1770 in Göttingen." *History of Anthropology Newsletter* 19, no. 1 (1992): 6–9.

Wallace, Anthony F. C. *Teedyuscung, King of the Delawares, 1700–1763*. (1949). Reprint, Syracuse, N.Y.: Syracuse UP, 1990.

Wallace, Paul A. W. *Conrad Weiser, 1696–1760: Friend of Colonist and Mohawk*. Philadelphia: U of Pennsylvania P, 1945.

———. *Thirty Thousand Miles with John Heckewelder*. Pittsburgh: U of Pittsburgh P, 1958.

Ward, John William. *Andrew Jackson: Symbol for an Age*. New York: Oxford UP, 1962.

Weaver, Ethan Allan. *The Forks of the Delaware*. Easton, Penn.: Eschenbach, 1900.

Weber, Samuel Edwin. *The Charity School Movement in Colonial Pennsylvania: 1905*. New York: Arno Press, 1969.

Welch, James, and Paul Stekler. *Killing Custer: The Battle of the Little Big Horn and the Fate of the Plains Indians*. New York: W. W. Norton, 1994.

Weslager, C. A. *The Delaware Indians: A History*. New Brunswick, N.J.: Rutgers UP, 1972.

Wessel, Carola. "Missionary Diaries as a Source of Native American Studies: David Zeisberger and the Delaware." *European Review of Native American Studies* 10, no. 2 (1996): 31-37.

————. *Missionsvorstellung und Missionswirklichkeit der Herrnhuter Brüdergemeinde in Nordamerika im 18. Jahrhundert.* Seminar paper, University of Göttingen, 1989.

Wharton, Clarence. *Satanta: The Great Chief of the Kiowas.* Dallas: Bank Upshaw & Co., 1935.

White, Richard. *The Middle Ground: Indians, Empires, and Republics in the Great Lakes Region, 1650-1815.* New York: Cambridge UP, 1991.

Whitt, Laurie Anne. "Indigenous Peoples and The Cultural Politics of Knowledge." In *Issues in Native American Cultural Identity,* edited by Michael K. Green, 223-71. New York: Peter Lang, 1995.

Wickham, Christopher J. "Oil and Water: The Development of the Portrayal of Native Americans by Nineteenth-Century German Painters." *Yearbook of German-American Studies* 31 (1996): 63-106.

Wojciechowski, F. *The Paugusset Tribes.* Nijmegen, Netherlands: Catholic U, 1985.

Wokeck, Marianne S. "Harnessing the Lure of the 'Best Poor Man's Country': The Dynamics of German-Speaking Immigration to British North America, 1683-1783," In *"To Make America": European Emigration in the Early Modern Period,* edited by Ida Altman and James Horn, 204-43. Berkeley: U of California P, 1991.

————. *Trade in Strangers: The Beginnings of Mass Migration to North America.* University Park: Pennsylvania State UP, 1999.

Wollschläger, Hans. *Karl May.* Fundus-Bücher 120-21. Dresden: VEB Verlag der Kunst, 1990.

Wood, W. Raymond. "The Role of the Romantic West in Shaping the Third Reich." *Plains Anthropologist* 35, no. 112 (1990): 313-19.

Woringer, August. "Ein waldeckischer Indianerhäuptling." *Nachrichten der Gesellschaft für Familienkunde in Kurhessen und Waldeck* 7, no. 4 (1932): 125.

Wright, Robin K. "The Traveling Exhibition of Captain Samuel Hadlock, Jr.: Eskimos in Europe, 1822-1826" In: *Indians and Europe: An Interdisciplinary Collection of Essays,* edited by Christian F. Feest, 215-33. Aachen: Rader, 1987. Reprint, Lincoln: U of Nebraska P, 1999.

Zantop, Susanne. *Colonial Fantasies: Conquest, Family, and Nation in Precolonial Germany, 1770-1870.* Durham, N.C.: Duke UP, 1997.

————. "Colonial Legends, Postcolonial Legacies." In *A User's Guide to German Cultural Studies,* edited by Scott Denham, Irene Kacandes, and Jonathan Petropoulos, 189-205. Ann Arbor: U of Michigan P, 1997. 189-205.

————. " 'Der Indianer' im Rasse- und Geschlechterdiskurs der deutschen Spätaufklärung." In *Das Subjekt und die Anderen,* edited by Herbert Uerlings, Karl Hoelz, and Viktoria Schmidt-Linsenhoff. Berlin: E. Schmidt Verlag, 2000.

Contributors

RUSSEL LAWRENCE BARSH has taught Native American studies at the University of Lethbridge and the University of Washington and currently teaches law at New York University. He has assisted the Mi'kmaq Nation in legal matters since 1978 and has served as a consultant to the United Nations Development Program, the International Labor Office (ILO), and Canada's Royal Commission on Aboriginal Peoples. His books and articles on Native Americans and other indigenous peoples include *The Road: Indian Tribes and Political Liberty* and *Effective Negotiation by Indigenous Peoples*.

COLIN G. CALLOWAY teaches history and Native American studies at Dartmouth College and chairs Dartmouth's Native American Studies Program. He is the author of numerous books, including *First Peoples: A Documentary Survey of American Indian History* (1999); *New Worlds For All: Indians, Europeans, and the Remaking of Early America* (1997); *The American Revolution in Indian Country* (1995); *The Western Abenakis of Vermont* (1990); and *Crown and Calumet: British-Indian Relations 1783–1815* (1987).

MARTA CARLSON (Yurok) is an accomplished filmmaker, an award-winning playwright, and a Ph.D. student at the University of Massachusetts. Her research interests are in Native American studies, anthropology of theater, and visual anthropology. She has served as a board member for the American Indian Community House in New York City since 1993 and has been on several film festival selection committees for the National Museum of the American Indian. Her latest film, *Das Pow-wow*, was screened at the American Anthropology Association's annual conference in San Francisco.

CORINNA DALLY-STARNA is a native of Bremen, Germany, and a professional German-English translator. She holds a B.A. in history and a B.S. in social studies secondary education from the State University of New York, College at Oneonta. She has translated over nine hundred manuscript pages of diaries and reports from the records of the Moravian missions to the Indians of Connecticut, a project that is sponsored by the Mashantucket Pequot Museum and Research Center, Mashantucket, Connecticut.

RENATE EIGENBROD completed her Ph.D. dissertation "(Im)migrant Readings of Canadian Indigenous Literature: Towards an Ethics of Positionality" at the University of Greifswald, Germany, in 2000. She taught Canadian First Nations literature at Lakehead University, Thunder Bay, Ontario, from 1986 to 2000 and is currently teaching at Acadia University in Wolfville, Nova Scotia.

LOUISE ERDRICH attended Dartmouth College from 1972 to 1976 and Johns Hopkins University (1978–1979) before becoming an independent writer. Now an internationally acclaimed author, her novels include *Love Medicine* (1984), *The Beet Queen* (1986), *Tracks* (1989), *The Antelope Wife* (1998), and, in collaboration with Michael Dorris, *The Crown of Columbus* (1991). Her forthcoming novel, *The Master Butcher*, is about the German side of her family.

CHRISTIAN F. FEEST teaches historical ethnology (North America) at the Johann-Wolfgang-Goethe-Universität, Frankfurt am Main. He served as curator of the North and Middle American collections of the Museum für Völkerkunde, Vienna, was a postdoctoral fellow in the Department of Anthropology at the Smithsonian Institution in Washington, and a Ford Foundation Fellow at the Center for the History of the American Indian, Newberry Library, Chicago. An indefatigable lecturer and prolific writer, Feest has published widely on North American Indians.

GERD GEMÜNDEN is professor of German studies and comparative literature at Dartmouth College. In his book *Framed Visions: Popular Culture, Americanization, and the Contemporary German and Austrian Imagination* (1998), he devotes a chapter to the "Indianerphantasien" of Herbert Achternbusch. His current project centers on German exile filmmakers in Hollywood during the 1930s and 1940s.

KARL MARKUS KREIS is professor of political science and pedagogy at the Fachhochschule, Dortmund, Germany. He received his Ph.D. in 1971 from the Universities of Innsbruck and Munich. His research areas include international relations, foreign policy, international education, and concepts of multiculturalism. He has published on the Vietnam War, German foreign policy, and German-American exchange.

UTE LISCHKE-MCNAB received her Ph.D. in German studies from the University of Cambridge, England, and is associate professor of German in the Department of Languages and Literatures at Wilfrid Laurier University in Waterloo, Ontario. She is the author of *Lily Braun, 1865–1916: German Writer, Feminist, Socialist* (Camden House, 2000). Her current projects include a book on women and the DEFA films of East Germany and, with David McNab, a study of the writings of Louise Erdrich.

HARTMUT LUTZ teaches North American studies at the University of Greifswald, Germany. He received his Ph.D. in English and American literature and education from the University of Tübingen in 1974 and wrote his postdoctoral

Habilitation thesis on the history of "Indian-stereotyping" in the U.S. and German cultures.

BERND PEYER received his Ph.D. from the Johann-Wolfgang-Goethe-Universität, Frankfurt, in American studies, ethnology, and Latin American studies. His publications include *The Elders Wrote: An Anthology of Early Prose by North American Indians 1768–1931; The Singing Spirit: Early Short Stories by North American Indians; Indianische Kunst Nordamerikas* (Indians arts of North America); and his latest, *The Tutor'd Mind: Indian Missionary Writers in Antebellum America*. He was the first Ford Foundation Fellow at the D'Arcy McNickle Center for the History of the American Indian at the Newberry Library in Chicago in 1986–1987, and he was the first Gordon Russell Visitor in Native American Studies at Dartmouth College in 1995.

LIAM RIORDAN has been an assistant professor in the Department of History at the University of Maine, Orono, since 1997. He received his Ph.D. in history in 1996 from the University of Pennsylvania with a dissertation titled "Identities in the New Nation: The Creation of an American Mainstream in the Delaware Valley, 1770–1830." He has written articles for *Pennsylvania History* and the *William and Mary Quarterly*.

JEFFREY L. SAMMONS is professor of German at Yale University. His many publications range from monographs on Heinrich Heine and Wilhelm Raabe to his most recent book on German travelers and novelists of the American West, *Ideology, Mimesis, Fantasy: Charles Sealsfield, Friedrich Gerstäcker, Karl May, and other German Novelists of America* (1998).

KATRIN SIEG is an associate professor of Germanic studies at Indiana University, with a special focus on drama and performance. Her book *Exiles, Eccentrics, Activists: Women in Contemporary German Theatre* was published by the University of Michigan Press in 1994. Her latest book, *Ethnic Drag*, is forthcoming from Duke.

WILLIAM A. STARNA is professor of anthropology emeritus at SUNY Oneonta. He has served as adjunct curator of ethnology at the New York State Museum and as litigation and historical consultant to twenty American Indian tribes and a number of law firms representing Indian people in the area of land claims, tax issues, hunting and fishing rights, and federal acknowledgment. He edited four books on the Iroquoian and Algonquian Indian populations of the eastern United States and Canada from the sixteenth century to the present and contemporary state-federal-Indian relations. He now lives in Bremen, Germany.

EMMA LEE WARRIOR grew up on the (Blackfoot) Peigan Reserve in Southern Alberta, Canada. She attended boarding school on the reservation and later received an M.A. from the University of Washington. Her short stories and poems have appeared in magazines and anthologies in the United States and Canada.

SUSANNE ZANTOP held degrees in political science/Latin American studies (Stanford) and comparative literature (Harvard). Since 1984, she was a member of Dartmouth's Department of German Studies, which she was chairing at the time of her death. Her research revolved around German fantasies and fictions about South American Indians (*Colonial Fantasies: Conquest, Family, and Nation in Precolonial Germany, 1770–1870* [1997]) and German colonialism. Her most recent publication, coedited with Sara Friedrichsmeyer and Sara Lennox, is titled *The Imperialist Imagination: German Colonialism and Its Legacy* (1998).

Index

Page references for illustrations appear in italics.

Index

critique of, 214-16; institutional structures of, 221-22, 223-24, 240 n.7 n.9, 242 n.19 n.21; politicized minority in, 230-31, 236-37; sensitivity to Native American issues in, 32, 213-14, 235-37. *See also* Indian hobbyism

East Germany: anti-Americanism in, 36, 235, 240 n.10, 241 n.18; foundational fiction of, 249; identification with Indians in, after German reunification, 182 n.5, 183 n.20, 215, 235-36; nostalgia for, after German reunification, 32, 247. *See also* DEFA *Indianerfilme*; East German hobbyism; Germany

Eastman, Charles, 69

Easton PA 102-14; Christian Indians in, 110, 118 n.57; French and Indian War in, 106-7; proprietary power in, 104; Revolutionary period in, 113, 119 n.67; treaty meetings at, 78 n.26, 98, 104-6, 107-12, 117 n.32 n.42 n.44, 118 n.45

Eber, Elk, 30

Edda, 174

Egmond, Florike, 28

Eigenbrod, Renate: "'Stranger and Stranger': The (German) Other in Canadian Indigenous Texts," 7-8, 12, 259-80

Eldridge, William, 129

Elwell, John, 134

Engels, Friedrich: *Der Ursprung der Familie*, 149

Erdrich, Louise, 7, 10, 281-86; *The Antelope Wife*, 9, 12, 14 n.15, 283-86, 287-94; *The Beet Queen*, 281, 282; *The Birchbark House*, 281; *The Blue Jay's Dance*, 281, 282; *Grandmother's Pigeon*, 281; *Love Medicine*, 281; *Tracks*, 281, 282

Erik the Red, 29, 48

Ethnic Drag (Sieg), 220

ethnic identity: as biological race, 169, 170-71, 174-75, 179-80, 188; changing of, as "ethnic drag," 219-20, 233, 239 n.4, 276-78, 280 n.48; essentialist notions of, 28, 174, 189, 273; as "ethnic competence," 219, 223-25, 227, 230, 238, 240 n.11 n.12; as hair and skin color, 3, 13 n.2, 99-100; instability of, in colonial Pennsylvania, 97-98, 102, 108-9, 111-14, 114 n.2 n.3, 115 n.12; instability

of, in Native American texts, 9, 12, 13 n.15, 259-78, 279 n.17 n.22, 280 n.35 n.38; "othering" of, 3-5, 98-99, 104-5, 106, 113-14, 114 n.2, 245-46; secondary nature of, 39; social constructedness of, 167-68, 170-80; terminology of, 181 n.4; Whiteness theory of, 214-15, 237

ethnography, 39-40, 64-65, 66-69

exoticism. *See* DEFA *Indianerfilme*; Indian hobbyism; Indians; Indianthusiasm; Wild West Shows

Fairfield, Ontario, 85

Fanon, Frantz, 114 n.2

Farny, Henry, 38

Faust (Goethe), 12, 13 n.15

Feest, Christian F., 238; "Germany's Indians in a European Perspective," 4, 10, 13 n.8, 25-43, 239 n.2

Ferry, Gabriel, 37; *Le coureur de bois*, 25

Feyl, Nancy, 281

Fiedler, Leslie, 175

Fife, Hans, 51

Finerty, John, 61

Fioz, Juan, 56

Fischer, Rudolph, 59

Foehse, Ludwig, 35

Fogleman, Aaron Spenser, 114 n.5, 116 n.22

Forbes, J. T., 160 n.3

Ford, John: *Cheyenne Autumn*, 255 n.14

Fort Clark ND, 65, 66

Frankfurt. *See* Third World Peace Congress

Frankfurter Journal, 163 n.25

Frankfurter Konversationsblatt, 154

Franklin, Benjamin: hostility of, to German settlement, 47, 99-100, 104-5, 113; Indian treaties of, 118 n.45; *Observations Concerning the Increase of Mankind*, 99-100, 115 n.7; role of, in Charity School movement, 100, 115 n.14

Fredericksburg TX, 57, 58-59

Freiligrath, Hermann Ferdinand: friendship of, with George Copway, 141, 144-45, 156-58; life of, 163 n.30; quarrel of, with George Copway, 159, 164 n.37 n.39

French and Indian War, 52, 106-7, 110, 113

French Company of the Indies, 50

Frey, W., 35

Index

Index

Index

Index

Index

Williams, Ted: *The Science of Hitting*, 274
Wilson, Woodrow, 147
Wimar, Charles, 38, 65
Windolph, Charles, 61-62
Winnetou trilogy (May): colonialist myth in, 3-4, 13 n.6, 175, 184 n.32, 225-26; German *Indianer* myth in, 10-11, 33, 191-92, 247-49, 275-76; male bonding in, 3-4, 175-76, 184 n.29, 248, 274; Nazi admiration of, 25-26, 177-80, 215, 247; translations of, 26
Wisconsin, 123, 124
Wokeck, Marianne S., 115 n.5
"Wompanoo" Indians, 84
The Works of Sitting Bull in the Original Latin and French (Clarke), 33

Wounded Knee, Battle of, 62, 205, 273
Wyoming PA, 54, 104, 111

Yakima Indians, 254
Yathe, Evelyn, 75
Yellow Robe, Chauncey, 73

Zantop, Susanne: "Close Encounters: *Deutsche* and *Indianer*," 3-14; *Colonial Fantasies*, 6, 13 n.2; "Der Indianer," 13 n.2
Zeisberger, David, 53-54, 55
Zeitschrift für Ethnologie, 66
Zinzendorf, Count Nikolaus Ludwig von, 53, 83
Zuni Indians, 188

CPSIA information can be obtained at www.ICGtesting.com
Printed in the USA
LVOW13s0337260214

375180LV00001B/34/A

9 780803 264205